Learning the Art of Helping
Building Blocks and Techniques

Mark E. Young
Stetson University

Merrill,
an imprint of Prentice Hall

Upper Saddle River, New Jersey   Columbus, Ohio

Library of Congress Cataloging-in-Publication Data
Young, Mark E.
    Learning the art of helping : building blocks and techniques / by
Mark E. Young.—1st ed.
        p.   cm.
    Includes bibliographical references and index.
    ISBN 0-13-834268-7
    1. Counseling.   2. Psychotherapy.   I. Title.
BF637.C6Y583   1998
158'.3—dc21

97-30515
CIP

Cover photo: © Diana Ong/Superstock
Editor: Kevin M. Davis
Production Editor: Sheryl Glicker Langner
Production Coordination: Tally Morgan, WordCrafters Editorial Services, Inc.
Design Coordinator: Karrie M. Converse
Cover Designer: Susan Unger
Production Manager: Laura Messerly
Electronic Text Management: Karen L. Bretz
Director of Marketing: Kevin Flanagan
Marketing Manager: Suzanne Stanton
Advertising/Marketing Coordinator: Julie Shough

This book was set in ITC Century by Carlisle Communications, Ltd. and was printed and bound by Book Press Inc., Quebecor America Book Group Company. The cover was printed by Phoenix Color Corp.

 © 1998 by Prentice-Hall, Inc.
Simon & Schuster/A Viacom Company
Upper Saddle River, New Jersey 07458

Printed in the United States of America

10 9 8 7 6 5 4 3 2 1

ISBN: 0-13-834268-7

Prentice-Hall International (UK) Limited, *London*
Prentice-Hall of Australia Pty. Limited, *Sydney*
Prentice-Hall of Canada, Inc., *Toronto*
Prentice-Hall Hispanoamericana, S. A., *Mexico*
Prentice-Hall of India Private Limited, *New Delhi*
Prentice-Hall of Japan, Inc., *Tokyo*
Simon & Schuster Asia Pte. Ltd., *Singapore*
Editora Prentice-Hall do Brasil, Ltda., *Rio de Janeiro*

Dedication

To my sisters, Sara, Carla and Ann
All professional helpers who are always there for me.

Preface

How to Read This Book

This book is somewhat different from other texts you may have read because it asks you to react to what you are learning at every step as you read. If you can identify experiences in your own life and in the lives of others, your learning will become more firmly established and more relevant to you. The journey to learn the art of helping is a personal one requiring you to know yourself as you learn to help others. Think about what you are reading, record your reactions, discuss them with your teachers and classmates and write to me personally with your ideas.

Organization of the Book

The first part of the book (chapters 1-8) focuses on helping you learn the 21 building blocks, or basic counseling skills. In the first chapter, we will look at the personal side of the helping journey, the stages that you will go through and the roadblocks that you can expect to face. In Chapter 2, you will be introduced to some important definitions, get an overview of the helping process, and receive an orientation to the book. The next six chapters each take up a different set of skills and techniques. They are categorized as invitational, reflecting, advanced reflecting, challenging, goal-setting and solution skills.

Chapters 9-14 help you learn more elaborate techniques, from muscle relaxation training to reframing. In these six chapters, about twenty major counseling techniques are described. In each chapter, two of the most important are explained in a step-by-step process; you will have the opportunity to practice these with your training group. These methods, while more complex, are constructed from the basic building blocks you learned in chapters 1-8.

Each of the chapters from 9 to 14 embodies one of the six therapeutic factors that form the foundation of all effective helping techniques: the therapeutic relationship, enhancing efficacy and self-esteem, practicing new behaviors, lowering or raising emotional arousal, and new learning experiences. You will learn to consider these common curative factors, select those that seem most helpful to the client, and identify specific techniques to address the client's goals. This simple treatment planning approach is called the REPLAN system, an acronym formed by the identifying letter for each therapeutic factor.

Organization of Each Chapter

Every chapter in this book follows a similar format. First, the skills and techniques are described. At two or three places in each chapter, you will encounter a section called *Stop and Reflect*. These sections ask you to pause and think about the personal implications of your learning. This is a way for you to evaluate, agree or disagree with what you are reading and attempt to compare the author's ideas with your own experience. At the end of each chapter, there are group exercises and additional exercises where you will have the opportunity to practice with fellow learners and discuss your experiences. Finally, there is *Homework* that contains assignments for independent exploration. As you use this book, then, you will have time for personal reflection, group work and individual practice. All of these can help you on your own personal journey.

Acknowledgments

There is an Indian saying, "At every step, I must bow to my teacher." The farther I progress on the journey of becoming a helper, the more I become aware of what I owe to those who have taken the time to inspire and encourage me as a person and a helper: Rajinder Singh, J. Melvin Witmer, James Pinnell, Thomas Sweeney, Harry Dewire, John Nolte, James Faulconer, Helen Rucker, Elene Milié Summers, Jesse Carlock and Judith Smith Wright.

I would also like to acknowledge friends who have encouraged me in my writing: Sam Gladding, Gerald Corey and Jeffrey Kottler. I need to recognize the many students and former students who challenged me, reacted to this text and tried out the exercises, including Shane Porter, Lori Porter, Peter Begalla, and Kristi Myers Sutter. Two colleagues at Ohio State University, Paul Granello and Darcy Granello, were instrumental in helping me conceptualize the book in its early stages. I appreciate Darcy's help with the first chapter. Ximena Mejia was especially helpful in encouraging me to keep a multicultural perspective in mind.

I appreciate the helpful comments of those who reviewed various drafts of the manuscript: Dale Blumen, University of Rhode Island; R. David Couch, Southwest Texas State University; Carroy U. Ferguson, University of Massachusetts–Boston; Dale E. Fish, Stephen F. Austin State University; Samuel T. Gladding, Wake Forest University; and Timothy Sewall, University of Wisconsin–Green Bay.

I would like to thank my editor, Kevin Davis, for his guidance and support throughout the project and especially for his choice of Barbara Lyons, the editor who challenged me at every turn and who made my best much better. Finally, I must recognize my most demanding critic and my staunchest supporter, my wife, Jora DeFalco Young, and my children Angela and Joseph, for their patience, encouragement and love.

Brief Contents

Contents

3 Invitational Skills, 37

4 Reflecting Skills, 54

5 Advanced Reflecting Skills, 74

6 Challenging Skills, 99

7 Goal-Setting Skills, 119

8 Solution Skills, 135

9   The Relationship as a Therapeutic Factor, 151

10   Enhancing Efficacy and Self-Esteem, 178

11 Practicing New Behaviors, 203

12 Lowering and Raising Emotional Arousal, 220

13 Activating Client Expectations, Hope and Motivation, 241

14   New Learning Experiences and Termination, 271

Helping as a Personal Journey

by Darcy Haag Granello and Mark Young

Introduction

Learning to be a professional helper is a journey that takes years. It is a personal journey; to do the work, you must be committed to understanding yourself as well as your clients. It is not enough to be skilled; at every turn, helpers face self-doubt, personal prejudices, and feelings of attraction, repulsion, and frustration. We experience self-doubt when our clients encounter complex and unfamiliar problems. We experience attraction and repulsion because of our own needs, and we experience prejudice based on our cultural conditioning. We become frustrated when our clients fail to reach the goals we expect of them. All of these reactions can be roadblocks on our journeys if they interfere with our client relationships. As fallible human beings, we all must keep watch on these tendencies and conquer them as they arise.

No matter how much experience you have with people, the most helpful attitude you can develop is that of the "reflective practitioner." This means that you make a commitment to personal awareness, gaining feedback from others and reflecting on how you can improve your client-oriented skills and attitudes. Many times in your training, you will become defensive, rationalizing your mistakes, discounting the giver of feedback, or calling the client "resistant." These are natural reactions to the threat of feeling uncertain or incompetent. A reflective practitioner examines and reflects upon critical incidents and strong personal feelings in the course of supervision, by keeping a journal of personal counseling or therapy.

Stop and Reflect

Learning the art of helping is a personal journey that asks you to examine your own ideas and reflect on what you are reading. Try to use the "Stop and Reflect" sections to think about the material, jot down your thoughts and reactions, and share them with another classmate or a small group. You will certainly find other points in the book where your own ideas are challenged. Learn to pause at those moments and contrast the two positions. If you can begin this habit now, you are well on your way to becoming a reflective practitioner.

Before you begin this course of study, we ask that you use the following inventory to reflect for a moment and think about your present attitudes about helping. Rather than writing what you think your teacher wants you to write, respond as honestly as possible. Toward the middle of this course and again at the end, you may wish to review this inventory to determine whether your attitudes have changed.

This quiz is one of two "Stop and Reflect" sections in this chapter that are designed to help you become a reflective practitioner. Others are scattered throughout the book. The "Stop and Reflect" sections have no right or wrong answers. They ask for personal reactions to specific topics. They can make your learning more interactive if you take the time to respond honestly, providing a chance to decide whether you agree or disagree with a particular presentation. You may or may not wish to share your answers with others during a class discussion.

Stop and Reflect

1. Write *A* or *D* next to each of the following statements, indicating whether you agree or disagree. Note as well any thoughts that may clarify or qualify your responses.

   a. In most cases, clients come for help because they are in a crisis. They need leadership. In order to help, you should generally be active and directive, providing guidance and advice.

   b. Clients may have different values about families, religious principles, and what is important in life. It is not up to you to change clients' values.

   c. The relationship between helper and client must be a good one. Without good chemistry the counseling process will be difficult, if not impossible.

   d. You must remain at a professional distance. Caring too much about a client makes you lose objectivity.

   e. People are responsible for their own problems. You must get clients to work on themselves, rather than blaming others.

   f. If you have not been through an experience personally, you cannot help another person deal with it.

   g. You should never disclose anything personal to a client; the client's issues should be paramount.

2. Answer the following questions:

   As a helper, which do you think you are most likely to focus on changing (you may circle more than one)?

   a. A client's feelings
   b. A client's thoughts and perceptions
   c. A client's behaviors
   Why? _____

   _____

   When talking with a client about a problem, which do you think you are most likely to focus on?

   a. The history of the problem
   b. The present difficulties caused by the problem
   c. The future goals
   Why? _____

   _____

   Do you think a helper is more responsible for helping a client adjust to the difficulties in the world, or for changing the society that causes mental health problems? How might the attitude you express in response to this question affect your actions as a helper?

   _____

   _____

   _____

3. Describe briefly a situation in which you displayed each of the following helper characteristics:

   Empathy (the ability to put yourself in the shoes of another, to understand the other person's subjective reality):

   _____

   _____

   _____

   Positive regard (the ability to respect another person, even though you may not like what he or she has done):

   _____

   _____

   _____

   Genuineness (the ability to be honest and open with another person, even though what you have to say may be difficult to express):

   _____

   _____

   _____

4. The following are some difficult situations helpers face.

   Rank-order them from 1 to 5, depending on how uncomfortable you might feel in each case. In this ranking, 5 is the most difficult and 1 is the least difficult.
   • A client is considering suicide.
   • A client is suffering from the death of a loved one.
   • A client is struggling over whether to get an abortion.
   • An adolescent client is trying to decide whether he is gay or straight.
   • A married client is having an affair.

How a Helper Develops: Perry's Stages

Susan has known for a long time that she wants to work with people. During her teenage years, a school counselor helped her cope during her parents' divorce. Since then, she has always hoped to work in a helping profession. She is finally sitting in her first course, a techniques class where she will begin her formal training. Suddenly she is filled with a combination of excitement and apprehension. What if she can't do it? What if she says the wrong thing in front of the class or to a fragile client? She is confident in her abilities to memorize facts from the textbook and to select the best answers in multiple-choice exams, but can she really learn and demonstrate her skills? Is she in the wrong place?

Three weeks into the class, Susan is still nervous. When her professor calls on her to practice a role play, her stomach is in knots. She feels light-headed as she heads to the front of the classroom. She fears that she will forget the skills she has just learned, that she will make a mistake, that her mind will go blank and she will appear foolish to her classmates and professor.

Beginning a new course of study can be simultaneously exciting, overwhelming, and intimidating. Perhaps you also feel apprehensive as you read this, wondering whether you will ever learn to make effective interventions. Maybe you have even watched an experienced professional at work and thought, *How does he or she know what to say? How will I ever know the right answers?*

The desire to learn the "right" answers and to make the "right" interventions, and the nervousness that accompanies it, are a natural part of the process of becoming a helper. It may be helpful to know that students often progress through a series of developmental stages, and that learning can be tailored to those stages. This book is based upon a developmental model of learning. This means that you will be asked to practice and learn the very basic therapeutic building blocks first, and then learn how those building blocks can be combined to form higher-order helping behaviors or interventions, called *techniques.*

Let us begin with an overview of developmental stages that you can expect to experience during your training. The stages of cognitive development presented here are based on the work of Perry (1970), who studied undergraduate students during a 20-year period. Later research found that Perry's stages are also applicable to graduate students learning a new profession (Simpson, Dalgaard, & O'Brien, 1986).

The Dualistic or "Right/Wrong" Stage

The first stage is a *dualistic* or absolutist position that can also be called the "right/wrong" stage. It is characterized by the belief that a helper's responses to a client are either right or wrong. In the beginning, trainees often believe there is only one right way to respond to a client's statement or situation. The internal pressure to find that answer is enormous, and students may feel they have failed if they give a response that seems less than perfect. Moreover, they may fail to listen fully to their clients because they are thinking about what they are going to say next. They feel that by planning their next statement, they will be able to construct a better response. Actually, they are losing the train of the interview. Students in this stage often ask for direct feedback with questions such as "Was that right?" "How long should I wait before giving advice?" "What should I have told the client when she asked me that question?"

The Multiplistic Stage

As you learn the therapeutic building blocks presented in the early chapters of this book, you will soon learn that there are actually many possible responses to each statement a client makes. Eventually you will become comfortable with the knowledge that there is no one right answer at any moment in the helping process. For example, a client considering leaving her boyfriend might say something like this:

> "I think that I should get out of the relationship, and then other times I think I should stay. Everyone is giving me advice. What do you advise?"

You might react in several different ways.
- You could respond with a question: "What about the relationship is making you question whether you should stay in it?"
- You could respond with a reflection of feeling: "You feel overwhelmed and confused, and you would like someone to guide you."

- You could respond with a confrontation: "On the one hand, you are saying that you are confused by all the advice; on the other hand, you want me to give my viewpoint. How will that help?"

Each of these responses can be valid. When you discover that there are multiple ways of responding to the same client statement, you will have moved into a *multiplistic* way of thinking. In fact, at this stage, all interventions and techniques may seem equally appropriate. You may find yourself feeling overwhelmed by so many possibilities and wonder what differentiates a good response from a great one.

Students at this stage often report being frustrated and defensive with supervisors who "correct" them because they have not yet learned how to prioritize the possible interventions. For example, a student may pose a series of probing questions to a client. The supervisor might point out in turn that the questions made the client feel interrogated and that the best idea would have been to identify and reflect the client's feelings. A student at the multiplistic stage knows that questioning can be a valid approach, but does not yet understand when this approach is most appropriate and therefore concludes that he or she has made a mistake. Students at this stage may feel that because there are many possible "right" responses to a given situation, there is no organized system in helping. In fact, the student's ideas may seem just as valid as the instructor's. Here are some common statements students make at this phase of development:

"I watched Albert Ellis on film. He didn't reflect a single feeling."
"I can't see why you told me not to ask so many closed questions when you told Ximena that it was all right with her client."
"I thought you said we weren't supposed to give advice, and now you're saying that I should have given this client direction."

The Relativistic Stage

When you have gained some experience through study and practice, you will move into a *relativistic* stage. At this stage you will learn that although many types of responses may be appropriate, depending on the circumstances, some are relatively better than others. You will learn to choose from the many possibilities based on the available information and on the goals for the session.

Let us reconsider the client we discussed earlier who was asking for help with a relationship problem. We identified three possible responses to the client's statement, " I think that I should get out of the relationship and then other times I think I should stay. Everyone is giving me advice. What do you advise?" Each response has merit and each leads in a different direction.

Question: "What about the relationship is making you question whether you should stay in it?"

Response: The client will probably discuss the good and bad points of the relationship.

Reflection of Feeling: "You feel overwhelmed and confused, and you would like someone to guide you."

Response: The client will talk about feelings and may indicate why she feels so helpless.

Confrontation: "On the one hand, you are saying that you are confused by all the advice; on the other hand, you want me to give my viewpoint. How will that help?"

Response: The client may respond with anger at the helper's perception that she is maintaining her confusion by asking people for advice. The client may also begin to explore her lack of confidence in her own decisions.

Obviously, none of these responses is necessarily wrong, but each will take the session in a different direction. At the relativistic stage, you will understand that a response is good or bad depending on whether it takes you in the direction you want to go. You will have moved past a belief in right or wrong answers, and toward an understanding that your choice of responses will have particular repercussions. This will happen when you have the knowledge and self-confidence to make effective choices among a wide variety of interventions and techniques. You may not feel comfortable with the relativistic stage until long after this course is over.

The Challenge of Development

Although the shift from dualistic thinking to relativistic thinking may be the most dramatic change you will make as you become a professional helper, you will meet other challenges in your early training. The frustration and feelings of incompetence that accompany learning the helping skills make many students feel like throwing in the towel. We hope that recognizing these issues will help you feel less alone and will help you deal with them.

Taking Responsibility for Your Own Learning

Helping-skills training requires courage. You must face the areas where you are having problems and report these to your teacher. For example, you may appear to be ahead or behind your classmates as you learn a particular skill in this book. If the class moves ahead, you may need to continue to work on a particular skill by practicing with fellow students, watching videotapes of your performance, reading, or getting special help from the instructor. You must take responsibility for educating yourself and request the training that you need, rather than seeing the process of learning as a "mug and jug" phenomenon, in which the teacher pours from the jug of knowledge into the student's mug. You must move from teacher-directed learning to student-directed learning (Caffarella, 1993). In your training, this means that you may face embarrassment if you are honest about what you do not know.

Finding a Mentor

One of the best ways to learn the helping skills is to watch effective models and to receive feedback from teachers. It is a challenge, though, to find experienced helpers who have the time to act as mentors. Teachers and supervisors are important throughout the journey, but especially in the beginning, and you must seek them out. As time goes on, you will learn to have more faith and confidence in your own judgment and abilities (Skovholt & Ronnestad, 1992). Even then, supervision and mentoring are essential for self-assessment.

Seeking the Perfect Technique

Beginning helpers are extremely eager to learn specific techniques and interventions. They gather techniques and tricks of the trade at workshops, hoping that one will be the magic pill that cures all clients. When you feel anxious or ineffective, it is normal to experience a desire to learn every technique available and assume a sort of cookbook approach to helping. There is nothing wrong with learning all you can. It is unlikely though, that you will find a perfect technique that will work for every client. Pursuit of a perfect technique is characteristic of dualistic or right/wrong thinking. In the relativistic stage, you will evaluate a technique to see whether it is best for a specific client, with a particular problem, in a particular situation.

Finding Yourself in Limbo

As you begin the process of learning to help, you may find that you abandon your "pretraining" self. Although beginning helpers are often naturally therapeutic, they typically find that they must temporarily set aside their old ways of helping. You may find that the new techniques and interventions feel artificial or "not like me" at first. Do not be surprised to hear yourself say, "I used to know what to do when a friend was upset. Now that I've begun to study helping, I no longer know what to say." Even your attempts to regain your old self will seem awkward and artificial. It is a little like the centipede who was asked how he could coordinate those hundred legs and walk. Once he started thinking about it, he couldn't do it. As you consciously learn the helping process, it may seem hard to be natural. The good news is that this feeling passes. Over time, you will find that you are able to integrate the old "therapeutic friend" with the new "therapeutic helper."

Accepting Feedback and Being Perfect

Your willingness to accept feedback will be another indicator of developmental change. As we have said, students in the dualistic stage accept feedback but feel discouraged when they "do it wrong." In the multiplistic stage, they may be defensive in the face of feedback and attempt to justify their actions rather than listening to critiques and suggestions. As you gain confidence and see how different responses take clients in different directions, it is easier not to take such criticism personally. The risk in the early stages is that you may be too hard on yourself, demanding perfection when you are just beginning. Try to focus on your strengths, build on what you are doing well, and learn from feedback.

Other Challenges

If you are a member of a minority group or a woman, have a disability, are one of the first in your family to attain higher education, or are going through a particularly stressful life stage (getting married or divorced, leaving home, having children), this can add an additional challenge to the process of becoming a helper. Students facing outside stressors may also have difficulty maintaining the flexible schedule that is required (Gaff & Gaff, 1981). Specifically, consider how the following differences may have an impact:

- Minority students may lack same-race peer interactions and minority role models (Cheatham & Berg-Cross, 1992).
- Female students raised in traditional families may have difficulty trusting in an internal authority (Bernard, 1981; Marx, 1990). As a profession, we train others to develop internal control and autonomy and we must model this.
- Some male students may not be as attuned to relationships and feelings as their female counterparts. Hypermasculine upbringing may cause male students to seek solutions quickly, before understanding the client. They may fail to recognize feelings such as fear and helplessness in themselves and may therefore have difficulty in recognizing them in others.

Such considerations should serve to illustrate that development is not the same for each person, rather than discouraging those with special situations. An individual's progress cannot be confined to a timetable (Barrow, 1987), nor is it necessarily a linear, step-by-step process. Sometimes you may feel that you are going two steps forward and one step back. Allow yourself time to move at your own pace. Development is not a competition with your classmates; it is a personal journey.

The Perfect Helper

When Do I Quit Developing?

Your development as a professional helper does not end with graduation; it is a life-long process. Academic training will give you the skills, but practice, supervision, networking, and experience will make you a helper. Neither a Ph.D. nor a certificate from a training institute will mean that you have "arrived." Just as students progress through developmental stages, so do professionals. In fact, interviews with professionals possessing more than 20 years of experience revealed that these helpers believed most of their development occurred after graduation (Skovholt & Ronnestad, 1992). Equipped with diplomas but not a lot of work experience, new professionals may feel the effects of the "imposter phenomenon." Beginning helpers also tend to see themselves as frauds who are vulnerable to being found out (Harvey & Katz, 1985). Professionals who have been out of school more than 10 years speak of a deeper authenticity in their work, the reassurance of accumulated wisdom, and the ability to make individual and personalized interventions with their clients. Do you have to wait 10 years until you can be a good helper? No—you can be the best helper you can be at your particular stage. Keep learning, keep receiving supervision, and do not pretend you know more than you do. One of the best books on this topic is *Finding Your Way as a Counselor* by Jeffrey Kottler (1996). It is a book of stories by practicing counselors about the issues they face as they develop. Besides making us feel that we are not alone, the writers give us help in thinking about how to get over the hurdles we continue to face.

To address ongoing developmental needs, the concept of lifelong learning is essential for helpers. Our knowledge of new techniques, advances in research in the field, new client populations, and emerging social issues can be updated through workshops, journals, classes, study groups, and conventions. The foundation you receive in your formal training is important—but it is not enough. The most important things you learn will be those that help you make contact with the needs, dreams, feelings, and viewpoints of your clients.

Who Can Be an Effective Helper?

Asking yourself whether you are really cut out for a job is a key developmental hurdle when you are entering a new field. Are you similar to the professionals you know? What must you know and what abilities must you possess going in? While there is no one personality configuration that defines the perfect helper, various writers have looked at specific traits that lead to effective helping. They have also looked at beliefs and attitudes most conducive to learning and working in the profession. Knowing more about these may help you because many of them can be learned.

The Legacy of Rogers

The writings of Carl Rogers (1967) have provided much of the framework for the core facilitative conditions that many see as the necessary ingredients for change and growth. Rogers believed that clients would move toward growth and positive outcomes if the helper provided the right environment. This environment, he felt, was more a reflection of the helper than an outcome of prescribed techniques or interventions. He considered three personal characteristics to be essential for a helper: congruence, positive regard, and empathic understanding.

Congruence   *Congruence* is the ability to be completely genuine with others; it means that there is consistency between what a person feels and says and how he or she acts. Helpers who are congruent are not afraid to take risks and to spontaneously share reactions and thoughts with clients. They react to clients in the here and now and do not hide behind the facade of the professional role. A simple example of incongruence is when verbal and nonverbal messages conflict. Suppose a helper tells a client that he or she will provide support on the phone during a period of crisis, but does not regularly return phone calls. The nonverbal message comes across more clearly than the verbal one. A helper who is incongruent will not be trusted.

Positive Regard   If helpers do not have *positive regard* for their clients, they will not be congruent in the relationship. It is not that helpers must approve of every client behavior. Rather, the helper must respect the personhood of each client and believe that all people have inherent worth. Hazler (1988) wrote about finding unconditional positive regard while working with a prison population. He described the insight that occurred when he was able to differentiate the prisoners (as real, valuable persons who had hopes and dreams and goals) from their crimes (which were brutal). A helper who works from unconditional positive regard never rejects a person, although he or she may reject that person's actions.

Empathic Understanding   *Empathic understanding,* or empathy, is the ability to understand another person's feelings or world view. Responding to another's feelings can be called *emotional empathy,* while taking the time to reflect an understanding of a person's motives, intentions, values, and thinking might be called *cognitive empathy.* Helpers suspend their own judgment as they learn the subjective world view of their client. Rather than evaluating the content of client statements, the purpose is simply to understand the client's feelings, beliefs, experiences, and goals. Most of us have had the experience of giving advice to a troubled friend and having that advice discounted or rebuffed. Advice giving conveys to a client that he or she is incapable of solving a problem and raises the helper to a superior position. This takes away power and demoralizes the client. Rogers believed that through empathy, clients feel understood and are empowered to solve their own problems.

Other Research on Effective Helping

In the writings of 14 different authors, we found 55 characteristics, attitudes, and beliefs of effective helpers. We have tried to boil these down to a few key elements (Combs, Avila, & Purkey, 1971; Corey, Corey, & Callanan, 1993; Gladding, 1996; McConnaughy, 1987; Patterson & Eisenberg, 1983; Spurling & Dryden, 1989; Truax & Carkhuff, 1967).

First and foremost, an effective helper has a positive view of other people. He or she accepts people who are different and is not judgmental about other people's lifestyles, values, cultures, and religions. He or she wants to help others and believes that people have the desire to change. The helper must be able to communicate his or her nonjudgmental attitude as well as warmth and caring.

Second, the effective helper has good self-esteem and is a secure and mentally healthy person. He or she is not attracted to helping in order to experience power over others. He or she seeks cooperation rather than control. Effective helpers appreciate themselves, but also know their limitations. They are able to dig deep and critically examine themselves. They have the courage to look at themselves under a microscope. They make personal growth integral to their lifestyles.

Most writers agree that effective helpers have good self-care skills. Many who are attracted to this profession want to help others, but soon find that in order to do so they must make certain they have something to give. It is easy to become emotionally bankrupt and burned out if one does not develop techniques for stress management, time management, relaxation, leisure, and personal self-renewal. The effective helper has a stable and fulfilling personal life with close family and friends to provide support as a buffer to the stress of helping.

The effective helper is both creative and intellectually competent, a renaissance person who appreciates both the science and the art of helping. The effective helper has specialized knowledge of human relationships, human motivation, and human development and understands how to create change. Those who remain vital in the profession have "insatiable curiosity" to learn and grow in their skills and knowledge (Spurling & Dryden, 1989). Creativity and flexibility are equally vital. Helping requires one to devise innovative ideas with different clients in different situations. A helper must be able to deal flexibly with ambivalence, unfinished business, and moral dilemmas. He or she must allow clients to work through difficult situations without moving them to premature decisions.

When Moreno, the founder of psychodrama, was once asked what the most important quality was for a group leader, his unexpected response was "courage." The courage displayed by an effective helper has two facets: First, the helper must be able to listen unflinchingly to stories of great pain. Like a physician who sets a broken arm, he or she must be able to look with a detached eye at human destruction and see where the healing can be started. Second, the helper's job requires risk taking and action, without the security offered by other sciences. Individuals who believe that they can control every circumstance and that there is a procedure and a solution for every crisis have a difficult time as helpers. For example, no psychological test can accurately predict a person's tendency to be violent. Helpers' decisions must be based on experience, training, and even intuition. Since human behavior is relatively unpredictable, effective helpers must be able to live with that uncertainty.

What Can You Offer a Client?

No one set of personal qualities makes an effective helper. There is room in the profession for many types of individuals, each of whom brings significant strengths and must simultaneously be aware of the limitations of his or her own personality style. The example of a former student will help to illustrate this. Maria, a graduate student, got under her teacher's skin sometimes because she had little patience for long theoretical discussions and did not like studying the research. She seemed to roll her eyes when the discussion got too intellectual. She was practical and concrete and liked people who were "down-to-earth." She wanted to solve problems and make a difference in the lives of children. She tended to be too quick to come to closure with adult clients who were stymied. Sometimes she pushed them to make decisions and seemed insensitive to their turmoil. However, Maria now works effectively as a school counselor. Her particular strength is that she knows how to manage crises. She instantly grasps what has to be done and takes bold and concrete steps to accomplish it. She has excellent judgment and is indispensable to her school because she knows how to take quick action. Maria's case illustrates that each of us brings strengths to the helping role. Much depends on knowing our own abilities and finding an environment where they can be put to good use.

As you consider the characteristics of effective helpers that we have identified, remember two things. First, many of the characteristics can be developed. They are not necessarily inborn. Second, each person brings unique characteristics to the helping profession and, as in Maria's case, the challenge is to find a place where these will help others. Do not look at the characteristics of effective helpers in order to identify which you do not have. We are not trying to produce clones. A client will have a relationship with you, not with a set of skills. By focusing on your strengths, you will have much to offer a client.

Stop and Reflect

The characteristics of effective helpers identified by the experts are listed in brief form in the following statements. Which of these qualities do you presently possess and on which do you want to improve? For those where you think you need to develop, think for a moment about what you might do to improve yourself or what extracurricular activities you might become involved with in order to grow in that area.

1. You believe that most people are basically good and strive for self-improvement. You enjoy people and believe that people can change.
   Is this true for you?_____ How can you grow?

   _____

   _____

2. You have good self-esteem and are basically a secure, mentally healthy person. (This is sometimes difficult to know about yourself, but friends and family can help you answer this question.)
   Is this true for you?_____ How can you grow?

   _____

   _____

3. You have good self-care skills. You do not become overly involved with those you are helping. You know your limits and are able to set boundaries to protect yourself from burnout.
   Is this true for you?_____ How can you grow?

   _____

   _____

4. You are an intellectually curious person who is interested in the psychological world of other people. You can appreciate both a scientific and an artistic approach to learning about helping.
   Is this true for you? _____ How can you grow?

   _____

   _____

5. You are a creative person in some aspect of your life. You are not rigid or inflexible in your attitudes. You are not burdened with prejudices about people, cultures, religions, and family customs that differ from your own.

Is this true for you?_____ How can you grow?

_____

_____

6. You have enough courage to examine your own personal problems and seek
   help and guidance for yourself when you need it. You are willing to admit that
   you need to change and grow. For the most part, you are able to deal with the
   cruelties that other people inflict on each other without being so disturbed
   that it disrupts your own life or your ability to help.

   Is this true for you?_____ How can you grow?

_____

_____

Summary

Entering a new kind of learning brings about uncertainty and challenges us to remain open and
nondefensive. Knowing that learning the art of
helping follows some predictable stages should
allow us to be less self-critical when we face the
normal developmental hurdles.

Learning to help is a personal journey because it means evaluating and analyzing oneself at
each step while simultaneously trying to understand a client. It is a long journey and everyone
travels at a different rate, bringing unique traits
and differing gifts to the helping process. While
experts have identified characteristics of effective
helpers, including self-acceptance, cooperative-
ness, and the ability to reach out to others, there
is not just one kind of person who can practice the
helping arts. The core conditions of Carl Rogers
remain a legacy to beginning helpers. They remind us that our job is to be personally honest, to
have a positive regard for our clients, and to convey empathy.

As you progress, you may find it helpful to
consider some methods for self-assessment and
self-improvement that other students have found
conducive to their own learning and development.

- Many have found it useful to keep a journal
  of their thoughts and feelings during this

course. Identify your fears and moments of
success, then look back from start to finish
to see how far you have come.

- Consider getting together on a regular basis with other students to practice new
  skills and to support each other.

- You may want to keep a record of unrealistic thoughts, self-criticisms, and exaggerated expectations that you may be holding
  for yourself.

- Think about recording your practice sessions and writing down all of your responses. Identify each of your responses
  and think about how they affected the
  client.

By now you might be thinking that learning
to help is a long journey requiring much of the
learner. It is that, but it is also a voyage of personal discovery and an opportunity to encounter and appreciate other people at a level
of intimacy that few professions allow. As you
begin, remember the adage of the mountain
climber: Don't look at the summit, but rather
keep your attention on your next step. One day
you'll get to the top; right now, appreciate
where you are.

Exercises

Exercise 1

In groups of three, discuss your reasons for wanting to become professional helpers. What are your expectations and concerns?

Exercise 2

Think of a time when you learned a new skill (for example, playing tennis or learning to sew). What stages did you go through? How did you improve? Were you self-critical at first? Can you identify any particular thoughts that you had during that time? Discuss them with classmates and see whether you can relate that experience to learning helping skills.

Homework

Make an appointment with a professional helper who has been working for about a year. Ask him or her the following questions about ongoing developmental changes. Then interview another professional helper with at least 10 years of experience. Compare his or her answers to those of the first helper. (Be sure to add a couple of questions of particular interest to you.)

- Are you supervised by another helper? If so, what do you value about these sessions?
- Are there any particular helpers you admire?
- When do you feel least confident in your job?
- To what theoretical orientation do you subscribe?
- What kinds of professional reading do you do?
- Do you benefit from conferences?
- Did you notice any big jumps or stages in your ability to help?

References

Barrow, J. C. (1987). Is student development "dissonance roulette?" *Journal of College Student Personnel, 28,* 12–13.

Bernard, J. (1981). Women's educational needs. In A. W. Chickering (Ed.), *The modern American college* (pp. 256–278). New York: Jossey-Bass.

Caffarella, R. S. (1993). Self-directed learning. *New Directions for Adult and Continuing Education, 57,* 25–35.

Cheatham, H. E., & Berg-Cross, L. (1992). College student development: African Americans reconsidered. *College Student Development, 6,* 167–191.

Combs, A. W., Avila, D. L., & Purkey, W. W. (1971). *Helping relationships: Basic concepts for helping professions.* Boston: Allyn & Bacon.

Corey, G., Corey, M. S., & Callanan, P. (1993). *Issues and ethics in the helping professions* (4th ed.). Monterey, CA: Brooks/Cole.

Gaff, J. G., & Gaff, S. S. (1981). Student-faculty relationships. In A. W. Chickering (Ed.), *The modern American college* (pp. 642–657). New York: Jossey-Bass.

Gladding, S. (1996). *Counseling: A comprehensive profession.* Columbus, OH: Merrill.

Harvey, C., & Katz, C. (1985). *If I'm so successful, why do I feel like a fake? The imposter phenomenon.* New York: St. Martin's Press.

Hazler, R. J. (1988). Stumbling into unconditional positive regard. *Journal of Counseling and Development, 67,* 130.

Kottler, J. A. (Ed.) (1996). *Finding your way as a counselor.* Alexandria, VA: American Counseling Association.

Marx, S. D. (1990). Phase I: On the transition from student to professional. *Psychotherapy in Private Practice, 8(2),* 57–67.

McConnaughy, E. A. (1987). The person of the therapist in psychotherapeutic practice. *Psychotherapy, 24,* 303–314.

Patterson, L. E., & Eisenberg, S. (1983). *The counseling process* (3rd ed.). Boston: Houghton Mifflin.

Perry, W. G., Jr. (1970). *Forms of intellectual and ethical development in the college years.* New York: Holt, Rinehart & Winston.

Rogers, C. R. (1967). *Person to person: The problem of being human.* Moab, UT: Real People Press.

Simpson, D. E., Dalgaard, K. A., & O'Brien, D. K. (1986). Student and faculty assumptions about the nature of uncertainty in medicine and medical education. *Journal of Family Practice, 23(5),* 468–472.

Skovholt, T. M., & Ronnestad, M. H. (1992). Themes in therapist and counselor development. *Journal of Counseling and Development, 70,* 505–515.

Spurling, L., & Dryden, W. (1989). The self and the therapeutic domain. In W. Dryden & L. Spurling (Eds.), *On becoming a psychotherapist.* London: Tavistock/Routledge.

Truax, C. B., & Carkhuff, R. R. (1967). *Toward effective counseling and psychotherapy: Training and practice.* Chicago: Aldine.

The Nuts and Bolts of Helping

Introduction

T he purpose of this chapter is to orient you to this book and to the way in which
we will be teaching the helping process. We will provide some important definitions
of the terms that we will be using. In addition, we want to introduce you to the basic
skills, or building blocks, that we will be teaching you in later chapters. We plan to
show that these building blocks are the basic elements that make up more complicated counseling techniques that you also will be learning. Because beginning
helpers often question how basic skills fit into the larger picture, we will present the
theoretical concept of common or therapeutic factors, which is a way of organizing
helping techniques based on what we are trying to achieve. We end the chapter by
taking you through the process of a basic helping session. After reading and completing the exercises in this chapter, you should have a framework that will help you
organize your learning.

Defining Some Important Terms

What Is Helping?

Helping is a broad term that encompasses all of the activities we use to assist another person, whether we have a professional relationship or not. For example, a
school administrator who takes time to listen to a crying first-grader can utilize helping skills. A foster parent can learn to listen to the child and to the biological parents.
A teacher's aide in a sixth-grade classroom can take a nonjudgmental stance when a
child talks about why homework is late. Husbands and wives can help each other.
Helping does not require a contract or a professional, confidential relationship.
Helping requires only a person desiring help (a client), someone willing and able to
give help (a helper), and a conducive setting (Hackney & Cormier, 1988). You can
learn helping skills and use them whether you are on the way to becoming a professional or you simply want to help those with whom you live and work.

While *helping* is the overarching term, different settings and different contracts
between helper and client mean that there are a variety of ways that the helping relationship can be defined. To the newcomer, this can be confusing. In the next sections we will clarify some of the most common terms, including *interviewing, counseling,* and *psychotherapy.*

Is Interviewing Helping?

According to the simplest definition, *interviewing* is the gathering and recording of
information about a client. The purpose of the interview may be to help a client or to
make a decision about a client. For example, many counseling centers hire intake in-
terviewers who talk with clients and then assign them to the appropriate counselor

or refer them to another service or treatment facility. Employers interview applicants for jobs and for promotions. Normally, interviewing involves one or two sessions. There is no long-term relationship.

Interviewing is not simply a mechanical procedure best accomplished by a computer. It usually has a purpose beyond completing a file folder. An interview may be used to help make a decision about an applicant for a job, for a promotion, or for entrance into special training programs; to determine the appropriateness of counseling for an individual; or to assess some skill, as in an oral examination in graduate school. Interviewing is an art whose medium is the relationship. A skilled interviewer knows how to quickly develop a working relationship with an interviewee in order to obtain the most relevant information for the decision-making process.

An interview may also be used to test the interviewee's skills, poise, or ability to think in a "live" setting. For example, some companies use a "stress interview" to determine which of their employees can operate best under pressure. The interviewee is "grilled" and even treated disrespectfully, so the employer can see his or her reaction. Many people think that this kind of interview is unethical, but the point is that an interview can provide an opportunity to observe the reaction of a student or employee in a contrived situation similar to actual situations that he or she may face.

In summary, interviewing is not necessarily helping. At times, an interview can lay the groundwork for helping by establishing a working relationship and collecting needed information. However, interviews are also conducted in a wide variety of settings for the purposes of companies, agencies, or institutions, rather than for the good of clients.

What Are Counseling and Psychotherapy?

Counseling and *psychotherapy* are professional helping services provided by trained individuals who have contracts with their clients to assist them in attaining their goals. Counselors and psychotherapists use specific techniques to persuade, inform, arouse, motivate, and encourage their clients. Sessions with a counselor or psychotherapist take place on a regularly scheduled basis, usually weekly, and last about one hour. A therapeutic relationship will last several months or even several years. While counselors and psychotherapists may help clients deal with emergencies, they also try to empower clients to address persistent problems in living and make changes in their lives that will lead to overall improvement rather than momentary relief.

In the literature and in practice, the words *counseling* and *psychotherapy* are now used interchangeably. Historically, however, different professional groups including mental health counselors, social workers, psychiatrists, psychologists, and marriage and family therapists have tended to prefer one or the other, and many people, including clients, are confused by the two terms.

Between 1920 and 1950, psychotherapy was practiced mainly with clients troubled by mental disorders. *Mental disorders* are defined as severe disturbances of mood, thought, and behavior for which there are specific diagnostic criteria. Examples include major depression, schizophrenia, and anxiety disorders. The criteria are outlined in *DSM-IV* (1994), the American Psychiatric Association's bible of mental disorders. Even today, these are the only problems that most health insurance companies recognize as reimbursable. From the beginning, the processes of assessment, diagnosis, and treatment planning have been integral aspects of psychotherapy.

Counseling was invented as psychotherapy for "normal people" in the 1960s. Medical terminology was shunned by counselors, along with words such as *treatment* and *diagnosis.* Counselors believed in seeing each individual as a unique person rather than a diagnostic label. For that reason, personality tests and other assessment activities were minimized in practice since they tended to categorize clients. Counseling was focused more on the counselor/client relationship as the medium for change.

Today, the distinctions between counseling and psychotherapy have blurred. Now, counseling includes helping people with mental disorders as well as those experiencing normal developmental problems. Modern counselors routinely learn diagnostic methods and engage in treatment planning. By the same token, professionals such as psychologists and marriage and family therapists who prefer the term *psychotherapy* or *therapy* also help clients with difficulties such as adolescent adjustment, marital issues, and the transition to college or work—what we might call "normal" problems. While some may still feel there are good reasons to make distinctions between the terms *counseling* and *psychotherapy,* they will be used interchangeably in this book. Both will refer to the contractual and professional relationship between a trained helper and a client.

How Is Professional Helping Different from Friendship?

As you learn the art of helping, you will be able to provide friends with a listening ear, a caring attitude, and emotional support, enhancing your relationships and aiding those you care about. There is, however, a difference between friendship and a professional helping relationship: each is built on a distinct contract. A friendship is based on the assumption that we are there for each other—it is a two-way street. In a professional helping relationship, it is the client's issues that are discussed and the client's welfare that is paramount. In exchange, the helper receives compensation for professional services rendered. Consider this analogy: You mention to your friend, who is a dentist, that you have a toothache. She may suggest you take some aspirin and that you make an appointment with a dentist as soon as possible. Despite her professional capabilities, she probably won't pull out her dental equipment and start drilling. While the comparison doesn't hold completely, counseling can also be a painful process best accomplished in a less personal setting. A professional helper is required to identify and articulate issues not normally broached in a friendship, from sex to painful childhood memories. Moreover, the professional helper is committed to hours of listening, confidentiality, responsibility for the outcome, and disregard for whether the client ultimately likes him or her. The helper's concern as a professional is to do a good job, not to maintain a relationship for its own sake.

One reason for drawing the distinction between a professional helping relationship and a friendship is that it is easy to make mistakes in both settings when you begin learning helping skills. You might be tempted to use elaborate techniques on your friends when all they are asking for is support. On the other hand, you might find yourself treating a client as a friend. Remember that with friends you have no contract to instigate change, but rather an opportunity to care, to show concern, and to provide support. In the helping relationship, you have a contract to help the client make specific changes in his or her life, not to make a new friend, enjoy each other's company, or discuss the weather, your family, or your favorite hobby. What makes this difficult is that we have learned our natural helping skills in the context of our friendships and family relationships. It is easy to find ourselves being sociable and sympathetic rather than thinking about how to help the client.

What Can You Expect from a Helping Relationship?

Beginners' hopes about what can be achieved in a professional helping relationship are often very grand. When, inevitably, they are dashed, naturally there is disappointment. In this section, we will identify some common unrealistic beliefs about the helping process that many struggle with, and we will examine the corresponding, more reasonable expectations.

Unrealistic Belief: "I must help clients solve all of their problems."

Reasonable Expectation: "If all goes well, we may make a good-sized dent in a problem or two and the client will continue to progress when the relationship ends."

Most agencies and private practitioners find that on the average helpers and clients see each other for 6 to 10 sessions. Most clients do not expect long-term relationships, and they come to a helper to deal with specific problems. Indeed, contrary to our expectations, clients who have even just a session or two with a helper are often very satisfied with the results. Helpers must not become disappointed when they want more changes than the client wants.

Unrealistic Belief: "If the client is not motivated, it is my fault."

Reasonable Expectation: "While I can stimulate clients to consider making changes, I cannot force them."

It is estimated that nearly a third of helpers' clients today are involuntary referrals by courts, government agencies, or others. While clients can be forced to attend sessions, helping is a voluntary relationship. Ethically, we cannot attempt to coerce clients to change. We can supply the opportunities for change, but the client must meet us halfway.

In the real world, some clients are genuinely opposed to changing their lifestyles, even self-destructive ones. Others know they need to change but require encouragement. The art of helping involves getting clients to envisage and consider a different kind of life and persuading them to change. For example, when an alcoholic client is sent by the court for treatment, the helper's job is twofold. First, the helper must intensify the client's awareness of the negative consequences of drinking; second, the helper must help the client see the advantages of sobriety. However, even with detoxification and Alcoholics Anonymous, the odds are less than even that the client will stop drinking.

Unrealistic Belief: "If I care about my clients or have good practical experience, that is enough."

Reasonable Expectation: "Besides caring and practical experience in the helping field, I must learn all the skills I can."

No matter how good our intentions are, caring about another person is not a substitute for professional knowledge of how to help him or her. A caring physician is of course better than one who is indifferent, but the physician must also be well trained and fully abreast of his or her specialty through continuing education. Similarly, caring will enhance your helping skills, but it cannot replace them.

Some helpers believe that they are already fully trained. They have practical skills gained in the helping field and they go on for formal education merely to "have their ticket punched." This is a potentially dangerous attitude. When we see the wide variety and severity of client problems and the new treatments that are cropping up everywhere, it is unreasonable to believe that we can ignore skills training in our formal education or that we can ever really be finished learning.

Unrealistic Belief: "If I am a good helper, my client will never need help again."

Reasonable Expectation: "If we are successful, the client may consult me again when a similar problem arises."

It is unrealistic to expect that clients should be "cured" in a single encounter with a helper. A family doctor model is a better analogy for the helping relationship. Such a relationship can be revived if the client needs help at a later developmental stage.

Unrealistic Belief: "If I am effective, I will be effective with every client."

Reasonable Expectation: "I will not be the best match for every client."

Even famous therapists have found that they are not effective with every person who consults them. There are many reasons why a helping relationship may not succeed; some are not under the helper's control. The client may perceive a mismatch because the helper is not of his or her gender, race, or social class. The client may instantly dislike the helper because the helper reminds him or her of someone in the past. It is easy to feel rejected and disappointed if a client does not wish to continue the helping relationship, especially if you feel positive about it.

Unrealistic Belief: "It is unacceptable to make a mistake."

Reasonable Expectation: "I am a fallible human being who can learn from mistakes."

If you attend workshops and seminars, you will see well-known counselors and psychotherapists showing videos of their amazing successes. In *The Imperfect*

Therapist (1989), Jeffrey Kottler and Diane Blau have suggested that we can learn just as much from our failures, but we rarely talk about them. It is both ego protection and a fear that we are incompetent that keeps us from discussing our mistakes with colleagues, supervisors, and teachers. However, if we do not examine these missteps, we are likely to repeat them.

Unrealistic Belief: "Sometimes I feel incompetent; therefore I am not competent."

Reasonable Expectation: "There will be many times in my training and work as a helper when I will feel incompetent. It goes with the territory."

No matter how long you have worked as a helper, clients will surprise you. They have problems you have never heard of and problems your supervisor has never encountered. This can be either an assault on your self-esteem or a reminder that you need to keep learning. Feeling incompetent should motivate you to learn more about a client and his or her problems, but it should not paralyze you. You can seek supervision or possibly refer your client, if an honest appraisal of the situation suggests that this would be in the client's best interest.

Helping Summary

Professional helping has as its basis a special therapeutic relationship involving a trained helper and a client wanting help. In the preceding paragraphs we alluded to some of these characteristics. They are:

1. The purpose for the relationship is the resolution of the client's issues.
2. An atmosphere of safety and trust is established, allowing honest disclosure by the client and the giving of feedback by the helper.
3. There is a sense of teamwork as both helper and client work toward a mutually agreed-upon goal.
4. There is a contract specifying what will be disclosed to others outside of the relationship.
5. There is an agreement about compensation for the helper.
6. There is an understanding that the relationship is confined to the counseling sessions and does not overlap into the participants' personal lives.
7. The relationship normally has regular meeting times over a period of time.
8. As a contractual relationship, the relationship can be terminated.

Stop and Reflect

Begin by considering each of the following questions:

- Have you ever given help to a friend that was not well received or that changed the friendship?
- Some people think that our mobile, stressful society has led to a lack of community and has separated us from our extended family. If friendships

and family relationships were closer, do you think that professional helping would be needed?

- What would you do if a friend told you he or she was thinking about suicide? In what other situations do you think a professional helper might have an advantage?

What Makes Helping Work?

Every system of counseling and psychotherapy has a slightly different answer to this question and each theory has its own set of techniques to produce change. Unfortunately, there are now between 100 and 460 systems of counseling and psychotherapy (Corsini, 1981; Herink, 1980; Parloff, 1979). In response to this confusion, many practitioners have adopted an *eclectic,* or integrative, point of view. Eclecticism can be defined as selecting what is best from many theories and also selecting "what works." As Paul (1967) stated, the task is to ascertain "what treatment, by whom, is most effective for this individual with that specific problem (or set of problems) and under which set of circumstances" (p. 111).

In recent years, eclectic approaches have been developed that attempt to reconcile the differences in the various theories, or at least try to take what is best from several points of view (Norcross, 1986; Young, 1992). One survey showed that as many as 75% of practicing counselors could be defined as eclectic (Young, 1990). Surveys of other professions, including psychologists and social workers, show similar results (Jayartne, 1982; Norcross & Prochaska, 1982; Smith, 1982).

Therapeutic Factors

There are several approaches to eclecticism, but one that merits a deeper examination is called *common curative or therapeutic factors.* Therapeutic factors are the activities that seem to be used by all effective helpers. For example, a positive, supportive, and confiding relationship between client and helper is considered to be a necessary condition for helping by nearly all theoretical positions.

The lifetime work of Jerome Frank (1971, 1981) showed how different theories rely on common therapeutic factors for their effectiveness. Although helpers seem to be utilizing different techniques, they are actually drawing on similar methods. Frank and Frank (1991) describe six common therapeutic factors that seem to cut across all theoretical persuasions:

1. A strong helper/client relationship.
2. Enhancement of the client's sense of efficacy and self-esteem.
3. Provision of opportunities to practice new behaviors.
4. Lowering and raising emotional arousal.
5. Methods that activate the client's expectations, hope, and motivation.
6. Provision of new learning experiences.

These therapeutic factors provide the basis for organizing much of chapters 9–14.

Learning to Help

Therapeutic factors are a way of understanding that many different theories and techniques seem to be effective because they are actually drawing on similar methods; however, this knowledge does not provide us with a starting point in our own journey. Which skills should we learn first? Over the last few decades, writers and educators have generally agreed upon a similar set of basic, "generic" helping skills, forming a good starting point regardless of the setting where the helper works or the theory that he or she follows. Chapters 3–8 of the book are devoted to teaching these basic skills or building blocks.

Basic helping skills are normally taught as small units called "microskills" (Ivey, 1971). Individual microskills often seem so insignificant, however, that students may experience difficulty in learning them. They have trouble seeing the big picture when they learn first one piece and then another. In this section, we want to help you to understand how all of the specific skills of helping fit together. With this structure in the back of your mind, it may be easier to learn the microskills one by one.

Therapeutic Building Blocks

Therapeutic building blocks is the phrase we use to describe the fundamental components, or microskills, of the helping interview, such as asking open-ended questions or maintaining eye contact. These building blocks are like the elements in the periodic table we all learned in high school chemistry. There are both simple elements like carbon and more elaborate elements like uranium; there are simple building blocks like paraphrasing and more complex ones like confrontation. The therapeutic building blocks represent the simplest behaviors used to create change. In this book, we identify 21 building blocks. They represent the combined wisdom of many theorists and helpers over time. While 21 may seem to be an overwhelming number, nearly half are quite simple (we call them invitational skills) and very easy to master. The building-block skills are divided into six categories (see Figure 2-1). Each category represents an important helping activity:

Invitational Skills (8 skills—Chapter 3)

Invitational skills are the basic means by which the helper invites the client into a therapeutic relationship. These skills encompass all the subtle verbal and nonverbal ways that helpers use to encourage a client to open up. For example, how would you feel if the helper constantly checked her watch or looked out the window? You may think that paying attention is only polite, but it is also a skill. Learning to keep your focus on the client with eye contact and body posture are two of the invitational behaviors you will learn and practice in Chapter 3.

Reflecting Skills (2 skills—Chapter 4)

Have you ever had an experience in which a friend listened to your story and understood completely what you were trying to get across? Maybe your friend identified your emotions or your thoughts before you spoke them. Reflections are "snapshots" of the client's story or of the client's emotional reactions to the story. Reflecting skills help us connect with the client at a deeper level than invitational skills and facilitate more in-depth exploration of the client's problem.

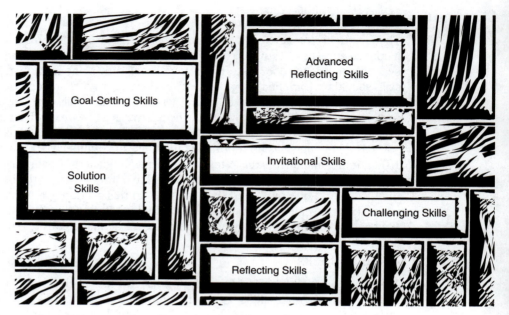

Figure 2-1
Building-blocks wall

Advanced Reflecting Skills (2 skills—Chapter 5)

Advanced reflecting skills include reflecting meaning and summarizing. These are advanced skills because they require an understanding of the client's issues beyond the basic facts and the client's feelings. For example, the loss of a job encompasses more than just the economics and the feelings of loss. Depending on the person, job loss may also be seen as a sign of failure or evidence of incompetence. Advanced reflecting skills are hunches that helpers make and repeat to their clients to see whether they understand the unique impact of the client's problem.

Challenging Skills (2 skills—Chapter 6)

While invitational skills and reflecting skills encourage and support clients, challenging skills push clients to deeper self-examination. Challenging skills identify incongruities in a client's story or give information on client strengths and weaknesses. For example, a client who says that he wishes to stop smoking but does not follow any of the suggestions of the helper might be challenged about the discrepancy between words and behavior. Challenging skills can strain the relationship. Challenging skills remind clients that the helping relationship is a work project, not a social encounter. Giving feedback and confrontation are fundamental challenging skills.

Goal-Setting Skills (2 skills—Chapter 7)

Goal-setting skills are needed to confirm that the client and the helper are on the same track. One method helpers use to keep clients on track is the skill of keeping the focus on the client, which means urging the client to avoid blaming others and encouraging him or her to take responsibility for finding solutions. The second key helping skill in this area is "boiling down the problem," which involves shaping a client's vague or unrealistic goals into specific and achievable targets.

Solution Skills (5 skills—Chapter 8)

A helper uses solution skills to help the client identify alternatives for action. Advice giving is a commonly misused skill whose advantages are usually outweighed by its drawbacks. Other solution skills include giving information, giving directives, using alternative interpretation, and brainstorming. Brainstorming, a Madison Avenue idea-generating activity, is a key skill that helpers can use to encourage clients to expand their options.

We have said that one of the problems confronting most beginning helpers is that they learn elementary skills in isolation and cannot see how they fit into a grand scheme. They do not understand how flashy theory-based techniques such as Gestalt's "empty chair" relate to the "baby steps" they are learning in class. They begin making fun of their own tendencies to say "Um hmm. . . ," and "What I hear you saying is. . . ." They secretly yearn to do what famous therapists do in training films: have a tremendous impact on clients.

Just as in basketball or baseball, every helper needs to practice the fundamentals. In sports, when fundamentals are mastered, they are linked into more complex movements, or plays. Without solid fundamentals, the plays are less effective. An example of this principle is shown in the film *The Karate Kid*. When he begins to study karate, the student, Daniel, is put to work sanding wood, painting, and waxing cars. At one point he rebels and angrily confronts his teacher for having wasted his time. Daniel wants to be Bruce Lee. In a moving scene, the teacher shows him how each of the seemingly unrelated tasks is a fundamental move in the art of karate. Through repetition, the movements become second nature; when combined in a combat situation, they form an impenetrable defense. Your training in the helping skills will be very similar. You will learn basic helping movements, many of which will seem awkward and repetitive. However, when they are properly learned and put in proper sequence, they form more elaborate and elegant techniques. The art of helping develops when the basics have become second nature.

Earlier, we used the metaphor of the periodic table of the elements. We said that basic helping skills are analogous to these elements. In Chapters 9–14 of this book, you will learn a few selected techniques that are combinations of the basic building blocks. In chemistry, elements in combination make up molecules. For example, a water molecule (H_2O) is composed of two hydrogen atoms and one oxygen atom. Similarly, more advanced techniques such as role playing are constructed from building blocks. We will be teaching a few fairly common and important counseling techniques in Chapters 9–14; we hope that you will recognize them as merely creative

syntheses of the skills you have already mastered. Once you have learned the building blocks, you must simply apply them in a specific sequence to perform a technique. In your life as a counselor, therapist, or helper, you will learn many more complex methods than the techniques presented here. But we think you will see that the
building blocks of each will be the same.

Stages of the Helping Process: A Road Map

Figure 2-2 shows the stages of the helping process over time. The diagram shows five
helper tasks that occur more or less sequentially from the first session to the last.
This five-part structure is based on the work of several different writers (Dimond &
Havens, 1975; Dimond, Havens, & Jones, 1978; Ivey & Mathews, 1986). The arrows
show the typical progression of a client problem. Helping starts at the center of the
diagram with relationship-building activities. Helpers use invitational skills and then
move to assessment activities. From there, helping moves through the stages clock-
wise to treatment planning, intervention, and finally to evaluation. The diagram follows the progression of a problem from its disclosure to resolution. Once a problem
has been resolved, the cycle either begins again with a new problem or leads to termination of the relationship. The stages of the helping process become clearer in a
case example described in the words of Jane, a counselor, whose client Barbara was
referred by her daughter because of depression.

Relationship Building: The Heart of Helping

Jane: "Barbara is 68 years old with gray hair, somewhat slim but apparently in good
physical condition. Barbara's husband died six months ago and while she felt that she
had handled the first three months well, recently she had become depressed and ap-
athetic about life. She reminded me a lot of my grandmother, and I felt an urgency to
help her when I realized how much her depression was interfering with her life. She

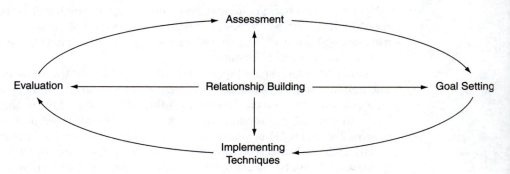

Figure 2-2
Stages of the helping process

had recently started taking antidepressant medication but her doctor had insisted that she also receive counseling. Barbara had never seen a counselor before, so I took some time to explain the process to her. She was skeptical that anything would help, so I spent about half of the first session listening, reflecting, and getting to know her better. I told her a little bit about myself because I sensed that we would not be successful unless she trusted me. Near the end of the session, I told her that we would be working on the feelings of depression that she was experiencing and I told her about the techniques we might use. We also discussed the issue of confidentiality and I explained that I could not even update her daughter without her permission. This seemed to alleviate some of her tension because Barbara saw asking for help as a weakness and was afraid that others would judge her for being depressed. We signed an agreement for treatment that outlined the limits to confidentiality and the fees. By the end of the session, Barbara seemed more hopeful about progress, but the work of dealing with depression was still before us."

At the heart of the helping process is the therapeutic relationship, which provides the core conditions or supports for the other activities of the helper. The relationship is the glue that holds the entire process together. The relationship has a special place in Figure 2-2 to emphasize its central role in the helping process. In relationship building, the helper uses invitational skills to allow the client to open up, to convey understanding, and to create a safe environment. This is exactly what Jane did with Barbara during their first session. Jane set out initially to allay any misgivings that Barbara might have had by giving her information, developing a personal relationship, and dealing with Barbara's real concern that entering a helping relationship was a sign of weakness. It is obvious in this case that if the relationship were not firmly established, assessment would be extremely difficult.

Assessment

Jane: "When I first saw Barbara, I was a little bit surprised to see that she was well-groomed, alert, and talkative. Her depression seemed to have started about three months after the death of her second husband, Carl. I took a complete history of Barbara's life and noted a number of losses. Barbara's mother died when she was 20 years old; when Barbara was 28, she lost a baby through a miscarriage, whose complications left her unable to have more children. Barbara's first husband subsequently died during military training. In addition to the death of Carl, her second husband, Barbara was now coping with financial problems. Carl's will had named her as the sole beneficiary, but the will was being contested by his children. The family problems and the lack of money were both sources of worry.

"One of the things I did in the very first session was to assess her suicide risk. Barbara denied any suicidal thoughts. She said, 'Sometimes I wish I were dead, but I would never kill myself.' Barbara had strong religious beliefs against suicide, did not own a gun, and her depression was not so severe that I was worried about her taking her own life. I did call the family physician and asked him to limit the number of antidepressant pills that were issued to Barbara each week to reduce the possibility of an overdose. I diagnosed Barbara's problems as mild depression stemming from grief and associated stress, with only a small risk of suicide.

"One of the things that I noticed was that any time Barbara identified something she was doing well, she discounted it and seemed to exaggerate the minor deficiencies in her performance. For example, she still went to church twice per week but she was very discouraged over the fact that it often took her 15 minutes to decide what clothes to wear in the morning. Barbara agreed to keep a journal of the negative thoughts so that we could deal with them in future sessions."

Assessment is the second stage of the helping process. As is apparent in Barbara's case, much of the assessment stage is inseparable from the relationship-building stage because helpers are observing their clients and collecting information from the moment that they first meet. This process continues throughout the helping relationship, but most of the background data pours in during the first few sessions. Some agencies ask that assessment forms be completed and a preliminary diagnosis be completed during the first session. That approach has an important drawback: it fails to take into account that the therapeutic relationship must be established before there is trust and a contract for helping. Figure 2-2 illustrates this premise. The relationship is drawn at the center of the diagram and is connected to each part of the process. Clearly, when the relationship is well established, assessment is more complete and easier to accomplish because clients are much better able to freely disclose information about the problem and about themselves.

Assessment includes formal and informal ways that helpers collect information about clients, among them paper-and-pencil tests, client reports, and helper observations. Collecting background data helps determine whether the services available are appropriate for a particular client and assures the helper that he or she is not missing a serious mental disorder such as schizophrenia, a substance abuse problem, or suicidal or violent behavior. Beyond this, assessment is the organizing of data on the client's problem, providing baseline data and relevant history.

Goal Setting

Jane: "In the second session, I started off by giving Barbara a summary of what I had learned so far. She had three major problems: feelings of depression that interfered with her life, financial problems, and disruption of family relationships caused by the fight over the will. We both agreed that there was little she could do at the present time to work on the money issues or deal with her husband's children. Instead, we decided to focus efforts on reducing her feelings of depression. In order to do this, I asked Barbara to think about what she would be doing if the depression lifted and what she would be feeling and thinking. This was easy for her. Barbara said, 'I would be able to play golf again. I would get dressed early every morning, and I would not have these negative thoughts going around in my head.' Using Barbara's ideas, we hammered out some goals for the next few sessions. First, we agreed that we would reduce the negative self-talk that Barbara was complaining about because this probably caused the depression or made it worse. Second, Barbara would become more physically active to help her get back to her old routine. Barbara resisted playing golf because she was afraid that friends would notice her depression, and she wanted to appear normal. I encouraged her to accept the fact that being depressed was a normal reaction to the loss of a spouse and that she did not have to expect so much of herself right now. I hoped that by acting 'normal,' Barbara would start to feel 'normal.' "

Once a helper has gained an understanding of the client's problem and the important background issues, it is time to identify the helping goals. Here, Barbara and Jane have identified two goals: reducing Barbara's negative self-talk and increasing her physical activity. In this book, we advance the theory that goals, such as those set by Barbara and Jane, are a collaborative construction of helper and client. While goals do not necessarily have to be defined behaviorally, if the desired outcomes are observable, it is easier to know when they have been achieved. In the goal-setting phase, professionals draw up treatment plans that identify agreed-upon goals and the interventions that will be used to achieve them. This plan instills hope in the client and invites his or her participation as a team player.

Intervention and Action

Jane: "The third session was spent in going over the negative thoughts that Barbara had recorded. When summarized, they seemed to have two persistent themes: 'I should not be depressed,' and 'I am a burden on everyone by being depressed.' These seemed to reflect Barbara's tendencies to be a perfectionist and her fear of relying on others. We discussed the fact that Barbara even felt she was a burden to me. During the session, we identified some ways of countering her negative thinking by examining the flaws in her negative conclusions. She readily admitted that the thoughts were not logical but did not see how to stop them. We suggested that she combat these thoughts in a two-step process. First, stop the thought when she noticed it; second, replace the thought with one that was more constructive. For example, when the thought came up, 'I am a weakling for being depressed,' she was to argue back, 'Feeling this way is a natural part of grieving. I am not perfect; no one is.' We decided to check on how effective these replacement thoughts were at the next meeting. She was to practice 'stopping and inserting' over the next week. During this session, I also encouraged Barbara to begin playing golf one time per week as an experiment and only temporarily. I explained that she might not feel 'normal,' but that the exercise would help to reduce the depression. She agreed reluctantly."

During the intervention stage, professional helpers utilize more advanced skills and ask clients to take active steps to reach their goals. In the case of Barbara, Jane taught Barbara how to identify negative self-statements and replace them. She also directed Barbara to begin some physical exercise and indicated that she would check on Barbara's progress on both goals at the next meeting. Note again in Figure 2-2 that the relationship occupies a central position and is connected to the intervention stage. In the case of Barbara and Jane, you might see how important a trusting, confiding, therapeutic relationship is to the implementation of techniques. At this stage, if Barbara did not have confidence and trust, she would not have wholeheartedly engaged in the activities suggested by Jane. Barbara was also more likely to complete homework assignments because Jane expected her to do so.

Evaluation

Jane: "We spent about five sessions working on Barbara's negative thinking and increasing her physical exercise. Although her physician decided to discontinue the antidepressant medication because of severe dizziness, Barbara's depression gradually lifted over this time. I asked Barbara to evaluate her progress after about two months of counseling. She said, 'Well, I am back to doing most of the things I used to do. I am still very sad sometimes when I think about Carl. I still have trouble making decisions. That is not totally over. I guess I won't be happy until that is resolved. I am still afraid to be around people too much because I don't want them to see how I feel.' Because Barbara focused on the missing elements only, I felt that I should also ask her to give herself a pat on the back for having reduced her depression and increased her physical activity. She was reluctant to do this, but admitted that things were substantially improved. I continued to see Barbara for three more months. The last month was mainly follow-up to make certain that changes were lasting and to reassure her that support was available."

Helpers regularly ask their clients to evaluate progress toward the treatment goals. Some time in each session is devoted to gauging the effectiveness of specific techniques and homework. Evaluation also occurs during the final sessions when the helper and client—like Jane and Barbara—review and celebrate the resolution of problems. When client and helper agree that the goals have been reached, either new goals are set (completing the circle in Figure 2-2) or the relationship is terminated.

Stop and Reflect

Let us think back for a moment to the case of Jane and Barbara. Jot down your answers to the following questions and discuss them with classmates or your training group.

Relationship Building   Jane was reminded of her grandmother when she first saw Barbara. Because Jane seemed to care about her own grandmother, this created a motive to help Barbara. Can you think of some situations that might arise between Barbara and Jane where Jane's feelings might not have been productive? In your own experience with different age groups, think about whether you feel more comfortable working with children, adults, or older people. Which group will create the biggest challenge for you?

Assessment   One of the first issues Jane assessed was Barbara's suicide potential. All helpers have to make judgments about this in the first few sessions, even those who work with young children. Since assessing suicide and violent behavior is not an exact science, how do you think you might handle a situation in which you are not certain about a particular client's suicidal intentions?

Goal Setting   In the case of Jane and Barbara, they both agreed that Barbara needed to deal with her depression, but it was Jane who suggested the goal of increasing physical exercise. Some feel that the helper's job is to accomplish the client's agenda.

Others feel that the helper's expertise and a diagnosis should be the basis of the goals. For example, some would say that because Barbara was depressed, she needed medication and a certain kind of therapy, whether Barbara wished to deal with her depression or not. Who do you think should set the goals in the helping relationship: the helper, the client, or both?

Intervention and Action   In thinking about which techniques to use, Barbara mainly focused on cognitive techniques: identifying and replacing negative thoughts. Barbara only reluctantly agreed to the procedure. How do you think you might deal with a client's lack of motivation to work on a problem or do homework assignments? What might you say?

Evaluation   In the evaluation stage, Jane highlighted Barbara's successes, but Barbara focused on the fact that she was not 100% back to normal. Why do you think Barbara made this statement? Could she be fearing the termination of the helping relationship? What other issues might be behind her unwillingness to recognize success? How do you think you might deal with her fears about termination or other reasons for her reluctance to celebrate success?

Summary

Helping, counseling, and *psychotherapy* are all terms that have been used to describe the processes involved in a professional relationship designed to identify problem issues and bring about positive change. Helping skills are best used within a professional relationship that includes a trained helper and a client seeking help. There are limits to how much one can employ helping skills with personal friends and family.

In this book, you will learn 21 basic helping skills or building blocks. When combined and elaborated, these building blocks form more complex techniques. It is important to take the time to practice the fundamental skills and gain mastery of them even if they seem overly simple or awkward.

A therapeutic relationship has special characteristics that differentiate it from other relationships. Among these are a contractual relationship between helper and client. In the case of Jane and Barbara, we emphasized how crucial this relationship is to accomplishing the goals of the helping relationship. Each of the other stages of helping—

assessment, treatment planning, intervention/action, and evaluation—is dependent on the quality of the helper/client bond.

As you learn the helping process, understand that you will encounter expected hurdles along the way. The process of learning helping skills is not merely an intellectual exercise involving memorization and taking tests. Unlike other courses you have taken, your ability to read and understand the textbook will probably not be sufficient to ensure success. You will need to demonstrate the skills taught in the textbook. For those who are "book smart," this might create anxiety. For those who learn best in a hands-on environment, this may be a refreshing change.

Finally, let us warn you against comparing yourself with others. Each person has a separate timetable for learning new skills. Some of us are so cognitively oriented that it takes longer. If you run into trouble, ask your instructor for help. Watch videos demonstrating basic helping skills; most of all, practice and get feedback from your instructor and classmates. Experience has shown that students with a desire to help can learn the requisite skills in time, but it is a personal journey and each person's timetable is different. To learn helping skills, you must be patient with your own pace, watch good models, and practice whenever possible.

Exercises

Exercise 1

Take a look at the list of eight characteristics of a therapeutic relationship contained in this chapter. Compare a therapeutic relationship to a friendship or a relationship with a favorite teacher. What are the similarities and differences? Discuss this in a small group.

Exercise 2

To get a better idea of the stages of the helping process, let us examine the five stages shown in Figure 2-2. Think about a problem that you are experiencing. It can be a small problem you are now facing, or an issue from the past that you can pretend is an issue today. Jot down your answers to the following questions about each stage of the helping interview.

a. Assessment:

What would a helper have to find out about you, your family, your environment, your goals, your cultural and religious background, and your history before he or she could help you?

_____

_____

_____

_____

b. Treatment planning:

Imagine yourself without the problem. What would you be doing, thinking, or feeling that you are not experiencing now?

_____

_____

_____

Can you turn your problem into a goal? For example, rather than stating the problem ("I bite my fingernails"), transform it to a future scenario, such as "I would like to have attractive nails that I would not be ashamed of in public."

_____

_____

_____

c. Intervention and action:

What kind of approach by a helper would you object to? What kind of help would you like? Respond briefly to each of the following interventions that a helper might use:

Advice about how to solve your problem

_____

Writing in a journal_____

Just someone to listen (no advice) _____

_____

Keeping a record of specific behaviors

_____

Role-playing your problem _____

Entering group therapy _____

Bringing a family member with you _____

_____

An assignment to say no more often

_____

d. Evaluation:

How would you know that you had definitely completed your goal? How would you be thinking, feeling, and acting?

_____

_____

_____

Homework

Homework 1

Go over the list of unrealistic beliefs about helping and the corresponding reasonable expectations given in this chapter. Identify two or three that you think might create difficulties for you in the helping relationship. Do you agree with the author's conclusions? Write a paragraph about each belief giving your reactions and indicate how you might deal with that belief if it should arise in your interaction with a client. Alternately, identify some of the beliefs you have about helping that you think are realistic.

Homework 2

You will sometimes hear helpers talk about being "overinvolved" with clients; they will sometimes suggest that you "keep a professional distance." What kinds of behaviors do you think would indicate that a helper was too involved in a client's life? What limits should the helper set in the relationship? Does this necessarily mean that the helper should not care about a client? What ethical guidelines do professional helpers rely on to determine whether the professional relationship has become too close? Write down your reaction to these questions in a page or two.

References

American Psychiatric Association (1993). *Diagnostic and Statistical Manual of Mental Disorders* (4th ed.). Washington, DC: Author.

Corsini, R. J. (Ed.), (1981). *Handbook of innovative psychotherapies.* New York: Wiley.

Dimond, R. E., & Havens, R. A. (1975). Restructuring psychotherapy: Toward a prescriptive eclecticism. *Professional Psychology, 6,* 193–200.

Dimond, R. E., Havens, R. A., & Jones, A. C. (1978). A conceptual framework for the practice of prescriptive eclecticism in psychotherapy. *American Psychologist, 33,* 239–248.

Frank, J. D. (1971). Psychotherapists need theories. *International Journal of Psychiatry, 9,* 146–149.

Frank, J. D. (1981). Therapeutic components shared by all psychotherapies. In J. H. Harvey & M. M. Parks (Eds.), *Psychotherapy research and behavior change* (pp. 175–182). Washington, DC: American Psychological Association.

Frank, J. D., & Frank, J. B. (1991). *Persuasion and healing* (3rd ed.). Baltimore: Johns Hopkins University Press.

Hackney, H., & Cormier, L. S. (1988). *Counseling strategies and interventions* (3rd ed.). Upper Saddle River, NJ: Prentice-Hall.

Herink, R. (1980). *The psychotherapy handbook: The A to Z guide to more than 250 different therapies in use today.* New York: New American Library.

Ivey, A. E. (1971). *Microcounseling: Innovations in interviewing training.* Springfield, IL: Thomas.

Ivey, A. E., & Mathews, J. W. (1986). A metamodel for structuring the clinical interview. In W. P. Anderson (Ed.), *Innovative counseling: A handbook of readings* (pp. 77–83). Alexandria, VA: American Counseling Association.

Jayartne, S. (1982). Characteristics and theoretical orientations of clinical social workers: A national survey. *Journal of Social Services Research, 4,* 17–30.

Kottler, J., & Blau, D. (1989). *The imperfect therapist.* San Francisco: Jossey-Bass.

Norcross, J. C. (1986). Eclectic psychotherapy: An introduction and overview. In J. C. Norcross (Ed.), *Handbook of eclectic psychotherapy* (pp. 3–24). New York: Brunner/Mazel.

Norcross, J. C., & Prochaska, J. O. (1982). A national survey of clinical psychologists: Affiliations and orientations. *The Clinical Psychologist, 35,* 4–6.

Parloff, M. B. (1979, February). Shopping for the right therapy. *Saturday Review,* 135–142.

Paul, G. L. (1967). Strategy of outcome research in psychotherapy. *Journal of Consulting Psychology, 31,* 109–119.

Smith, D. S. (1982). Trends in counseling and psychotherapy. *American Psychologist, 37,* 802–809.

Young, M. E. (1990). Theoretical trends in counselling. *Guidance and Counselling, 8,* 1–16.

Young, M. E. (1992). *Counseling methods and techniques: An eclectic approach.* New York: Merrill.

Invitational Skills

Yes, there is no doubt that paper is patient and as I don't intend to show this
cardboard covered notebook . . . to anyone, unless I find a real friend, boy
or girl, probably nobody cares. And now I come to the root of the matter, the
reason for my diary: it is that I have no such real friend.

Anne Frank
(in Moffat & Painter, 1974, p. 15)

Introduction

The entry in Anne Frank's diary that introduces this chapter reminds us of the
great human need to be understood and to communicate. James Pennebaker is the
author of some of the most interesting research on the benefits of self-disclosure and
confession (1989). He became interested in the phenomenon while talking to poly-
graph operators who interviewed people suspected of crimes. These technicians told
him stories of suspects who admitted their guilt under questioning and even thanked
the operator of the lie-detecting apparatus. Some said they even received Christmas
cards from some of the subjects! Pennebaker found in his own research that college
students who wrote diaries about their most troubling experiences showed better
immune-system responses and better health. Pennebaker's work exemplifies a growing body of evidence that confession is good for the soul *and* the body.

When clients come for help, they are seeking to explain themselves to a nonjudgmental listener. They want to untangle the knots of traumas, miscalculations,
and resentments that are troubling them. They do not simply want absolution; they
want to understand how things got so mixed up and how to deal with the unfinished
business they are left with. The confiding relationship can provide the opportunity
to heal the body and the mind if the helper can get out of the way and allow the client
to open up and investigate all the nooks and crannies of the problem.

In this chapter, you will learn and practice the first building block: invitational
skills. These skills will allow you to convey to clients that you are listening to them and
that you are concerned. Clients respond to this atmosphere by disclosing and exploring their problems more fully. The invitational skills are especially useful early on in
the helping session when they do not interfere with the client's recitation of the story.
But they are useful as well throughout the entire helping process, session after session, as the helper listens to the client tell about his or her progress and setbacks.

Listening to the Client's Story

Is there such a thing as "therapeutic listening"? Is it possible that merely giving someone your full attention is healing in and of itself? Some writers have called this *active*
listening, a way of attending and encouraging without intruding on the client's
telling of the story. Too often, we want to stir things up, make things happen, and cre-

ate a change. This tendency is what prompts friends to offer advice. But frequently the best approach in the professional helping relationship is to allow clients to fully describe a situation to you and to themselves.

Therapists such as Sheldon Kopp (1978) have emphasized the importance of clients' telling their tales. The tale is a recitation of the problem from the client's unique perspective. Egan (1994) calls this the client's "story." Michael White, the Australian therapist, describes it as a "narrative." It often seems that a client wants to get the story told as completely as possible before he or she will allow the helper to make an intervention. Hidden in each client's story are the keys to understanding how that person views the world.

Sometimes clients will open the floodgates during the first session, pausing only to take a breath and seemingly ignoring all of the helper's comments. It is difficult for others even to indicate their reason for coming. In either case, the role of the helper *seems* passive, waiting for the client to finish the tale. Actually, however, the helper is listening with complete attention so as to fully understand the import of the story and the unique perspective of the client. Many client stories are as ironic and full of twists and turns as a Shakespearean comedy or tragedy. You cannot make a comment that a client will respect until you know the names of all the players and their relationships. It is difficult for many beginning helpers to listen. Their own personal anxiety and wish to help propel them to rely on the skills they have used all of their lives: support and advice giving. The art of helping, however, requires the helper to place his or her own concerns on the back burner and to focus on the client.

Nonverbal Skills: Sending the Right Message as a Helper

Nonverbal communication is body language. In therapeutic communication, we talk about eight kinds of nonverbals: eye contact, body position, attentive silence, voice tone, gestures, facial expressions, physical distance, and touching. The importance of nonverbals in communication cannot be overemphasized; they are crucial to getting the full message. The most honest and persuasive messages are delivered in person. We have a friend who spends thousands of dollars each year traveling to local offices of her company scattered around the state. If communication simply consisted of an exchange of words or data, all of her business could be transacted by e-mail, telephone, or written correspondence, but in fact these approaches are only the next best thing to being there. To communicate fully, you have to look into the other person's face. Perhaps nonverbals can be compared to the musical score in a movie. It can influence us tremendously, but we rarely notice that it is there.

Have you ever participated in a conference call on the telephone? This can be a frustrating ordeal. In face-to-face conversations, knowing when to speak and when to listen are communicated nonverbally. Without access to nonverbals, everyone talks at once or there are long silences. Written communication can be even more frustrating because we cannot hear the tone of voice or we imagine the wrong tone.

Some writers have suggested that as much as 80% of communication takes place on the nonverbal level. Certainly the most persuasive communication takes place when we can see another person's face, when we are standing in the same room. It is much easier to say no to a salesperson on the phone than to one who has a foot in the door. The art of helping is also a persuasive art. We are persuading clients to open up to us and to themselves. To that end, we have to be aware of the nonverbals we are sending. We want to use nonverbals that invite the client to greater openness.

Nonverbal Skills in the Helping Relationship

One maxim says that you can't *not* communicate. Our bodies are not very good liars. Folded arms and drooping facial muscles tend to give us away. Astute helpers learn to read the body language of their clients as clues to the depth and meaning of each client's problems. But helpers must also be aware of the signals that *they* are sending. The client is interpreting and reacting to the nonverbal messages of the helper. Nonverbals sent by the helper are interpreted by the client on first contact by voice tone on the phone and even by the arrangement of the office where client and helper meet.

This discussion brings up an important caution about nonverbal messages: they are *ambiguous*. A client whose voice seems monotonous and depressed may be suffering from a cold. Crossed arms may be a better signal that the air conditioning is too high than that the client is "closed." Because of the ambiguous nature of nonverbal communication, most helpers are cautious about interpreting a client's posture, facial expressions, or voice tone, or about drawing serious conclusions about a client's mental state from a single piece of information. On the other hand, we have no control over what conclusions clients may draw from inadvertent nonverbals that we as helpers send. For this reason, from the beginning, helpers try to present the most welcoming, nonthreatening, and facilitative nonverbals that encourage the client to talk and do not interfere with the client's telling of the story.

Eye Contact

Eye-to-eye contact is the first and most important indicator of listening. It conveys confidence and involvement (Ridley & Asbury, 1988). In Western culture, we normally associate lack of eye contact with dishonesty, indifference, or shame. The helper uses eye contact to communicate full attention. Eye contact implies that the client and helper are sitting at the same level and facing each other squarely. Remember, however, that a fixed stare can be disconcerting and should be broken naturally and intermittently if the client becomes uncomfortable.

More care needs to be taken when dealing with people who may be offended by direct eye contact. In some situations, such as in the military and in some cultural groups, direct eye contact can be considered defiant, rude, or a sign that you consider yourself superior.

Body Position

Actions speak louder than words. Posture may be the most often noticed aspect of body language, so it becomes important to have a "posture of involvement." A relaxed alertness communicates, "I am comfortable with myself and I have time to listen to you." A relaxed and attentive posture is one of the fundamental tools for putting the client at ease. Lounging or sprawling in the chair may put the person more at ease, but it may also communicate that the level of the helper's involvement is minimal. Leaning slightly forward is suggested, since it decreases personal distance and conveys caring during moments of peak emotion and attentiveness at other times. It is also suggested that the helper maintain an open posture—no crossed arms or legs (Egan, 1994). Open postures seem to relax the client and discourage defensiveness.

Attentive Silence

In social settings, it is vital to keep a conversation flowing. A deadly silence is a disaster at a party, but therapy does not follow the same rules. Allowing for periods of silence gives the client moments for reflection (Cormier & Cormier, 1991) and the helper time for processing. Silence is often the most appropriate response to a client's disclosure of loss. Words often seem somehow to deny the validity of a person's grief or are perceived as attempts to sweep feelings under the rug. At these times, the helper falls back on attentive silence in order to be present without interfering. Finally, the most powerful use of silence is to nudge the client to disclose. When there is a gap in the conversation, there is a pressure to talk to fill in the void. If the helper is able to endure this discomfort, it may prompt the client to open up more.

Voice Tone

A client's voice can give clues to his or her emotional state. We can tell from the client's voice which issues are the most painful. Similarly, clients respond to the helper's voice tone. Helpers attempt to show calm concern and empathy with their voices. In addition, they try to mirror the client's emotional tone. The helper does not try to *match* the intensity of the client's feelings, but instead raises the voice slightly or gives emphasis to words that give the client the message that the importance of his or her experience has been understood. For example, suppose a client describes a situation in which he did not get an expected promotion. The helper may respond to the client's situation by saying, "You were really angry," or "You were *really* angry." In the second sentence, the helper's voice tone emphasized the word *really* to reflect the client's intense feelings.

Gestures and Facial Expressions

Originally, Freudian analysts were trained to avoid reacting to the client's expressions of emotion. Those trained in the client-centered approach of Carl Rogers feel that gestures and facial expressions can be useful tools. Facial expressions that convey the helper's reactions to the client's joy or sadness, anger or fear, or excitement or boredom can serve as attending responses (Fretz, Corn, Tuemmler, & Bellet, 1979; Maurer & Tindall, 1983).

Sometimes expressive body movements by the helper can also be distracting to the client. Fidgeting, playing with a pencil, drumming fingers, frequent shifting of body position, checking a watch, and other such movements can be read by the client as anxiety, impatience, or lack of interest. On the other hand, a motionless, statue-like pose is likely to be perceived as aloof and controlled. A listener who is moderately re-active to the client's content and affect is more likely to be viewed as friendly, warm, casual, and natural. Specifically, this includes occasional head nodding for encour-agement, a facial expression that indicates concern and interest, and encouraging movements of the hands that are not distracting.

Physical Distance

Most one-on-one dialogues in mainstream U.S. culture take place at a distance of 1 to 4 feet. Normally, about 3 feet is a comfortable space for personal interaction. In general, the smaller the physical distance, the more personal the interaction. Physical barriers such as desks increase distance and add a feeling of formality to the relationship. On the other hand, extremely close quarters can also feel intimi-dating. Stone and Morden (1976) suggest 5 feet as an optimal distance between client and helper. In general, the helper should determine the distance between chairs and allow the client to arrange the chair in a comfortable way if it is too close or too far.

Touching

While there is much to be said for the healing power of the human touch, certain taboos must be observed (Goodman & Teicher, 1988). Touch can communicate car-ing and concern, especially during moments of grief (Driscoll, Newman, & Seals, 1988). Willison and Masson (1986) contend that research supports the appropriate use of touch, which can have a positive impact on clients. Holroyd and Brodsky (1980) recommend touch with socially immature clients to foster communication and bonding and with clients in grief, depression, or trauma as a way of showing sup-port. They also encourage the use of touch as a greeting or at termination. In addi-tion, touch may be used to emphasize or underline important points (Older, 1982).

Touch can also engender powerful sexual and transference reactions in the client (Alyn, 1988). For a client who has been sexually abused, a good deal of anxi-ety may be aroused. Perhaps fears about physical contact are overblown in the liter-ature, but many writers have cautioned that it is important to know the client well before initiating touch. Probably the safest helper/client touching is a handshake or a pat on the shoulder or back. One guideline is to use touch sparingly to communi-cate encouragement and concern, with the knowledge that even slight gestures may evoke sexual or fearful feelings in the client. The helper must be prepared to recog-nize this reaction in the client and be willing to deal with it when appropriate.

Fisher, Rytting, and Heslin (1976) established three useful guidelines to deter-mine the appropriate use of touch: touch should be appropriate to the situation, should not impose a greater level of intimacy than the client can handle, and should not communicate a negative message (such as a patronizing pat).

It must be recognized here that there is a "pro-hug" school of thought. A hug may be a special gesture at the time of termination, but it seems to be a sort of forced in-timacy when used routinely. An embrace may be seen as phony, and the helper may actually be seen as less trustworthy (Suiter & Goodyear, 1985).

Table 3-1

Nonverbal cue	Warmth	Coldness
Tone of voice	Soft	Hard
Facial expression	Smiling, interested	Poker-faced, frowning, uninterested
Posture	Lean towards other; relaxed	Lean away from other; tense
Eye contact	Look into other's eyes	Avoid looking into other's eyes
Touching	Touch other softly	Avoid touching other
Gestures	Open, welcoming	Closed, guarding oneself, and keeping other away
Spatial distance	Close	Distant

From Johnson, D. W. (1997). *Reaching Out.* Boston, MA: Allyn & Bacon, p. 179.

While touch has its dangers, the helper still wants to convey warmth and caring nonverbally. Warmth is not a skill but a synthesis of nonverbals that can have a powerful effect on a client's willingness to open up. In Table 3-1, David Johnson (1997) shows how nonverbals can communicate either warmth or coldness.

Stop and Reflect

Differences in nonverbal communication can be a stumbling block in forming a relationship with someone from a different cultural background. We make assumptions about people based on the way they talk, look, or dress. In this section, Andrew Daire, who works in a university counseling center, describes how talking about these perceived differences can lead to a better helping relationship.

I am the only black counselor at a small, private, predominantly white institution in the South. Once I was called to the office to meet a new client named Ray. When I came downstairs, I saw a burly young man in western wear and cowboy boots who possessed a strong Southern drawl. He seemed very guarded initially, which I attributed to his discomfort in talking about his relationship problems. Soon, I realized that we were not talking about the obvious differences between us, so I made the decision to cautiously open a discussion about his upbringing and how it differed from my own.

During that first session, he talked about his father being a racist and then admitted that he had almost walked out the door when he saw that his counselor was black. Despite this first encounter, we were able to form a good counseling relationship and over the next nine sessions, we talked about his relationship issues as well as stereotypes and prejudice. When I saw my client for the first time, based on his clothing and accent, I expected him to be racist and I was tempted to pull back and not even address our differences. I now believe that treating him in that way would probably have reinforced his stereotypes and prejudice rather than providing an opportunity for him to examine them. I also began to understand a little about the fears that drive the attitudes of people like Ray and his father. Most important, we were able to develop a relationship that helped him deal with the issues he had come to work on. Had I not brought up the impressions we shared of each other, he probably would not have come back after the first session.

- Have you ever thought about attitudes you might have about people from various parts of the country? Do certain accents lead you to make unfair assumptions about people at times?

- Have you ever thought of clothing as a communication? Clothing choice is a nonverbal that can be culturally influenced. Think about your own background. What customs can you identify in your own culture that help you decide what clothes to wear? Are certain colors best for certain occasions? What can you tell about a person from his or her clothing? Is there a risk in "pigeonholing" people based on their clothing choice or the kind of car they drive?

- Think for a moment about your experience with people from different cultural backgrounds. Which cultural groups do you have the most experience with through friends or family? Which groups do you know the least about? How important do you think it is for a helper to experience a variety of cultural groups during his or her training? Do you think it is possible for a helper to cross over cultural lines, as Andrew did, and help someone who seems to be so different?

- In Andrew's story, both helper and client reacted to the nonverbals of the other person—clothing, accent, skin color, and probably many other tiny cultural differences—but they were hesitant to mention them. When do you think it might be important in a helping relationship to notice these and talk about them? When do you think it is best to ignore them? Discuss this with your classmates.

Opening Skills: Inviting Client Self-Disclosure

The best atmosphere for encouraging client self-disclosure is free of coercion, manipulation, and "game playing." The first step in creating this climate is to communicate to the client that you, the helper, are present intellectually and emotionally. Opening skills are verbal encouragers by the helper that help create coercion-free environments. Opening skills include door openers, minimal encouragers, open and closed questions, and clarifiers.

Door Openers

A *door opener* is "a noncoercive invitation to talk" (Bolton, 1979, p. 40). The door opener is initiated by the helper, but the client determines the depth of the response. It is more than a passing social response or greeting; the door opener's purpose is to signal availability on the part of the listener and encourage exploration and discussion. By contrast, valuative or judgmental responses are door closers. A door opener is generally a positive, nonjudgmental response made during the initial phase of a contact. It may include observations by the helper such as the following:

"I see you are reading a book about Sylvia Plath. (observation) How do you like it?"

"You look down this morning. (observation) Do you want to talk about it?"

"What's on your mind?"

"Tell me about it."

"Can you say more about that?"

"What would you like to talk about today?"

Minimal Encouragers

Minimal encouragers are brief supportive statements that convey attention and understanding. Most of us are most familiar with minimal encouragers from the media's image of the Freudian analyst behind the couch, stroking his beard and saying "Mm-hmm." Like door openers, minimal encouragers are verbal responses that show interest and involvement but allow the client to determine the primary direction of the conversation. They are different from door openers in that they communicate only that the listener is on track. Such phrases reinforce talking on the part of the client and are often accompanied by an approving nod of the head. The following are examples of minimal encouragers:

"I see."

"Yes."

"Right."

"Okay."

"Hmm."

"I've got you."

"I hear you."

"I'm with you."

Of course, these responses are not sufficient to help a client achieve the goals of therapy, but if they are *not* used frequently enough (especially in the beginning of the session), the client feels stranded and uncertain. Clients present complex problems and scenes with many players. It is crucial that the helper convey that the information painfully revealed by the client has been received.

Questions

Of all opening skills, *questions* are the most easily abused. Research suggests that beginning helpers ask more questions than experienced ones (Ornston, Cichetti, Levine, & Freeman, 1968). Excessive questions get in the way of listening, and the client usually feels interrogated and evaluated.

In a vain search for causes, helpers sometimes ask a lot of "why" questions. If you ask a five-year-old why he or she stepped in the mud, the inevitable and truthful answer is "I don't know." It is only when we become adults that we are able to come up with lengthy rationalizations for our behavior. A few decisions that people make, such as buying a car or a house, may have been the result of a lengthy rational process. But the best answer to most *why* questions is usually, "It seemed like a good idea at the time." Certainly this is true even about why people get married or why they make other important life changes. A helper soon learns to avoid this dead end, which seems to question the client's logic. With experience, the helper learns to ask more open questions and determine the *why* of the client's behavior from the whole of a client's story rather than from the client's quick explanation.

Still, questions are often needed to get the client to explain the hidden or painful aspects of the story. This became apparent in a recent demonstration session in which a client discussed the trauma and aftereffects of a serious two-car accident. The helper, using door openers, minimal encouragers, and appropriate nonverbals, was able to get the client to talk about many of the important issues. However, the student helper failed to ask whether the other person in the accident had been killed or injured, which was the key to the client's shame and remorse about the incident. It is vital to get this kind of question answered, but clients often talk about a problem on a superficial level at first. The helper must delve to get the important facts. The difficulty is in knowing which aspects of the story are likely to be important. In this incident, for example, it was the seriousness of the accident that needed to be explored. Many beginning helpers might ask about less relevant details. They might ask when the accident occurred, how bad the damage was to the cars involved, where the incident took place, and so on. These sorts of questions sidetrack the client from the important issues.

Open and Closed Questions

There are two major categories of questions: open and closed. *Closed questions* ask for specific information and usually require a short factual response. There are certainly times when closed questions are called for; for example, when a closed question is used as a *clarifier:* "What do you mean when you say you 'can't breathe' in this relationship?" Certainly, it is important to get the important facts straight and to focus in on areas that the client seems to gloss over, but closed questions usually interrupt the client and are less productive.

Open questions allow more freedom of expression. The difference between the two question types is something like the comparison between multiple-choice and essay questions used by teachers. Multiple-choice tests check the facts, but essays show deeper levels of understanding. Here are some examples of open and closed questions and likely client responses.

Closed

Helper: "Are you getting along with your parents these days?"

Client: "Yeah. Pretty good."

Open

Helper: "Can you tell me how you and your parents have been dealing with your differences recently?"

Client: "Well, we haven't been, really. We're not fighting but we're not talking either. Just existing."

Closed

Helper: "Are you married now?"

Client: "No, divorced."

Open

Helper: "Can you tell me a little about your personal relationships during the past few years?"

Client: "Well, I've been divorced for six months from my second wife. We were married for over seven years and one day she left me for this guy at work. Since then, I haven't really been up to seeing anyone."

As these examples suggest, open questions elicit more information than closed questions. Open questions also persuade the client to answer by giving the client the opportunity to refuse.

Stop and Reflect

Are You an Opener?

This scale was developed by Miller, Berg, and Archer (1983) to identify individuals who are good listeners and are able to get others to disclose information about themselves. If you score yourself as low on this scale, it does not mean that you cannot learn the basic helping skills in this book; consider it to be a self-assessment of where you are right now, not what you can become. At the end of the book, we will direct you to answer again to see what changes you have made. Answer as honestly as you can. Don't compare your score to other people's, since the scale was not devised for that purpose.

Rate each statement as it applies to you on a scale of 0–4 (4 = strongly agree; 0 = strongly disagree).

1. People frequently tell me about themselves.
2. I've been told that I'm a good listener.
3. I'm very accepting of others.
4. People trust me with their secrets.
5. I easily get people to "open up."

6. People feel relaxed around me.

7. I enjoy listening to people.

8. I'm sympathetic to people's problems.

9. I encourage people to tell me how they are feeling.

10. I can keep people talking about themselves.

People with high scores on the Opener Scale are more successful in eliciting self-disclosure, even in people whose self disclosure is normally low. High scorers are able to take the viewpoint of others more easily than low scorers. Purvis, Dabbs, & Hopper (1984) found that high scorers show more comfort, enjoyment, and attentiveness than low scorers and are more verbally and nonverbally engaged. What reaction do you have to your results?

Summary

Every client has a story to tell. Invitational skills let the client know we are interested in that story and encourage him or her to open up even more. Invitational skills have two basic building blocks: nonverbal and opening skills. Nonverbal skills are body language used by helpers to provide the right conditions for the client to open up. The skills are eye contact, body position, attentive silence, voice tone, gestures and facial expressions, physical distance, and touching. Opening skills are the verbal messages helpers send to facilitate the client's disclosure. Opening skills include door openers, minimal encouragers, and open and closed questions.

Invitational skills are relatively simple to learn but they count for a lot in the relationship between client and helper. Getting the relationship off on the right foot means establishing that the client has free rein to explore the deepest issues in a nonjudgmental atmosphere. Besides their importance in the beginning, invitational skills are needed at all stages of the helping process. As each new issue comes to the surface, the helper relies on these skills and the nonjudgmental attitude to provide the medium for change.

Group Exercises

Practice and Feedback Session Using Invitational Skills:
Some Notes on the Helper/Client/Observer Training Group
For many of the practice sessions in this book, we will be asking you to break into groups of three or four. Generally, the way this works is that person A counsels person B, who counsels person C, who counsels person A. Depending on how your instructor likes to work, you may be assigned to the same groups for all practice sessions, or you may frequently change groups.

Such practice on fellow students is a method used in medical and dental schools as well as with mental health professionals. One of its benefits is that you learn just as much in the client role as in the helper role. You learn how it feels to be challenged or supported. You also get a feeling about what is too invasive or too superficial. In the role of observer, you are able to step out of the helping situation and look at it objectively. All three roles are instructive. As a member of a practice group you will be challenged ethically, too. While you may be role playing part of the time, some of the situations are real; you should have an agreement for confidentiality just as if facing an actual problem. It has been our experience that students respect this confidentiality and take it very seriously. Still, it needs to be discussed explicitly in each group.

Exercise 1

Form groups of four. One person is the helper, another the client, and two act as observers. Before the "session" begins, the helper should take time to review the Quick Tips section. The client can decide on the topic, and the observers can look over their checklists. Observer 1 will use Feedback Checklist 1 to give the helper data on his or her nonverbal skills. Observer 2 will use Feedback Checklist 2 to rate the helper on opening skills. For 5–8 minutes, the helper invites the client to discuss one of the following topics:

- How I chose my present job
- A trip I took that was very important to me
- My relationship with a close friend
- A topic of the client's choice
- The problem of a friend or acquaintance whose role the client assumes.

Feedback

At the end of the time period, the observers and client give feedback to the helper. The client is encouraged to give feedback that may include qualitative evaluation of the helper's manner. The client should indicate whether or not he or she felt genuineness, empathy and respect from the helper. The observers will give feedback based on their checklists. The participants switch roles, giving each person a chance to experience helper, client, and observer roles. The entire process will take about 45 minutes.

Quick Tips: Invitational Skills

- Once you have adopted a facilitative body position, take a deep breath and relax.

- Remember that the ball is in the client's court: Invite the client to talk and to tell the story.
- After an open question or two, use the first few minutes to listen to the client using minimal encouragers and head nodding.
- When a silence occurs, don't rush to fill the void. Wait for the client to do it first.
- Rely on door openers such as "Go on," "Say some more about that," rather than asking too many questions at first.
- Use closed questions sparingly but ask yourself if you have understood the crucial facts. If you are unsure, stop the client and ask a closed question or two.

Feedback Checklist 1 (to be completed by Observer 1) During the practice session, try to work through the checklist systematically, writing down comments for each skill as you observe it. If you have time left over, start at the beginning and review again to check your observations. When you are finished, write down any suggestions for improvement. Be as honest as possible so that the helper can benefit from feedback.

1. Draw a stick figure sketch of the helper's body position.

What does the body position convey? (circle all that apply)

Openness	Relaxation
Tension	Stiffness
Interest	Aloofness

Comments for improvement:

2. Evaluate the helper's ability to maintain appropriate eye contact (Circle one)

Avoids   Occasional

Constant with breaks   Stares

Comments for improvement:

3. Circle all that apply as you listen to the helper's voice tone:

Too loud   Too soft

Confident   Hesitant

Moralistic

   or smug   Warm

Cold   Soothing

Clipped   Interested

Bored   Other

Comments for Improvement:

4. Evaluate the helper's gestures and facial expressions (circle all that apply).

Gestures: Nervous movement

Occasional

Inviting gestures

Rigid

Nodding: Head nodding

appropriate

Head nodding

too frequent

Too infrequent

Expression: Helper's face shows

concern and

interest

Face shows

lack of interest

Face reflects client's

feelings

Face is unchanging/

mask-like

Other:

Comments for Improvement:

Feedback Checklist 2 (to be completed by Observer 2) You are to give feedback on the helper's use of minimal encouragers and questions. Your task is to write down everything the helper says during the interview. At the end categorize each response, and give the helper feedback.

Categories: Door openers (DO); Minimal encourager (ME); Open question (OQ); Closed question (CQ)

Helper Question or Statement	Category
1. _____	_____
2. _____	_____
3. _____	_____
4. _____	_____
5. _____	_____
6. _____	_____
7. _____	_____
8. _____	_____
9. _____	_____
10. _____	_____
11. _____	_____
12. _____	_____
13. _____	_____
14. _____	_____
15. _____	_____

Feedback on the Use of Minimal Encouragers

Did helper supply enough minimal encouragers during the initial two minutes of the interview to encourage the client? Were minimal encouragers used too often instead of open questions?

Feedback on the Use of Questions

1. Examine the closed questions with the helper and determine whether they were used as clarifiers or to gain important information (appropriate uses), or as attempts to get the client to open up and talk, a less useful means of encouragement.

2. Were there more open or closed questions? Does the helper need to increase the use of open questions or decrease the use of closed questions?

Additional Exercises

Exercise 1

View 10–15 minutes of a videotape that shows a client/helper interaction. While viewing, write down any observations you may have concerning the client's body posture, gestures, and movements. Afterward, discuss the relationship of these nonverbals to the client's concerns. Alternately, half of the class can observe the client and the other half can focus on the helper. Check the helper's invitational skills against the list in Table 3.2.

Exercise 2

Form dyads and sit facing each other with your eyes closed. Discuss your activities over the past week for about 5–8 minutes. In the class discussion that follows, take turns giving your reactions to the experience. What nonverbal behaviors did you and your classmates find it most difficult to do without?

Exercise 3

Set up a simulated office for a role-playing situation. Provide one chair for the client and another for the helper. Use a third chair to represent a desk if one is not available. Place the chairs about 10 feet apart and ask two participants to hold a conversation at that distance concerning a minor problem one of them is having. Ask the group to comment on how the distance has affected the conversation.

Next, allow the participants to move the chairs to a comfortable distance. Once the chairs have been moved and the participants are seated, measure the distance from knee to knee with a yardstick or tape measure and see if it is approximately 18 inches, an average distance for helpers and clients. Next move the chairs so close that the participants

feel uncomfortable. Measure that distance. If participants from diverse ethnic backgrounds are members of the group, interesting variations can occur. Try the exercise with participants standing instead of seated. Some people will feel comfortable with an interpersonal distance of 6 inches or less!

Exercise 4

Conduct a group discussion on the implications of touching clients. What constitutes sexual touching? Whose needs are being fulfilled by touching? Is it all right for the helper's emotional needs to be met by hugging a client? In what circumstances would a hug be beneficial or harmful? What about hugging in group therapy?

Exercise 5

Videotape two trainees, one of whom acts as the client and the other, the helper, for 15 minutes. The client discusses a minor problem he or she is having at work or at school. Focus the camera for half of the session on the helper's face and the other half of the session on the helper's whole body. Replay the tape and ask the helper to evaluate his or her own facial expressions, body position and gestures.

Exercise 6

Form dyads. The leader or instructor will keep time and signal the completion of the activity at the end of two minutes. Maintain eye contact with your partner and assume the appropriate helper's posture while remaining completely silent. Afterward, discuss your personal reactions to this exercise with your partner and then with the larger group.

Homework

1. Record a television show or movie and re-play it with the sound off. Try to see if you can guess emotional content by examining the characters' body language. Write a one-page reaction to this assignment.

2. Conduct a survey among a few friends or family members. How would they feel about being hugged or touched by a professional helper? Try to be objective and prepare a one-page summary of their answers and your conclusions.

3. In conversations with coworkers, family, and friends, instead of immediately responding to what they say, build in attentive silence and notice the effect. The purpose of the assignment is to observe the effect of silence on the communication of others. Make notes and report findings to the group. Write a one-paragraph reaction to this exercise.

Table 3-2
Glossary of Building Blocks for Invitational Skills

Nonverbal Skills
Nonverbal skills are the use of body position, direct eye contact, appropriate voice tone, attentive silence, and nonverbal encouragers such as head nodding or hand gestures which invite the client to talk.

Opening Skills
Opening skills are verbal encouragers. They ask the client to explore a little deeper but are not very invasive. They also reassure the client that you are following the story.

Skill	Example
Nonverbal Skills	
Eye contact	Direct eye contact with occasional breaks for client comfort
Facilitative body position	"Open" attentive body position, squarely facing the client
Appropriate use of silence	Allowing the client to fill in the "voids" in the conversation
Gestures	Encouraging the client to open up with appropriate gestures and head nodding.
Voice tone	Using a voice tone that reflects the client's, is appropriate in volume and rate, and shows warmth and support.
Opening Skills	
Minimal encouragers	"Uh, huh" "Okay"
Door openers	"Say some more"
Open questions	"Can you tell me what has been going on at work?"
Closed questions	"Is she your ex-wife?" "What do you mean by 'trapped?' " (clarifier)

References

Alyn, J. H. (1988). The politics of touch in therapy. *Journal of Counseling and Development, 66,* 155–159.

Bolton, R. (1979). *People skills: How to assert yourself, listen to others, and resolve conflicts.* Upper Saddle River, NJ: Prentice-Hall.

Cormier, W. H., & Cormier, L. S. (1991). *Interviewing strategies for helpers* (4th ed.). Monterey, CA: Brooks/Cole.

Driscoll, M. S., Newman, D. L., & Seals, J. M. (1988). The effect of touch on perception of helpers. *Counselor Education and Supervision, 27,* 113–115.

Egan, G. (1994). *The skilled helper* (5th ed.). Pacific Grove CA: Brooks/Cole.

Fisher, J. D., Rytting, M., & Heslin, R. (1976). Affective and valuative effects of an interpersonal touch. *Sociometry, 39,* 416–421.

Fretz, B. R., Corn, R., Tuemmler, J. M., & Bellet, W. (1979). Counselor non-verbal behaviors and client evaluations. *Journal of Counseling Psychology, 26,* 304–311.

Goodman, M., & Teicher, A. (1988). To touch or not to touch. *Psychotherapy: Theory, Research and Practice, 25,* 492–500.

Holroyd, J., & Brodsky, A. (1980). Does touching patients lead to sexual intercourse? *Professional Psychology, 11,* 807–811.

Johnson, D. W. (1997). *Reaching out.* Boston, MA: Allyn & Bacon.

Kopp, S. (1978). *If you meet the Buddha on the road, kill him!* New York: Bantam Books.

Maurer, R. E., & Tindall, J. H. (1983). Effect of postural congruence on client's perception of helper empathy. *Journal of Counseling Psychology, 30,* 158–163.

Miller, L., Berg, J. H., & Archer, R. L. (1983). Openers: Individuals who elicit intimate self-disclosure. *Journal of Personality and Social Psychology, 44,* 1234–1244.

Moffat, M. J., & Painter, C. (Eds.). (1974). *Revelations: Diaries of women.* New York: Vintage.

Older, J. (1982). *Touching is healing.* New York: Stein and Day.

Ornston, P. S., Cichetti, D. V., Levine, J., & Freeman, L. B. (1968). Some parameters of verbal behavior that reliably differentiate novice from experienced therapists. *Journal of Abnormal Psychology, 73,* 240–244.

Pennebaker, J. W. (1989). Confession, inhibition, and disease. In L. Berkowitz (Ed.), *Advances in experimental social psychology* (Vol. 22, pp. 211–214). New York: Academic Press.

Purvis, J. A., Dabbs, J. M., & Hopper, C. (1984). The "Opener": Skilled use of facial expression and speech pattern. *Personality and Social Psychology Bulletin, 10,* 60–66.

Ridley, N. C., & Asbury, F. R. (1988). Does counselor body position make a difference? *The School Counselor, 35,* 253–258.

Stone, G. L., & Morden, C. J. (1976). Effect of distance on verbal productivity. *Journal of Counseling Psychology, 23,* 486–488.

Suiter, R. L., & Goodyear, R. K. (1985). Male and female counselor and client perceptions of four levels of counselor touch. *Journal of Counseling Psychology, 32,* 645–648.

Willison, B. G., & Masson, R. L. (1986). The role of touch in therapy: An adjunct to communication. *Journal of Counseling and Development, 64,* 497–500.

Reflecting Skills

Introduction

The invitational skills you have learned thus far encourage the client to open up and let the client know that you are willing to listen. Invitational skills convey that you are present and available, although they do not indicate a deep understanding of the client's world. Invitational skills are commonly used by friends, family, and acquaintances as well as by helpers. Reflecting skills, on the other hand, are specialized interventions used by helpers to stimulate deeper exploration of the facts and feelings of a client's problem.

In general, reflecting entails repeating back to the client his or her own thoughts and feelings in a condensed way, using different words, and in a manner that communicates nonevaluative, nonjudgmental understanding. Consider the following client/helper exchange:

Philippe (Client): "When I was 16, I stole a car with some other kids. We went joyriding and had an accident. The driver was drunk and one of the kids in the car was killed. Every time my own kid goes out on Saturday night, I think of that. I yell and scream and maybe I am too strict with him."

Joyce (Helper): "It is difficult for you to know whether you are being overprotective because you remember that incident and worry that the same thing might happen to him."

Philippe: "Yes, sometimes I get really scared. My own parents didn't care what I did. I don't want to keep him at home all the time, but I don't want him doing something stupid."

Joyce: "Your own upbringing is not a good model for how you would like to be with your son, and so you're not sure how strict to be."

Reflecting skills go beyond invitational skills by facilitating a greater depth of understanding and getting at the real meaning the person is trying to express. With the example of Philippe and Joyce in mind, let us look at the four functions served by reflecting skills in helping:

1. *Reflecting acts as a verbal means for communicating empathy.* In this example, Joyce does not have to say to Philippe, "I understand what you are going through." Instead, she communicates that she understands his situation through his eyes rather than a similar experience of her own. Her statement is a you-message rather than an I-message.
2. *Reflecting acts as a form of feedback or mirror that enables the person to confirm or correct the impression he or she is giving.* In Philippe's second statement, he confirms that Joyce has correctly identified the key elements of his story. Had circumstances been different, he might have corrected Joyce's reflection by saying, "It is not that I think I am being overprotective; I just don't want to lose the

friendship my son and I have developed." In other words, even if your reflection is inaccurate, your reflection gives the client opportunities for clarification.

3. *Reflecting stimulates further exploration of what the client is experiencing.* Notice that following the reflection, in Philippe's second statement, he discusses his own upbringing and talks about the conflict between being overprotective and too lenient. Even if it is not on target, a reflection can encourage further self-disclosure.

4. *Reflecting captures important aspects of the client's message that otherwise might remain camouflaged.* In Philippe's first statement, he makes no mention of the fact that he is scared or worried about his son. The helper's reflection pulls out this feeling, which was hidden in his first statement.

Reflecting Content and Reflecting Feelings

Every client message has two basic components: the factual content and the underlying feelings. The feelings are often hidden and it is up to the helper to bring these to the surface, as Joyce did with Philippe. However, the content—the facts about the situation—is also important and the client needs to know that this has been understood. In the following story, a helper describes a situation that brought home to him the distinction between reflecting content and the often unexpressed feelings implicit in the client's statements.

> *Once I ran a private practice in a small town. The house next door to my office was guarded by a huge German shepherd that frequently growled at my clients when they approached the front door. When I greeted my clients, I was always interested in how they framed their reaction. They often said, "That is the biggest dog I've ever seen." If I had responded to the content of the message, I might have said, "Yes, that is exceptionally large for a German shepherd," or, "Actually, I've seen bigger," or even, "Yes, he weighs over 100 pounds and is in excellent health!"*

This example brings out the fact that every communication has at least two dimensions: the content or perceptions of the event described and the unspoken set of feelings that underlie the content. In this case, the hidden emotional message concerned the fear that the dog evoked but that very few people felt comfortable expressing. In our culture many people are reluctant to express their feelings and are much more comfortable talking about content or facts. However, because the content and the emotional side are equally important, a response that recognizes both will lead to the deepest communication of understanding. At the beginning of the helping relationship, clients are often more comfortable when the helper is able to reflect the content of their story. Later, a helper can show that he or she also grasps the underlying or hidden emotional side.

Two separate skills are used to reflect two different aspects of the client's message. The first, paraphrasing, is primarily a reflection of content; the second skill reflects feeling. Sometimes the helper combines these two responses to capture both sides of the messages, as you will see.

The Skill of Paraphrasing: Reflecting Content

In the discussion of invitational skills in Chapter 3, you were warned not to ask too many questions at the beginning stages of the helping relationship. Questions, especially closed questions, can interrupt the flow of the client's story and make the client feel that he or she is under the microscope. But it is important to have a clear grasp of the important facts relating to the client's problem and also, at times, to repeat important thoughts, behaviors, or intentions embedded in the client's statements. *Paraphrasing* is a reflecting skill that serves both purposes. The paraphrase is not a word-for-word reiteration, but rather a distilled version of the content of the client's message that restates the content in different words and in a nonjudgmental way. As a client tells his or her story, the paraphrase is used as a mirror to let the client know that you are following, but does not pressure the client by asking a question. It is short and sweet and therefore does not slow the client down while he or she is disclosing. It does not take sides with the client by supporting his or her version of the story, but rather points out that this is the client's perspective.

How to Paraphrase

Paraphrasing involves two steps: listening carefully to the client's story and then feeding back to the client a condensed version of the facts. Helpers must select quiet environments so that listening is not impaired by external noises, but the biggest distractions come from mental "noise." You cannot grasp the client's message when you are listening to your own thoughts. Helpers sometimes experience internal noise when the client's story evokes a personal memory of a similar situation. Internal noise may interrupt because the client is expressing something that you find distasteful or that evokes moral outrage.

Worrying about what to say next is perhaps the biggest impediment to listening for the beginning helper. Rather than responding to the client's statement, the helper is sidetracked by thinking about what his or her response ought to be. Because it is difficult to do two things simultaneously, when you become focused on your own thoughts, you lose track of the client's story.

The second step in paraphrasing is collapsing the important information from a large volume of client material into a succinct summary. If the paraphrase goes on too long, it will disrupt the client's story and he or she will not stay on track. Using a boxing analogy, the paraphrase is more like a jab. The helper gets in and out quickly. A common mistake is to simply list the major points the client has made in exactly the same way. A good paraphrase is actually a miniature version of the client's story; it keeps the client's story on track by mentioning only the important aspects, not issues that sidetrack the client. Here is an example of a paraphrase that assists the helper in understanding the facts of the story and also allows the client to feel that the helper is on track:

Peter (Client):   "I've been taking three medications from three different doctors. Of course, I stopped taking two kinds right away. But that was before the operation and now I am on some painkillers, too. I get confused sometimes when I drink a beer or two."

Marina (Helper):   "OK, let me stop you for a moment. Right now you are taking one medication besides the painkillers and you are drinking alcohol, too."

Marina stops Peter and feeds back what she has heard—that Peter is mixing medications and alcohol. Suppose Marina had chosen to paraphrase Peter's statement as follows: "So you started using drugs after the operation." Can you see how this would be missing the most essential element of his message? The conversation might then veer off into a discussion of the operation. As the dialogue continues, Peter gives more of the story:

Peter: "Yes, I am taking a muscle relaxant and pain pills and I do drink a little bit, but I have always enjoyed partying. Sometimes when I drink with this medication, I get really groggy. But if I don't take the medication, I have a lot of pain. I'm not sure whether I should still drink with those pills."

Besides identifying the essential facts of the story, a paraphrase can also summarize the client's thoughts, behaviors, or intentions. Here is a paraphrase of Peter's second statement, in which Marina reflects Peter's thinking:

Marina: "On the one hand, you want to avoid the pain, but you are starting to realize that mixing drugs and alcohol is dangerous."

A final point to keep in mind is that a paraphrase should be nonjudgmental. This tone helps encourage further exploration. A common mistake is to paraphrase in a way that gives a moral lesson. This makes the client defensive, and further exploration is blocked. For example, what if Marina had paraphrased Peter's problem in the following way: "Sounds like you are flirting with disaster"? Such a response may stymie the helping process by evoking Peter's defenses rather than urging him to consider the danger of his actions.

When to Paraphrase

Paraphrases can be used early on in any helping session, as soon as the helper gets a grasp of the facts or, conversely, needs to clarify the facts. Paraphrases interrupt the client's story and demand a response and can be overused. Paraphrasing should follow a sequence of opening and invitational skills.

Paraphrasing after every client statement would seem to make the helper's responses trivial. It is therefore better to wait until the client has gone on at some length before paraphrasing. In the following conversation between a child and a school counselor, a paraphrase is shown in the normal progression of a therapeutic discussion:

Chris: "The teacher said I have to tell you what happened yesterday."

School Counselor: "Do you want to give me an idea about what went on?" (open question)

Chris: "So, I was walking around the playground, not really looking at anything, you know? I was bored."

School Counselor: "Yes; um-hmm." (minimal encouragers)

Chris: "And then these three second graders came around the corner and started calling me names. I said, "Shut up." And later I punched William in the nose. It was bleeding and he was crying but I didn't care because he is mean."

School Counselor: "So you got into a fight with William. He got hurt but you don't think it was your fault."

Notice that the counselor's paraphrase is not just a restatement of what Chris said. It is a summary of the child's story, giving its essence in a nonjudgmental way. The paraphrase is brief and therefore does not interrupt the child unduly as he talks. It does not take sides by supporting one version of the story, but recognizes instead the child's perspective.

Quick Tips: Paraphrasing

- Don't paraphrase too early. Wait until you have a firm grasp of the important details, then compress them into a short paraphrase.
- Early on, use minimal encouragers and door openers liberally to encourage the client to supply essential information.
- Don't repeat the client's exact words. Give a distilled version in slightly different words.
- Don't add a moral tone to your paraphrase.
- When you can, paraphrase the client's thoughts and intentions as well as the basic facts.

Stop and Reflect

Listed here are some client stories. Try to paraphrase them. See whether you can reflect the client's thoughts and intentions as well as the basic facts of the story. Compare your paraphrases with those of your classmates and discuss any differences in your approaches.

1. "I had to tell one of my co-workers he couldn't go on the trip. He had not put in enough time with the company. I was forced to follow the rules. It wasn't really my fault and I couldn't do anything about it. When I told him, he didn't say much. He just walked away."
2. "I met this woman. She seems too good to be true. I don't know too much about her. We only met last week. But since then, everything I find out about her makes me feel more like she is 'the one.' I believe there is only one person out there for everyone, you know. But how can you be sure?"

3. "I called my husband's hotel room Tuesday night and when the phone picked up all I heard was the sound of a woman giggling. Then she hung up. I tried calling back and there was no answer. The next morning I called my husband's room again. He answered and I told him what had happened the night before. He said I must have dialed a wrong number. I guess I believe him. But we went through something similar before when he was younger. There was more than one woman then. I won't go through that again."

- Do any of these stories challenge your ability to be nonjudgmental?
- What might you be tempted to say that would indicate that you are taking sides?

The Skill of Reflecting Feelings

The building block of *reflecting feelings* involves essentially the same technique as paraphrasing. This time, however, the focus is on feelings rather than content. Reflecting feelings involves expressing in one's own words the emotions stated or implied by the client. Feelings can be reflected from both verbal or nonverbal responses of the client.

A number of therapeutic events occur when feelings are reflected. For one thing, the client becomes more keenly aware of the emotions surrounding a topic. For example, suppose the helper makes a reflection such as, "I can tell that you are terribly angry about that." The client's response may be one of surprise: "Yes, I guess I am." Because a reflection is done in a non-evaluative manner, it communicates understanding of feelings—anger, guilt, and sadness—that the client may not be consciously aware of and that the client may feel he or she has no right to feel.

Another important effect is that reflection of feelings brings the client to deeper levels of self-disclosure. An accurate reflection focuses the client on emotions and teaches the client to become aware of and to report feelings. Even if the reflection is not quite accurate, the client will provide a correction that is more on target.

In addition, an accurate reflection of feelings has the almost magical power to deepen the relationship between client and counselor. Nothing transmits nonjudgmental understanding more completely. This is why this technique, which originated in the client-centered tradition of Carl Rogers (1961), has gained such wide usage. It taps the enormous healing properties of the therapeutic relationship. A beginning helper who can accurately reflect feelings can provide supportive counseling and understanding without any other tools.

Finally, reflecting feelings brings on feelings of genuine relief as the client gains some understanding of what he or she is feeling. Take, for example, the client who found his wife in bed with another man. He came to counseling crying about his loss of the relationship. He ran the gamut, on an emotional roller coaster, from shock to disgust to affection to rage. Experiencing all of these conflicting emotions in one session can make anyone feel "crazy." Even though there were conflicting feelings, by the end the client felt more in control simply because he had sorted out his feelings and labeled them. Untangling the emotional knots seems to promote healing even if no real action is taken. Somehow we can accept our feelings as normal reactions when we bring them to the surface. Reflecting feelings, such as "You feel so betrayed yet you still feel a bond of affection," can help to normalize what the client perceives as a deeply conflicting emotional experience.

Why It Is Difficult to Reflect Feelings

Reflecting feelings is one of the most valuable tools of the helper, but it is not an easy one to learn. Theodore Reik, the famous analyst, claimed that in order to hear these feelings one must learn to become sensitive to the unexpressed and listen with the "third ear." Referring to the fact that the client may not even be aware of these feelings, Reik said, "The voice that speaks in him speaks low but he who listens with a third ear, hears also what is expressed almost noiselessly, what is said *pianissimo*" (Reik, 1968, p. 165).

Feelings are often implicit in a client's statements and require hunches and guesses on the part of the helper to identify them. The reason for this is that our upbringing, family background, and culture affect the way we express emotions. For example, speaking in generalities, individuals with Appalachian and English roots tend to express emotions in very subtle ways. Open expression of emotions is considered to be a weakness and a burden on those around you. Some Italians are quite comfortable with public expression of their feelings. In that culture, being too contained may suggest indifference and selfishness.

Gender also has a bearing on emotional expression. Men, more than women, have been trained to suppress emotional expression; big boys don't cry (see Kottler, 1997). However, women are also sometimes expected not to express certain emotions, such as anger or even confidence, that are not considered "ladylike."

How to Reflect Feelings

Like paraphrasing, reflecting feelings involves two steps. The first step is identifying the client's feelings; the second step is articulating the underlying emotions that you detect in his or her statements. You can learn the first step in your practice sessions as you listen intently to a client's statements. Imagine how he or she feels in this situation. The best way to do this is to think of yourself as the client, taking into account all the facts and also thinking about what you know about the client's personality and history. In other words, do not try to think about how *you* would feel in this situation; instead, become the client and think about how he or she might feel.

The second step is making a statement (not asking a question) that *accurately* mirrors the client's emotions, whether the client has actually stated them or whether they are hidden in the client's words. While this sounds easier than the first step, actually it is harder because you must accurately express emotions in words. In our experience, these two steps to reflecting feelings are often learned independently;

learning to identify feelings is a precursor to actually reflecting them. You will probably be able to identify feelings before you can accurately reflect them.

Reflected-feeling statements take two forms. The simple version of reflected feelings is a helper statement with the structure, "You feel _____." The simple form, as illustrated here, lets the client know you understand the emotional aspects of the story:

Latrice (Client):   "You can imagine how everyone in the family reacted when Grandpa got married six months after Grandma's death."

Tim (Helper):   "It must have been quite a shock." (simple reflection of feelings)

After one or two reflections of feeling, a helper may then use a reflection of feelings that connects emotions and content. The format of this combination response is: "You feel _____ because _____." The first blank contains a reflection of the client's feelings. The second blank explains the feelings by paraphrasing the content while at the same time showing the connection between the feelings and the content (Carkhuff, 1987). As the conversation between Latrice and Tim continues, Tim begins to understand and articulate the reason for Latrice's resentment and anger:

Latrice: "I was floored. Besides, Grandma and I were close. I didn't want that new woman going through her things. I bet she and Grandpa were carrying on for years!"

Tim: "You really resent your grandfather because he seems to have let go of your grandmother's memory so easily."

The reflection of feeling, "You really resent your grandfather," is connected to the paraphrase, "he seems to have let go of your grandmother's memory so easily." This is content, the client's perception of what has happened. The connection is the word *because,* which demonstrates to Latrice that Tim understands why she feels resentful.

Not every reflection of feeling must contain a paraphrase. Sometimes it is sufficient to reflect the feeling using the simple statement, "You feel _____." When you understand the connection between feeling and content, you can then utilize the combined form to convey deeper understanding of the *reasons* for the client's feelings.

Students often report that they feel "phony" when they use a response such as "You feel _____ because _____." The formula is merely a training tool that you can modify later, when reflecting feelings has become second nature. Then you will want to vary the way you reflect so that it feels natural to you and to the client.

Improving Your Feeling Vocabulary

To learn the first step in reflecting feelings, identifying feelings, it is important to recognize that emotions have many shades and variations, and they also vary in strength. Thus it is difficult to classify them in a way that fully captures their scope.

Table 4-1 is an attempt to categorize feelings in a way that will help you recognize the basic emotions. They are like the primary colors in the light spectrum. The color analogy is useful because emotions of clients are often mixed together, producing a completely unique "hue." The primary emotions are listed from top to bottom on the left-hand side of Table 4-1.

The emotions that have been identified as primary, or basic, are joy, sadness, anger, guilt/shame, fear, disgust, surprise, and interest/excitement. People around the world can recognize facial expressions of these emotional states whether they are from remote parts of New Guinea or New York City (Izard, 1977). They appear to have deep biological roots. In addition to the primary emotions, three other categories of emotions are indicated in the table: feelings of weakness and strength and feelings of overall distress. Normally, the helper should try to identify the specific feeling that a client is experiencing. Sometimes, though, especially in the beginning of a client's story, it is necessary to reflect a sense of general distress before homing in on the target feelings.

Across the top of Table 4-1, the emotions are categorized by intensity, much as colors can be described in terms of brightness. Besides finding precise words that suggest different intensities, you can qualify your reflections by using adjectives like *a little, somewhat,* and *very* to home in on the client's exact feeling. In fact, some clients will not have large feeling vocabularies; it may be better to say, "You were very angry," rather than, "You were filled with consternation."

You can use Table 4-1 to familiarize yourself with a wider variety of words. The more closely you express the exact shade of feeling, the more the client will sense that you understand his or her frame of mind.

Stop and Reflect

To consider further the distinction between content and feelings, take a look at the following client message and see whether you can respond as a professional helper would. Answer the related questions and compare your responses with those of your classmates.

Teresa: "First we went to the drugstore, then we went to the grocery; we went to two or three other places and ended up in a bad part of town. All because he wanted this particular kind of candy. I had a lot to do that day. This wasn't the first time this kind of thing had happened, but he's a lot of fun most of the time. Other times, he is a pain!"

- What might Teresa be feeling? (Identify as many emotions as you can.) Try to pinpoint her feelings using Table 4-1. Use qualifiers like *a little* or *very* as needed to try to get the right shade of emotion. Your answers and those of your classmates may vary because in a written example we cannot hear the client's voice tone to cue us in as to how strong her emotions are.

- Why do you think Teresa does not express her feelings about the situation?

Table 4-1
Feeling Words

Feeling	Mild	Moderate	Strong
Joy	at ease pleased satisfied content	glad happy	overjoyed jubilant elated
Sadness	down sad low	glum downhearted melancholy	depressed dejected despondent
Anger	annoyed irritated miffed ticked	angry mad	furious outraged enraged
Guilt/shame	responsible at fault chagrined	guilty embarrassed	ashamed humiliated mortified
Fear	apprehensive nervous uneasy wary insecure	anxious scared worried afraid	frightened terrified panicked
Disgust	offended put off	turned off disgusted	repulsed sickened revolted nauseated

- Try to summarize the content (not the feelings) of Teresa's message in a single sentence. Remember that the content includes thoughts, intentions, behaviors, and facts that she relates.

  _____

  _____

  _____

- Try to make a connection between what Teresa is feeling and the content of her story: Teresa feels _____ (emotion) because _____ (reason you identify from content).

- What facts about Teresa's cultural or family upbringing might affect her willingness to express her feelings?

  _____

  _____

  _____

- Now think for a moment about your own upbringing, family background, and culture. What rules does your own family have about expressing emo-

Feeling	Mild	Moderate	Strong
Surprise	perplexed puzzled stumped	amazed bewildered baffled	awed stunned astonished shocked
Interest/excitement	bored interested	amused curious inspired engaged	excited stimulated thrilled

Feelings Associated with Power and Confidence

Weakness	unimportant awkward unsure	inadequate incompetent inept	worthless helpless dependent powerless impotent
Strength	able capable	confident strong authoritative secure competent	self-assured potent powerful

Feelings of General Distress

	upset concerned troubled bothered	frustrated disturbed perturbed	distressed pained miserable anguished agitated

tions such as anger or sadness? How do you express affection? What would be the most difficult feelings for you to admit to a helper if you were a client?

_____

_____

_____

Common Problems in Reflecting Feelings

In many classes on helping skills, learning to paraphrase and reflect feelings takes up a large portion of the class time. These skills may take many weeks to develop, and there is no substitute for practice. To assist you in developing your ability to reflect, we analyze some common problems that tend to sidetrack students at the early stages, and we suggest methods for overcoming these normal difficulties.

Waiting Too Long to Reflect

In the opening minutes of the helping session, utilize invitational skills to help elicit the client's story. A common mistake is to wait 10 or 15 minutes before going on to reflect the client's feelings. To avoid this mistake, work to become proficient in the identification of feelings. To practice, make full use of the written exercises in this chapter. Also, watch television shows, particularly daytime dramas, to listen to people's statements and then reflect their feelings immediately after they speak, picking up on nonverbal as well as spoken cues.

Being Judgmental and Taking Sides

Beginners are often too quick to take the client's side and agree that the problem is caused by other people. The tendency to be judgmental is often expressed in the paraphrase component of a combined reflection of feeling. For example:

Client: "At work, the other girls ignore me because I don't go drinking with them on Friday night and they think I am the boss's favorite. The boss always compliments me on my work. I can't help it if they don't work as hard as I do."

Helper: "You are a little sad because your co-workers mistreat you."

With a judgmental paraphrase, the helper has essentially agreed that the co-workers are at fault. Shifting the blame to other people will not help the client to gain greater self-awareness.

A related error is being judgmental of the client, as in this alternative scenario:

Client: "At work, the other girls ignore me because I don't go drinking with them on Friday night and they think I am the boss's favorite. The boss always compliments me on my work. I can't help it if they don't work as hard as I do."

Helper: "You feel left out because you haven't been a team player."

Sometimes, helpers show a judgmental attitude when they try to sneak in a little free advice. In the preceding example, there is a hidden message: "If you want to be liked, be more a part of the team." A nonjudgmental response would be: "You feel left out and you think it is because of the different way the boss treats you compared to the way he treats your co-workers." The purpose of a reflection should be to help the client explore more deeply, not to end the exploration by supplying a solution or placing blame.

Turning the Reflection into a Question

When a paraphrase or reflection of feeling is made, it is best to put it in the form of a statement rather than a question. Think back on the purpose of the reflecting skills: to show clients that you are with them, that you understand what they are saying and feeling, and that you are there to help them explore deeper feelings. Asking a question indicates that you are interested but not that you understand, as in the following exchange:

Client: "I've had a very difficult time. My mother died about a month ago and now my dad is in the hospital with pneumonia. I'm here, 2,000 miles away, and I can't get any time away from work."

Helper: "Are you feeling sad over the death of your mom and a sense of helplessness as you worry about your dad?"

Can you see how the client might respond with a simple yes or no? The question suggests that the helper is confused, and it does not provide as many options to explore. Had the helper reflected the client's feelings with a statement, he or she might have said: "It must be a very helpless feeling for you to be so far away when you are worried and trying to deal with the sadness of your mom's death." Such a statement seems to more effectively communicate understanding of the client's situation and also seems to be more compassionate. Rather than responding to a question, the client can go on to explore whatever issues seem important to him or her.

Combining a Reflection and an Open Question

In the early stages of learning helping, it is tempting to add an open question after the reflecting statement. This confuses the client because he or she has been asked to do two things: respond to the reflection and answer the open question. For example, a helper might say, "You feel really alone since your wife died. Do you have any close friends?" Clients often respond in such cases by reacting to the open question rather than to the reflection of feeling. If you have this tendency, try eliminating open questions altogether for a while in your practice sessions.

Focusing on the Wrong Person

Reflecting skills are aimed at the client. Clients, on the other hand, frequently complain about other people and launch into long stories about them. The helper must be careful to keep the focus on the client and not on others. For example, the helper can respond in different ways when a client makes a statement such as: "My best friend and I are not as close as we used to be. Sometimes I think she just wants to neutralize our relationship. It seems like she has no time for me, like she doesn't care." The helper can paraphrase, focusing on the client's friend: "She neglects you." Or the helper can keep attention centered on the client: "You miss the relationship you used to enjoy so much."

Can you see how focusing on the other person can send a judgmental message about the friend? Because you do not know anything directly about the other person, such a statement is unfair and perhaps inaccurate.

Letting the Client Ramble

Many helpers tend to let their clients talk too long without responding. However, clients need encouragers and reflections in order to know that their story is making sense to the helper. When they are talkative or anxious, clients leave little room for the helper to slow the pace and focus on a particularly important message. Beginning helpers need to give themselves permission to stop rambling clients and make reflections. Surprisingly, this often serves to reassure clients that each aspect of their story is being heard in a systematic way. Here is one example in which a helper politely requests a pause to verify that the right message is being received:

Helper: "Let me stop you here for a second and see if I understand correctly. You feel both angry and hurt that your friend is not spending time with you, but you are afraid to mention it because she may simply terminate the friendship."

Using the Word *Feel* Instead of *Think*

In the beginning, you may hear yourself or your classmates make a reflection along these lines: "You feel that your husband should have been more respectful of your need for privacy." This is not a reflection of feeling because the client's underlying feelings are not being identified. More accurately, the word *think* may be substituted for *feel:* "You *think* that your husband should have been more respectful of your need for privacy." In a case like this, if you can substitute the word *think* without changing the meaning of a statement, you have not reflected a feeling; rather you have paraphrased the client's thoughts, which are part of the content. In this example, a true reflection of feeling would be: "You feel angry (or hurt) because you think your husband should have been more respectful of your need for privacy." It is important to choose your words carefully. Otherwise, you may not be conveying to the client that you understand both the content and the feeling levels of his or her story.

Undershooting and Overshooting

Undershooting and overshooting are two common mistakes in reflecting feelings (Gordon, 1975). *Overshooting* means reflecting a feeling that is more intense than the feeling expressed by the client; *undershooting* means reflecting a feeling that is too weak to adequately mirror the client's emotion. Consider this client statement:

Client: "Becky told Mrs. Gordon that I was not a good typist, so she started giving the most interesting work to Ronaldo instead of me."

Helper: "You must have been mad enough to kill!" (overshooting)

Helper: "You were a little annoyed." (undershooting)

Helper: "You were angry." (accurate intensity)

Overshooting and undershooting are beginners' mistakes; this tendency normally corrects itself as you gain a larger feeling vocabulary. If your feeling vocabulary seems limited at present, study lists of feeling words like those in Table 4-1. You may also try using qualifiers such as *a little angry, somewhat angry,* or *very angry* to convey levels of emotional intensity.

Parroting

Parroting is another common mistake caused by an inadequate feeling vocabulary. Parroting means repeating back to the client the very same feeling words he or she has just used. For example, a client might say, "The whole party I planned was rather frustrating because no one came for the first hour and then people stayed past the time limit we had indicated in the invitation." The helper then responds (parroting): "You were frustrated that they disregarded your instructions." The tendency to parrot arises when the client seems to have beaten you to the punch and to have already expressed a feeling. What do you do? The answer is to discern what other feelings the client might have experienced at the same time or to identify a feeling more accurate than the one the client has expressed. In the previous exchange, for example, the helper might have responded to the client's expressed frustration by reflecting, "I'd guess you were a little angry that they didn't seem to get the message after all the planning you put into it." By studying lists of feeling words like the one in Table 4-1, you may be able to select slightly different wording that will accurately reflect but not parrot. Another alternative is to temporarily ignore the feeling identified by the client and to imagine instead how you might have felt in the situation described. Reflecting that feeling might lead the client to the awareness of even deeper emotions. The following dialogue uses the same client statement, but this time the helper gives a reflection based on what he or she might have been feeling:

Client: "The whole party I planned was rather frustrating because no one came for the first hour and then people stayed past the time limit we had indicated in the invitation."

Helper: "If I had been in your shoes, I guess I might have felt a little hurt that very few of the people seemed to have honored my wishes."

Letting Your Reflections Go On and On

Long and rambling helper reflections are normally due to anxiety. Silences are thought to be deadly. In reality, silence can add a little pressure for the client to talk. Helpers must learn to be comfortable with silence.

Sometimes helpers tend to continue to reflect and paraphrase for several sentences until they see the light of recognition in the client's eyes. This is a kind of shotgun approach. The student thinks, "If I reflect several different things, one of them is bound to be right." But making a reflection is necessarily a kind of gamble. You must wait until you think you understand and then place your bet on a single brief reflection, paraphrase, or combination. If you are wrong, the client will correct you and proceed to describe the accurate feeling. An inaccurate reflection is still an effective interchange and leads to clarification, deeper exploration, and greater self-awareness in the client.

Summary

The reflecting skills are a quantum leap from the invitational skills because they do more than encourage clients to tell their stories. The reflecting skills move clients to greater self-awareness and encourage them to address deeper issues beneath the surface. Reflecting skills have two building blocks: paraphrasing and reflecting feelings. Paraphrasing is a distilled version of the content of the client's message; reflecting feelings involves identifying and labeling the client's feelings, whether such feelings have been openly expressed or not. The feeling component of the message is often hidden because disclosure of feelings is bound by cultural and family rules.

The emotions that helpers identify when reflecting feelings have many nuances and variations. However, helpers can consider some basic or primary feelings when trying to home in on a client's unique emotional experience. Helpers need to improve their feeling vocabularies in order to communicate understanding of the client's message. Labeling and reflecting feelings can be one of the most difficult processes to learn. There is a great variability in how quickly students learn to reflect feelings. Some come to it very naturally and quickly. Others take longer but can learn the skill eventually through persistence and practice.

Group Exercises

Group Exercise 1: The Alter-Ego Technique for Identifying Feelings

One of the best action methods for learning to identify feelings is the *alter-ego technique,* which comes to us from psychodrama (Moreno, 1958). The alter-ego technique involves taking on the role of the client so as to imagine the client's feelings. This exercise requires four members: the client, the helper, the alter ego, and the observer.

The Client's Role   The client discusses an experience with either positive or negative ramifications, such as a good or bad vacation, a relationship that ended abruptly, a missed opportunity, or another minor problem.

The Helper's Role   The student who plays the part of the helper has little to do in this exercise. The job of the helper is to listen with appropriate body position, using only open questions and minimal encouragers, providing a focus for the client but rarely intervening.

The Alter Ego's Role   The third student stands behind the client and speaks for the client, identifying anything the client might be feeling but has left out. The alter ego speaks using the word *I* as if he or she is speaking for the client: "I am angry," "I am embarrassed," and so on. The client should be directed to ignore the alter ego except when the alter ego really hits the mark. At that point, the client should incorporate the alter ego's comment into his or her statements. For example, suppose the alter ego says, "I am angry and embarrassed." The client may then respond, saying, "I *am* embarrassed." The client always directs his or her response to the helper, even when reacting to the alter ego. Though the client and the helper sometimes find this frustrating, the alter ego learns to identify feelings by taking on the role of another person. After 5–8 minutes, the group members exchange roles.

The Observer's Role The fourth member of the group is an observer recording the alter ego's remarks on a blank sheet of paper. In the subsequent discussion, the client gives the alter ego feedback on which were the most accurate and the least accurate reflections and paraphrases.

Quick Tips: Reflecting Feelings

- You will probably need to use invitational skills and paraphrasing before you have enough information to reflect feelings. When you have heard enough of the client's story to grasp the emotional content, stop the client to make a reflection.
- If you don't know how the client is feeling, imagine yourself in the client's shoes. What would you be feeling if you were the client?
- Use different feeling words from those used by the client to avoid parroting.
- Don't agree with the client when he or she is placing blame on someone else. Convey that you understand the client's viewpoint without taking sides.

Group Exercise 2: Reflecting During the Helping Interview

The alter-ego technique is a good way to develop the initial skill of imagining oneself as the client and identifying thoughts and feelings. The next step is to incorporate the skill within the helping interview. Break into groups of three with a helper, client, and observer. During a 5-to-8-minute session, the client describes a small problem that he or she has been having with a friend, family member, or someone at work. The helper uses invitational skills and paraphrases and, whenever possible, reflects feelings. The helper's goal is to reflect *at least three feelings* during the practice session.

The observer makes certain that the time limits are observed and, during the period, records every helper response verbatim on the Feedback Checklist. At the end of the time, the observer codes the helper's responses as shown on the checklist. The client gives the helper feedback on which responses on the checklist were most accurate and which were least accurate. The client makes a check next to those that seem to "hit the mark." The group exchanges roles until everyone has had a chance to practice the role of helper and receive feedback.

Feedback Checklist: Reflecting Skills

Observer Name _____ Helper Name _____
During the session, the observer records the helper's responses verbatim (except minimal encouragers). After the session, the group categorizes the responses with the following symbols:
OQ = open question
CQ = closed question
 P = paraphrase
 R = reflection of feeling
P/R = combination paraphrase and reflection of feeling

Helper Response	Coding*	Client Check Mark
1.		
2.		
3.		
4.		
5.		
6.		
7.		
8.		
9.		
10.		

*Do not include minimal encouragers.

Additional Exercises

Exercise 1: Practice in Identifying Feelings—*In Vivo* (Porter, 1996)

Form groups of four for this exercise. One student (the client) briefly describes a recent situation, or one in the distant past, that caused a strong emotional reaction—for example, being turned down for a job, breaking up with a girlfriend or boyfriend, or experiencing angry feelings toward a teacher or co-worker. During the description, the student who is relating the story is not to use any feeling words—for example, "All day, I tried to talk to my boss but she kept cutting me off and avoiding me." The remaining three students listen to the story and write down the emotions they might have felt in this situation. The students compare the feelings they identified.

Exercise 2: Identifying Feelings and Reflecting Feelings in Writing

Listed here are eight client statements. First, identify the major feeling or feelings in each client statement. Then write out a full reflection of feeling. If more than one feeling exists, reflect all of them.

    a. "There I was, standing in front of the entire assembly, and I froze. Everyone was staring at me. My heart was pounding and I started to shake. I thought I was going to die right there on the spot. I could never show my face again after that."

    ————————————————————

    ————————————————————

    b. "And for the third time in a row, he failed to show. What a jerk! My daughter looks forward to these outings with her father and I hate to see him treat her this way. Don't you think he is a jerk?"

    ————————————————————

    ————————————————————

    c. "I can't wait to go to Europe with the French club. It's the opportunity of a lifetime! Yet it's going to be expensive. In addition to the obvious things, I'm going to need spending money too. I'll have to bring my boyfriend something. I don't know how I am going to come up with all the money I need."

    ————————————————————

    ————————————————————

    d. "The more I do, the more the boss seems to expect. He's never satisfied and is always finding fault. I think I should start looking for another job because I can't take it anymore."

    ————————————————————

    ————————————————————

    e. "I can't believe I trusted my sister-in-law. She is such a back-stabbing witch. I hate her. She'd start bad-mouthing my mother-in-law and get me going. Then after she got me saying negative things, I found out she was going back and repeating everything I said to her! Now my mother-in-law hates me."

    ————————————————————

    ————————————————————

    f. "We just moved here and I'm working two jobs. But somehow I've got to find time to take my kids to their schoolmates' houses so they can get to know people and have some friends. I just don't seem to have time."

    ————————————————————

    ————————————————————

    g. "My son keeps staying out late at night with his friends. He won't tell me where he goes. I'm afraid he'll get hurt. He's probably able to take care of himself. I don't know what to do."

    ————————————————————

    ————————————————————

h. "My boss just stays in her office doing her personal paperwork. She won't come out to help us and sometimes we get so busy. We get tired and then we get behind."

_____

_____

Homework

In this homework exercise, you will be keeping an emotions diary. Make a copy of Table 4-1 and keep it with some blank paper on a clipboard near your bed. Choose one of the emotions you experience that day. For example, if you often feel angry at work or with family, this might be a good emotion to choose. Before going to sleep, review the day and identify the situations in which you experienced the emotion, then answer the following questions:

- What was the emotion? _____

_____

- Think of a synonym for the emotion as you experienced it today. _____

_____

- Describe the situation in which you experienced the emotion. _____

_____

- Who was present when you experienced the emotion? _____

_____

- What do you think caused your emotion? Do you blame other people for your emotion? Which of your personal values and beliefs might have given rise to this emotion? In other words, what did you say to yourself that seemed to spark this emotional response?_____

_____

- How did you express the emotion? _____

- What family or societal rules come to mind when you think about expressing this emotion? _____

_____

- Record any other thoughts you have about your experience today._____

_____

References

Carkhuff, R. (1987). _The art of helping VI._ Amherst, MA: Human Resource Development Press.

Izard, C. E. (1977). _Human emotions._ New York: Plenum Press.

Gordon, T. (1975). _PET: Parent effectiveness training._ New York: Wyden.

Kottler, J. (1997). _The language of tears._ San Francisco: Jossey-Bass.

Moreno, J. L. (1958). _Psychodrama_ (Vol. 2). New York: Beacon House.

Porter, S. (1996). _Reflecting feelings._ Unpublished manuscript.

Reik, T. (1968). _Listening with the third ear._ New York: Pyramid Books.

Rogers, C. R. (1961). On becoming a person. Boston: Houghton Mifflin.

Advanced Reflecting Skills

It is not just what we inherit from our mothers and fathers that haunts us. It's all kinds of old defunct theories, all sorts of old defunct beliefs, and things like that. It's not that they actually live on in us; they are simply lodged there and we cannot get rid of them. I've only to pick up a newspaper and I see ghosts gliding between the lines.

Henrik Ibsen, Ghosts, Act 2

Introduction

In the remake of the movie *Father of the Bride,* the bride-to-be calls off the wedding when her fiancé buys her a blender for the eight-month anniversary of their meeting. The bride-to-be is tearful and angry because, for her, the blender is a sexist symbol. She interprets the present as an expression of his wish for her to take on a traditional female role—in the kitchen. The example illustrates two points about the perceived meaning of an event. First, each person's interpretations, values, and perceptions are unique. They are formed by the person's history, current needs, values, and world view. Two people experiencing the same event will have different takes on its significance. As many cognitive therapists like to quote, "It is not what happens to us, but what we make of it." Second, the meaning of an event for an individual can be uncovered only with some deeper knowledge of that person. Had the fiancé understood that being independent and being recognized as more than wife and mother were very important to his future bride, he would have been able to anticipate her reaction to the gift of a blender!

Advanced Reflecting Skills: Understanding the Client's World View

In this chapter, we will look at how a helper can identify and respond to the meanings of a client's story by using advanced reflecting skills. These skills are a step beyond paraphrasing and reflecting feelings because they tap the unique world view of the client.

Consider the case of Joan, who had been having problems at work for two years. Her co-workers had split into two factions that everyone on the job called the "redbirds" and the "bluebirds." There was considerable animosity because of a power struggle between the two leaders of these groups. Joan found herself allied with the bluebirds. During one of their after-work gripe sessions, she revealed that she knew that one of the redbirds, Bob, had sought treatment for alcoholism. Bob had told her this several years ago when they were on good terms. Once this information leaked, Bob's boss called him on the carpet because the company was working on several government contracts, and had Bob investigated as a security risk. A couple of weeks later, Joan went to the company's employee assistance program (EAP) and asked for counseling. During the interview, she and the counselor (Lynn) had the following exchange.

Joan: "There is just so much turmoil. It used to be a good place to work. Now it's dog-eat-dog."

Lynn: "You are a bit sad that things have changed and there is so much competition."

Joan: "Yes, that among other things."

Lynn: "So what is it about the situation that bothers you the most?"

Joan: "Well, Bob told me about his treatment for alcoholism one night when we were working late, sort of offhand. I even thought of him as a friend."

Lynn: "You're afraid of his reaction when he finds out that you leaked the information."

Joan: "Not really. It just seems a nasty thing to do to someone who was trying to be friendly."

Lynn: "In other words, you are disappointed in yourself for having betrayed a confidence."

Joan: "Yeah, that's the thing. I'd like to apologize to him but I'm not sure how he would take it."

If Lynn had merely paraphrased the story of Joan's problems at work and her underlying feelings, they would have had a productive session. However, Lynn chose to probe more deeply, not only paraphrasing Joan's feelings about recent events but also looking at the underlying meaning—the perceptions and values her client attributed to herself, the office situation, and the other workers involved. Figure 5-1 shows that every client story, like Joan's, has several layers. As if peeling an onion, a client is likely to give us first the content of the story, then the feelings it evokes, and finally its personal meaning. Sometimes the deeper feelings and meanings evoke embarrassment and shame, and much time and trust are needed before the full meaning of the story becomes apparent. Sometimes the client is not even aware of the fact that his or her feelings stem from the meanings that he or she has attributed to events.

Notice that Lynn begins by reflecting feelings and paraphrasing Joan's story before using advanced reflecting skills. As a client, it is less threatening to respond to content than to feelings. When a helper uses advanced reflecting skills that get at the deeper meanings of the client's statements, the client may feel threatened. That is a good reason to use reflecting skills first and then to step into deeper waters as the client feels more comfortable.

Joan's response to Lynn is in partial agreement with her initial reflection, but she goes on to indicate that there are deeper issues by saying, ". . . among other things." Lynn makes the transition to meaning by trying to understand what is behind Joan's

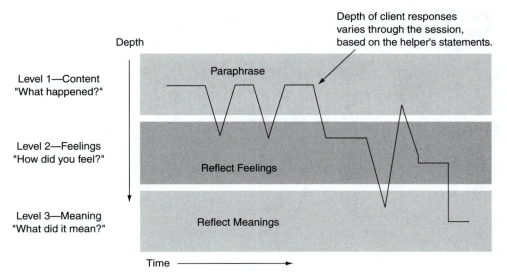

Figure 5-1
Levels of disclosure

discomfort. She asks a closed question about meaning to try to get Joan to identify the source of her feelings.

Joan responds by sending a rather cryptic message. She says, "Well, Bob told me about his treatment for alcoholism one night when we were working late, sort of off-hand. I even thought of him as a friend." Lynn makes an inaccurate reflection that Joan rejects. But as is often the case, even a blind alley like this one helps the process, because Joan corrects Lynn's reflection by describing an even more important issue. Joan is disappointed in herself for being "nasty." In her final reflection, Lynn sees this and gives an accurate reflection of meaning.

It is clear that the events in Joan's story have a deeper significance than Joan herself is able to identify. Why is it important for the helper to bring this deeper level of meaning to the surface? One reason is that for a client to feel truly understood, the helper must see the story through the eyes of the client. The meanings that a person attributes to the story are unique, based on his or her cultural and family background and on his or her personal history of similar situations. Also, as the helper uses meaning-oriented questions and reflects meanings, the client begins to have insight into the connection between feelings and meanings. For example, Joan begins to see that the reason for her sadness is a disappointment in herself for not living up to her own standards. Finally, reflecting meanings enables the client to begin to develop some objectivity about his or her personal perspective on life. In effect, the helper says to the client, "This is your unique perspective on the problem. I respect it, but your perspective is not the whole truth. Perhaps you could change your outlook." In other words, helping clients examine the meaning that an issue has for them is a first step in changing negative attitudes, prejudices, and faulty ideas about the world.

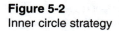

Figure 5-2
Inner circle strategy

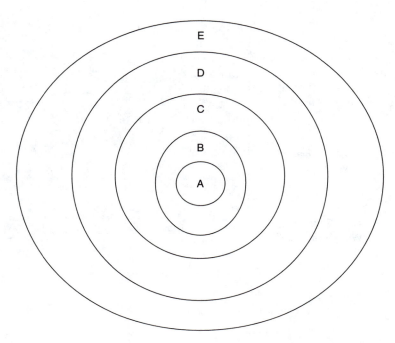

Challenging the Client to Go Deeper: The Inner-Circle Strategy

In Joan's case, Lynn used questions and reflections of meaning to get at the deeper levels of the story. Sometimes clients have difficulty recognizing that their stories have these deeper layers; it is useful to challenge them to move from a superficial recounting to the area of personal meanings. Arnold Lazarus, the multimodal therapy founder, uses what he calls an "inner-circle strategy" for getting clients to identify deeper, more personal issues (1981, p. 55). The helper draws a series of concentric circles labeled A, B, C, D, and E (see Figure 5-2), identifying ring A as issues that are very personal and ring E as issues that are essentially public. For example, at level E is information about the client's appearance and occupation. At level A are very personal issues such as sexual problems, anger and resentment toward people, negative views of the self, and secrets that the client feels are immoral or dishonest. Once the circles are identified, the client might be asked to write in the names of individuals, including the helper, who have access to the various levels from A to D. Lazarus likes to use the diagram to confront the client when counseling is too superficial. For example, the helper might say, "It seems to me that we are discussing issues that fall in the D or C category. The most effective work occurs at levels A or B. I am wondering whether you do not feel comfortable talking about these deeper levels yet."

Stop and Reflect

We have been talking about the fact that the best information is forthcoming, and the most therapeutic relationships are developed, when clients reveal their deepest thoughts, feelings, and perceptions. Clients who venture to this level of disclosure are risking a great deal, however. One way to realize this is to imagine yourself in the client's position. Think for a moment about what is unique about you. What would a person need to know about you before you would feel that they were sufficiently informed to help you? How long would you have to know someone before discussing your deepest secrets? Read each topic in the following list, and identify something relevant about yourself that you would be willing to discuss with a helper during the first session and something else that you probably would not discuss. Write down brief notes under each heading; what do you fear might happen if you disclosed the thoughts, feelings, and perceptions that you would prefer not to discuss?

	I would disclose	**I would not disclose**
Your family values and history		
Your religion or spiritual beliefs		
Your history of intimate relationships		
Your personal dreams and ambitions		
Happy and unhappy childhood memories		
Times when you were dishonest or unethical		

Draw an inner circle for yourself like the one in Figure 5-2 and write down the names of people who have access to the deeper issues in your life. Now think of one or two issues that you would not discuss with anyone, even a professional helper. What would stop you? Are there also issues at levels B and C that would be difficult to discuss with a helper? What issues would you discuss only if there were safeguards of confidentiality? Share your inner circle with a small group of classmates if you feel comfortable in doing so. There is no need to discuss the issues at each of the levels. But it might be interesting to compare the numbers of people who have access to the various levels. Who are these people and how did they gain access to this kind of trust? Do you spot any gender differences?

Helping Clients Understand Meaning in Their Statements

In *Reality Isn't What It Used to Be,* Walter Truett Anderson (1990) points out that as far back as Plato, we have marveled about how people from different backgrounds can have such different views of the same situation. One of Plato's great metaphors is the allegory of the cave. With apologies, I am extending it here to make a point. In this story, people are living in a cave chained together so they must all face the cave wall. They never see the outside world; their ideas about it are based entirely on the shadows they see reflected on the walls, which constitute their reality. Similarly, we are all caught up in the restrictions of our cultures and backgrounds and we see other points of view as odd, misguided, or even ignorant.

Like the people in the cave, those who possess similar views and a similar culture see things the same way and reinforce each other's views. Only when we look at ourselves from outside our usual vantage point do we perceive the chains that hold us within a narrow point of view.

The helping relationship leads the client to look at himself or herself from a different perspective. The helper holds up a mirror to the client, reflecting rather than agreeing with what the client says. The helper lets the client get a good look at his or her own values and viewpoint about the self, others, and the world. When a client sees himself or herself honestly in this way, he or she begins to envision how to make constructive changes.

Within our meaning system, or world view, we translate every life event into a language we can understand. For example, if someone is driving fast on the freeway, we assume that he or she is a "maniac," not that he or she is rushing to the hospital with an injury. Although we have no evidence for what is motivating the other person, we supply it. Such a tendency to supply an instant interpretation of every new event can be counterproductive. It can be especially problematic when sudden and traumatic events arise. One example is survivor guilt. Many people who live through airplane or car crashes in which others die experience psychological troubles later. They often feel guilty for having survived, yet most are not even aware that they have drawn this conclusion. They feel troubled, sad, and uneasy, but need to fully express themselves before they realize that they feel selfish for being alive. This is what Alfred Adler called *private logic:* the human tendency—consciously or unconsciously—to search for causes even if they are superstitious or dead wrong. Life seems more manageable if we assign reasons to events, but these reasons we invent are not necessarily constructive. When held up to the light of the confiding relationship, these perceptions can be acknowledged and evaluated. If this is not done, inappropriate conclusions can be drawn, sometimes leading to years of unhappiness and regret.

World View and Values: The Source of Meaning

World view is a term coined to refer to a person's view of self, others, and the world. Language, gender, ethnicity/race, religion/spirituality, sexual orientation, age, physical issues, socioeconomic situation, and trauma all influence the development of world view (Ivey, Ivey, & Simek-Morgan, 1997).

In counterdistinction to world view, *values* are assumptions about what is right and wrong. By understanding a client's values, we begin to grasp his or her internal struggles and moral dilemmas. Values are a person's basis for self-evaluation and may explain his or her conflicts with others. A client's values tell us about what the client expects of himself or herself, defining his or her ideals and aspirations. They are the internal guidance system of the individual (Young & Witmer, 1985).

The helper's job is to understand the client's world view and values so that the client's viewpoint—and the meaning of his or her story—can be appreciated and an appropriate solution to the client's problems can be found. Following are examples of client statements that give a window to world view or values:

Self-Concept

"I am essentially (a good person) (evil) (selfish) (OK/not OK) (smart/dull) (damaged) (unlovable)."

"Nothing I do seems to work out."

"I always land on my feet."

Notice that these statements express general notions about the self rather than defining specific abilities, such as being a good piano player or having a good sense of direction.

Views of Others

"People are (unreliable) (essentially good) (selfish) (trustworthy) (kind)."

"Men are all alike."

"People will take advantage of you if they can."

"White people are . . ."

Views of the Environment or the World in General

"It's dog eat dog."

"It's a vale of tears."

"You can't get ahead."

"It's bad luck."

"God punished you."

"God rewarded you."

"Things always turn out for the best."

"Stuff happens!"

Values

"People should treat each other fairly."

"Men should be the providers."

"Family secrets should not be told to others."

"Conflict is bad."

"You should always try to do your best."

Helping a Client Whose World View Is Different from the Helper's

The following are some general approaches helpful in dealing with clients who have a world view that is distinctly different from that of the helper:

1. Especially at the beginning of the helping relationship, focus on listening rather than on telling. Recently, a psychologist on the radio told a welfare mother with three daughters that she should go back to work, even though she could not arrange good day care for her three-year-old. This advice was offered in the first minute of the interview; the psychologist had not taken the time to

assess the client's support system, the ages of the other children, or the importance the client placed on being a good mother. Anyone who offers advice so quickly is not respecting or understanding a client's world view. Such advice is likely to be culturally insensitive and ultimately irrelevant to the client.

2. Helpers should expose themselves to knowledge and experiences that help them appreciate different cultures and special populations. At the minimum, helpers should have studied the culture and history of Asian Americans, African Americans, Hispanic Americans, and Native Americans (Sue & Sue, 1990). In addition, helpers should probably have training in more than one language.

   Beginning helpers may feel overwhelmed when they realize the amount of information that they need to assimilate to become culturally sensitive. A rational approach to an overload of information is to accept that any one helper cannot be prepared for all possible differences between helper and client. The best approach is a tutorial one. Let your client teach you about his or her background. Be open and sensitive and do not try to examine the client under the lens of the dominant culture. Helpers must recognize that strategies and techniques useful with the majority population will probably need to be modified or even eliminated when working with members of other groups.

3. Helpers must be sensitive to nonverbal communication and to uses of language that might be offensive to special groups. For example, a client who was filling out the initial paperwork for a counseling appointment objected to the federal requirement that she choose a particular cultural group. As a Cuban, she felt angry at having to choose the category "Hispanic," which she felt only focused on her language, not her cultural background. During the session, she talked about the importance of her Cuban heritage.

4. Helpers must become sensitive to differences in emphasis on the role of the family among different cultures. Because families in North America are mobile and less than cohesive, we usually assume that becoming independent of the family of origin is a sign of maturity. However, in some Asian and Latino cultures, becoming independent of the family is not a valued goal of adulthood.

5. Helpers must recognize that therapy may be unacceptable to some groups and that in some cases indigenous methods should be explored. For example, the World Health Organization recommends that Western medical personnel work jointly with traditional and folk-medicine providers. Closer to home, a priest or minister in the African American or Mexican American communities may have more influence and insight than an external helper.

6. Helpers also need to examine their personal and cultural attitudes. The counselor must possess or adopt attitudes of empathy (rather than sympathy), tolerance for ambiguity, open-mindedness, and an openness to experience (Corey, Corey, & Callanan, 1988). In addition, Sue (1981) asserts that counselors who are skilled in dealing with special populations understand their own value systems and basic assumptions about human behavior and can appreciate that the views of others will differ. They understand that different cultures have been shaped by different social and political forces than those

that molded the helper's world view (Pedersen, 1987). Most important, culturally effective helpers honor the world view of the client, can share it in some way, and constantly strive to avoid the pitfall of believing that their own culture is superior and provides the right way of looking at life. A final point is that helpers who hope to work effectively with those who are culturally different should become truly eclectic, using skills, methods, and techniques and forming goals that are congruent with the views, values, lifestyles, and life experiences of each client.

Changing a Client's World View

Our discussion has focused on respecting and understanding a client's world view and values, which compose his or her basic cultural underpinning. But clients come to a helper to change. How can we honor the client's cultural heritage and yet help him or her change? The best guideline is that a helper works for the client and both should be certain that this change is desirable. It is important not to make a snap decision about this issue until the client understands the ramifications of the proposed change. At the same time, the helper must examine himself or herself and be certain that the change is what is desired by the client rather than one that merely reflects the helper's values or that of the majority culture.

Stop and Reflect

A helper is not always aware that his or her assumptions about good mental health are culturally bound. In this case, a counselor named Don was tempted to encourage a client to accept a Western concept of maturity even though she came from an Asian culture. As you read the case, think how you might help such a client solve the problem in a way that is best for her.

Don was a counselor practicing in a small town near Denver, Colorado. He was born and raised in that area. One of his clients was a 25-year-old woman named Mira who had been born in the United States, although her parents were from northern India. She described the difficulties she was encountering with friends because she still lives at home. She was embarrassed because many raise their eyebrows when she tells them she is living at home. However, in her culture and family, any other living situation would be considered unacceptable before marriage. A previous helper had pushed her to move out of the house and told her, "If your parents don't like it, too bad."

- If the client were of European descent, aged 25 and still living at home, what assumptions might you make about her? Do you think you might be tempted to make these same assumptions about Mira?
- In talking about her previous counselor, what was Mira communicating to Don?
- What cultural values do you imagine Don might possess that would conflict with the client's upbringing?
- If you were Don, how might you begin helping this client? What more would you like to know about the client?

Jot down your answers to the questions raised here. Discuss them with your classmates.

Uncovering Meaning

Reflecting meaning denotes counselor attempts to restate the personal impact of the event the client is describing. This sometimes means employing intuition or hunches (Egan, 1990). Just as the helper can ask a client what he or she is feeling or reflect the feelings implicit in the client's statements, the same two approaches can be used to help the client get in touch with meaning.

Using Open Questions to Uncover Meaning

Sometimes, especially if the client is not very forthcoming, an open question focusing on meaning is useful. You are already familiar with open questions as a building block from Chapter 3. Open questions can be employed to facilitate a client's identification and expression of meaning. Consider the following exchange between a client, Sonia, and a helper, Chris:

Sonia: "There was a big family problem because I didn't pick up my sister at the airport. Everyone in the family jumped on me. I guess I was wrong, but I was busy and no one seemed to understand. Now my mom is mad at me and so is my brother."

Chris: "You feel confused about what happened."

Sonia: "Yeah, and I am mad!"

Chris: "Can you tell me what makes you so angry?"

Sonia: "My time isn't important. The family is important. My sister Camilla is important, but not me."

In this interaction, Chris reflected a feeling of confusion that was on target, but Sonia added that she also felt angry. Because Chris could not quite identify the meaning in Sonia's statement, she used an open question to try to understand the deeper issue. Sonia responded by indicating that this event reinforced her view that she is not an important part of her family.

How to Reflect Meaning

In Chapter 4, you learned to reflect feelings using the following formula: "You feel ____ because ____." The first blank was to be filled in with the client's emotion and the second with paraphrased content—for example, "You feel angry because you didn't get the promotion." To reflect meaning, we use the same formula, but in this case, we place an accurate reflection of feeling in the first blank and a reflection of meaning in the second blank, as in the following statement: "You feel disappointed in yourself because being a good daughter is an important value to you." Sometimes it may be necessary to include both a reflection of feeling and a short paraphrase of content in the first blank so that the client knows exactly which event you are referring to—for example, "You were excited (feeling) when you received your driver's license (paraphrase) *because* it meant you were becoming an adult (meaning)." The word *because* shows the connection between the content and feelings of the story and the underlying meaning for the client.

Here are some examples of helper reflections of meaning. Assume that each reflection of meaning comes after a period of listening during a helping session.

Example 1

Client: "I don't know what to do now. Everything I worked for is going down the drain."

Helper: "You must feel pretty lost because the dream of having your own business was so important to you."

Here the helper reflects the feeling of being lost. The helper then ties this feeling with the unique meaning that the client's dream has died. The helper may make a reflection like this only when he or she has adequate knowledge of the client's hopes and ambitions from previous statements.

Example 2

Client: "My daughter isn't living right. She stays out late and now she's moved in with that boy and I don't have the heart to tell anyone where she's staying."

Helper: "You are ashamed about your daughter's living situation because you think you have failed as a parent to convey your values."

The helper reflects the client's feeling of being ashamed and briefly paraphrases by mentioning her "daughter's living situation" in a nonjudgmental way. Then, the helper connects these to the underlying meaning: The client feels that she has failed.

Example 3

Client: "I never thought about being divorced. We were married for so long that I never thought about it. Since he left six months ago, I don't know how to act."

Helper: "You feel disoriented by your husband's leaving. Never in your wildest dreams did you expect to get divorced."

Here the helper reflects the client's specific feeling of shock and disorientation. The source or meaning of the shock is that the client had developed a world view that did not include this possibility. The helper reflects this meaning by saying, "Never in your wildest dreams did you expect to get divorced." This variation from the client's own words is a bit risky, but if it is correct, the client might feel understood at a deeper level.

Reflecting meaning is one of the most difficult skills to learn. It requires that the helper think intuitively and it also means that the helper must fully comprehend the client's unique situation and values. While we can guess what meaning most people might derive from a situation, as we saw in the case of Mira, to accurately reflect the meaning of an event we must also have some understanding of its cultural context. The surest route to reflection of meaning is to patiently and persistently use the basic invitational and reflecting skills. These provide the best atmosphere for clients to tell their stories. The more fully we understand the content and feelings, the easier it will be to reflect the underlying meanings.

Summarizing

Summarizing is the second advanced reflecting skill. Summarizing pulls together everything a client has said in a brief synopsis of the session up to that point. The summary helps the client make some sense of the tangle of thought and feeling just evoked in the session. In other words, it serves a reflecting purpose, letting the client hear his or her own viewpoint in a more organized way. The summary ties together some of the major issues that have emerged. It may include any of the following: content, major feelings, meaning issues and themes, or history or future plans. Of the reflecting skills, summarizing could be considered the broadest brush, bringing together main content, themes, and feelings in the client's story by concisely recapping them. Summaries may be used at all points during a therapy session—beginning, middle, and end. Since summaries have different purposes, they can be divided into four types: focusing, signal, thematic, and planning.

Focusing Summaries

When used at the beginning of a session, a summary serves the function of a focusing statement. A *focusing summary* brings the discussion back to the major issues and themes, places the spotlight on the client's responsibility for the problem, and reminds the client of the goals. For example:

> "In the last few sessions, it seems that we have been dealing with two major issues. The first is the way that you are trying to renew your social network and find some supportive friends since your breakup with Alicia. The other issue is your mixed feelings about living back home with your parents."

Focusing summaries can even be used at a first session with a new client. For example:

> "Let's review what I know so far. Your mother called and made this appointment for you because you were arrested about a month ago for public intoxication. One of the conditions of your probation is that you receive help for your drinking problem. Your probation officer referred you to our agency. So you're here to do something about the problems you've been having with alcohol. Is this about right?"

Brammer (1973) points out that a focusing summary at the beginning gets the client on track immediately. Contrast this with the normal opening statements such as, "How have things been going this week?" or "What would you like to talk about today?" When a client begins the session by reacting to a focusing summary, he or she gets back on track more quickly and immediately addresses the agreed-upon goals.

Signal Summaries

In the middle of a session, the *signal summary* can serve as a sign to the client that the helper has digested what has been said and that the session can move on to the next topic. If the helper does not summarize, the client may go over an issue several times until full understanding is communicated. An effective signal summary is used at a pause in the session when it appears to the helper that it may be time to move on to the next step.

Client: "So that's about it . . . (pause)."

Helper: "Before we move on, let's just summarize where we've been so far. You have tried to get professional help for your daughter's drug problem and she has rejected it. Since she is an adult, there is not much force you can apply. This makes you feel helpless and when you see her, your relationship is very superficial because you can't talk about the drug issue without getting into a fight. You've always been the kind of person who likes to leap into action when a problem arises and here is a situation where there is little to do. That's what makes it especially frustrating."

Client: "Yes, but that's the way it is. Now I guess I need to talk about how I can go on with my life under these circumstances."

Helper: "Okay, let's talk about that."

Thematic Summaries

A theme is a pattern of content, feelings, or meanings that the client returns to again and again (Carkhuff, 1987). The *thematic summary* is an advanced reflecting skill because it means that the helper has to be able to make connections among the content, emotions, or meanings expressed in many client statements or even during many sessions. When this kind of reflection is made, it often provides new information to the client, who may be unaware that the issue is resurfacing so often. Rather than signaling a transition to a new topic, the thematic summary tends to push clients to an even deeper level of understanding or exploration. Here are some examples of thematic summaries:

"There seem to be two issues that keep coming up. One of them is the anger you feel in a number of different close relationships (emotional theme) and the other is your sense that you haven't been able to reach your potential in your career (content theme)."

"As you have been talking, I seemed to notice a pattern and I'd like to check it out. You seem to want to end relationships when they begin to lose their initial excitement and romance (content theme)."

"From everything we've talked about over these past few weeks, one major issue seems to be that over and over again, you hesitate to make a commitment to a career or to a relationship or to take any important action because you are afraid you might let your parents down by failing (meaning theme). Is this right?"

It is difficult to practice using thematic summaries because it presumes that you have seen a client over some time and usually for more than one session. It usually takes time for important themes to emerge, and identification of themes is an intuitive process. The helper must think back on the whole of his or her experience with the client and try to cull the big issues.

Planning Summaries

A summary can be employed to terminate a session with a review of progress, plans, and agreements made. The *planning summary* brings a sense of closure and ends the session on a hopeful note. Here are two examples:

"Well, it seems that we've identified several things in this first session that we will want to pursue. First, you are unhappy with the way you tend to become overly dependent on your friends. You want to pursue your own interests. In fact, you

Table 5-1
Reflecting Skills

Skill	Example
Paraphrase A distilled restatement of the content of the client's message	"So what you're saying is that you suspect your friend is the one who informed on you to the boss."
Reflection of Feeling A statement that reveals the underlying emotions "You feel _____ (feeling) because _____ (content)."	"You're feeling anxious about your son's involvement with a new set of friends."
Reflection of Meaning A statement of content and meaning "You feel _____ (feeling) because _____ (meaning)."	"You were excited by the promotion because your longtime ambition to be accepted by the company's leaders"
Summary Distilled content and/or major feelings, meanings, or themes	"It's been a difficult two years with the divorce and the court battles. Now you're feeling lost because you had not imagined how your life would be when all of this fighting ended."

want to get to know yourself better. With this in mind, we thought about your entering a counseling group at the local mental health center. Besides that, you'd like to identify some goals for your career. That is something you and I can begin to work on right away. We'll set up an assessment program and talk more about this in the next several weeks. How does all this sound?"

"Let's recap what we have talked about so far. On the one hand, you have accomplished your financial goals but you are far from satisfied with your relationships with friends and family. You have said that this is because you are not very assertive. It sounds as if this is the area we need to discuss in our next session. What do you think?"

The Nonjudgmental Listening Cycle

When Do You Use Each Skill?

A question that students frequently have when they complete their learning of the building-block skills is, "How do you know when to use each one?" The nonjudgmental listening cycle is a way of conceptualizing a normal or average helping session as a series of discussions on various topics. The building blocks can be thought of as following a set of sequential procedures as each topic is discussed and comes to closure. As shown in Figure 5-3, each topic forms a circle that is completed before a new cycle begins. The invitational skills open the topic; the reflecting and advanced reflecting skills move the discussion to deeper levels (see Table 5-1). A signal summary normally makes the transition from one topic to another. Because each person and each helping relationship is different, this map of the average session should not be seen as the way that every helping session must unfold. Instead, it is a guide for the student to follow in the beginning. A cycle like the one shown in Figure 5-3 is typical of a discussion that might occur later in a helping session. Early on, a client and helper move through several more superficial cycles, focusing initially on content

Figure 5-3
A complete nonjudgmental listening
cycle moving from open questions
to summary

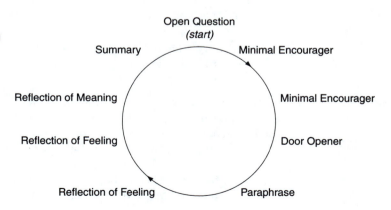

issues. The helper would probably move from utilizing open questions to paraphrases several times before finding an opportunity for a deeper discussion.

Why Is the Cycle Described as Nonjudgmental?

We have focused a great deal on the skills that a helper uses to understand a client's story. Beyond specific skills, however, the attitudes displayed by the helper can make a great difference in the willingness of the client to open up. Carl Rogers (1957), a pioneer in counseling and psychotherapy, identified positive regard as one of these important attitudes. As the name suggests, positive regard is not a neutral stance. The helper actively demonstrates a nonjudgmental approach to the client by showing respect and interest in the unique life of the client. It is a continual challenge to hold such an attitude, especially when we are confronted by clients who have perpetrated violence. Positive regard means responding in an accepting and nondefensive way to others who are different in culture, language, ethnicity, and religion. The listening cycle is called *nonjudgmental* because the attitude of positive regard must be in place when the helping skills are being employed. Without this underpinning, the skills are perceived as cold and robotic. The client will feel dissected rather than understood.

The following are examples of helper responses to client statements that represent a complete nonjudgmental listening cycle. It might take more than one such cycle to reach a summary. The session is condensed here to illustrate the major components in sequence:

1. Open questions: "Tell me more about the accident."
2. Minimal encouragers and door openers: "Okay," "Uh-huh," "Yes"; "Can you tell me more about that?"
3. Closed question (initial assessment or important facts): "How badly were you hurt?"
4. Paraphrase: "So you had to be in the rehabilitation center for several weeks and you're still unable to work."
5. Reflection of feeling: "You're embarrassed about what has happened and a little afraid that people blame you."
6. Reflection of meaning: "Your identity has always been tied up with your job. Now that you cannot work for several months, it is hard to feel good about yourself."
7. Summary: "Though you're recovering on a physical level, several issues continue to worry you, including how you might perform at your job and how other people will see you."

Figure 5-4 shows a relatively unproductive but common cycle, called a *questioning cycle,* typically found in the beginning of training. In this cycle, the helper starts with a good opening question and is able to paraphrase the content. Because the helper is unable to use reflecting or advanced reflecting skills yet, the helper utilizes a question to keep things moving. The question focuses the client back on content and the helper follows this with a series of questions or minimal encouragers. After several such cycles, the helper is tempted to give advice because he or she has understood essential facts

Figure 5-4
A questioning cycle typically
found early in training

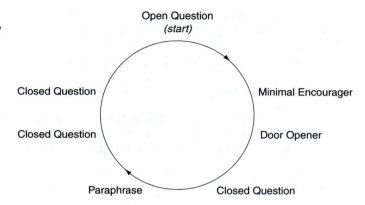

Open Question
(start)

Closed Question

Minimal Encourager

Closed Question

Door Opener

Paraphrase

Closed Question

and expects that the client is simply in need of direction. In fact, the discussion has not really scratched the surface. The helper/client exchange might go something like this:

Helper: "Tell me more about the accident."

Client: "It was horrible—what can I say? It was a financial problem, I felt terrible for months and there were the physical problems too."

Helper: "Can you tell me more about what happened?"

Client: "I ran into another car and that car hit some people on the sidewalk."

Helper: "How badly were you hurt?"

Client: "I had two weeks in the hospital with a broken femur and a broken ankle. I had to go to the rehab center for the entire month of May. I'm not walking yet without a cane. I don't know when I will be able to go back to my job."

Helper: "So you had to be in the rehabilitation center for several weeks and you're still unable to work."

Client: "Yes, but I'm in no hurry to face people. I'm a little afraid to see everybody."

Helper: "What is it like being out of work for so long?"

Client: "I am bored and I focus a lot on the pain in my legs."

Helper: "How much pain would you say you are in?"

Can you see that the helper's fourth response, "What is it like being out of work so long?" is not responsive to the client's statement, "Yes, but I'm in no hurry to face people. I'm a little afraid to see everybody"? Here the helper has a golden opportunity to reflect the client's feelings of fear and embarrassment. Instead, the helper falls back on questioning, taking the client off track. When the helper is struggling to understand but cannot make a quick response, he or she is better off using a minimal encourager or a door opener. These do not interrupt the client's story and they encourage further exploration. It also gives the helper time to ponder the client's message. Now consider how the use of minimal encouragers, leading to reflecting feelings and meaning, might be altered from the preceding helper/client exchange:

Helper: "How badly were you hurt?"

Client: "I had two weeks in the hospital with a broken femur and a broken ankle. I had to go to the rehab center for the entire month of May. I'm not walking yet without a cane. I don't know when I will be able to go back to my job."

Helper: "So you had to be in the rehabilitation center for several weeks and you're still unable to work."

Client: "Yes, but I'm in no hurry to face people. I'm a little afraid to see everybody."

Helper: "Go on."

Client: "Well, I don't know what they are thinking."

Helper: "Okay."

Client: "I think everyone blames me for what happened."

Helper: "You're worried that some of your friends will reject you because of the injuries to the other people."

Client: "I guess it's not rational."

Summary

Reflecting feelings and content are important tools for helping a client disclose. For a client to deeply sense understanding from the helper, it is also important to identify and reflect the meanings behind the client's experiences. Meanings consist of the world view or values that clients bring with them from their culture and from their experiences of life. Culture includes influences of family, religion, and ethnicity.

The inner-circle strategy is a method used to indicate to clients that they are not disclosing at the deepest levels, where the best helping occurs. It also helps us recognize that everyone maintains some secret areas. When we consider how scary it might be to expose these to others, we can begin to understand a client's need for a therapeutic alliance built on trust and time.

Reflections of meaning are helper responses that go beyond the superficial, getting at the implicit messages rather than the explicit. This means that the helper must use intuition to go beyond the surface of what the client says, extrapolating the underlying meanings. When the facts, feelings, and meanings of a client's story are reflected, he or she feels that the helper has understood at a very deep level.

Summarizing is the second major skill described in this chapter. Summaries pull together the content, feelings, and meanings in a distilled form. Summaries serve to focus the client on the major issues, signal a transition in the session, and provide a basis for planning the next steps.

The nonjudgmental listening cycle is a way of explaining the sequence of skills that a helper normally employs in the first few hours of interaction. Understanding the nonjudgmental listening cycle can help new helpers decide which skills to use at various points in the initial stage of helping.

Group Exercises

Exercise 1

Form groups of three with a client, helper, and observer. The client is to pick a topic that evokes some deeper meaning such as:

> "My greatest ambition is . . ."
> "My biggest disappointment has been . . ."
> "Something I am not very proud of is . . ."
> "My ideas about divorce are . . ."
> "What I like about this country is . . ."
> "Something I would like to improve about myself is . . ."

The helper is to use minimal encouragers and open questions to keep things moving, but the main goal is to advance hunches about the personal meanings that lie behind the client's disclosures. The helper should review the list titled "Quick Tips: Reflecting Meaning" that follows and give reflections of meaning to the client's story.

The observer is to write down all helper responses on a sheet of paper. After 5 minutes or 10 attempts at reflection of meaning, the observer calls time. Together, look at the helper's responses and see how many are accurate reflections of meaning. The client, in particular, should give the helper feedback on issues that were missed. Group members should then change roles and continue until each person has had a chance to take on the role of the helper.

Quick Tips: Reflecting Meaning

- Ask yourself, "Why is this story important to the client?" "Why is he or she telling me this?" "What is it that bothers the client so much about the event?"
- Be patient! Wait until you have heard enough of the story to understand its importance, then reflect meaning.
- Think about the client's background, then tie in what you know about his or her unique viewpoint from previous topics.
- When you have established a good reflecting relationship and the client knows that you understand the situation, take a risk and play your best hunch about underlying meaning.

Exercise 2

Look back in this chapter to the scenario of Joan and Lynn. After reading the dialogue again, write down a brief planning summary and share it with your classmates in a small group. Next, write a focusing summary that you might use to begin the next session. Summaries should be about two or three sentences in length. They should contain a brief synopsis of the thoughts, feelings, and meanings expressed by the client. Use these criteria to give each other feedback.

Quick Tips: Summarizing

- Use a summary when the client appears to be stuck. This will tend to get things back on track.
- At the end of a summary, it is often useful to finish with a quick "checking" question, such as, "Have I got that right?" or "Am I correct?"
- When you feel like asking a question, try summarizing to signal the client to move on to the next topic.
- Use a summary when the client is moving too quickly and you want to slow the session down.
- Try to finish every session with a planning summary.

Additional Exercises

Exercise 1: Identifying Meanings

Look at the following client statements. Begin by paraphrasing each, to help you get a sense of the client's situation. Next, identify the client's world view, values, or attributions in a sentence or two. Finally, use this background to construct a reflection of meaning and write it down. Take into account the fact that there may be more than one possible answer since, in practice, inflection or word emphasis might change the meaning of these responses.

   a. "I am extremely depressed and have been for about six months. I am now taking medication and things are a little better. But every day I go to the refrigerator and look in. I can't decide what to eat. In the morning I can't decide what to wear. This isn't me. If a friend calls on the phone, I am not sure what I will talk about, so I dread anyone calling. How long do you think this is going to last? Never has anything like this happened in my family. I feel so bad that my daughter has to come and take care of me. She has a life too. I even feel like I am burden to you."

Paraphrase the situation (content):

_____

_____

_____

_____

Client's underlying meanings or unspoken assumptions:

_____

_____

_____

_____

Your reflection of meaning (content + feeling + meaning):

_____

_____

   b. "I am a 31-year-old construction worker. Lately, I've had thoughts of hitting my child, Barbie. She is the light of my life. But she doesn't mind me. I have to yell and scream. My wife and I don't seem to see eye to eye on how she should be raised. Maybe we don't agree on a lot of things. When I tell my daughter something, my wife rolls her eyes and belittles me. So of course Barbie won't do what I say. I tried to talk to my wife, but she won't listen any better than my daughter does. Now, I was brought up with a belt. But only when I needed it. I don't necessarily think she has to be spanked, but she needs to learn to mind. I am embarrassed when I have to take her to my mom's house or anywhere else because she won't listen."

Paraphrase the situation (content):

_____

_____

_____

_____

Client's underlying meanings or unspoken assumptions:

_____

_____

_____

Your reflection of meaning (content + feeling + meaning):

_____

_____

_____

   c. "My main problem is that I am overweight. I know that. And I want to lose weight. Look at the television and magazines. Everybody's skinny! I guess I am supposed to go along with the crowd. But my husband doesn't realize that I have tried everything. He never says it, but I know he doesn't find me attractive anymore. But is a slim body all that is important? How about love? If I lost weight, what would I have to do next? Dress some particular way? He says he is concerned about my health, but do you believe that? Last week, my seven-year-old son and I went to the mall and one of his classmates was there. In front of everyone, the other kid said to my son, 'You have a big fat mom!' Children can be so cruel. And his mother didn't even correct him. Don't you think she should have?"

Paraphrase the situation (content):

_____
_____
_____
_____

Client's underlying meanings or unspoken assumptions:

_____
_____
_____
_____

Your reflection of meaning (content + feeling + meaning):

_____
_____
_____
_____

Exercise 2

Once your training group has completed the first typescript (see Homework 2), you will have a way to look at the nonjudgmental listening cycle. Make a list, in order, of all of the skills you used during your taped practice session. Can you discern a cycle from open questions to minimal encouragers to paraphrases to reflections of feelings and meaning? Do you stick with a topic long enough to get at deeper feelings and meanings, or do you tend to go into a questioning cycle? Get feedback from your training group, your instructor, or a classmate about how you can deepen your nonjudgmental listening cycles.

Exercise 3

Form groups of four. Each member is to write down a three- or four-line statement that a fictitious client might give as a summary of a problem. It should be written in the first person, as follows: "I am having trouble getting my children to mind me. That's not all. I've been very depressed and I'm not going to be able to pay my bills this month. What am I supposed to do?" When writing the example, students should remember to include enough information so that a reflection of meaning is possible. The trainer or leader reads each one anonymously and the training group takes turns giving a reflection of meaning using the formula, "You feel _____ because _____." The trainer or leader asks for feedback from the group concerning the accuracy of the reflection. Another option is to ask one participant to reflect the feeling and the next participant to rephrase it in more natural terms.

Homework

Homework 1: A Mid-Course Checkup

You have now learned something about invitational, reflecting, and advanced reflecting skills. Although you have probably not mastered all of them, it is time for a brief review and checkup. Try to be as honest as possible; this will help you identify areas where more practice is needed. Review the feedback you have received during group exercises and your individual practice. Then take a look at the building blocks that follow and rate your current level of mastery for each skill. Next to each, indicate how you can improve.

1 = I understand the concept

2 = I can identify it and give examples

3 = I can do it occasionally

4 = I do it regularly

_____ Eye contact

_____ Body position

_____ Attentive silence

_____ Voice tone

_____ Gestures and facial expressions

_____ Physical distance

_____ Door openers and minimal encouragers

_____ Open and closed questions

_____ Paraphrasing

_____ Reflecting feelings

_____ Reflecting meaning

_____ Summarizing

Take a look at the pattern of your responses. If you are like most learners, your invitational skills are strong. You may also be doing fairly well with paraphrasing but you may well be at level 2 or 3 on the reflecting and advanced reflecting skills.

Homework 2: First Typescript

Now that you have read about and practiced the building blocks of the helping relationship, it is time to make a record of your present skill level by recording a longer session (20–30 minutes) on audio or videotape and convert-

ing it to hard copy, or, as we will call it, a *typescript.*

Your goal as a helper in this typescript is to demonstrate your ability to move from cycles of questioning and paraphrasing to use of the higher skills of reflecting feelings and meanings. Rather than asking questions, fall back on paraphrasing, door openers, minimal encouragers, and even silence until you are able to make a reflection.

Step 1

With a partner from your training group, conduct and tape-record a session based on a concern that he or she is willing to discuss. Alternately, your client may role-play the problem of a friend or acquaintance or fabricate a problem he or she might someday encounter in his or her own life.

Step 2

Choose the best 15 minutes of the tape and transcribe every word of both client and helper using the format of Table 5-2. It is important that the client's comments appear directly *below* your helping responses so that the connection between the two can be examined. Be sure you have permission from the client to record the session. You can verify permission aloud on the tape and in writing.

Step 3

Listen to the tape or read the typescript and make comments, naming each of the skills that your response exemplifies. Sometimes, students describe their responses rather than categorizing them. It is important to identify the skills you are using to determine their frequency and appropriateness. Use only the names of the building blocks you have learned. The "Comments" column is a place for you to reflect on your responses. Do not just note weaknesses; identify strengths as well. In the "Comments" column, you may also wish to identify any other issues that come to mind as you review the typescript.

Table 5-2
Typescript Example

In your write-up, include a short description of the client and the nature of the issue to be discussed. Note that each helper and client response is numbered so that the instructor can refer to them.

Client and Helper Responses	The Skill You Used	Comments
H1: "What would you like to talk about today?"	Open question	Looking at this now, it seems a little trite. I think I will try something else next time.
C1: "Well, I've been having a problem with a nosy neighbor."		
H2: "Really? Tell me more."	Minimal encourager and door opener	Seems appropriate at this stage.
C2: "Well, she comes over every day. I can't get anything done. I need to work on the computer. I need to do some work around the house. But she won't let me."		I notice that the client is blaming the neighbor. She is not owning the problem. Maybe next time I will get the client to focus more on that.
H3: "She doesn't have anything else to do?"	Closed question	Whoops, I missed the boat. I think it might have been better to reflect the client's frustration.

References

Anderson, W. T. (1990). *Reality isn't what it used to be.* San Francisco: Harper.

Brammer, L. (1973). *The helping relationship: Process and skills.* Upper Saddle River, NJ: Prentice-Hall.

Carkhuff, R. R. (1987). *The art of helping* (6th ed.). Amherst, MA: Human Resource Development Press.

Corey, G., Corey, M., & Callanan, P. (1988). *Issues and ethics in the helping professions.* Monterey, CA: Brooks/Cole.

Egan, G. (1990). *The skilled helper* (4th ed.). Monterey, CA: Brooks/Cole.

Ivey, A. E., Ivey, M. B., & Simek-Morgan, L. (1997). *Counseling and psychotherapy: A multicultural perspective.* Boston: Allyn & Bacon.

Lazarus, A. A. (1981). *The practice of multimodal therapy.* New York: McGraw-Hill.

Pedersen, P. B. (1987). Ten frequent assumptions of cultural bias in counseling. *Journal of Multicultural Counseling and Development, 14,* 16–24.

Rogers, C. R. (1957). The necessary and sufficient conditions of therapeutic personality change. *Journal of Consulting Psychology, 21,* 95–103.

Sue, D. W. (1981). *Counseling the culturally different: Theory and practice.* New York: Wiley.

Sue, D. W., & Sue, D. (1990). *Counseling the culturally different.* New York: Wiley.

Young, M. E., & Witmer, J. M. (1985). Values: Our internal guidance system. In J. M. Witmer, *Pathways to personal growth* (pp. 275–289). Muncie, IN: Accelerated Development.

6

Challenging Skills

Introduction

Sometimes it becomes necessary for helpers to "dare" clients to change by giving them feedback and confronting discrepancies in their stories. For most of us, this step in the journey of helping is a giant one. While the invitational and reflecting skills are supportive and persuade a client to open up, the challenging skills push the client to critically examine his or her choices, feelings, and thoughts. When the helper uses challenging skills, he or she is giving the client an honest reaction or pointing out inconsistencies and conflicts. Supportive behaviors such as the invitational and reflecting skills do not necessarily encourage the client to follow through with plans and goals.

When challenging skills are used, the aura of safety and support, so carefully constructed by the helper, is at risk. There is a fundamental shift from relationship building to a focus on the goals set by the client and helper, conveying to the client that the helping relationship is not a friendship but a business partnership.

During the initial stages of the relationship, the helper strives to understand the client's unique world view by getting the client to open up. As the client tells his or her story, the helper listens attentively using the nonjudgmental listening cycle. After several cycles, the helper begins to detect distortions, blind spots, and inconsistencies. He or she may then use feedback and challenging skills, not so much to straighten out the client as to teach the client the method of self-challenging. The essential aim of the challenging skills is to help clients function with unclouded information about themselves. With heightened self-awareness, they are better able to make decisions and operate free of illusions. This is consistent with the goal of helping: to empower clients by encouraging them to explore their own thoughts, feelings, and behaviors. Clients need to be challenged when:

- They are operating on misinformation about the self. For example, a client may underestimate her intelligence, feeling that she is not capable of attending college.
- They misinterpret the actions of others. This tendency is called *mind reading* and is a common problem among couples. A client may act on assumptions without confirming them, making statements such as the following: "I could tell by the way he acted that he did not want to date me anymore."
- They blame others rather than examining themselves. For example, a client may blame the boss at work but refuse to look at his own responsibility for the poor relationship or his own work performance.
- Their behavior, thoughts, and feelings are inconsistent. For example, a client talks about how much he values honesty, but at the same time discusses how he hides his financial difficulties from his wife.

In this chapter, we will discuss two building blocks used to challenge clients: giving feedback and confrontation.

Giving Feedback

Why Is Feedback Important?

The invitational, reflecting, and advanced reflecting skills that you have already learned are the primary methods for enhancing client self-disclosure. The mere act of confiding in another person seems to have many health benefits (Pennebaker, 1990), and the ability to be "transparent" to others has been linked with mental health (Jourard, 1971).

Learning to receive *feedback* is the other key to self-awareness and growth. Clients need accurate feedback in order to confront inconsistencies in their own attitudes and to know how they are affecting others. Most problems that people face are "people problems." The major difficulties they suffer from are in their interpersonal worlds. Yet, unfortunately, they often receive less-than-useful or conflicting messages about themselves from other people. Even family members and close friends may be afraid to give each other information about how they are affecting others. A friend may say, "You look like a lunatic when you dance," or "Your driving makes me nervous!" because he or she is embarrassed or afraid of crashing rather than because of a desire to provide good information. On the other hand, close friends and relatives may also withhold feedback because they do not wish to jeopardize the relationship. Egan (1977) calls this tendency the "mum effect."

The Johari Window

The *Johari window* (Luft, 1969) is a visual way of explaining that information about the self comes from two sources: things we observe about ourselves and feedback from those around us (see Figure 6-1). The Johari window (named after Joe Luft and Harry Ingram, who invented it) helps to explain how we can gain greater self-awareness through two tools of growth: self-disclosure and feedback. The window has four "panes":

	Known to self	Not known to self
Known to others	I Public area	II Blind spot
Not known to others	III Hidden area	IV Unknown area

Figure 6-1
The Johari window
Source: From Luft, J. (1969). *Of human interaction* (p. 13). Palo Alto, CA: National Press. Reprinted by permission.

I. Information Known Both to Others and to the Self (Public Area)

According to the model, the behavior of self-disclosure widens the public area (pane I) and shrinks the private area (pane III). A client who has a broader public area is able to disclose more deeply, will experience greater relief, creates better relationships, and supplies the helper with more complete information about problems. The contents of this area vary depending on how open or transparent an individual is. However, most people do not keep secret such information as their occupation, the car they drive, their ethnic background, and perhaps their religion or party affiliation.

II. Information Known to Others but Not to the Self (Blind Spot)

Feedback shrinks the blind spot (pane II). There is much about ourselves that we cannot know because we are not objective. As the poet Robert Burns said, "O wad some pow'r the giftie gie us / to see ourselves as ithers see us." One example of a blind spot is that we do not know what we really look like to others; when we look into a mirror, we are really seeing the reverse of our image. We often do not know if we have bad breath, if we are annoying someone, if we appear judgmental, or if we have a whining tone in our voice. Conversely, we may miss our positive traits as well, unaware that others see us as attractive, kind, or a good listener.

III. Information Not Known to Others but Known to the Self (Hidden Area)

This is the area of secrets. People with large private areas (pane III) usually are not known or liked by others. There is a saying in Alcoholics Anonymous that you are "only as sick as your darkest secret." This phrase suggests that through appropriate self-disclosure, many problems that have been lurking in our minds—our deepest secrets—tend to vanish in the light of a confiding relationship. When we keep secrets from others, we do not have to face our negative traits and bad habits. Most people keep secrets about their sexual activities, their drug or alcohol use, and the times when they have been dishonest or cowardly.

IV. Information Not Known to Others or the Self (Unknown Area)

The helping relationship reduces the size of the unknown area (pane IV). Unconscious or preconscious information comes to light when the client opens up. Clients have moments of insight, or "aha!" experiences, that occur when they consolidate information gained through self-disclosure and feedback. Invitational, reflecting, and challenging skills help clients gain more information about themselves and reduce this unknown area.

When we think about whether a helping session has been successful, we can evaluate it in two ways. We can look at whether the helper has demonstrated the invitational and reflecting skills as well as other building blocks. On the other hand, the Johari window gives us a glimpse of the big picture. A session is successful if the client has disclosed important material to the helper and if he or she has reduced the blind spot by receiving feedback from the helper.

How to Give Feedback

In the helping relationship, giving feedback means supplying information to a client about what you see, feel, or suspect about him or her. Feedback helps people grow because they are receiving helpful, specific information about themselves. When a professional helper gives feedback, the purpose is solely to help the client. Feedback from a professional—unlike that of family and friends—does not consider the needs of the helper or whether this will produce a strain on the relationship. Helpers give feedback only when clients ask for it or when the client needs information to progress. They give feedback for three purposes: (1) to indicate how the client's behavior affects the helper, (2) to evaluate a client's progress, and (3) to supply a client with information based on the helper's observation. When a helper says, "You say you want to be assertive but I experience your behavior as passive when you look away and avoid eye contact," the feedback indicates the effect of the behavior on the helper. The statement, "As I see it, you have been successful in overcoming your anxiety by facing the situations you have been avoiding," is an evaluation of the client's progress. The helper is making an observation when he or she says, "I notice that you never seem to talk about your father."

Feedback may be rejected by clients because the truth hurts. Clients use defense mechanisms to avoid accepting the information they receive. Therefore, helpers endeavor to present feedback so that it will be more palatable. In his classic book about raising children, *Parent Effectiveness Training* (1975), Thomas Gordon described the process of delivering feedback as "I-messages." Most feedback statements delivered by helpers are I-messages because using the word *I* conveys that the helper is expressing his or her own perspective. When a person starts a conversation by saying, "This is my viewpoint," we are more likely to listen nondefensively.

Here are some suggestions about how to give effective feedback. These are good rules for helpers and for students, who may be giving feedback to each other in group exercises.

1. Do not give people feedback on their personality traits. It is hard to see how one can change a description of one's character.

Poor Feedback: "You are a procrastinator."

Good Feedback: "For the past three months, your report has been late. That is unacceptable."

2. Be specific and concrete.

Poor Feedback: "You're bugging me."

Good Feedback: "I find it annoying when you whistle during my favorite music."

3. Ask permission before giving feedback.

Good Feedback: "You say that people at work are angry about your behavior. Would you like some feedback?"

Good Feedback: "I would like to give you some feedback on something I have noticed. Is that all right?"

    4. Sometimes, feedback about touchy subjects is accepted more easily if it is offered tentatively. You do not have to dilute the feedback; rather, find an acceptable route to get the client to think about what is being reported.

Poor Feedback: "Last time we talked about your feelings that you deserted your father when he was ill. This time, you avoid the topic when I try to reopen it."

Good Feedback: "I got the impression last time that talking about your father was difficult for you and you seemed to steer away from that topic. Maybe it is because you think you deserted him when he was ill. Am I right about this?"

    5. Give only one or two pieces of feedback at a time. When too much feedback is given, client defenses rear up like impenetrable walls and little gets through.

Poor Feedback: "I think you should improve your appearance at work. You look disheveled and you need to wear a tie. By the way, you left the copy machine on again last night and you forgot to call Darlene back."

Good Feedback: "I think you should improve your appearance at work. You look disheveled and you need to wear a tie."

    6. Remember to give feedback that emphasizes the client's strengths. It is easy to assume that clients are aware of their strengths and to focus on their foibles. We tend to give feedback that points out unknown weaknesses rather than unrecognized assets. More often, clients need to know what is going right, what is working, and what resources the client has to bring to the problem.

Poor Feedback: "You asked someone out for a date but you did not work on the other part of the assignment, where you were to confront your friend on her behavior. Let's talk about that."

Good Feedback: "Based on what you've said today, I'm picking up that you have made real progress. Even though it was a little scary, you asked two people for a date and one of them said yes."

    7. Use a checking question to determine whether feedback was received and how it was accepted.

Helper: "A minute ago, I pointed out that you have spent the last few weeks talking only about your ex-husband. What is your reaction to that feedback?"

Stop and Reflect
_____

- Think about a particularly difficult piece of feedback you have received. It may have been a friend's comment about a weakness in your appearance or your boss's comment during a job evaluation; it may even have been feedback you received in this class. How did you respond emotionally to the feedback? Did it make you angry, hurt your feelings, or just make you feel incompetent? Did you try to protect yourself by denying or discounting the feedback? Did you learn anything constructive from the negative feedback?
- Now think about a time when you received some positive feedback on a personal strength—for example, about a job well done or some aspect of your appearance or personality. What made the feedback positive?
- Finally, have you ever had an experience in which you received no feedback after expending considerable time and effort? For instance, have you ever turned in a lengthy project or paper and received no comments other than a grade? How did you react emotionally? What effect do you think a lack of feedback would have on a person's behavior in the long run?

Of the three kinds of feedback mentioned here—positive, negative, and none—which helped you the most? How might you apply your reactions to your future dealings with clients?

Confrontation
_____

Confrontations are interventions that point out discrepancies in client beliefs, behaviors, words, or nonverbal messages and that are followed by a push to resolve the inconsistencies. Confrontation creates emotional arousal and can lead clients to develop important insights.

A *discrepancy* is an inconsistency, a mixed message or conflict among a client's thoughts, feelings, and behaviors. In fact, every problem a client presents contains discrepancies. For example:

A client says she wants an equal sharing relationship, but dates only domineering men.

A client says she that loves her job, but complains about it constantly.

A client states that he wants to improve his marriage, but forgets to come to marriage counseling sessions.

Why Should Inconsistencies Be Confronted?

Ivey and Simek-Downing (1980) say that "the resolution or synthesis of incongruities may be said to be a central goal of all theoretical orientations" (p. 177). As a result of confrontation, client awareness of inconsistencies is stimulated, and the client moves to resolve them. In essence, it is an educational process that brings information to the client's attention that has been previously unknown, disregarded, or repressed.

Confrontation is a skill that is developed after the early helping building blocks are well established. As you gain more training and experience, you will realize increasingly that clients need to be challenged as well as supported. Recent research confirms that highly trained (doctoral) counselors use confrontation more often than students (Tracey, Hays, Malone, & Herman, 1988). At the same time, doctoral-level counselors demonstrate less dominance and verbosity than student helpers. It appears that experience and training teach helpers to use confrontation more frequently, to talk less, and to be less domineering with clients.

Cognitive Dissonance and Confrontation: Why Confrontation Works

Do you remember the concept of cognitive dissonance from Psychology 101? Cognitive dissonance theory states that we are motivated to keep cognitions such as values, beliefs, and attitudes consistent (Festinger, 1957). When people experience inconsistencies in their thoughts, feelings, and behaviors, this creates tension and they are motivated to reduce the tension. We often convince ourselves that the incongruity is unimportant or try changing one of the incompatible elements. For example, a client describes her good-paying but repetitive and boring job and says that she wants to go to college because she is not intellectually challenged in her present position. She deals with the tension caused by these conflicting thoughts by stating that intellectual challenge is not really important; it is better to be financially secure. We use such defense mechanisms to distort reality so that we can reduce anxiety. Many times, clients are using defense mechanisms to escape tension rather than making choices based on thinking and planning. When clients are confronted with these discrepancies, their anxiety often resurfaces.

Kiesler and Pallak (1976) reviewed dissonance studies and found a link between dissonance and physiological arousal (Cooper, Zanna, & Taves, 1978; Croyle & Cooper, 1983; Pittman, 1975; Zanna & Cooper, 1974). Attitude change occurs because clients are driven to reduce the arousal caused by the helper's discrepant messages. In short, when a helper confronts a client, the client becomes anxious when he or she realizes that there is a discrepancy in his or her story. The confrontation causes anxiety because the client must become aware of this split, which is normally kept out of awareness by his or her defenses. The client is then invited to change his or her ideas to ones that are more reality based and productive (Claiborn, 1982; Olsen & Claiborn, 1990).

Types of Discrepancies

Discrepancies in a person's life can exist in three major realms: the cognitive-perceptual, the affective, and the behavioral (Hammond, Hepworth, & Smith, 1977, pp. 287–313). An example of a discrepancy in the cognitive-perceptual realm would be a client's refusal to take responsibility for his or her actions. There is a discrepancy between the client's perception of himself or herself as a victim and his or her cognition that change is possible and requires personal effort. Clients can also be confronted on affective inconsistencies between verbal and nonverbal messages—for example, when a client laughs as she tells you about a terrible car accident in which she was involved. Behavioral confrontations might help clients face inconsistencies in such areas as lifestyle and values. For example, a client may say he wants to develop a long-term relationship but never calls anyone back for a second date.

The helper's confrontational statement usually takes one of the following forms:

"You said _____ , but acted _____ ."

"You said _____ , but also said _____ ."

"You acted _____ , but also acted _____ ."

"You said _____ , but I see _____ ."

Five of the most common contradictions or incongruities expressed by clients are illustrated in the following dialogues:

Incongruities between Verbal and Nonverbal Messages

Client: "It's been hell. This whole thing. It's almost funny (laughs). You know. Sometimes he loves me, sometimes he hates me."

Helper: "Your laughing and smiling make me think the problem is not serious, and yet I can tell by what you've said that it has been very painful for you." (confrontation)

Incongruities between the Client's View of the Self and the View of Others

Client: "I do the best I can. But I'm not really good-looking. I've been dating the same two guys for about four months now. They say I'm pretty, but I don't believe it."

Helper: "You tell me you're not attractive and then you describe going on a lot of dates." (confrontation)

Incongruities between What the Client Says and How the Client Behaves

Client: "I've been going to Cocaine Anonymous as I said I would. But it's not really helping. Every time I see one of my old friends, I'm back into it again."

Helper: "I'm confused. You say you want to give up cocaine, and yet you continue to see your old drug friends." (confrontation)

Incongruities between Client Plans and Helper Perception

Client: "Sure, my girlfriend and I have been having a lot of problems lately. But if we moved in together, I think things would improve."

Helper: "Isn't part of the problem that whenever you spend any length of time together, you fight violently for days? How will living together and spending even more time together help the relationship?" (confrontation)

Incongruities between Two Verbal Messages

Client: "My wife makes twice as much money as I do. It doesn't bother me. But I always feel that she looks down on me because of it. I should be making a lot more than I do. I often think about getting another job."

Helper: "OK, on the one hand, you say it doesn't bother you, and yet you feel inadequate in her eyes and often consider a career change!" (confrontation)

How to Confront

Step 1   Use the nonjudgmental listening cycle to fully understand the client's message and ask yourself whether the timing is right or whether a confrontation will prematurely strain the relationship. Have you earned the right to confront? The following example shows a helper using closed questioning and reflection of feeling as a lead-in to a confrontation.

Helper: "Can you tell me what you mean by the word *independence?*" (closed question—clarifier)

Client: "Well, what I mean is that I am tired of having to report to my wife. I don't know what I'd do without her. But she is a pain in the neck most of the time."

Helper: "You really resent her interference as if she were your boss at work." (reflection of feeling)

Client: "But she's a wonderful wife. I don't really mean it when I say those things, you know."

Helper: "You think she's wonderful, and yet you find yourself angry at her a great deal of the time." (confrontation)

Step 2   Whenever possible, follow up with a second confrontation that maintains the pressure. Because clients often respond to confrontation either by denial or superficial agreement, the helper must be ready to follow up with additional exploration, another confrontation, or clarification. A confrontation can be uncomfortable, and it is easier, but not productive, to allow the client to move away from the issue.

Helper: "I'm a little confused. You have been telling me for the past four weeks that all you want to do is reunite with your wife. Now a marriage counseling session has been scheduled and you don't want to attend." (confrontation showing tentativeness)

Client: "I do want to get back together, but I'm just not ready."

Helper: "When you say, you're not ready, I feel very surprised. You've been ready for months now. Have you been saying that you want to get back together and feeling at the same time like you don't want to?" (maintaining the pressure)

Client: "Yes, I dread the idea of going back to that fighting. I have to admit, I've been enjoying the peace and freedom."

Stop and Reflect

The following is a reflection by Cindy Yee, a counselor working in Phoenix, about her upbringing and how her family and cultural values helped her become a nonjudgmental listener and also presented a challenge when she was forced to confront her clients.

Respect is a core value around which Chinese culture is based. "Respect your parents and do as they say." "Respect your teachers and don't question or challenge them." "Respect your family and don't discuss concerns or problems outside the family circle." "Respect your elders and don't talk back to them." These were the values and expectations instilled in me by my parents, and especially my mother. She was born in China and believed most strongly in these rules.

When I first began working as a counselor, my job was to facilitate a group for court-ordered drunk drivers, one of the most angry and difficult client populations. You can imagine the challenges I had to face. For someone who is assertive, open, and willing to confront others, regardless of age or status, this would be a difficult job. For someone like me who was taught to listen, not interrupt, and agree with others, especially older people and those in higher positions, it was a daunting task.

Frequently, there were older clients in the group who tended to "ramble on" in their discussions. Interrupting them, in Chinese eyes, would have been very disrespectful. When doctors, lawyers, and teachers were in the group, and expressed opinions contrary to my curriculum, it was nearly impossible for me, at first, to disagree with them. It has taken quite a while for me to overcome this reluctance to be what my culture would consider "disrespectful," and to develop the necessary skills as a counselor to be assertive in confronting others. This is still an area I am trying to improve. My cultural style of passive acceptance has helped me develop unconditional acceptance regardless of differences. This has helped me in developing rapport with clients and getting to the point in a relationship where they can accept confrontation. Chinese cultural values and beliefs have been both helpful and challenging to me as an emerging helper.

- Cindy Yee indicates that respect is one of the core values in Chinese culture. Thinking back on your own upbringing, what cultural or family values were stressed? What were your family's values about contradicting others, keeping the peace, and disclosing weaknesses? Was family business to be kept within the family? Do you think any of your own core values might have an effect on your willingness either to talk with clients about their deepest issues or to confront certain individuals?

- One of the most common difficulties for most of us is overcoming the "mum effect," that is, the social rule that says to keep feedback to yourself. As a helper, your contract with the client implies that you will give honest feedback despite your personal discomfort. Think about some specific situations that will create discomfort for you, such as refusing an expensive gift from a client, informing a client that his or her personal hygiene is poor, dealing with tardiness, talking about sexual problems, discussing whether the client is having an affair, or asking whether the client is being honest with you. Which do you think will be the most difficult for you? How might you increase your comfort with these topics?

- Would you find it more difficult to confront someone of a different ethnic or racial background, someone older or younger than you, someone who has a high-status profession, or someone of the same or opposite sex? How do you plan to overcome these limitations? Discuss with a small group some strategies for overcoming some of these roadblocks to confrontation.

Evaluating Confrontation

The Helper Confrontation Scale

One way to evaluate the potency of a confrontation is to score the helper's statement on a 5-level scale that is similar to Carkhuff's levels of empathic response (Hammond, Hepworth, & Smith, 1977). We call this the *Helper Confrontation Scale*. Higher scores on the scale reflect a better ability to confront effectively.

At level 1, the helper overlooks or accepts the discrepancies, inconsistencies, or dysfunctional expressions of the client or uses a harsh or abrasive confrontation. An example of a harsh confrontation is one that breaks the rules of good feedback given earlier—for instance, "Your unwillingness to make this decision shows that you are a dependent person."

At level 2, the helper does not focus on discrepancies, but responds with silence or reflects without noting the inconsistency. This category also includes poorly timed confrontations, such as a strong confrontation that is delivered in the first few interchanges between helper and client, before a therapeutic relationship is established.

At level 3, the helper focuses attention on a discrepancy by questioning or by pointing out the inconsistency. At level 3, the timing is appropriate and the confrontation is not abusive—for example, the helper points out, "After hearing your story, I am struck by the fact that you talk about your unhappiness with your choice of college, but at the same time it sounds like there are things you like about being there as well."

Level 4 involves a direct confrontation by the helper that includes a challenge to the client to modify the behavior or to resolve the inconsistency, while at the same time protecting the client's self-esteem. To guard the client's self-esteem, the helper uses a nonjudgmental tone and a tentative approach. For example, a helper might say, "What I am hearing is that on the one hand you love your mother, but on the other, at age 30, you feel that you need a place of your own. This sounds like a really important issue for you to resolve and I would like to help."

Finally, level 5 includes all of the positive characteristics of the lower levels but is conveyed by the helper in a caring and helpful way along with enthusiasm for growth. For example, the helper might say, "You really care for Angela but you are afraid of the consequences when the boss finds out you are dating his ex-wife. This sounds like a problem that really deserves some quick attention and it could really help you because you desire to be more honest and straightforward about your feelings."

The Client Acceptance Scale

Another method of evaluating a confrontation is to look at how the client responds to it. Clients react to a confrontation in three basic ways. Each represents a different level of acceptance of the confrontation and can give the helper important feedback. A client response can be rated on the *Client Acceptance Scale* as a 1, 2, or 3, depending on the extent to which a client agrees with a discrepancy pointed out by the helper. The three levels of acceptance are:

Level 1:   A client may deny that a discrepancy even exists. Examples of denial include attempts by the client to discredit the helper, to change the topic, to seek support elsewhere, or to falsely accept the confrontation. The helper must decide in such cases whether to pound away continually until the confrontation is accepted or to bring the topic up again at a later date. The combative approach can be detrimental to the relationship.

Level 2:   The client may choose to accept one part or aspect of the confrontation as being true while finding another hard to swallow. Partial acceptance can lead to further dialogue on the issue.

Level 3:   The client appears to fully accept the confrontation and agrees to try to resolve the inconsistency that has been pointed out with new behavior.

A client who fails to agree with a confrontation is not necessarily resistant. The confrontation may have been inaccurate or too discrepant with the client's experience. Very often, a client's response at levels 1 and 2 precedes full acceptance. The client has not yet identified the issue as a problem and may need some time to change viewpoints.

An example was given earlier in which a helper confronted an individual who stated that he wanted to give up cocaine, yet continued to associate with his old drug-using friends. The continuation of their conversation is presented here to show how the helper can promote exploration even when the client does not fully accept the confrontation. It also shows how a confrontation can lead to the setting of a new goal when the helper points out a discrepancy and then asks the client to resolve it.

Client: "I've been going to Cocaine Anonymous as I said I would. But it's not really helping. Every time I see one of my old friends, I'm back into it again."

Helper: "I'm confused. You say you want to give up cocaine and yet you continue to see your old drug friends." (Helper Confrontation Scale—3)

Client: "I do want to stop using. But what am I supposed to do? Stay by myself all the time?" (Client Acceptance Scale—2)

Helper: "So what you really need is to be around people, socialize, have friends. So how could you do this—stay away from cocaine and still have friends?"

Client: "You tell me."

Helper: "Hold it. I don't have all the answers to this. But you said you want to have friends and you want to stop using. Is this possible?"

Client: "It must be. People do it."

Helper: "Yes, but how do they do it?"

Client: "I don't know. I guess they have new friends that don't use. But it's hard to start all over again."

Helper: "I'm not an expert on this. But some people who have been off cocaine for a while must be familiar with this problem. It seems like it might be fairly common. Between now and when we next meet, would you be willing to think about this? Go to your next Anonymous meeting and ask one or two people about this, then let me know what they have to say."

Client: "All right. And I'll talk to my friend, Michelle. She's been sober for a year now."

Shock Confrontation

Confrontation can also act as a shock treatment. Provocative therapy, Gestalt therapy, and some others use confrontive language to arouse emotions rather than to promote learning. Sometimes clinicians use loud voice tones or even curses to intensify confrontations. Some early group therapy methods, such as the Synanon approach, used personal attacks and abusive confrontation to create movement in dealing with deeply ingrained behavior patterns. Many alcohol and drug treatment facilities still favor these methods. Such confrontation is designed to provoke an emotional response, such as anger or sadness, in "hardened" clients. These confrontations compare the client to some external standard set by the helper—they are judgments. Below is an example of this shock-treatment type of confrontation:

Client: "I'm always, you know, the last one, the fifth wheel. My parents favor my sister. At work everyone ignores me. *You* talk to me only because I pay you. What's wrong with me? Why doesn't anybody like me?"

Helper: "Maybe it's because they don't want to be around a whiner!"

Prochaska (1984) describes an experience in which his co-helper confronted a husband about his domineering behavior toward his wife by saying, "You make me want to vomit!" The man returned to an individual session filled with consternation over this abuse. His anger triggered a great deal of discussion, introspection, and therapeutic movement because the client was able to see how he brought out these responses not only in the helper but with his wife.

The helper responses in both these examples could be called feedback. They are verbalizations of the helper's genuine reaction to the client (Prochaska, 1984). The client must either agree or become defensive, refuting the helper's statement, but an important aspect of this type of confrontation is that it is unexpected and promotes emotional arousal. Confrontive helpers such as Fritz Perls are able to get away with this kind of behavior because of their charisma and reputation, and the piercing accuracy of their confrontations. However, shock confrontation cannot be recommended, especially to the beginning helper, because of its effects on the therapeutic alliance and on client self-esteem. The reason for discussing it here is that such methods are often portrayed in films, books, and dramatic demonstrations. They are appealing in their power and cleverness, but the implications for the helping relationship should be the primary consideration.

Problems and Precautions

Confrontation, if mishandled, may arouse the defenses of the client rather than increasing his or her awareness of discrepancies. Therefore, confrontational interventions must be advanced carefully. Although the force of the confrontation should not be watered down with qualifiers, confrontation must be presented in a way that does not damage self-esteem and that is palatable to the client. Earlier, the notion of timing was mentioned. Timing means knowing when in the relationship and when in the course of therapy confrontation will do the most good. Obviously, confrontation should wait until the client/helper relationship is well established. Knowing when confrontation will do the most good is a more tricky clinical judgment. It has been our experience that frequent and premature confrontations based on very little information tend to erode the credibility of the helper. Consider waiting to confront an issue until after it has been raised on several occasions and the chances of acceptance by the client are high.

Confrontation can have other negative effects on the therapeutic relationship. Confrontations, if made too forcefully, may seem to blame or humiliate the client and therefore can be contradictory to the goal of raising self-esteem. Inappropriate confrontations place the helper in a judgmental and superior position, arousing defenses rather than providing insight.

Before confronting, the helper must understand that the reason for the intervention is to increase client awareness, not just to unload a sense of frustration. Egan (1994) has always contended that one needs to earn the right to confront one's friends. The same is also true in the helping relationship. Biting confrontation without the client's trust is not likely to be successful.

A general caveat is that any helper intervention that is in opposition to the client's social and cultural values may not be only disrespectful but also ineffective. Confrontation is an excellent example of a technique with cultural implications. For example, Lazarus (1982) discusses how this technique can backfire with some Native American children in a school counseling setting. Others have recommended a gentle approach in using confrontation with African American clients (Ivey, 1994).

Summary

The nonjudgmental listening cycle creates the proper conditions for a therapeutic relationship to take place. In that relationship, the client feels accepted and explores the thoughts, feelings, and meanings that are implicit in his or her story. But the story also has inconsistencies and conflicts or else the client would not be seeking help. The helper must give the client feedback and use confrontational skills to help the client become aware of the discrepancies and encourage the client to act to resolve them. Ironically, this places a strain on the therapeutic relationship because the client begins to realize that the helper is not going to stick to safe topics but will explore the touchy ones as well.

In this chapter, we presented the Johari window as a way of envisioning the big picture in the helping process. The client needs to gain information about the self as well as disclose. Growth involves greater self-knowledge, which goes hand in hand with self-disclosure. This chapter presented some guidelines for giving feedback to increase clients' knowledge about themselves and how their behavior might be affecting others.

A confrontation is a serious challenge to the inconsistencies and discrepancies in the story and pushes the client to act. Confrontation is an art in that one must present discrepancies clearly, yet kindly. The Helper Confrontation Scale assists new helpers in evaluating the quality of their confrontations. On the other hand, the Client Acceptance Scale rates client reactions to confrontations to determine how much impact a confrontation is having and whether another tactic should be tried.

Group Exercises

Group Exercise 1: Feedback—The Fishbowl

This exercise works best with groups of eight to ten people. Four or five people sit in chairs facing each other to form an inner circle. The same number of participants form an outer circle. Each member of the outer circle is paired with an inner-circle member. The outer-circle members sit behind the inner circle and across from the members they are paired with so they can observe them. (See Figure 6-2.) For 10–15 minutes, the inner-circle members engage in a leaderless discussion on a topic such as "What are the most important personal characteristics of a helper?" or

Figure 6-2
Fishbowl activity
diagram

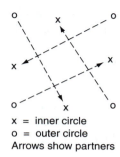

x = inner circle
o = outer circle
Arrows show partners

"What do you see yourself doing personally and professionally, five years from now?"

During the discussion, outer-circle members are instructed to carefully observe nonverbals and listen to the words of their partners in the inner group. At the end of the discussion, the groups break down into dyads of the inner-circle members and their outer-circle partners. Outer-circle members give feedback to inner-circle members using the following guidelines. When this is completed, inner-circle members should comment on the quality of the feedback they received. How accurate was it?

Feedback Guidelines

1. Do not give people feedback on their personality traits.
2. Be specific and concrete.
3. Ask permission before giving feedback.
4. Sometimes, feedback about touchy subjects is accepted more easily if it is offered tentatively.
5. Give only one or two pieces of feedback at a time.
6. Give feedback that emphasizes the client's strengths, not just weaknesses.
7. Use a checking question to determine whether feedback was received and how it was accepted.

Time permitting, the exercise can be repeated with inner- and outer-circle members changing places. Following the feedback in dyads, a class discussion can be held in which members compare their experiences of giving and receiving feedback. Which role was more difficult, giver or receiver of feedback? Were you surprised by the accuracy of the feedback on your interpersonal style?

Group Exercise 2: Confrontation

Break into groups of three students who will assume the roles of helper, client, and observer. As the exercise continues, each member should have the opportunity to assume each role.

The Client's Role   Discuss a problem that is causing an internal conflict or moral dilemma. The problem might be the result of:

- conflict about a job or whether to relocate.
- conflict about whether or not to be honest in a relationship—for example, whether to tell a friend she depends on you too much.
- conflict about something you have done that you do not feel good about, that you regret, or that you wish you could change.

The Observer's Role   Write down verbatim the helper's responses on the Feedback Checklist and evaluate the helper on the ability to use confrontation using the 5-point Helper Confrontation Scale. Code the helper's responses as indicated on the Feedback Checklist.

The Helper's Role   Review the list titled "Quick Tips: Confrontation" that follows this exercise. Use the nonjudgmental listening cycle to get the basics of the client's story. Do not spend too much time on setting up the relationship. While this is critical in real helping situations, in this exercise the main purpose is to practice identifying discrepancies and delivering them to a client. As soon as possible, identify discrepancies by pointing them out, then encourage the client to resolve the inconsistency.

Post-Exercise Discussion   The observer shares his or her feedback with the helper. The client gives qualitative feedback concerning the effectiveness of the confrontation and the degree of discomfort caused by the confrontation. For example, were the confrontations presented as observations rather than accusations? Were they presented nonjudgmentally? The helper and observer can also attempt to recall the client's reaction to the confrontation and score it according to the Client Acceptance Scale.

Quick Tips: Confrontation

- Wait until you have heard the client's whole story before you identify discrepancies. What seems to be a discrepancy may be a minor point once you know more about the situation.
- If you are having trouble identifying discrepancies, remember that there would

not be a problem if there were no discrepancy. Ask yourself, "What makes this a dilemma?" or "What are the two sides to the client's problem that make this situation so bothersome?"

- Note the impact of your confrontation on the client. Does he or she deny, partially accept, or fully accept your identification of the discrepancy? Follow up denial and partial acceptance with invitational and reflecting skills.
- After you identify a discrepancy, try using a checking question such as, "Am I on target with that?" Often the client will correct you and clarify the discrepancy.

Additional Exercises

Exercise 1

Break into groups of three or four. Come up with a client problem, then construct a role play in which the client uses a defense mechanism to reduce anxiety. The helper's job is to point out the discrepancy and encourage the client to reevaluate his or her choices.

Exercise 2

Listed here are four client situations. Try to identify the discrepancy in each. Respond in writing beneath each example. Try using this formula: "On the one hand, _____ , yet on the other hand, _____ ." This will help you get a feel for identifying discrepancies.

In some of the following situations, the conflict is implied rather than actually stated. Imagine what conflicts you might be experiencing if you were in that situation. When you have written your answers, meet with a small group and discuss them. Looking both at the clients and the issues, which would be most difficult for you to actually confront?

  a. An 18-year-old client describes how sad she is that she has to leave her parents

and go off to college. She smiles as she talks about this.

  b. The client is very religious and is very judgmental about nonbelievers. At age 22, he has only a few friends and has never had a longstanding romantic relationship. He comes for help because he has become "addicted" to 900-number telephone sex lines.

  c. The client says that he loves his sister and that she is very important to him. During their last encounter, she "exploded" because he did not attend her wedding.

  d. The client states that she has just been offered a job as a manager at a new company. They are very excited about having her because of her years of experience. She has worked for her current company on weekends and during the summer since she was 17. She says that she feels the owner relies on her, but her pay and responsibilities are unlikely to improve. She feels that she has made as much advancement as she can and would like a new challenge.

Feedback Checklist: Confrontation

Observer Name _____ Helper Name _____

During the session, the observer records the helper's responses verbatim (except minimal encouragers) and categorizes the responses with the following symbols:

OQ = open question
CQ = closed question
P = paraphrase
ROF = reflection of feeling
ROM = reflection of meaning
CON = confrontation

Helper Response	Coding*	Helper Confrontation Scale (1–5)	Client Acceptance Scale (1–3)
1. _____ _____	_____	_____	_____
2. _____ _____	_____	_____	_____
3. _____ _____	_____	_____	_____
4. _____ _____	_____	_____	_____
5. _____ _____	_____	_____	_____
6. _____ _____	_____	_____	_____
7. _____ _____	_____	_____	_____
8. _____ _____	_____	_____	_____
9. _____ _____	_____	_____	_____
10. _____ _____	_____	_____	_____

*Do not include minimal encouragers.

Homework

In a single page, identify an incongruity or discrepancy in your own life that you are willing to talk about. Alternately, you may write, in a disguised fashion, about a discrepancy you have noticed in another person. Write down the two sides of the dilemma. Can you think of ways that you have used defense mechanisms or other methods to alter the situation? What action would be needed to resolve the discrepancy?

References

Claiborn, C. D. (1982). Interpretation and change in counseling. *Journal of Counseling Psychology, 29,* 439–453.

Cooper, J., Zanna, M., & Taves, P. A. (1978). Arousal as a necessary condition for attitude change following induced compliance. *Journal of Personality and Social Psychology, 36,* 1101–1106.

Croyle, R. T., & Cooper, J. (1983). Dissonance arousal: Physiological evidence. *Journal of Personality and Social Psychology, 45,* 782–789.

Egan, G. (1977) *You and me.* Pacific Grove, CA: Brooks/Cole.

Egan, G. (1994). *The skilled helper.* Pacific Grove, CA: Brooks/Cole.

Festinger, L. (1957). *A theory of cognitive dissonance.* Stanford, CA: Stanford University Press.

Gordon, T. (1975). *PET: Parent effectiveness training.* New York: Wyden.

Hammond, D. C., Hepworth, D. H., & Smith, V. G. (1977). *Improving therapeutic communication.* San Francisco: Jossey-Bass.

Ivey, A. E. (1994). *Intentional interviewing.* Pacific Grove, CA: Brooks/Cole.

Ivey, A. E., & Simek-Downing, L. (1980). *Counseling and psychotherapy: Skills, theories and practice.* Upper Saddle River, NJ: Prentice-Hall.

Jourard, S. (1971). *The transparent self.* New York: Van Nostrand Reinhold.

Kiesler, C. A., & Pallak, M. S. (1976). Arousal properties of dissonance manipulations. *Psychological Bulletin, 83,* 1014–1025.

Lazarus, A. A. (1982). Counseling the Native American child: Acquisition of values. *Elementary School Guidance and Counseling, 17,* 83–88.

Luft, J. (1969). *Of human interaction.* Palo Alto, CA: National Press.

Olsen, P., & Claiborn, C. (1990). Interpretation and arousal in the counseling process. *Journal of Counseling Psychology, 37,* 131–137.

Pennebaker, J. W. (1990). *Opening up: The healing power of confiding in others.* New York: Morrow.

Pittman, T. S. (1975). Attribution of arousal as a mediator in dissonance reduction. *Journal of Experimental and Social Psychology, 11,* 53–63.

Prochaska, J. O. (1984). *Systems of psychotherapy.* Chicago: Dorsey Press.

Tracey, T. J., Hays, K. A., Malone, J., & Herman, B. (1988). Changes in counselor response as a function of experience. *Journal of Counseling Psychology, 35,* 119–126.

Zanna, M. P., & Cooper, J. (1974). Dissonance and the pill: An attribution approach to studying the arousal properties of dissonance. *Journal of Personality and Social Psychology, 29,* 703–709.

Goal-Setting Skills

Introduction

Helping begins with establishing a therapeutic relationship, progressing ultimately through five basic stages as described in Chapter 2 and shown in Figure 7-1. At the initial relationship-building stage, most of the helper's activities are based upon the invitational, reflecting, and challenging skills, which invite the client to open up and examine himself or herself within the confiding relationship. Early in the relationship, the helper does not try to narrow the field of discussion. A clear idea of the whole landscape of the client's life is needed before the helper tries to identify a single issue or two.

While invitational and reflecting skills encourage clients to open up, the skills at the goal-setting stage are methods for narrowing down the tasks and goals of the therapeutic relationship. It is necessary to pass through several listening cycles covering the major topics in the client's story in order to have enough information to help the client move on to the goal-setting stage. It then becomes important for the helper to change the focus of counseling sessions from the introduction of new topics to the identification of the most crucial issues to be addressed in the therapeutic relationship.

As shown in Figure 7-1, the helper moves from relationship building to the process of assessment and goal setting before implementing and evaluating strategies or techniques. In this book, we will not delve very deeply into the process of assessment because we have found that it is more effective and less confusing to learn the basic helping skills without getting into too much detail on assessment. Most training programs consider assessment and testing in a separate course. For the time being, you can gather the information you need in order to set client goals by asking open and closed questions.

In this chapter, we will be considering helping skills that narrow the discussion and focus on a smaller range of issues for the purpose of goal setting. Goal setting has an extremely positive effect on the client because it separates the tangled mass of a problem into manageable units. Once a few goals have been identified, future ses-

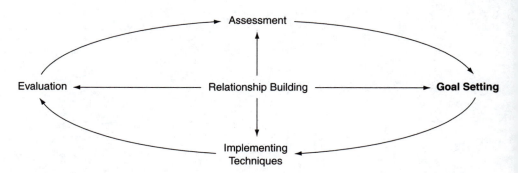

Figure 7-1
The counseling relationship: goal setting

Who Owns the Problem? Focusing on the Client

121

sions have a focus and the client begins to have hope that his or her issues are solvable. We will look at two helping skills that narrow the discussion: (1) focusing on the client, and (2) boiling down the problem.

Who Owns the Problem? Focusing on the Client

Thomas Gordon (1975) suggested that helpers think about a key question as they begin the goal-setting stage of the helping process: Who owns the problem? The question can be most clearly answered by determining who is emotionally upset by the problem. The emotional reaction not only provides the motivation to seek help, but acts as a red flag for the helper by identifying the person most affected. For example, if both members of a couple are unhappy with the relationship, the couple will own the relationship problem and may seek counseling together. On the other hand, the man who complains about his employer's stinginess owns the problem and must decide how to solve the problem either by seeking another job, becoming more assertive, or modifying his feelings and perceptions to better handle the situation. It is unlikely that the employer owns the problem, since he or she is probably not upset by stinginess toward others.

One of the reasons this is such a critical question is that early on in their practice, helpers can be easily sidetracked into helping a client change some other person: a spouse, employer, or significant other. One of the clearest examples of this occurs in the case of an alcoholic's family. At first, the affected family members seek professional help to try to control the drinking of the alcoholic member. Sometimes they can actually force the alcoholic into treatment. Eventually, however, the helper must confront other family members with the fact that they are troubled and need to deal with their own emotional disturbance and develop their own goals. The family members must come to realize the senselessness of trying to stop the alcoholic's drinking and instead try to regain their own self-esteem and handle their own negative feelings, regardless of the alcoholic's behavior. The proper view of problem ownership is a central theme of Alcoholics Anonymous and is crystallized in their prayer, "God grant me courage to change the things I can change, serenity to accept the things I cannot change, and wisdom to know the difference." In short, before a client can set a goal or solve a problem, he or she first must own it. The helper must encourage the client to deal with his or her own issues first and not to focus on changing the values, feelings, and behaviors of others.

Stop and Reflect

A 65-year-old client, Rhoda, complained that her 40-year-old son, Jorge, was irresponsible with money. According to her two other children, Rhoda always bailed Jorge out whenever he had difficulties. She was both resentful and worried about his spendthrift ways, wanting suggestions about how to get her son to become more responsible. Her family was concerned about the fact that in her will, she was leaving most of her money to Jorge.

- If you were Rhoda's counselor, what would you identify as the main problem that Rhoda owns?
- What problems are owned by other members of the family?
- Assuming that you cannot help change any other family members, including Jorge, what do you think are the main goals you and Rhoda might agree upon?

How to Focus on the Client

Around the turn of the century, a famous yogi came to the United States to give lectures. His newspaper ads said, "Wanted: Reformers—Not of Others but of Themselves." One of the major issues we face in dealing with clients is getting them to deal with issues that they can control and trying to coax them to give up on the project of reforming others. The skill of *focusing on the client* is the skill of asking the client to take responsibility and ownership of his or her problems. Nearly all major theoretical orientations conclude that effective helping involves getting the client to see that he or she alone is the person who can best initiate change. The skill of focusing on the client is most easily explained by contrasting it with responses that focus on others or on the environment:

Bradley: "With the economic slowdown and my bills, I can't change jobs right now, no matter how angry I get with my boss."

Helper: "Your boss makes the job miserable but you can't leave because you don't have many options right now." (Here, the helper is paraphrasing with a focus on others and the environment.)

Bradley: "Yeah, my boss is a jerk, but what can I do?"

Helper: "You feel angry because your boss is unfair." (Here, the helper is reflecting feelings with a focus on others and the environment.)

Bradley: "Yes, and besides that he doesn't seem to care about any of us."

Helper: "What does the boss do that makes you angry?" (Here, the helper asks a closed question, again with a focus on others and the environment.)

Bradley: "He is always on me, criticizing my work. He never has a good word to say."

When the helper keeps the focus on external issues—the working conditions, the boss, and so on—the client's responses center on others or the environment rather than on thoughtful self-examination. In effect, when the helper asks the client to focus on others or the environment, the helper is agreeing that other people or external events are the cause of the client's problems.

Focusing on the client empowers the client and prevents him or her from blaming other people and external circumstances, a time-draining sidetrack. Focusing on the client does not encourage passive acceptance of the behavior of others or the vicissitudes of life; rather, it encourages the client to act to change them. While there are certainly times when it is helpful to analyze others and the environment, we recommend that at this stage of the helping process, the helper should keep the focus primarily on the client, reducing interventions that would direct the focus elsewhere.

Let us take another look at the example of Bradley, this time with the helper keeping the focus on the client:

Bradley: "With the economic slowdown and my bills, I can't change jobs right now, no matter how angry I get with my boss."

Helper: "It is a difficult situation you find yourself in, caught between a problem at work, financial pressure, and fewer job opportunities." (Here, the helper is paraphrasing with a focus on the client.)

Bradley: "It is difficult. But one thing I would like to work on is getting rid of some of my bills so that I have more freedom."

Helper: "You feel trapped in your job right now, and you're experiencing stress from financial problems too." (Here, the helper is reflecting feelings with a focus on the client.)

Bradley: "I don't feel like I have one place in my life where things are calm and going right. I feel like everything is out of control."

Helper: "What kind of financial pressures do you have?" (Here, the helper asks a closed question with a focus on the client.)

Bradley: "I have a big car payment, student loans, and a lot of credit card bills."

Can you see that with these interventions, the helper is keeping the focus on the client as the one who needs to make decisions? The helper acknowledges that external forces are at work and that they affect the client's decisions, but the helper indicates that the client is responsible for the outcome. The examples reflect our experience that focusing on the client rather than on other people and external circumstances leads in a more productive and positive direction, with more client self-examination and surfacing of the most important issues. Focusing on problems owned by the client—rather than being railroaded into attempts to change others—should be characteristic of the helper's first efforts to set goals.

Goal Setting: An Overview

In this section, you will learn about ways to help clients develop clear and realistic goals for the counseling process. We believe that goal setting is often overlooked or touched upon too briefly, yet goal setting can make the difference between success and failure in counseling, and poor goal setting can demoralize both helper and client. In this section, we will pose and attempt to answer three questions that are important to helpers: "How will we know when we are finished with the helping relationship?" "Why must we narrow down the issues to specific goals?" and "What are the characteristics of constructive goals?"

How Will We Know When We Are Finished?

Steve de Shazer says that one of the most important questions a helper can ask is, "How will we know when therapy is done?" (de Shazer, 1990). This question can be answered in several ways. Some helpers use a time-limited approach, in which the client attends counseling only for a certain amount of time or a certain number of sessions. Helping is finished when the time is up, typically between 6 and 20 sessions (Grayson, 1979). Another commonly accepted method is for either the helper or the client to declare unilaterally that helping is completed. Clients are frequently terminated despite their protests if the helper feels that the client has obtained the maximum benefit from helping, or if the helper feels that the client's problems have been solved. Even more commonly, the client independently terminates.

The best measure of whether the work is done is to see whether the treatment goals have been reached. If we have formulated goals at the beginning of the helping relationship, client and helper will have a shared vision throughout the relationship and will know when it is time to end.

Why Must We Narrow Down the Issues to Specific Goals?

One quick answer to this question is that when clients have specific goals, they make better progress (Borelli & Mermelstein, 1994; Hart, 1978). According to Cormier and Cormier (1991, p. 217) one of the most important reasons for developing clear helping goals is that the process helps to modify client expectations about what can realistically be achieved. In addition, at least six other favorable outcomes accrue from a joint process of helper/client negotiation of goal statements:

1. When based on individual goals for the client, the counseling process is more likely to be aimed at the client's needs rather than derived from the helper's theoretical orientation alone.
2. When goals are clearly understood by client and helper, the helper can determine whether he or she possesses the requisite skills to continue with the counseling or whether a referral is needed.
3. Many clients have problems imagining or envisioning success. Visualizing a positive outcome has the tendency to focus the client's resources and energies and increase hope.
4. Goals provide a rational basis for selecting treatment strategies in helping.
5. Goals enable helpers to determine how successful helping has been for the client. Goal statements also provide feedback to the client, who can be asked to evaluate the outcome based on the degree to which goals have been achieved.

6. Setting goals can be therapeutic. The client feels less "stuck." The client who is clear about his or her goals will be able to work on these goals in and out of session. The setting of goals also motivates the client to work harder.

What Are the Characteristics of Constructive Goals?

Constructive goals (1) are mutually agreed upon by helper and client; (2) are specific, clear, and easily restated; (3) are realistic; (4) are conducive to general improvement in the client's life; and (5) address crises first.

Constructive Goals Are Mutually Agreed Upon by Helper and Client

The likelihood of goal attainment is increased by the identification of goals that the client really wants to achieve (Barbrack & Maher, 1984; Evans, 1984; Goodyear & Bradley, 1986; Hart, 1978). However, when goals are selected *solely* by the client, they will not reflect the helper's professional insights and may lead to the pursuit of superficial or unrealistic aims. The professional helper brings expertise about relationships and problem solving and has a duty to challenge clients to develop realistic, far-reaching goals. The professional helper actively participates in goal setting, neither dictating the goals of helping nor passively accepting the client's goals.

Students often raise the question, "What if the client's goals are morally unacceptable to the helper?" While helpers are generally nonjudgmental and accepting of differences, there are times when a helper cannot help a client set and achieve a goal because of personal religious convictions or ethics. For example, many helpers will refuse to take sides in custody cases when they have seen a couple for marriage counseling. Often, as well, helpers may choose not to help clients achieve goals related to sexuality, such as accepting homosexuality or conducting extramarital affairs. Professional helpers inform clients early in the counseling process about issues they will not address, so that the relationship does not develop too far before a referral is needed.

Frequently, helpers are informed that their job is to achieve the goals of a third party, such as parents or school officials. Since neither client nor helper participates in the goal-setting process, they may not feel personally involved or motivated to achieve the third party's aims, and the likelihood of success is low. This third-party problem is evident in the example of a client who has been referred by a probation officer following an incestuous relationship. The probation officer wants the client treated for sexual dysfunction to ensure that this kind of thing does not happen again. The client is divorced now and has had no contact with his teenage daughter, the incest victim. At this point, the client's concerns center on forming new relationships and dealing with family members' rejection. He is not willing to rehash the incestuous relationship and is resentful of the helper's intrusions. This kind of situation is quite common (Ritchie, 1986), and clients pressured to attend by a third party may make up as much as one-third of all new clients referred for counseling (Haley, 1989). Helpers must therefore be clear about whose goals will be the focus with each client. Sometimes they are forced to accept the goals of third parties, but goal setting involving both client and helper provides the best opportunity for success.

Constructive Goals Are Specific, Clear, and Easily Restated

One of the first problems that a helper faces in goal setting is dealing with a client whose goals are vague and elusive. Unfocused goals, which are hard to put into workable form, are goals that either are not in the client's conscious awareness or are too broad (Rule, 1982). An unfocused goal is exemplified in this type of client statement: "I don't really know what's wrong; it's just that I am uneasy with everything." A specific, clear, and easily restated goal looks more like this: "I want to be able to be more assertive with my friends and co-workers."

Developing simple goals that have a high probability of success is especially important when the client is demoralized. Whenever small goals are achieved, the client will be encouraged to continue with more difficult or more time-consuming projects (Dyer & Vriend, 1977; Egan, 1994). As Milton Erickson once said, "Therapy is often a matter of tipping the first domino" (Rossi, 1980, Vol. 4, p. 454).

A rule of thumb in developing a goal is that it should be extremely simple, so simple that an "eight-year-old could understand it" (Steiner, 1976). In other words, even if helping goals are not quantifiable, they can still be concrete (Goodyear & Bradley, 1986). For example, the helper might not want to accept the following goal: "I want to improve my relationship with my mother." The helper might be willing, though, to accept the following revision: "Well, I would like to be able to politely stop her when she starts trying to give me advice."

Constructive Goals Are Realistic

The helper's expertise is important in defining goals when a client has unrealistic aims. Consider the following client statements:

"I don't like science or math and I am not very good at them. My aptitudes in those areas are not very good, according to the national exams. I want to be a doctor, though, because I need to have a good salary and I want to be respected as a professional."

"I want to get my girlfriend back. She's living with someone else right now and she won't even return my calls. She hates me because I was dating other people behind her back while we were going out. I still have a problem with being faithful to one person but I know if I got her back, we could make it work."

"I want to stay married and enjoy the safety and security of the married relationship. Myra and I have a problem with communication and that is something we can work on. But there is someone else that I am seeing right now. The excitement and romance is something that is missing in my marriage. I can't hurt Myra or the kids by letting it come out in the open. So I have decided to keep it a secret. When Myra and I come in for marriage counseling, I don't want to bring up this other relationship."

Helpers have to evaluate goals that clients present based on how likely it is that some improvement can be made. When a client is operating on faulty information or is engaging in self-deception, as in the preceding cases, the helper uses challenging skills and helps the client gain self-knowledge or knowledge about the problem that will help him or her set better goals. For example, in the case of the student who wants to be a doctor, the helper might help the client gain experience and knowledge of medicine in several ways, including volunteering in a hospital, looking at the courses medical schools teach, and asking physicians directly about how important it is to enjoy and do well in math and science.

Constructive Goals Are Conducive to General Improvement in the Client's Life

As an expert, the helper has a duty to help the client focus on the key problems so as to set goals that will lead to lasting or generalized improvement (Weinberger, 1982). For example, a client once initially stated that her problem was a "bad marriage." She was tired of being dominated by her husband, although she had been married only 18 months. She went on to say that she had an ongoing conflict at work with her boss, who was too demanding, and that another major problem was her mother, who was always telling her what to do. The client wished to have the helper assist in dissolving her marriage. The helper suggested, however, that the client's difficulties encompassed more than just her poor third marriage. The helper felt that unless the client developed better communication skills and improved her capacity to be assertive generally, she would continue to have relationship problems. The helper offered a contract to deal with these general problems first, before addressing the marital issue in particular, and the client agreed.

William Nicoll (personal communication, August 5, 1996) talks about the Bobo doll as a metaphor for the danger of choosing superficial goals. The Bobo doll is a large punching bag that looks vaguely like a person and is often used in therapy. The bottom of the bag is weighted so that when it is punched in the head, Bobo tips over but inevitably stands up again. The only way to push the doll over is to hit or kick it at the base. Nicoll uses this image as a way of teaching that in these days of brief and time-limited approaches to helping, we must carefully decide where we should take our "shots." Dealing with superficial symptoms is similar to hitting Bobo in the head and having it bounce right back to the original position. Instead, we should focus on issues that lead to major improvement in the client's life—the base.

Constructive Goals Address Crises First

As clients move through nonjudgmental listening cycles at the beginning of the helping relationship, they explore different facets of the story they are telling. They jump back and forth from problems at work, to families, to personal relationships, to spiritual yearnings, to moral dilemmas, to financial crises. In Maslovian terms, clients discuss problems in getting their needs met at all levels, from basic physiological needs to safety, belonging, self-esteem, love, and self-actualization.

If a client has many issues to deal with, it can be confusing for the helper to decide which issues should take priority. As a rule, help the client choose goals that ameliorate emergent problems first. *Crises* are fast-developing situations that are normally unexpected and threaten the client's functioning. Generally speaking, crises that are lower on the Maslovian hierarchy of needs (food, clothing, shelter, and security needs) must take precedence over crises in higher needs categories, such as relationships and self-esteem (Bruce, 1984). For example, a client who is being evicted from an apartment needs immediate help in finding shelter, not in looking at long-term issues such as finding a new job or learning to manage money better.

Stop and Reflect

There is a saying among career- and life-planning counselors that if you don't know where you are going, you will arrive somewhere else. The meaning is that if we do not set goals for our lives, other factors besides our own plans will intervene. A well-known football coach is said to have identified a list of 400 personal goals over 20 years ago. Recently he indicated that he had completed over 300 of them. Think about the following areas of your own life and write down a goal under each heading that you would like to accomplish in the next 5 to 10 years:

1. A job that I would like to have:

   _____

2. A project that I would like to be involved in:

   _____

3. The kind of friendship or intimate relationship that I would like to develop:

   _____

4. An area of learning that I would like to master or a formal degree program that I would like to complete:

   _____

5. A hobby or interest that I would like to develop:

   _____

Next, evaluate each of the goals that you have identified according to the following criteria:

- Is the goal specific, clear, and easily restated?
- Is the goal realistic, considering your abilities?
- How motivated are you to accomplish this goal?

Choose one of the goals that appears to meet some or all of these criteria and rewrite it in a simple, specific sentence or two. List the steps you must go through to accomplish this goal.

- As you look at the steps that you have identified, does the goal seem more manageable or more difficult now that it has been broken down into parts?
- Discuss this exercise with a friend who knows you well. Ask him or her to evaluate the goal as to how realistic it is and how clearly it is stated. What are your conclusions?

Boiling Down the Problem

Usually, clients do not arrive with clearly defined questions and problems; more often they present tangles of feelings, people, and events that can easily sidetrack both client and helper. Achieving clarity of purpose is a major task of helping. At some point, the helper must choose areas to develop and others to set aside for the moment. Just sorting the work into "piles" or cutting the job into "pieces" reduces client anxiety and offers fresh hope. Most of us are aware of the experience of motivation and relief that accompanies making a "To Do" list when we feel overwhelmed.

As we said earlier, goal-setting skills are narrowing skills. One therapist used to say to clients, "Well, we've chased a lot of rabbits out of the bush; now let's track down a few of them." This metaphor worked well to signal that a more specific focus was needed. *Boiling down the problem* follows this metaphor. First, the client is encouraged to open up; then specific issues are identified and evaluated. The steps in boiling down the problem are as follows:

Step 1: Summarizing

The helper uses summaries, advanced reflecting skills, and paraphrasing to determine agreement on the overall content of the counseling session to that point.

Helper: "So let me pull this together a little. You're living at home and feel embarrassed because you think you should be out on your own. The man you have been dating for a year has called it quits, and in the middle of all this upset, your teenage sister is causing turmoil in the home. Meanwhile, your mother's illness worries you. You're feeling overwhelmed since everything has happened at once."

Tricia: "That's about it. I'm living at home, my life is going nowhere, and right now everyone needs me to be strong."

Step 2: Asking Closed Questions

Next the helper uses one or more closed questions to ask the client to evaluate which problems are the most critical, thereby narrowing down the number of issues to be addressed.

Helper: "I realize that all of these issues—your mother's health, your sister's problems, getting over your boyfriend, and becoming financially able to have your own place—are all important issues to you. Of these, which do you think are the most critical and are ones that we can deal with in these sessions?"

Tricia: "There is nothing I can do about my mother's illness, and unfortunately there is not much I can do about my sister, either. But I want to get on my feet financially and emotionally. I need help in thinking about where I am going in my career so I can earn enough to live on, and I've got to think about how I am going to make it through the next few months without my boyfriend. I need to focus on myself for a little while."

Step 3: Selecting the Problem

In this activity, the helper uses a mental checklist to evaluate client goals and advocates for those that:

- Are mutually agreed upon by helper and client.
- Are specific and easily restated.

- Are realistic.
- Lead to general improvement in the client's life.
- Address crises first.

Helper: "So it sounds like one of the emergency issues is to help you find some ways to take care of yourself emotionally so that you can cope with your loss. At the same time, you want to look at the future a little bit too. You want to explore some career ideas."

Tricia: "I know I can get some help with the career thing; you've already offered to do the tests and talk about that. The main thing is how I can deal with my angry and depressed feelings all the time. I am bored and angry and alone. I feel like a baby."

Step 4: Changing the Problem to a Goal

In this step, the helper encourages the client to think about success—what will the problem look like when it is solved? When a clear vision of success is formulated, it is easier to see the steps needed to attain it (O'Hanlon & Weiner-Davis, 1989).

Helper: "You have told me that you are in a lot of distress about losing your boyfriend and we have discussed that topic pretty thoroughly. As you think about the future, I wonder if you can envision your life when this is no longer a problem. What would you be doing then that you are not doing now? What would you be feeling and thinking?"

Tricia: "I would be going out with my friends and enjoying life again. I wouldn't be thinking about him all the time, sitting there waiting for him to call. I would be able to concentrate at work."

Helper: "So these are the goals that you would like to work toward."

Tricia: "Sure!"

Step 5: Reaching a Final Goal Statement

Here, the helper summarizes the goals that have been mutually agreed upon. In addition, the helper may ask the client to state them aloud or write them down, so that the agreement is clear. At this point, clients often need encouragement and a message from the helper that the goals are reachable.

Helper: "Let's see if I can restate them. You would like to go out with friends, enjoy life again, and not spend so much time thinking about your ex-boyfriend. Is that about right?"

Tricia: "Yes, but it's not that easy."

Helper: "I agree, it won't be easy. But these are our three goals over the next few weeks, right?"

Tricia: "Right."

Helper: "Would you mind restating the goals as we talked about them so that I am sure we are both operating with the same understanding?"

Tricia: "Okay. I am going to find a way to have fun again and spend time with friends and stop thinking so much about my boyfriend."

Helper: "Like you said, it won't be easy, but I am confident that you can make this happen. Let's talk about how you can go about this."

Summary

The first stage of the helping process can be summarized as *opening*. The second is *assessing*. The next stage, described in this chapter, is *narrowing*: once the client's important issues have been identified, it is time to select and target the important ones. One of the key questions in narrowing is "Who owns the problem?" Helpers develop the skill of focusing on the client to keep the client directed toward the issues that are causing pain. This compels the client to deal with issues on which he or she can really make an impact.

This chapter advocates that the helper should develop goals collaboratively with the client, melding the helper's expertise with the concerns and needs of the client. Constructive goals are therefore mutually agreed upon; they are also specific, realistic, conducive to general improvement rather than symptomatic relief, and focused on important crises first. The skill of boiling down the problem uses summarizing and questioning to help clients clearly define and negotiate specific, significant, and achievable goals.

Group Exercise

The purpose of this exercise is to practice the process of boiling down the goal of the counseling relationship to a workable agreement between helper and client. To accomplish this in a short period of time, the helper and client should spend only a small portion of the interview (perhaps 5 minutes) on the invitational and reflecting skills, to enable the helper to understand the basics of the problem, and jump into a discussion of what the client would like to accomplish as soon as possible.

One or two observers can be used in this exercise. One observer can write down the helper's interventions that help the client develop a goal. The other can note the final goal and facilitate discussion about how closely the goal matches the ideal characteristics.

Part I: Instructions to the Observer Record what you feel are the key statements by the helper that help the client boil down the goal to a workable contract.

1. _____

_____

2. _____
   _____
3. _____
   _____
4. _____
   _____
5. _____
   _____

Part II: Instructions to the Observer

In the space provided, write down your understanding of the goal finally arrived at by the client and the helper.

_____
_____
_____
_____

_____

Read this to the client and the helper to determine whether your articulation of the goal is accurate. Then give the helper feedback on how closely the goal matches the following characteristics. Is the goal, as written:

1. Mutually agreed upon by helper and client?
2. Specific and easily restated?
3. Achievement and success oriented (versus eliminating or reducing)?
4. Realistic?
5. One that will lead to general improvement in the client's life?
6. One that addresses crises first, before less pressing issues?

Additional Exercises

Exercise 1

In the helper/client interview, one of the mistakes beginners make is to ask too many closed questions that focus on others and the environment. Examine the client situations listed here and formulate one question or paraphrase that focuses on the client and another that would take the client off track.

High School Student: "I don't know where I am going with my life. My grades are good enough to get into college and my parents want me to go. But I am more interested in music. My music teacher thinks I should go that route. What do you think?"

Client Focus: _____

_____
_____

Other Focus: _____

_____
_____

Client Whose Spouse Has Been Unfaithful: "What is wrong with people today? They have no morals. They can't be honest. I can't believe I was stupid enough to marry someone like that. I wasn't raised that way and I don't intend to live that way."

Client Focus: _____

_____
_____

Other Focus: _____

_____
_____

Parent of a Teenager: "He smokes pot continually. I am caught between him and his father. I found some pot under his bed. He says that he is not smoking now and I am afraid to tell his father. He will blow up. What am I going to do about his drug problem?"

Client Focus: _____
_____
_____

Other Focus: _____
_____
_____

Client Who Has Accepted a Job out of State: "My family is upset with me. They can't see

that this is my best chance for success. They want me around to come over for Sunday dinner. I want that too, but it is so hard to balance these things."

Client Focus: _____
_____
_____

Other Focus: _____
_____
_____

Homework

One aspect of boiling down the problem that takes practice is changing a problem to a goal. Create two short dialogues between client and helper where the client is helped through the five steps of boiling down the problem. Following each dialogue, identify the problem as stated by the client and the goal as reformulated by the helper.

References

Barbrack, C. R., & Maher, C. A. (1984). Effects of involving conduct problem adolescents into the setting of counseling goals. *Child and Family Behavior Therapy, 6,* 33–43.

Borelli, B., & Mermelstein R. (1994). Goal setting and behavior change in a smoking cessation program. *Cognitive Therapy and Research, 18,* 69–83.

Bruce, P. (1984). Continuum of counseling goals: A framework for differentiating counseling strategies. *Personnel and Guidance Journal, 62,* 259–263.

Cormier, W., & Cormier, L. S. (1991). *Interviewing strategies for helpers: Fundamental skills and cognitive behavioral interventions.* Pacific Grove, CA: Brooks/Cole.

De Shazer, S. (1990, May). Brief therapy. Symposium conducted at Stetson University, DeLand, FL.

Dyer, W. W., & Vriend, J. (1977). A goal-setting checklist for counselors. *Personnel and Guidance Journal, 55,* 469–471.

Egan, G. (1994). *The skilled helper* (5th ed.). Pacific Grove, CA: Brooks/Cole.

Evans, M. H. (1984). Increasing patient involvement with therapy goals. *Journal of Clinical Psychology, 40,* 728–733.

Goodyear, R. K., & Bradley, F. O. (1986). The helping process as contractual. In W. P. Anderson (Ed.), *Innovative counseling: A handbook of readings* (pp. 59–62). Alexandria, VA: American Association for Counseling and Development.

Gordon, T. (1975). *PET: Parent effectiveness training.* New York: Wyden.

Grayson, H. (1979). *Short-term approaches to psychotherapy.* New York: Human Sciences Press.

Haley, J. (1989, May). Strategic family therapy. Symposium conducted at Stetson University, DeLand, FL.

Hart, R. (1978). Therapeutic effectiveness of setting and monitoring goals. *Journal of Consulting and Clinical Psychology, 60,* 24–28.

O'Hanlon, W. H., & Weiner-Davis, M. (1989). *In search of solutions: A new direction in psychotherapy.* New York: W. W. Norton.

Ritchie, M. H. (1986). Counseling the involuntary client. *Journal of Counseling and Development, 64,* 516–518.

Rossi, E. (1980). *Collected papers of Milton Erickson on hypnosis* (Vols. 1–4). New York: Irvington.

Rule, W. R. (1982). Pursuing the horizon: Striving for elusive goals. *Personnel and Guidance Journal, 61,* 195–197.

Steiner, C. (1976, April). Radical psychiatry. Symposium conducted at the University of Dayton, Dayton, OH.

Weinberger, A. (1982). The "consumer" in psychotherapy. *Canadian Psychology, 2,* 37–41.

Solution Skills

Introduction

In this chapter, we will introduce five new skills: giving advice, giving information, giving directives, brainstorming, and alternate interpretation. These building blocks are called *solution skills* because they are all methods that helpers use to challenge clients to find solutions to their problems.

The solution skills represent the final set of building blocks you will need to know about in order to construct more complex techniques later on. For example, when you learn relaxation training in Chapter 12, you will be giving clients directives to tense and then relax muscles. When you encounter the technique of reframing in Chapter 14, you will already know how to provide clients with alternate interpretations, which is the pivotal step in that technique. Brainstorming, on the other hand, is an effective tool that you can use immediately in a wide variety of circumstances in conjunction with the nonjudgmental listening cycle.

Solution skills can be used inappropriately. By their very nature, they place the helper in a superior position; this can change the client/helper relationship. Also, the helper could breed dependency in the client by overuse of these skills. Properly applied, however, solution skills can stimulate clients to work toward resolving their problems.

Giving Advice, Information, and Directives

Giving Advice

When a helper makes a statement that attempts to solve a client's problem for him or her, the helper is giving advice. Like salt, *advice giving* is beneficial but only in the right amount. Advice giving can be beneficial in emergency situations when a client is engaging in unsafe behavior, such as practicing unsafe sex, considering an affair, or using drugs, or when a client is being exposed to physical violence.

Because beginning helpers like to give advice too liberally, many teachers tend to ban it outright in the initial stages, and as a consequence, textbooks often have little to say about it. However, because advice giving is rarely addressed, students tend not to be aware of its drawbacks, and may find it an easy habit to fall back on. In fact, advice giving is a veritable minefield. It lures us into thinking that we are actively helping a client. After patiently inviting and reflecting, we are eager to produce change. But there are good reasons for leaving this skill out of your practice sessions for the present. If you have a tendency to give advice, we urge that you consider retiring that skill at this point and that you develop other alternatives.

Why Are Professional Helpers Reluctant to Give Advice?

Everyone is familiar with the *Peanuts* cartoons in which Lucy sits at the psychiatrist's booth with a sign that says, "Advice: 5 cents." If helping were merely giving advice, we could set up such a booth at the local grocery store. However, as one writer notes, "Clients can get all the advice they want from acquaintances, friends, and family members. They hardly need to pay a therapist to tell them what to do" (Kleinke, 1994, p. 9). Another reason that professional helpers avoid giving advice is that people do not listen to it. Real helping involves getting people to solve their own problems, which is much more difficult than supplying solutions by giving advice. When we give advice, we feel that we have accomplished something: we have solved the problem by giving the client an answer. Sometimes advice does stimulate a client's thinking about the problem, but more often, it is simply disregarded (Mallett, Spokane, & Vance, 1978). Eric Berne (1972) identified a "game" that helpers and clients often play called, "'Why don't you. . . .' 'Yes, but. . . . ,' " or WDYYB. When helpers give advice they begin, "Why don't you. . . .," and the client responds, giving reasons why the advice will not work: "Yes, but. . . ." Most of us are familiar with this "game" from work and social situations. The advice giver feels frustrated when good suggestions are rejected. What we need to remember is that while a client may appear to be asking for advice, he or she is really looking for opportunities to think aloud, to be understood, and to explore the options.

Another crucial drawback to advice giving is that if the client follows the helper's advice, the helper is responsible for the resultant change. If the helper gets the glory for having supplied good advice, how has this empowered the client to solve future life problems, an important goal of helping? There is an aphorism that states, "Give me a fish and I will eat today; teach me how to fish and I will eat forever." Sometimes, advice may be needed to solve immediate problems, but when clients resolve their own difficulties, they gain confidence and skills. Thomas Gordon (1975) considers lecturing and preaching to be one of the "dirty dozen" of bad communication practices because they communicate to a client that he or she is incapable of solving the problem. Lecturing and preaching are disguised advice giving (Patterson & Eisenberg, 1983). Another persuasive argument against giving advice is that the consequences of being wrong can be severe, both to the client's life and to the client's faith in the therapeutic relationship.

A final reason to avoid advice giving is that it may violate the values of an individual's family, culture or religion. Such advice will probably be rejected and it may also harm the therapeutic relationship. Consider these examples of inappropriate advice:

> "I advise you to get an abortion."
>
> "I suggest you learn to be more assertive with your mother."
>
> "If you don't like all the arguing, why don't you get a divorce?"

When Is It Appropriate and Inappropriate to Give Advice?

A helper who gives advice must have the following characteristics:

- Has special knowledge and training in the specific issue the client is facing.
- Has been through the experience personally or has helped many people go through such an experience.

- Has learned that his or her own experiences are not the same as the client's experiences.
- Gives advice in a way that outlines the risks as well as the opportunities that following a certain course of action entails.
- Has a thorough knowledge of the client, including the client's ethnic, religious, and cultural background.

Appropriate advice is concrete and invites reaction and discussion. It is presented as one alternative along with other solutions generated by the client. It suggests that the client should alter the instructions to fit the circumstances. Advice about what to expect from certain courses of action may be quite helpful. Advice is also appropriate when the client is in some physical danger and a helper's directive can reduce the risk. Here are some examples of advice that might be appropriate:

"Your statement that you are drinking too much has me concerned, especially since you drive home in that condition. If you continue to drink, you can expect to be in an accident or in court. I want you to go to an alcohol treatment center for an assessment interview. Would you be willing to do that?" This advice is given to inform the client about the likely outcomes of drinking and also identifies potential physical danger.

"You know, my wife and I always try to spend 15 minutes playing cards or backgammon at the end of every day. It has been a way of building a moment of contact into our hectic lives. Do you think something like that might work for you?" This advice invites discussion and asks the client to tailor the advice to fit his or her particular situation.

"You've outlined several possibilities; let me add one more. Have you considered directly confronting your co-worker about her unsafe behavior on the job? What effect do you think that might have?" This advice asks the client to think and to discuss the alternative suggested by the helper.

Advice is inappropriate and harmful to the therapeutic relationship:

- When the client seems to be dependent on others to make decisions and needs to learn to choose his or her own course of action. He or she might ask, for example:

  "Do you think I need a new haircut?"
  "Do you think I should go home this weekend as my parents ask or do what my boyfriend wants?"

- When the client has not heeded advice previously.
- When the client is asking for assurance on issues with unpredictable outcomes, such as:

  "Should we have a baby?"
  "Should I get married?"
  "Should I move to Saudi Arabia?"

- When the purpose of obtaining advice is to influence another person:

"My husband believes in spanking our child, but I don't. What do you think?"

"My mother thinks I am too old to date. Do you agree?"

- When the client has information available and is capable of solving the problem without advice.
- When the advice conflicts with a client's basic values, upbringing, or culture. The helper is giving inappropriate advice, for example, when he or she says:

"You may come from an Indian culture, but you live in America now. You have to do what you want and your parents will have to understand."

Clearly, the times when advice giving is useful are limited. Advice giving is appropriate only at carefully considered moments rather than as standard procedure.

Stop and Reflect

Think back for a moment on pieces of advice you have received from teachers, guidance counselors, friends, parents, grandparents, or other family members. It might have been about the purchase of a car or house, which college to attend, or what to do in a relationship. Identify one piece of good advice and one that was not very helpful, then consider the following questions:

- What was it about each piece of advice that made it helpful or not helpful?
- When considering the helpful advice, did the person giving it have particular expertise in that area?
- What other characteristics did the person giving the advice have that encouraged you to accept it?
- If you cannot recall any advice given by friends, teachers, counselors, parents, or family members, what conclusions might you draw from this?
- When you have a problem, do you want advice or is it more important to have someone listen?
- What can you conclude about the role of advice in helping you make decisions in your own life? Will your conclusions have a bearing on your willingness to give advice as a helper?

Discuss your answers with a small group of classmates.

Giving Information

Information giving is the supplying of data or facts to help a client reach his or her goal. Information giving might include providing ideas about how to gain access to social services or community resources. It can include correcting erroneous ideas about topics such as sexuality, drugs, parenting, and stereotypes about different ethnic groups. A helper uses information giving sparingly because too much information will be ignored. Information giving can also subtly change the relationship between client and helper. It can become a lecture that clients may disregard. Here is an example of an appropriate use of giving information:

"Based on what you have told me, your financial problems are significant and you could use some professional help. I would like to refer you to the Consumer

Credit Counseling Service. They can help you make the decision about whether bankruptcy is a good answer for you. Would you be willing to go?"

Giving Directives

Directives are helper instructions that specify behaviors that a client is to perform. The helper is not giving advice but specifying an action that the client is to take. Some common directives include giving a client instructions on how to relax, how to engage in a role-playing activity, or how to do a homework assignment. The following is an example of a directive given to a client as a homework assignment:

"You are trying to decide between staying at your current job and taking a job in New York. As homework, I was wondering if you would be willing to write down the pros and cons of each decision, to stay or to leave. Place a star beside the pros or cons that are important or weighty reasons as opposed to minor ones. Discuss the important ones with family and friends before we meet next week."

Follow-up questions might include:

"Would you be willing to try this for next week?"

"Would you mind saying back to me what you understand the task to be? This will help me know if we are on the same page."

Note that the directive identifies the task as being related to the goals that the client is trying to accomplish. Second, it specifies concrete steps that the client should take to complete the task. Third, it asks for the client's cooperation. Finally, the helper checks the client's understanding of the task by asking the client to restate the essence of the assignment.

Directives have important drawbacks. Like advice and information, directives make the relationship between client and helper less equal. When helpers give directives, the client may attribute success to the technique or the helper rather than personal effort.

Helping and Creativity

According to Holland's typology of personalities and career environments (Holland & Gottfredson, 1976), helpers frequently show three personality traits: investigative, social, and artistic. Clearly, a helper must have investigative interests to untangle the client's issues in the same way that a detective or scientist tries to solve a puzzle. Helpers also have strong interpersonal interests, represented by the social trait; they want to help people. The artistic aspect of helping is perhaps less obvious but, as the title of this book suggests, there is a side to helping that cannot be quantified and is purely artistic. Artists use different media to express themselves and create beauty. The helping arts are focused not on self-expression by the artist but on the helper's desire to create something beautiful out of human disarray: harmony, peace, wholeness, and fulfillment. This holistic sense cannot be achieved merely through application of a scientific process any more than it is possible to use a formula to reproduce a Picasso.

Helpers are often creative people. They are open to considering options when a problem arises and they try to help clients devise novel ways of thinking and problem solving. Indeed, they may at times use artistic media—drama, poetry, painting, sculpture, and music—to help clients express themselves (Gladding, 1996). Helpers also encourage their clients to think creatively when they have problems. A major difficulty in problem solving is that we tend to see things through the lens of our outmoded ideas, social conventions, and our personal history. As Emerson noted, consistency can be a hobgoblin, leading us into foolish repetitions when what we need is to break out of our old ways of thinking.

Perhaps you have heard of the nine-dot problem. Take a look at the nine dots in Figure 8–1. The problem is to take a pencil and draw four straight lines that connect all of the dots without lifting your pencil from the page. The answer to this puzzle appears in Figure 8–2, but try to solve it yourself.

Whether you have seen this puzzle before or not, it illustrates an important aspect of human thinking. We tend to rely on previous experience. When we try to solve the nine-dot problem, we recall that we have usually been told to "color in the lines." We see a box shape represented by the points and conclude that we must stay within the shape rather than expand into the page beyond. This same kind of thinking affects us when we encounter a problem in life. During a crisis, when we become even more conservative and less creative, a sort of tunnel vision occurs that convinces us that we have very few options. For example, people with suicidal thoughts often conclude that killing themselves is the only option available.

When a client experiences a problem, he or she sees the problem and the possible solutions in terms of past experience, and with the narrowed vision of stress. It is well known, for example, that battered women see few options to their abusive relationships because their experience tells them that the situation has no exit. The concept of learned helplessness has been advanced to explain why people fail to look for alternatives. When people seem to find that nothing works to solve their dilemmas, they stop trying, even when circumstances change. The job of a helper is to be

Figure 8-1
The nine-dot problem

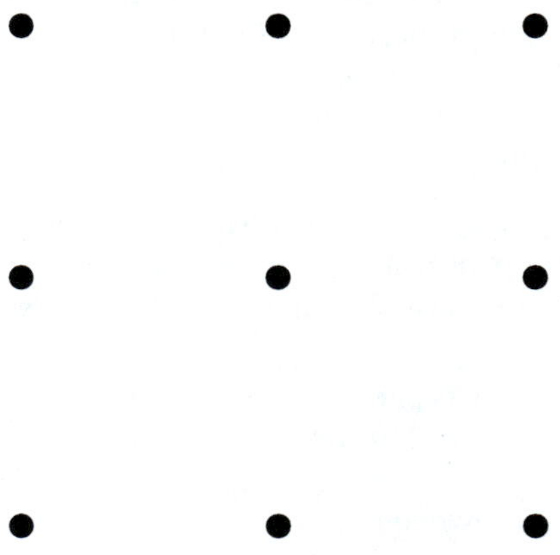

Figure 8–2
Solution to the nine-
dot problem

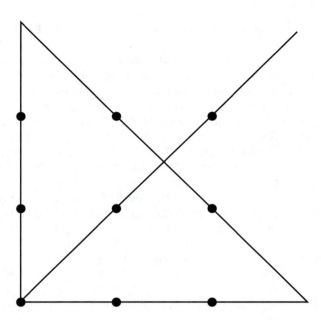

an "expander" (not a "shrink") who tries to help clients expand their possibilities, open up their thinking, and engage their creativity.

What Is Brainstorming?

Brainstorming originally was developed by Madison Avenue advertising firms to increase the creativity of staff members responsible for commercials. To brainstorm, a group of people sit around a table and generate ideas. The conditions and ground rules, however, are a little different from those of an average meeting. The atmosphere is relaxed and even playful. Cooperation rather than competition is encouraged. Everyone in the group is called upon to participate and no one is allowed to dominate. All ideas are recorded, but the focus remains on a specific problem that the group wants to solve. Beyond these general conditions for brainstorming, some specific rules differentiate it from other problem-solving activities:

1. Ideas generated by brainstorming are not evaluated. They are simply brought before the group and recorded. Evaluation involves a critical function of mind rather than a creative one. Creativity flows best in a nonjudgmental atmosphere.

2. Freewheeling is encouraged. Practical considerations are not brought up during a brainstorming session. In fact, the wilder the ideas, the better, so that the limits of creativity can be reached. A playful attitude by the facilitator can increase freewheeling.

3. The quantity of ideas is more important than the quality. The more ideas the better. A large pool of ideas is needed as a source of good solutions. Seemingly unimportant ideas can spark thoughts from other members of the group.
4. Hitchhiking is encouraged. Hitchhiking, or "piggybacking," is building on the ideas of other people. By combining ideas, a concept grows and develops.

Research has suggested that sometimes when two or more people brainstorm together, they do not generate as many new ideas as they would if they constructed their lists separately (Diehl & Stroebe, 1991; Mullen, Johnson, & Salas, 1991). The reason sometimes given is production blocking. *Production blocking* means that people are sometimes too polite in a group situation to spontaneously blurt out their ideas while others are talking. Brainstorming requires that each person be allowed to express his or her ideas without having to wait for others to stop speaking (Johnson & Johnson, 1997). This same situation often occurs in a therapeutic relationship. The client is reluctant in that setting to really think in a spontaneous and freewheeling way because of the weight that he or she gives the helper's ideas. Sometimes it is more effective for each person in a brainstorming session to write down his or her ideas, or for one person to generate ideas and the other to record them. This allows for more freewheeling than the start-and-stop approach that a conversation entails.

How to Brainstorm

Brainstorming between a helper and a client involves the same basic activities that groups use, with slight modifications. The helper acts as a facilitator and participant, but a major aim is to help the client develop skills of creative thinking, which can be generalized to other situations.

In the helping relationship, brainstorming should not be an activity that keeps a client talking about options rather than taking action. Brainstorming is a solution skill. At the end of a brainstorming session, both helper and client should have a clear idea about the next steps to take to solve the problem. Brainstorming takes a client through three basic steps:

1. Challenging the client's assumptions and identifying the problem
2. Generating ideas
3. Evaluating and agreeing upon potential solutions

Brainstorming with a client does not differ much from the steps in group brainstorming except that, at the outset, more attention is devoted to identifying and challenging assumptions. The client thinks about the assumptions he or she has about the problem and tries to shake free of them. Otherwise, pre-existing ideas will color the next idea-generating step, leading the client to substitute previous solutions rather than to think creatively.

One tactic for dealing with assumptions is to reverse them. For example, while designing an innovative program for training school counselors, participants listed all their assumptions about school counselors. One of them was, "School counselors work during school hours." This assumption was reversed and written down on the blackboard as "School counselors do not work during school hours." Ideas based on this new concept were then generated. Participants began thinking about how school counselors should be available to parents after school and in the evenings. This led them to include family counseling training as part of the curriculum. A nearby public school system is now incorporating this idea in its new school. The plans for next year allow flexible working hours for school counselors so that they can meet with parents several evenings per week.

Another story illustrates how assumptions about problems can be challenged and how, in turn, creative thinking leads to better solutions. David and Gloria have been married for 5 years. David's job requires that he move to another state for a 2-year period to work on an exciting project. David cannot refuse the assignment or he risks losing the job. The couple came for help because they have come to an impasse in their decision-making process. David wants Gloria to quit her job as a part-time graphic designer and move with him. Gloria wants to stay where she is and she wants David to stay too, even if he gets demoted or loses his job. Neither wants to live alone for the 2-year period. Acting as a facilitator, the helper took them through the three basic steps of brainstorming to help them arrive at a solution.

Step 1:   Challenging Assumptions and Asking the Right Question

The first step is to ask the right question. This can be determined by asking what is to be achieved in the end. What is the goal? The reason this step is so crucial is that often, clients are examining previous solutions rather than the current problem. A good example of how this happens comes from the food industry. For several years, the following question was often asked: "How can we make a better can opener?" This formulation generated a number of new can openers, both manual and electric; however, a can opener is a previous solution, not the real problem. Someone ultimately asked the question in a different way: "How do we open a can?" When the problem was stated in this way, a whole new set of creative opening features developed. Helpers assist clients in identifying the key issues by asking closed questions, such as:

"What do you want to achieve by solving this problem?"

"What is it you are afraid of losing?"

"What is the most important thing you want to accomplish?"

Similarly, David and Gloria might argue over who is going to move, but what is the real question? With the assistance of the helper, the couple realized that the question that really needed to be asked was, "How will we be able to spend enough time together and feel close to each other if David goes out of state for 2 years?" Previously the couple had assumed:

"Someone is going to have to move."

"Someone is going to be unhappy."

"Someone is going to lose his or her job."

Once the problem assumptions had been put aside and the real problem identified, the couple was ready to start generating ideas.

Step 2:   Generating Ideas

In a freewheeling and cooperative atmosphere, David and Gloria took a few minutes to identify creative answers to the question, "How can we remain close if David takes the job for two years?" Since quantity is wanted, the helper insisted that they generate at least 10 ideas. They came up with the following list:

1. We will e-mail every day.
2. We will call every day.
3. We will meet halfway every weekend.
4. David will come home once a month and Gloria will travel to see David once a month.
5. We can send telegrams.
6. We will spend our vacations and holidays with each other for the next 2 years, not with other family members.
7. We will install a video phone or videoconferencing software on the computer.
8. We will send recordings to each other.
9. Gloria will take some of her work with her to David's place and stay for a week at a time.
10. David will ask the company for time off to come home.
11. We can take pictures of things that happen and share them with each other.
12. We could each take a class to fill our time and discuss them with each other.
13. We can send smoke signals.
14. We can meet halfway in Mexico.

As the ideas got crazier, they began to hitchhike on each others' ideas. When Gloria said, "We could take a class," David suggested that they take a Spanish class and share their learning when they meet in Mexico.

Step 3.   Evaluating and Selecting a Solution

The final step of brainstorming is evaluating and selecting a solution. David and Gloria went through the list at this point and discussed each possibility. They settled on four or five suggestions to implement that best fit the goal of keeping their relationship vital while they lived separately. Although the case of David and Gloria may seem too good to be true, many clients and helpers have learned to use brainstorming in just this way. When a client and helper devise a creative solution to a knotty problem, the therapeutic relationship is enhanced and the client's confidence and sense of hope is increased.

The Skill of Alternate Interpretation

The skill of brainstorming encourages clients and helpers to collaborate and create new solutions. When we challenge our assumptions in the first steps of brainstorming, we begin to recognize that there are many different ways to frame a problem, and that the way we conceptualize it has important implications for the eventual solution. *Alternate interpretation* is another method to help clients recognize that problem situations can be seen in many different lights. The method of alternate interpretation does not attempt to reach into the past to find the correct interpretation or meaning of an event. Rather, its sole purpose is to convince the client that there are several possible alternatives to a negative first impression or catastrophic appraisal. For instance, many people continue into adulthood to misinterpret events that happened when they were children. The method of alternate interpretation tends to loosen the hold of outmoded ideas and to convince clients that there are many possible ways of looking at a problem, some of them helpful and some of them self-defeating.

How to Teach a Client to Use Alternate Interpretation

The decision to use alternate interpretation usually comes within a session when a client describes an event that has occurred and then begins to catastrophize about it. The helper stops the process and asks the client to stop imagining the worst-case scenario and examine the premises that led to the conclusion that a catastrophe has occurred or is imminent. Consider the case of Jan, who has been working at a new job for only a short while. She was recently fired from another position and is feeling very insecure about her new situation:

Jan: "On Monday my boss mentioned that I had not finished last week's reports. My boss is criticizing me. Things are starting all over again. I know I'll lose this job now."

Step 1.

The helper listens to the client's problem and then previews and explains the concept of alternate interpretation.

Helper: "I recognize that you are concerned about losing your new job, but I wonder if I could stop you for a moment and ask you to try something."

Jan: "Okay."

Helper: "This technique is called alternate interpretation. The way it works is that we take the situation and try to identify some different conclusions than the one you have drawn. As I understand it, your boss stopped you and mentioned you had not done last week's reports, right?"

Jan: "Right."

Helper: "And your conclusion was that the same thing is happening that occurred at your old job and that you will probably be fired, right?"

Jan: "It sounds kind of silly when you say it that way."

Helper: "Well, what I would like to do is get you to try to generate some other interpretations of the facts. For example, perhaps your boss needed that information for some reason and was more interested in the content of the reports than in firing you."

Jan: "All right, I see."

Step 2.

The helper asks the client to make a list of three or four other interpretations that fit the facts at least as well as the catastrophic conclusion of the client.

Helper: "I wonder if you could think for a moment about some other ways of interpreting the same situation."

Jan: Well, in the past, I have not received this kind of criticism. It is unfamiliar. Perhaps she is trying to help me improve and become a better employee."

Helper: "That's good. What else?"

Jan: "Um, I guess I could realize that I have just received feedback that will help my performance. Maybe it will actually help me *keep* the job."

Helper: "Very good. Can you think of any other way to interpret this situation?"

Jan: "Like I said, this is the first time that my work has been criticized. My boss probably doesn't place that much importance on a single instance like this. She's probably forgotten about it. I'm just nervous because of my past history."

Step 3.

The helper assigns a homework task of developing three or four alternate explanations to the first interpretation of any disturbing event that occurs between sessions. The only requirement for the alternatives is that they have as much likelihood of being true as the first impression.

Stop and Reflect

1. Think about the following scenario and consider how you might help the client develop alternate interpretations of the same situation.

   "My best friend Pam isn't talking to me. We were out together on Friday night. Well, I met someone that I knew from work and wanted to spend more time with. He and I left the coffee shop. It was crowded and I didn't see Pam, so I didn't say good-bye. When I saw her at church, she waved but didn't stay to talk. I know she hates me now. We have been so close for two years and now it's over."

2. Now, take a moment to consider an event in your own life where your first impression was incorrect. Might the skill of alternate interpretation have been helpful in your situation? As you think about it, list two or three other possible interpretations you might have made had you been able to be more objective.

3. What client problems do you think might respond best to the technique of alternate interpretation? Compare your ideas with those of your classmates.

Summary

Up to this point, we have looked mainly at skills for developing the therapeutic relationship, exploring client problems and setting goals. In this chapter, we talked about five building blocks that help move clients toward solutions: giving advice, giving information, giving directives, alternate interpretation, and brainstorming. Advice giving is the most controversial skill presented and the one that can potentially create the most harm to the therapeutic relationship. It is discussed because helpers need to understand appropriate and inappropriate uses of advice rather than ignoring it completely.

The major focus of this chapter was on the skills of brainstorming and alternate interpretation. Both skills are aimed at getting clients to free themselves from their first interpretations of events or the mental constraints that keep them from developing creative solutions to their difficulties.

Group Exercise

In this exercise, students work in groups of three or four. One student becomes the client, another the helper, and the others act as observers. The client discusses a dilemma with a helper. The dilemma should be a situation in which the client is forced to make a difficult choice between two alternatives. It may be a current dilemma or it may be one that the client faced in the past. Suggestions of possible topics for the client to discuss include:

- Whether or not to commit to a relationship.
- Whether or not to end a relationship.
- Whether to move or stay in the same place.
- Whether or not to begin an academic degree program.

Before beginning the brainstorming process, the helper uses the nonjudgmental listening cycle for several minutes to understand a little more about the client's problem. Next, the helper moves with the client through the three steps of brainstorming:

1. The helper challenges the client to review his or her assumptions about the problem and to identify the real issue.
2. The helper and client brainstorm solutions.

3. The helper and client agree on a solution.

Following the brainstorming session, the client and observer(s) give the helper general feedback on:

1. The handling of the nonjudgmental listening cycle.
2. The helper's success in getting the client to think creatively.
3. The final solution. Was it realistic and appropriate for this client?

Quick Tips: Brainstorming

- Use closed questions to help the client pinpoint the real problem.
- Create a playful and cooperative atmosphere in the session by modeling freewheeling. Come up with a few unusual ideas yourself to encourage the client's creativity.
- The helper should take the role of facilitator and write down all of the ideas that are generated.
- Add humor when possible and exaggerate to encourage a sense of play.
- Make sure that the final creative solution between helper and client meets the reality criterion: it must effectively address the problem.

Additional Exercises

Exercise 1

This activity can be used as a whole-class activity or for groups of at least six or eight students. One student acts as the client and describes a real problem to the group. The client is asked to identify a problem that is not too personal so that he or she does not feel uncomfortable discussing it in some detail. The helper (student or teacher) uses the nonjudgmental listening cycle to understand the issue. When the story has been fully articulated to the helper, the group thinks about the client's story and each person writes down a piece of advice.

In the second part of the exercise, the helper collects the written advice and reads each student's advice to the client. After hearing the advice, the client discusses with the class which advice he or she is most likely to follow and why.

In the third part of the exercise, the helper uses a brainstorming approach to get the client to think about the issue and come up with his or her own plan. Finally, the client is asked to review both the advice-giving and brainstorming sessions and indicate what course of action he or she is most likely to take. The class or group discusses the results.

Exercise 2

This exercise is suitable for a large class or for groups of six to eight students. It is designed to help students learn to identify assumptions and generate ideas.

Begin by generating ideas about how to improve the blackboard. The task is to produce as many as possible in 2 minutes. These are recorded on the board so that everyone can see. For the first part of the activity, remember that it is important to let go of the mind's evaluative function and allow creativity to flow. Do not think about how practical the ideas are at first. Give equal time to wild ideas.

Next, list on the board the assumptions you have about blackboards—for example, they are black, you write on them, and so on. Next to each assumption, write a reversal of the assumption—for example, blackboards are not black, you do not write on them, and so on. Then brainstorm any ideas about improving the blackboard that seem to come out of these reversals. Add any new ideas to the list. Now, see whether you can force-fit any two ideas on the list together, or hitchhike, to devise any new creative ideas. If so, add them to the list.

As the final step in the process, evaluate each idea and select the best. Can any of the good ideas be combined to create a new product? The final design should meet the reality criterion: Is the product really an improvement? How likely would it be to sell?

Homework

Homework 1

a. Consider the case of Arnold, a 30-year-old man who had recently broken up with a woman he had been dating for a short time. The client described the problem like this: "I can't seem to make a relationship last. I thought this one was it! There must be something wrong with me. I think that women can see how incapable I am at maintaining a relationship." Identify three or four alternate interpretations for Arthur's first impression.

b. Next, identify two alternate interpretations for each of these client statements.

- "My marriage is on the rocks. We're not in love anymore."
- "Everybody else has a direction for their lives by the time they're my age. What's wrong with me?"
- "I can't stand this anxiety anymore. I want it to go away."
- "My life is not going anywhere. I'm in graduate school and I'm working, but when does it get to be fun?"

Homework 2

It has been said that creativity is an important trait of helpers. According to Witmer (1985), creative individuals are said to possess the following characteristics:

Curiosity

Openness to new experience

Independence

Sense of humor and playfulness (spontaneity)

Persistence

Flexibility

Originality

Ability to accept that opposing points of view may both be right

Do you see yourself as a creative individual? Is this something you would like to develop? Write a paragraph or two about why you think creativity might be useful in helping others. Indicate specifically how you might employ creativity in homework assignments for clients.

References

Berne, E. (1972). *What do you say after you say hello?* New York: Grove Press.

Diehl, M., & Stroebe, W. (1991). Productivity loss in idea-generating groups: Tracking down the blocking effect. *Journal of Personality and Social Psychology, 61,* 392–403.

Gladding, S. T. (1996). *Counseling: A comprehensive profession* (3rd ed.). Columbus, OH: Merrill.

Gordon, T. (1975). *PET: Parent effectiveness training.* New York: Wyden.

Holland, J. L., & Gottfredson, G. D. (1976). Using a typology of persons and environments to explain careers: Some extensions and clarifications. *The Counseling Psychologist, 6,* 20–29.

Johnson, D. W., & Johnson, F. P. (1997). *Joining together* (6th ed.). Boston: Allyn & Bacon.

Kleinke, C. L. (1994). *Common principles of psychotherapy.* Pacific Grove, CA: Brooks/Cole.

Mallett, S. D., Spokane, A. R., & Vance, F. L. (1978). Effects of vocationally relevant information on the expressed and measured interests of freshman males. *Journal of Counseling Psychology, 25,* 10–15.

Mullen, B., Johnson, C., & Salas, E. (1991). Productivity loss in brainstorming groups: A meta-analytic integration. *Basic and Applied Social Psychology, 12,* 3–25.

Patterson, L. E., & Eisenberg, S. (1983). *The counseling process* (3rd ed.). Boston: Houghton Mifflin.

Witmer, J. M. (1985). *Pathways to personal growth.* Muncie, IN: Accelerated Development.

The Relationship as a Therapeutic Factor

Introduction

This chapter marks a shift in our discussions. From this point on, the book is organized according to the six curative factors in the REPLAN system (see Figure 9-1). As we discussed in Chapter 2, a curative or therapeutic factor is a common or underlying factor that explains why many different therapy systems seem to be effective. All therapeutic systems evoke the healing potential of one or more of these underlying curative factors. The whole range of helping skills and techniques can be organized under one of these six factors. For example, assertiveness training and decreasing negative self-talk are two techniques from different theories, but both aim at improving a client's self-esteem. Before examining the first curative factor, the therapeutic relationship, we will take a look at how the concept of curative factors not only helps us categorize the wide variety of helping techniques but can also aid us in setting up a plan for helping.

Treatment Planning and the REPLAN System

Treatment planning is a systematic way of reviewing client problems and developing a list of strategies or techniques to treat these problems. Most people are famil-

Figure 9-1
Six curative factors in
the REPLAN system

iar with a diagnostic treatment planning method. It is the medical methodology that begins with assessing the client and arriving at a diagnosis. The diagnosis becomes the basis for determining what treatment the client will receive. If you have major depression, for example, you receive a certain treatment; if you have obsessive compulsive disorder, you receive another.

REPLAN is the goal-oriented treatment planning model based upon the six curative factors: (1) Relationship between helper and client, (2) enhancing efficacy and self-esteem, (3) practicing new behaviors, (4) lowering and raising emotional arousal, (5) activating expectations, hope, and motivation, and (6) new learning experiences. The REPLAN system does not conflict with making diagnoses, but it does assert that many clients with the same diagnosis need different treatments and techniques. Therefore, treatment strategies are tailored to the client's goals and the unique characteristics of the client, rather than to a specific diagnosis.

The REPLAN system is distinguishable from other forms of treatment planning because it focuses on a relatively small number of client goals, using strategies associated with one or two curative factors. This approach has the benefit of helping clients achieve a few goals at a time rather than planning an elaborate treatment regimen. The approach is not incompatible with long-term therapy, but it approaches client problems as distinct goals that must be regularly evaluated and replanned. Replanning occurs frequently in the therapeutic relationship, since client goals shift as some problems are resolved and new insights on old problems emerge.

REPLAN treatment planning entails two basic steps.

1. On the basis of assessment, mutually agreed-upon treatment goals that are understandable to both client and helper are formulated. These goals are then boiled down to a workable, solvable form and placed in priority order.

2. The curative factors (relationship, enhancing efficacy and self-esteem, practicing new behaviors, lowering and raising emotional arousal, activating expectations and increasing hope and motivation, and providing new learning experiences) are used to generate a list of possible treatment strategies or techniques to achieve the goals. The helper narrows down the list of potential techniques by asking himself or herself two questions: "What curative factors are most likely to help the client reach the goals?" and "What strategies, methods, or techniques will be most effective and acceptable to the client?"

To illustrate how the REPLAN system works in practice, let us look at the case example of Matthew, a 25-year-old single white male, a chemist, who is shy and wishes to meet and date women but has not been successful. Matthew's main problem is anxiety in social situations. Together he and the helper, Nadia, agree upon two goals: (1) to ask two women for dates during the next 2 months, and (2) to reduce anxiety in social situations.

To initiate the REPLAN method, Nadia asks herself which curative factors would be most helpful for Matthew in achieving his goal (see Figure 9-1). Based on her knowledge of Matthew and his situation, it seems clear that practicing new behaviors and lowering emotional arousal would be the most useful place to begin. Nadia then selects strategies to address both curative factors. The strategies she developed to address the first curative factor, practicing new behaviors, are shown in the following list. These strategies, together with those she develops to address the second curative factor, lowering emotional arousal, will constitute her initial treatment plan.

Curative Factor	Strategy
Practicing new behaviors	1. Practice self-disclosure and listening skills with helper and a friend.
	2. Role-play with helper, asking someone out for a drink.
	3. Ask any friend out for a drink.
	4. Ask a female friend out for a drink.

As this first part of Nadia's treatment plan shows, the notion of curative factors aids the helper in selecting a general approach to the client's problems. The use of curative factors stimulates thinking about possible techniques to employ, and the helper in turn narrows down the list of potential techniques depending on the client's particular situation. One rationale for this approach is that it encourages the helper to contemplate a variety of interventions and to plan these interventions as soon as the helping process begins. Table 9-1 is a REPLAN worksheet that shows how a helper might select techniques to address more serious specific problems of depression and family dysfunction.

Table 9-1
REPLAN Strategy Worksheet

Counselor asks self the following questions: (1) Which general curative factors are most likely to lead to improvement for this client? (2) What particular strategies will be most effective and acceptable to the client?

Curative Factor	Strategy
1. Decrease Depression and Suicidal Thoughts	
*R	A. Continue relationship building; encourage self-disclosure
*E	B. Ask client to generate list of positive self-statements—homework
	C. Challenge client's irrational self-downing
P	
L	
*A	D. Explain the cyclical nature of depression; encourage client to see
N	it as time limited
2. Resolve Family Problems; Make Brief Comfortable Contacts	
R	
E	
*P	A. Ask client to practice assertiveness skills in session
L	
A	
*N	B. Refer client to ACOA meeting to help client gain insight into family

The Therapeutic Relationship as a Curative Factor

> *Do not believe that he who seeks to comfort you lives untroubled among the simple and quiet words that sometimes do you good. His life has much difficulty and sorrow. Were it otherwise, he would never have been able to find those words.*
>
> *Rainer Marie Rilke*

The development of a working alliance, or therapeutic relationship, has long been identified as crucial to success in helping (Belkin, 1980; Fiedler, 1950). Most theorists, from behaviorists (Kanfer & Goldstein, 1986) to Carl Rogers (1957), have emphasized that without a strong therapeutic alliance, the goals of therapy cannot be reached. Always, the first goal is to develop a positive feeling in the client through the creation of a warm and accepting environment where the client has confidence that help is available.

Table 9-2 is an adaptation of a chart designed by Frederick Kanfer and Arnold Goldstein (1986, p. 21). The authors identified key relationship enhancers or helper behaviors that improve the quality of the helper/client relationship. As the table shows, the behaviors lead to the emotional qualities of liking, respect, and trust, which become components of the relationship. These in turn result in consequences that promote change: communication, openness, and persuasibility. Without the development of the relationship components and their consequences, therapeutic change is unlikely.

Table 9-2
Relationship Enhancers

Relationship Enhancers	Relationship Components	Relationship Consequences	Outcome
Physical closeness, posture, and warmth (invitational skills)	Liking ⟶	Communication	
Helper empathy (reflecting and advanced reflecting skills)			Change
Helper expertness and credibility	Respect ⟶	Openness ⟶	
Helper self-disclosure and good helper/client match	Trust ⟶	Persuasibility	

Source: Adapted from Kanfer, F. H., & Goldstein, A. P. (1986). Introduction, Figure 2.1. In F. Kanfer and A. Goldstein, *Helping people change: A textbook of methods* (p. 21). New York: Pergamon.

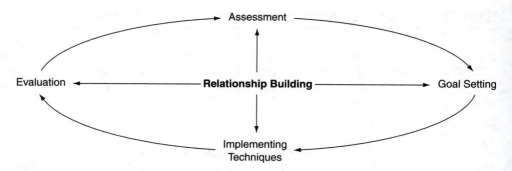

Figure 9-2
Stages of the therapeutic relationship: Relationship building

Relationship Enhancers

You have already learned important skills for relationship enhancement; the invitational, reflecting, and advanced reflecting skills are themselves powerful tools for creating a bond with a client. Here, we will consider the other three relationship enhancers mentioned in Table 9-2: the helper's expertness and credibility, the helper's capacity for self-disclosure, and the quality of the helper/client match.

The Helper's Expertness and Credibility

For the relationship to gel, the helper must first qualify for the job (Yalom, 1985). In other words, it is important for the client to perceive the helper as a competent professional. Researchers have called this client perception "credibility" (Sue & Zane, 1987) or "expertness" (Barak, Patkin, & Dell, 1982; Heppner & Dixon, 1986; Strong, 1968). Clients' expectations of competence are increased by objective evidence of competency: the helper's office, therapeutic rituals, reputation, and even the certificates and diplomas hanging on the walls (Frank, 1961; Loesch, 1984).

If a client perceives the helper as an expert, the client also is more likely to be attracted to and respect the helper. Ultimately, experts are more persuasive (Corrigan, Dell, Lewis, & Schmidt, 1980; Strong, 1968). In a review of the literature, Heppner and Dixon (1986) indicate that objective evidence of training as well as certain helper behaviors and "prestigious cues" affect ratings of helper expertness by their clients. These behaviors and cues include (1) appearing confident, organized, and interested and (2) nonverbal behaviors associated with attentiveness. Using interpretive statements and psychological jargon was also found to increase ratings of expertness. While the latter may seem phony, they are consistent with Frank's (1961) idea that one of the ways that helpers influence clients is to induct them into a therapeutic ritual and set of procedures. According to Frank, the office setting, the ritual, and therapeutic procedures all help to reassure the client and to combat the demoralization that has caused the client to seek help.

Sue and Zane (1987) identify credibility as a crucial relationship issue in helping someone who is culturally different. Although knowledge of the client's culture lends credibility to a helper who is dealing with someone from a different background, other factors are also important. Sue and Zane distinguish between ascribed and achieved credibility.

Ascribed credibility is that status given to the helper by the client that is often due to sex, age, experience, and similarity of life experiences and attitudes. For example, in some cultures, an older person is ascribed more credibility than a younger person.

Achieved credibility refers to the helper's skills and demonstrated abilities. If the helper cannot be ascribed much credibility with an individual from a special population, he or she may be able to achieve it over time. For example, a helper who is not recovering from alcohol or substance abuse will be ascribed very little credibility by clients in treatment programs for these problems. If the helper possesses special knowledge and skills, however, it may be possible to achieve some measure of acceptance among substance abusers. According to Sue and Zane (1987), the helper can achieve credibility by conceptualizing problems in a way that is congruent with the client's beliefs and values. For example, it has been suggested that framing a problem as medical, rather than psychological, is more acceptable to a Hispanic client (Meadow, 1982). It has also been suggested that African American clients prefer educational and practical strategies for dealing with problems to methods that focus only on feelings (Parker, 1988).

The Helper's Capacity for Self-Disclosure

Helper self-disclosure has been shown to increase trust in the relationship (Johnson & Matross, 1977), deepen client self-disclosure, and encourage expression of feelings (McCarthy, 1982; Nilsson, Strassberg, & Bannon, 1979; Sermat & Smythe, 1973). Helpers are self-disclosing when they are providing personal information about themselves. Moderate levels of self-disclosure have been shown to improve the helper/client relationship more than highly personal or only mildly personal disclosures (Banikotes, Kubinski, & Purcell, 1981).

Too much self-disclosure is a serious mistake in the helping relationship. One of the best discussions of this is contained in Kottler & Blau's book, *The Imperfect Therapist* (1989). According to the authors, "Whether the therapist's ignorance, insensitivity or narcissism are at fault, more than a few clients have been chased out of treatment because they felt negated by the repeated focus on the therapist's life" (p. 137). Kottler and Blau go on to say that clients are "frightened away" because helpers who talk about themselves make the client feel less important. Clients with low self-esteem do not want to hear about the successes of others. Helpers may lose their authority as transference figures and might be less able to influence the client through modeling. Finally, the client gets bored with the repetition of therapist stories and anecdotes. The mistake here is that the helper simply spends too much time in self-disclosure. Taking too much time for helper self-disclosure puts even more of a burden on the client (Egan, 1990). Kottler and Blau contend that the saddest aspect of this situation is that the helper is usually unaware of the problem.

The following are some examples of other common mistakes in self-disclosure made by helpers.

Mistake 1: *The helper's self-disclosure is too deep.* The client has to react to the helper rather than consider how the story might apply to the client's problem.

Situation: The client says that she feels like a failure because she is going through a divorce.

Inappropriate Disclosure by the Helper: "When I was going through my third divorce, I thought there must be something wrong with me. After all, I am supposed to help other people with their problems. So I went into therapy for over a year."

Appropriate Disclosure by the Helper: "I went through a divorce once myself and I can relate to those feelings. I guess they are pretty common."

Mistake 2:   *The helper's self-disclosure is poorly timed.* When one person self-discloses, it tends to reduce disclosure in the other person (Levin & Gergen, 1969). When a person is going through a stressful period, it is a poor time to get him or her to focus on the helper's story. Instead, the client should be encouraged to disclose more about himself or herself.

Situation: The client's mother died last week. (In this case, the client cannot really appreciate or focus on another person's story.)

Inappropriate Disclosure by the Helper: "I know just how you feel because my mother died about five years ago after a long illness. It was a long time before I got over it."

Appropriate Disclosure by the Helper: "I don't know exactly what you are going through, but I know a little bit about what it means to lose someone that close. I can guess that this whole thing has been very painful for you."

Mistake 3:   *The helper's self-disclosure does not match the client's experience.*

Situation: The client is fairly certain that she will be offered a basketball scholarship to go to college, but she is having trouble achieving satisfactory college board scores for admission.

Inappropriate Disclosure by the Helper: "Once I wanted to get into a prep school that cost $20,000 per year. But I had to go to one that cost a lot less because my family couldn't afford it."

Appropriate Disclosure by the Helper: "I can relate to your story in that I have had some goals in my life that I wanted that badly. It must be frustrating to be almost there and run into this new hurdle."

The Quality of the Client/Helper Match

Chances for success in the helping relationship are maximized when there is a good match between helper and client. We sometimes use the mystical term *chemistry* to describe a good fit in a relationship. On the other hand, a poor match makes the relationship and the possibility for change more unlikely. Elkind (1992) suggested that "lack of fit" can be due to differences in stage of life between helper and client. Sometimes clients want older, "wiser" helpers; others may find a better match with someone closer in age. Mismatches can occur when the client brings up issues or life experiences of which the therapist has no knowledge. For example, a Vietnam veteran may find it difficult to relate to a therapist who was born after the war. Personality differences can also cause mismatches. Clients who are very practical and concrete may not relate to a helper who wants to explore ideas and possibilities. Extroverted helpers may find introverted clients difficult to reach. Finally, Elkind identifies mismatches that occur as a result of differences in theoretical orientation or life philosophy. For example, an ardent feminist might have difficulty accepting the premises of a traditional psychodynamic approach.

Kanfer and Goldstein (1986) identify several characteristics research has found to produce good matches. First, the helper and the client agree on the roles and obligations of each person in the helping relationship. When the expectations of helper and client are congruent, a better match is obtained. Helpers can create a better match between client expectations and the content of the sessions by explaining the process and structure of the helping process. Some helpers use a handout that discusses fees, confidentiality, access to records, and other common concerns.

Second, a match is improved when both the client and the helper have a positive feeling about success, beginning at the first meeting. A helper can instill hope without false reassurance and select clients about whom he or she feels hopeful.

Third, a better match is obtained when clients and helpers come from similar cultural, economic, social, and racial backgrounds. Clients tend to prefer individuals who are similar to them in attitudes, personality, and ethnicity (Atkinson, Poston, Furlong, & Mercado, 1989), and helpers also seem to prefer clients who are similar to them. The helper's ability to be seen as competent and trustworthy may be influenced by gender, race, ethnicity, language, and socioeconomic status. In terms of gender, some clients may find a better match with same-gender helpers; others match better with opposite-gender helpers.

Most of the places where helpers work cannot take the time to match clients and helpers. The question therefore becomes not how to avoid mismatches but how to deal with them. A mismatch can be minimized when the helper has specific knowledge about the client's background. Besides seeking training in specific areas of knowledge about special populations, helpers need to examine their personal and cultural attitudes toward special populations. They must possess or adopt attitudes of empathy (rather than sympathy), tolerance for ambiguity, open-mindedness, and an openness to experience (Corey, Corey, & Callanan, 1988).

In most cases, client expectations and differences can be explored by a sensitive helper and resolved if the client is able to see the helper as accepting of the differences and perceives him or her as competent. It is important to address the differences directly, when it seems appropriate, and to ask the client how he or she feels about being helped by someone who is different. Another strategy to reduce the strength of the mismatch is to ask the client to teach you about his or her background. Also, a mismatch can be reduced by finding areas of commonality with the client. Many of these approaches require self-disclosure on the part of the helper. It is not necessary or even advisable to try to overcome all mismatches when they are identified. An appropriate referral, if available, can save time for both the helper and the client.

Stop and Reflect

Consider the following questions and then discuss them with a small group of fellow students.

- As you were growing up, did you have any friends, family, or acquaintances who were from a different racial, ethnic, or cultural background?
- How recently have you entertained someone in your home who comes from a different racial or ethnic background? How recently have you been in the home of someone from a very different background?
- As you think about different ethnic groups, which one (that is different from your own) evokes the greatest sense of discomfort when you think about working with this population? Which group, other than your own, would you be most comfortable working with?
- Describe a negative experience with someone from a different cultural group. Did this experience affect how you viewed other people from this background?
- Describe a positive experience with someone from a different cultural background. Does this experience make you more eager to work with people like him or her?
- What experiences might you plan as a student in order to have more contact with a different cultural group? How can you encourage your teachers to include this kind of experience in your coursework?
- What experiences do you think would help you become more comfortable dealing with someone who comes from a different cultural background?
- Can someone who comes from a completely different social, cultural, or ethnic background really help a person who has lived a completely different set of experiences? If so, what would a helper need to do or what attitudes must he or she possess to make this possible?

Therapeutic Faux Pas

Faux pas is a French term meaning "false step" or "wrong turn." Those who are at the dualistic, or right/wrong, stage in the helping process, might call these "mistakes." It is better to think of *faux pas* as detours that can potentially harm the relationship but that can be corrected. Thomas Gordon (1978) identified 12 such "wrong turns" that may occur in the development of a helping relationship. These are listed—with examples—in Table 9-3.

Gordon feels that two general messages are communicated by these twelve types of roadblocks. One message is that the client is incapable of solving his or her own problems. The second is that the client needs another person to tell him or her what

Table 9-3
Roadblocks to Communication

1. **Ordering, Directing, Commanding**
   You must do this.
   You cannot do this.
   I expect you to do this.
   Stop it.
   Go apologize to her.

2. **Warning, Admonishing, Threatening**
   You had better do this, or else . . .
   If you don't do this, then . . .
   You better not try that.
   I warn you, if you do that . . .

3. **Moralizing, Preaching, Imploring**
   You should do this.
   You ought to try it.
   It is your responsibility to do this.
   It is your duty to do this.
   I wish you would do this.
   I urge you to do this.

4. **Advising, Giving Suggestions or Solutions**
   What I think you should do is . . .
   Let me suggest . . .
   It would be best for you if . . .
   Why not take a different approach?
   The best solution is . . .

5. **Persuading with Logic, Lecturing, Arguing**
   Do you realize that . . .
   The facts are in favor of . . .
   Let me give you the facts.
   Here is the right way.
   Experience tells us that . . .

6. **Judging, Criticizing, Disagreeing, Blaming**
   You are acting foolishly.
   You are not thinking straight.
   You are out of line.
   You didn't do it right.
   You are wrong.
   That is a stupid thing to say.

7. **Praising, Agreeing, Evaluating Positively, Buttering Up**
   You usually have very good judgment.
   You are an intelligent person.
   You have so much potential.
   You've made quite a bit of progress.
   You have always made it in the past.

8. **Name-Calling, Ridiculing, Shaming**
   You are a sloppy worker.
   You are a fuzzy thinker.
   You're talking like an engineer.

Table 9-3—*continued*
Roadblocks to Communication

You really goofed on this one!

9. **Interpreting, Analyzing, Diagnosing**
You're saying this because you're angry.
You are jealous.
What you really need is . . .
You have problems with authority.
You want to look good.
You are being a bit paranoid.

10. **Reassuring, Sympathizing, Consoling, Supporting**
You'll feel different tomorrow.
Things will get better.
It is always darkest before the dawn.
Behind every cloud there's a silver lining.
Don't worry so much about it.
It's not that bad.

11. **Probing, Questioning, Interrogating**
Why did you do that?
How long have you felt this way?
What have you done to try to solve it?
Have you consulted with anyone?
When did you become aware of this feeling?
Who has influenced you?

12. **Distracting, Diverting, Kidding**
Think about the positive side.
Try not to think about it until you're rested.
Let's have lunch and forget about it.
That reminds me of the time when . . .
You think you've got problems!

Source: Adapted from Gordon, T. (1978). *Leadership effectiveness training* (pp. 60–62). New York: Bantam.

to do. Such responses engender resistance to change. Also, they take the responsibility for change away from the client and place it in the hands of the helper.

Besides these 12 major categories, Wolberg (1954) has identified several other specific helper behaviors that have a negative effect on the therapeutic relationship and should be avoided. These include:

- Being punitive.

Client: "I don't think you are giving me the help I need."

Helpful: "You feel stuck, that you are not making any progress."
           "What kind of help do you think would be useful to you at this time?"

Not Helpful: "Then I will just refer you to someone else."
               "You are not making progress because you are not working on the problem."

- Giving false reassurance.

Sometimes clients want us to give them hope that the helping process will be successful. This can backfire if the helper makes promises that cannot be kept.

Client: "Will I ever get over this completely and be normal?"

Helpful: "Tell me how you would like your life to be. What would normal look like to you?"
"You are unsure about whether you can conquer this problem. I am hopeful that we can make a significant change if we work together."

Not Helpful: "Of course you will."
"You will be better in six weeks."

- "Psychobabble" and premature interpretations.

Psychobabble is a word describing the overuse of psychological terminology. When the helper identifies a technical term for every issue, the client feels that his or her problems are trivialized or that they have become clinical syndromes. *Premature interpretation* consists of suggesting deep meanings before adequate information has been collected to support these interpretations.

Client: "My father was an alcoholic and my mother seemed to tolerate it. We lived in denial our whole lives."

Helpful: "Tell me more about what you mean by denial."
"Tell me more about your family relationships."

Not Helpful: "That's because your mother was co-dependent and you are an ACOA (adult child of an alcoholic)."
"That is why you are a dependent person yourself."

- Probing traumatic issues when the client strongly resists.

Respecting the client's wish to avoid a topic can be handled by noting it, reflecting, and suggesting that it can be put off until later. Damage to the relationship can take place when the helper mercilessly pursues a topic. It is a question of timing. Sometimes it is best to nurture the relationship and address the topic later.

Client: "I don't want to talk about sex."

Helpful: "It is a painful subject for you."
"All right, we can come back to that another time if you want."

Not Helpful: "We have to talk about it sometime."
"What about your own sex life?"

Challenges in Developing the Client/Helper Relationship

Although developing facilitative conditions through invitational and reflecting skills is important, maintaining the therapeutic relationship does not end there. In fact, in the helping process, when goals are being set and helping techniques are being implemented and evaluated, a variety of issues can potentially disrupt or change the therapeutic alliance, diminish trust and safety, and decrease the efficacy of helping techniques. One important challenge that arises is dealing with the client's and helper's feelings about each other, which can impede progress toward the client's goals. *Transference* and *countertransference* are terms that originated among psychoanalysts to denote the strong feelings that develop between helper and client because of the personal needs of these two individuals.

Transference: Dealing with the Client's Feelings

Transference is a client's carryover of feelings from past relationships into a new one—the client/helper relationship. These feelings can be described as positive, ranging from liking to sexual attraction, or negative, ranging from suspiciousness to hatred (Watkins, 1986). Relationship-building activities, such as reflecting feelings and providing conditions of safety, increase feelings of intimacy. Along with this closeness, through transference, other feelings and thoughts come to the surface. Gelso and Carter (1985) indicate that all helpers engender a "magnetism or transference pull" in their clients. Negative transference reactions are thought to be an important reason for treatment failures (Basch, 1980), since clients often drop out of therapy rather than face them.

Many therapeutic relationships never develop into intimate relationships, and serious transference issues do not surface. Some helpers believe it is even possible to achieve therapy goals without a deep personal relationship (Lazarus, 1981), though mutual respect and liking are extremely helpful. Others feel that every therapeutic relationship involves transference, and to avoid it is to miss the most crucial aspect of therapy.

In practice, many clients are able to achieve therapy goals without needing to work through transference issues. For others, it is vital to examine the therapeutic relationship as a first step in setting other relationships straight. Other clients experience such strong feelings with regard to the helper that the transference is literally an obstacle that must be overcome in order for helping to continue. When issues of transference interfere with the attainment of goals, they must be dealt with, either in an isolated fashion, or in conjunction with other relationship problems the client may be experiencing.

Stop and Reflect

It is possible to experience transference reactions immediately on meeting an individual, that is, without the presence of intimacy. Most of us are familiar with automatic feelings of liking or disliking a person on sight. This emotional reaction is most likely due to experiences with a similar person in the past. These emotional reactions are often vague and impressionistic. They can be expressed as valences, positive or negative.

Take a look around at your classmates and mentally note your feelings for each one. Write a one-word description of your emotional reaction or place a plus or minus next to each one to quantify your feelings. You may think it is unfair to assign a value to your feelings without taking into account the fact that you do not really know all about your classmates. That is true, but these impressions, like all first impressions, can be powerful. Are there reasons for your positives and negatives, or are they the result of experiences with similar people? Think about the names of your classmates. Do any evoke an emotional reaction? Is there anything about their style of dress that you like or that puts you off? If you had to choose two people in the class to play your parents in a role play, whom would you choose? Are you transferring any of your experiences with your parents to these people in your other interactions?

When you are finished with this exercise, erase your ratings of your fellow students. How might you begin to see them afresh without bringing previous experiences with you?

Causes of Transference

Some believe that transference is caused by unfinished business from the past. This notion is central to psychoanalysis, which asserts that issues surface from the unconscious because they are unresolved. Freud believed that resolution of transference was the most important aspect of therapy because it allowed the client to address remnant emotional issues about parents and siblings.

One alternative viewpoint that has emerged is to conceptualize transference as a set of cognitive distortions rather than as unresolved conflicts or unfulfilled needs (Sullivan, 1954). These distortions are learned patterns of thinking, like the irrational ideas that have been described by Albert Ellis (1985). Still, there is a common thread that binds the modern viewpoint to the psychoanalytic idea. In both conceptualizations, the client is seen as focused on the outside (external causes of behavior) versus the inside (self-direction). The more cognitive viewpoint stresses that a client who has strong positive feelings toward the helper sees the helper as the answer to all problems. Conversely, negative transference feelings are primarily due to the client's disappointment in the helper's inability to meet unrealistic expectations. Watkins (1986) has identified five major transference patterns that reinforce the concept of transference as cognitive distortion. Table 9-4, adapted from Watkins, shows these patterns along with the client's attitudes and the helper's experience of them.

Why Must Transference Be Addressed?

Some writers (Fine, 1975, p. 105) insist that the transference of feelings by the client onto the helper is mainly the result of childhood experiences and one's family of origin. Others (Watkins, 1986) indicate that transference does not necessarily have to reach so far into the past; it may be based on more recent relationships. For example, it is just as likely that a client may have positive feelings for a helper because of a physical resemblance to her best friend as it is that the helper reminds the client of her mother. Regardless of when the historical situation occurred, by definition the transference reaction is a reliance on old learning that may not be appropriate in present

Table 9-4
Major Transference Patterns

Client Behaviors/Attitudes	Counselor Experiences
Counselor as Ideal	
Compliments counselor profusely	Feels pride, satisfaction, and all-competent
Imitates counselor	
Wears similar clothing	Experiences tension, anxiety, confusion, anger, and frustration
General idealization	
Counselor as Seer	
Ascribes omniscience and power to the counselor	Experiences "God complex" and self-doubt
Views counselor as expert	Feels incompetent and pressure to be right and live up to client's expectations
Sees self as incompetent	
Seeks answers, solutions, and advice	
Counselor as Nurturer	
Experiences profuse emotion and sense of fragility	Experiences feelings of sorrow, sympathy, depression, despair, and depletion
Cries	Has urge to soothe, coddle, and touch
Feels dependent, helpless, and indecisive	
Desires to be touched and held	
Counselor as Frustrator	
Feels defensive, cautious, guarded, suspicious, and distrustful	Feels uneasy, on edge (walking on eggshells), tense, hostile, and hateful
Experiences "enter-exit" phenomenon	Withdraws and becomes unavailable
Tests counselor	Dislikes and blames client
Counselor as Nonentity	
Shifts topics	Feels overwhelmed, subdued, taken aback, used, useless
Lacks focus	
Is voluble and desultory	Experiences resentment, frustration, and lack of recognition
Meanders aimlessly	
Exhibits thought pressure	Characterizes self as a nonperson

relationships. It is a defensive reaction and an attempt to maintain the status quo (Paolino, 1981).

In addition, a client with strong emotional reactions to a helper has reduced self-awareness and is focused on the helper rather than the self. In the case of strong hero worship, for example, the client may be diminishing himself or herself by comparison with the helper (Singer, 1970).

When Must Transference Be Treated?

Under what conditions should the helper negotiate resolution of transference as a therapeutic goal? According to Wolberg (1954), transference is to be confronted only when it acts as resistance. *Resistance* can be understood as any conscious or unconscious effort by the client to avoid accomplishing therapy goals or to take on antitherapeutic goals. It is an attempt to return to the pre-therapy situation for reasons of safety or habit (Cavanagh, 1982). In Chapter 13, we will take up the topic of resistance and motivation in more detail.

In addition, transference must be dealt with when the negotiated treatment goals relate directly to the client's behavior toward the helper (Strupp & Binder, 1984). Using the therapeutic relationship as a laboratory, client and helper can identify and change inappropriate cycles of interpersonal behavior. For example, if a man who has a problem with extramarital affairs begins acting seductively toward his female helper, this behavior must be discussed since it relates to his original therapy goal—to decrease this behavior. By the same token, it can be argued that mild transferences and attractions need not be dealt with if they do not interfere or create resistance.

The Technique of Dealing with Transference

A client's strong emotional reactions to the helper may be the result of transference or may be honest reactions to the helper's behavior. In both cases, the task of the helper is the same: to help the client gain more awareness and explore the source of these feelings.

Dealing with transference is a technique because it is composed of several building blocks: questioning, reflection of feeling, and reflection of meaning. The general approach is to help clients explore their feelings toward the helper and then help them place the feelings in the proper context. To explain this more fully, let us look at how a helper can deal with angry or hostile feelings in a way that leads to growth in the client. A similar process applies to client feelings of dependency and strong attraction.

How to Deal With Hostility as Transference

Step 1: *Use invitational and reflecting skills to convey acceptance of the client's remarks.* Hostility is certainly the most difficult transference reaction for most helpers. It tends to evoke anger in the helper, and a defensive response can be perceived by the client as a weakness, an admission of guilt, or a punishment. The client's anger may be triggered by frustration over lack of progress or by the perception that the helper is unfriendly, inept, or destructive. After having expressed this hostility, the client may be concerned about angering or hurting the helper or may fear retaliation. The helper must explain that anger and frustration are a normal part of the process, and refrain from becoming defensive. The nonjudgmental listening cycle helps the client feel accepted as he or she expresses troubling feelings:

Client: "I don't think we're getting anywhere. When are we going to deal with the real issues? I'm sick of coming in here and paying all this money."

Helper: "I can tell you're mad. I'm glad you had the courage to be so honest. I can't think of anything that will be of more help to you than dealing with this issue."

Step 2: *Use questions to clarify and explore the client's feelings.* Following an expression of hostility toward the helper, the client may retreat, fearing punishment, losing control, or hurting the helper. Exploration of a client's hostile feelings involves continuing to encourage the expression and labeling of feelings while trying to clarify the source of the anger.

Client: "I don't think this is working, and I am tired of coming in here and being told that it is all my fault."

Helper: "What made you feel that it was all your fault?"
"Do you have the sense that I am blaming you for not changing?"

Step 3: *Reflect the meaning of the event so that the client explores the issue more fully.* It is difficult to become detached when someone expresses anger toward you. The helper must learn to reject any defensive reaction and to silently consider, "How can I help the client identify the true source of the anger?" The helper uses reflection of meaning to accomplish this. Reflection of meaning often means playing a hunch and asking the client to try to understand the hostile feelings as more than mere frustration with the helper. This approach is taken by the helper in the two examples that follow. Remember, these methods are useful when the client's anger appears to be transference. Helpers should not hide behind reflection when clients have legitimate complaints.

Client: "You think it's easy for me to give up smoking dope? How would you like to work at that plant, earning minimum wage, not enough money to get an apartment and having to live with your mom? How would you like it?"

Helper: "I don't think you are just angry at me. You're discouraged about life in general and I'm the closest target."

Client: "This is just a job to you. You're just like all the rest. Just collect your paycheck."

Helper: "You're angry, not just at me, but because you suspect that no one cares enough to help you."

Step 4: *Help the client find new ways of expressing feelings and meeting his or her needs.* Clients who express anger toward the helper may require assertiveness training. Assertiveness training is an attempt to help people learn to express their feelings in the actual problem situation while asking specifically for what they want. Clients who exhibit excessive anger or who are indirect or revengeful may be alienating others and thereby engaging in self-defeating patterns. Dealing with transference has the effect of making clients aware of these patterns, but they still may need assistance either individually or in a structured group to learn new and more productive behaviors. Assertiveness training is explained in detail in Chapter 10.

Countertransference: Dealing with the Helper's Feelings

Dealing with countertransference is not a skill utilized by the helper in the presence of the client. This is primarily an ethical and supervisory issue. However, because countertransference can seriously disrupt the therapeutic relationship, it merits discussion here.

Countertransference is an issue not fully appreciated by the beginning helper. When intellectualizing about the therapeutic relationship, one can hardly imagine the powerful feelings that some clients may elicit. In practice, helpers need ongoing supervision to help monitor the tendency to be too helpful, and to deal with feelings of sexual attraction as well as anger, fear, and insecurity.

Table 9-5 describes common helper emotional reactions, based on information collected by Corey, Corey, and Callanan (1988). The essential point apparent in the table is that countertransference issues are generally emotional reactions to clients, which can lead to certain behaviors on the part of the helper. Instead of helping the client achieve mutually defined goals, the helper develops a second (you might say unconscious) agenda that changes the helper's view of the client as a contractual partner in the therapy process. The helper has come to see the client as a project, a sexual object, a friend, or even a reflection of the self.

Table 9-5
Common Patterns of Countertransference

Counselor Emotional Response to Client	Counselor Behavior	Client Seen As
Paternal/maternal nurturing	Overprotective Failure to challenge	Fragile
Fear of client's anger	Reduction of conflict Attempts to please	Aggressor
Disgust, disapproval	Rejection	Needy Immoral
Need for reassurance	Socializing	Friend
Need for liking	Failure to challenge	
Anxiety	Avoidance of emotionally charged topics	
Insecurity		
Feelings of identification	Advice giving Overinvolvement Failure to recognize client's uniqueness	Self
Sexual	Seductive behavior	Sexual object
Romantic	Inappropriate self-disclosure Reduced focus on presenting problems Inappropriate exploration of sexual topics	Romantic partner
Frustration	Extreme confrontation	Product
Anger	Scolding Criticizing	Success

Countertransference is as common as transference reactions, and most helpers regularly fall prey to these feelings. A great deal of the unethical behavior in which helpers indulge is probably due to the strong emotions elicited in the therapeutic relationship, which make us forget our "asocial," contractual role. This is one reason why a supervisory relationship is so crucial for every helper. The supervisor's role is to appeal to the helper's professional sense and remind the helper to act in accordance with therapeutic goals.

Of all countertransference reactions, frustration and anger are probably the most common. Research by Fremont and Anderson (1986) found that the most exasperating clients are those who (1) show resistance to help, (2) impose on the helper's personal life and time or become too dependent, (3) verbally attack the helper, and (4) draw the helper into their personal dynamics, perhaps even seeing several helpers and pitting them against each other.

The Technique of Immediacy

In meeting someone for the first time, think about what issues are the most difficult to discuss. It is easier to talk about past problems and relationships than about present issues and relationships. It is easier to discuss issues that are positive and uplifting than those that are negative or depressing. It is easier to talk about issues that concern neither of us, such as the weather, than about our relationship (Egan, 1977). By the same token, it is sometimes difficult for the helper to bring up issues affecting the helper or the relationship. However, the ability to give honest feedback and openly discuss the helper/client relationship gives it a special meaning that separates it from other social interactions. Nothing is taboo. The relationship can be a laboratory where the client can learn about his or her effect on others.

Immediacy, a technique that helpers use to give clients immediate feedback of their effect on others, is a comment by the helper about what he or she thinks or feels at a given moment. Immediacy statements by the helper should have four characteristics:

1. The helper uses the word *I* in the statement to indicate that this is the helper's perspective.
2. The helper describes the client's behavior or the helping relationship issue in nonjudgmental terms.
3. The helper expresses his or her feelings in a way that does not overload or burden the client.
4. The helper includes a checking question to get the client involved and to underline further that this is an issue to consider, not the absolute "truth."

These four characteristics are apparent in the following helper statement and question:

1. "I am aware that
2. When I make a suggestion, such as the one just presented, we seem to end up in a struggle and the issue gets dropped.

3. I am a little concerned about this.

4. Do you agree that this is the case?"

There are three types of immediacy that the helper might want to employ: client immediacy, helper immediacy, and relationship immediacy (Cormier & Cormier, 1991). *Client immediacy* is specific feedback given by the helper to the client about what is going on at the present moment—for example, "You keep looking at the clock and glancing at the door as if you would like to leave," or "I can tell by your eyes that the memory of that person is still very close to you."

Helper immediacy, on the other hand, is self-disclosure by the helper about what he or she is feeling or thinking at a given moment. It is focused on the helper, but its purpose is to give the client information about how he or she affects others. For example, it is said that Carl Rogers once told a client that he felt bored. This turned out to be important data for the client and actually enhanced the relationship because the client began to see the helper as honest. The following are some other appropriate ways of using helper immediacy that are not quite as confrontational:

"I am excited about the progress that we have made so far. I look forward to the challenges that are still out there for us."

"I'm having trouble following you because I'm still concerned about the first thing you said, that you used to abuse your wife. Let's talk about that."

Murray (1986) cites the example of a young woman who came to therapy because she felt she was overly dependent on her father. For example, whenever she had car trouble, she turned it over to him. After a month of therapy, she brought in her auto insurance policy, which she was having trouble deciphering, and handed it to the therapist, who began reading it. After a moment, the therapist laughed and exclaimed, "Look, I'm behaving just like your father."

Relationship immediacy is "you-me" talk. It asks the client to focus on the helper's impressions of the therapeutic relationship. Relationship immediacy invites the client to reflect on the relationship by reacting to the helper's statements. Relationship immediacy can enhance intimacy in a relationship because it acknowledges the mutual bond and gives the client liberty to look at his or her feelings toward the helper. Relationship immediacy is one of the best ways of dealing with so-called resistance and transference reactions. Relationship immediacy is also an invitation to examine the client/helper relationship as a microcosm of the client's difficulties. It should be used only if it seems that the relationship issues between client and helper relate to the client's goals or if the therapeutic relationship is strained and needs to be repaired.

Relationship immediacy can be of the "here and now" variety, such as, "Right now, I feel a lot of tension between us because we brought up the alcohol issue. What is your reading on that?" Alternately, relationship immediacy can ask the client to reflect on the relationship as it has progressed up to that point—for example, "Over the past few weeks, I have found that our relationship seems to have changed. My experience is that the sessions are much more fun and productive. What do you think?"

While immediacy can be extremely valuable, the helper must be careful not to give himself or herself liberty to dump feelings on the client or vent frustration. Expressing feelings of disappointment, disapproval, or anger can produce a rupture in the relationship that is impossible to repair. Several therapeutic *faux pas*, such as exclamations of surprise and being punitive, can masquerade as immediacy. Before a helper uses immediacy, he or she must ask, "Am I doing this for myself or to help the client?"

Summary

The REPLAN system is a way of organizing therapeutic techniques based on six common therapeutic factors: the therapeutic relationship; efficacy and self-esteem; practicing new behaviors; lowering and raising emotional arousal; activating expectations, hope, and motivation; and new learning experiences. The REPLAN system is also a simple way to develop a treatment plan for a client. The helper asks himself or herself which therapeutic factor or factors would most help the client achieve the goals and then selects techniques associated with that factor.

Most of this chapter is devoted to exploring the curative factor associated with the therapeutic relationship. The therapeutic relationship is the keystone to change. Enhancing the therapeutic relationship makes other techniques more potent. The helper can enhance the therapeutic relationship by utilizing invitational and reflecting skills to establish an amiable relationship. The helper can also increase trust by showing expertise and appearing credible to the client. Helpers can deepen the relationship by utilizing self-disclosure and making sure that there is a good client/helper match.

Clients and helpers prefer people who are similar to them. Sometimes mismatches are the result of differing cultural backgrounds. One of the major challenges to developing an effective client/helper relationship is trying to achieve understanding and to convey acceptance when the client is culturally different from the helper or comes from some other special population. The helper must be flexible enough to try to view the problem situation from the client's unique cultural perspective, if the therapeutic bond is to be maintained.

Transference reactions are strong feelings of the client that have been carried over from past relationships. Transference must be resolved when it interferes with the accomplishment of goals. Resolution of major transference feelings of hostility, dependency, and strong affection involves accepting and normalizing the client's feelings, clarifying and exploring the transference, reflecting the underlying meanings, and helping the client find new ways of meeting needs.

Countertransference is the name given to the helper's strong emotional reactions to the client that may encourage the helper to respond to his or her own needs rather than the needs of the client. Immediacy responses are disclosures by the helper that invite the client to examine his or her effect on others by opening the therapeutic relationship to scrutiny.

Group Exercises

Group Exercise 1: Immediacy

In this exercise, students break into groups of three. In each group, one student plays the part of a client, one plays the helper, and the third records observations about the relationship. In this scenario, the client and helper have been meeting for several weeks to deal with self-esteem issues.

The Client's Role   In this session, the client reports success, but in the course of 3 or 4 minutes indicates that he or she is dependent on the helper and says the following kinds of things:

> "Before I came for help, I couldn't do anything. You have really helped me."
>
> "I can't do it by myself."
>
> "What should I do next?"
>
> "Can I call you every day to get suggestions?"

These are only suggestions of things the client might say. The client should improvise. The student playing the part of the client takes on the following characteristics and behaviors:

- The client has no confidence in his or her own abilities.
- The client needs the helper's permission in order to discuss a particular problem.
- The client indicates that he or she is reluctant to make any changes without checking with the helper.

The Helper's Role   The helper should:

- Use invitational, reflecting, and even advanced reflecting skills to understand the client's story.
- Take a moment to utilize helper or relationship immediacy.
- Include a final summary that makes mention of the immediacy response.

The Observer's Role   The observer writes each helper response verbatim. After the helper has given an immediacy response, the observer may prompt the helper to make a summary and conclude the session. The observer should then facilitate an examination of the helper's responses, reading them aloud to the group and getting consensus on the category of the response: minimal encourager, open question, closed question, paraphrase, reflection of feeling, or reflection of meaning.

The observer can ask the training group this question: Did the helper's immediacy response contain the components listed in this chapter? When the group has had a minute or two for discussion, roles should be exchanged until each person has had a chance to assume each.

Quick Tips: Immediacy

- Don't use immediacy to ventilate personal frustration.
- Do not use immediacy early in the session. Some trust must be established before immediacy responses are well received.
- Ask yourself two questions to test whether immediacy is appropriate: "Is the client aware that he or she is creating this feeling in others?" and "Would it be valuable for the client to know the effect he or she is having on others?"
- Use immediacy when the session feels "stuck."
- Use immediacy to identify problems with trust—for example, "I wonder whether your reluctance to talk about that means that you do not yet feel quite safe in this relationship."
- Use immediacy to deal with differences between helper and client.

Group Exercise 2

Form small groups of four or five and read the following case:

Dr. Melvin is a 62-year-old Cuban man who was referred for counseling by his physician. He has been diagnosed with gastric ulcers and is being treated for that with medication. However, the physician believes that the patient's medical complaints are exacerbated by his emotional condition. Dr. Melvin has been a dentist with his own practice for almost 35 years. The neighborhood where he practices has deteriorated and the number of new clients is decreasing. He is losing many of his affluent patients to younger, more technologically sophisticated dentists. In addition, Dr. Melvin is experiencing stress at home. He was divorced 10 years ago and remarried about 5 years ago to a woman 20 years younger than he. He works long hours in an effort to improve his practice. He is rarely at home and has few friends and leisure activities. He has trouble verbalizing his feelings. When he came to the first session, he described his problem as follows: "I am at the end of my rope. Nothing in my life is working. If only there were some way to get back the good feelings between me and my wife, I am sure that things would turn around."

a. After reading the case, examine the list of curative factors and identify two that you think would be most helpful for Dr. Melvin. What does this client need? What problem do you think he would be most interested in solving?

b. After you have selected the curative factors, list two or three skills or techniques you might use that are compatible with this client's unique situation. Discuss your answers with your group.

c. Based on the fact that Dr. Melvin is 62 and of Cuban origin, how might you modify the treatment plan you have constructed?

d. What other information would be important for a helper to know about this client?

Additional Exercises

Exercise 1: Case Study

In a small group, read and discuss the following example:

Ricardo is a counselor in private practice. The following is his description of a client who was referred for counseling by her family physician. She had come to the doctor's office crying and the doctor referred her for counseling.

The client began the therapeutic relationship with much enthusiasm and high expectations for achieving her goals. She was a 23-year-old only child who felt she could not maintain a serious relationship. After a few weeks, her enthusiasm waned and she expressed disappointment in me as a helper. By this time, enough assessment had been done to identify this denouement as being similar to her history of intimate relationships. She began relationships with an idealized picture of her boyfriends and then was quickly disappointed. She came to the session one day indicating that she was angry that I had not been able to give her an earlier session. During her earlier phone call, she had said it was important but not urgent that she see me soon. She admitted that she expected me to know how upset she was and to set up an emergency appointment. When we examined our relationship, the client was able to pick out several times when she left hints and clues about her needs but failed to ask for things directly. I shared my feelings of surprise, being unaware of her real feelings. Naturally, this led to a discussion of how her behavior might have affected other relationships. It was a very significant insight when she realized that she was undermining relationships by her failure to send clear messages about her needs. In her case, this pattern of behavior could be traced back to her upbringing, which did not require that she state her needs and rewarded indirect suggestions. In therapy, she was able to learn some assertiveness skills and practice them in a group setting.

a. Do you think it was necessary to examine the client's past to help her with the problem in the helping relationship?

b. Is it possible that the client has a legitimate gripe and that Ricardo is "saving face" by making it the client's problem?

c. In a case such as this, how much responsibility should the helper take for the miscommunication about the client's needs? Would it have helped the client if the helper had apologized or assumed partial responsibility for the misunderstanding?

d. If you were Ricardo, how would you have handled the client's expression of anger? Construct a sentence that uses helper immediacy and another that uses relationship immediacy.

Exercise 2: Barriers to Communication

Divide into groups of four or five. The instructor will assign each group one of the roadblocks in Table 9-3. (Roadblocks 4, 7, 10, and 12 are especially effective.) Each group is to put together a presentation that demonstrates their roadblock to the class in a role play and then shows helper behaviors that enhance the relationship in that situation. Following each demonstration, the class can discuss the effects of the roadblock on the helping relationship.

Homework

Relationship immediacy is a skill that can be used therapeutically to help a person obtain feedback or to enhance an ongoing relationship. Identify three friendships you have that might benefit from talking about the relationship, and explain your reasoning.

- Think about a situation with each of the three people that defines your relationship in some way—for example, you tend to avoid each other, you contact each other only when there is a problem, you have silently agreed to keep the relationship superficial, and so on.
- Imagine talking to each of these three people.
- Formulate a response that includes the four components of a good immediacy response. Write down the response and evaluate it.

Next, respond to the following questions:

- If you were the receiver of this immediacy response, how do you think you might respond? Would you feel hurt or violated that the person had chosen to bring it up?
- If you shared your immediacy response with the person you identified, do you think it would be beneficial?
- Before utilizing relationship immediacy, it is important to know why you are sharing your reactions. What reasons can you identify in support of sharing your feelings about these three relationships?
- In what situations could this kind of honesty be detrimental?

References

Atkinson, D. R., Poston, W. C., Furlong, M. J., & Mercado, P. (1989). Ethnic group preferences for counselor characteristics. *Journal of Counseling Psychology, 36,* 68–72.

Bannikotes, P. G., Kubinski, J. A., & Purcell, S. A. (1981). Sex role orientation, self-disclosure, and gender related perceptions. *Journal of Counseling Psychology, 28,* 140–146.

Barak, A., Patkin, J., & Dell, D. M. (1982). Effects of certain client behaviors in perceived expertness and attractiveness. *Journal of Counseling Psychology, 29,* 261–267.

Basch, M. F. (1980). *Doing psychotherapy.* New York: Basic Books.

Belkin, G. S. (1980). *Introduction to counseling* (2nd ed.). New York: Brown.

Cavanagh, M. E. (1982). *The counseling experience.* Monterey, CA: Brooks/Cole.

Corey, G., Corey, M. S., & Callanan, P. (1988). *Issues and ethics in the helping professions* (3rd ed.). Monterey, CA: Brooks/Cole.

Corrigan, J. D., Dell, D. M., Lewis, K. N., & Schmidt, L. D. (1980). Counseling as a social influence process: A review. *Journal of Counseling Psychology, 27,* 395–441.

Cormier, W. H., & Cormier, L. S. (1991). *Interviewing strategies for helpers.* Pacific Grove, CA: Brooks/Cole.

Egan, G. (1977). *You and me: The skills of communicating and relating to others.* Pacific Grove, CA: Brooks/Cole.

Egan, G. (1990). *The skilled helper* (4th ed.). Monterey, CA: Brooks/Cole.

Elkind, S. N. (1992). *Resolving impasses in therapeutic relationships.* New York: Guilford.

Ellis, A. (1985). *Overcoming resistance: Rational-emotive therapy with difficult clients.* New York: Springer.

Fiedler, F. E. (1950). The concept of an ideal therapeutic relationship. *Journal of Consulting Psychology, 14,* 339–345.

Fine, R. (1975). *Psychoanalytic psychology.* New York: Jason Aronson.

Frank, J. D. (1961). *Persuasion and healing.* Baltimore: Johns Hopkins University Press.

Fremont, S., & Anderson, W. P. (1986). What client behaviors make counselors angry?: An exploratory study. *Journal of Counseling and Development, 65,* 67–70.

Gelso, C. J., & Carter, J. A. (1985). The relationship in counseling and psychotherapy: Components, consequences and theoretical antecedents. *The Counseling Psychologist, 13,* 155–243.

Gordon, T. (1978). *Leadership effectiveness training.* New York: Bantam Books.

Heppner, P. P., & Dixon, D. N. (1986). A review of the interpersonal influence process in counseling. In W. P. Anderson (Ed.), *Innovative counseling: A handbook of readings* (pp. 8–16). Alexandria, VA: American Association for Counseling and Development.

Johnson, D. W., & Matross, R. (1977). Interpersonal influence in psychotherapy: A social psychological view. In A. S. Gurman & A. M. Razin (Eds.), *Effective psychotherapy: A handbook of research* (pp. 395–432). Elmsford, NY: Pergamon.

Kanfer, F. H., & Goldstein, A. P. (1986). Introduction. In F. Kanfer & A. Goldstein, *Helping people change: A textbook of methods.* New York: Pergamon.

Kottler, J. A., & Blau, D. S. (1989). *The imperfect therapist.* San Francisco: Jossey-Bass.

Lazarus, A. A. (1981). *The practice of multimodal therapy.* New York: McGraw-Hill.

Levin, F. M., & Gergin, K. J. (1969). Revealingness, ingratiation, and the disclosure of the self. *Proceedings of the 77th Annual Convention of the American Psychological Association 4,* 447–448.

Loesch, L. (1984). Professional credentialing in counseling. *Counseling and Human Development, 17,* 1–11.

McCarthy, P. (1982). Differential effects of counselor self-referent responses and counselor status. *Journal of Counseling Psychology, 29,* 125–131.

Meadow, A. (1982). Psychopathology, psychotherapy and the Mexican-American patient. In E. E. Jones & S. J. Korchin (Eds.), *Minority mental health* (pp. 331–362). New York: Praeger.

Murray, E. J. (1986). Possibilities and promises of eclecticism. In J. C. Norcross (Ed.), *Handbook of eclectic psychotherapy* (pp. 398–415). New York: Brunner/Mazel.

Nilsson, D., Strassberg, D., & Bannon, J. (1979). Perceptions of counselor self-disclosure: An analog study. *Journal of Counseling Psychology, 26,* 399–404.

Paolino, T. J. (1981). *Psychoanalytic psychotherapy: Theory, technique, therapeutic relationship and treatability.* New York: Brunner/Mazel.

Parker, W. M. (1988). Becoming an effective multicultural counselor. *Journal of Counseling and Development, 67,* 93.

Rogers, C. R. (1957). The necessary and sufficient conditions of therapeutic personality change. *Journal of Consulting Psychology, 21,* 95–103.

Sermat, V., & Smythe, M. (1973). Content analysis of verbal communication in the development of a relationship: Conditions influencing self-disclosure. *Journal of Personality and Social Psychology, 26,* 332–346.

Singer, E. (1970). *Key concepts in psychotherapy* (2nd ed.). New York: Basic Books.

Strong, S. R. (1968). Counseling: An interpersonal influence process. *Journal of Counseling Psychology, 15,* 215–224.

Strupp, H. H., & Binder, J. L. (1984). *Psychotherapy in a new key: A guide to time-limited therapy.* New York: Basic Books.

Sue, S. & Zane, N. (1987). The role of culture and cultural techniques in psychotherapy. *American Psychologist, 42,* 37–45.

Sullivan, H. S. (1954). *The psychiatric interview.* New York: W. W. Norton.

Watkins, C. E., Jr. (1986). Transference phenomena in the counseling situation. In W. P. Anderson (Ed.), *Innovative counseling: A handbook of readings.* Alexandria, VA: American Association of Counseling and Development.

Wolberg, L. R. (1954). *The technique of psychotherapy.* New York: Grune & Stratton.

Yalom, I. (1985). *Theory and practice of group psychotherapy.* New York: Basic Books.

Enhancing Efficacy and Self-Esteem

Introduction

In the REPLAN system developed in this book, the letter E represents the second curative factor, enhancing efficacy and self-esteem (Figure 10-1). There is wide agreement that a positive self-concept is a keystone of mental health and that raising self-esteem is a fundamental task of helping (Frey & Carlock, 1989; Kurpius, Rockwood, & Corbett, 1989; Walz, 1990). Likewise, low self-esteem has long been identified as a cause or contributing factor in many psychological diagnoses and symptoms, especially anxiety (Rosenberg, 1962), depression (Wilson & Krane, 1980), stress, dependency, pathological guilt, borderline personality (Ingham, Kreitman, Miller, & Sasidharan, 1986), and substance abuse (Brehm & Back, 1968).

Self-esteem has two aspects: efficacy (competence) and self-worth (Branden, 1969, 1971; Witmer, 1985). *Efficacy* is an expectation that one can perform a specific task (Bandura, 1982). For example, when an experienced driver sits behind the wheel of a car, he or she feels a sense of confidence or expectation that driving a car is a manageable task. Efficacy is tied to specific activities, though it may generalize to similar situations. It is also subject to modification by experience. Having an auto accident could undermine one's sense of efficacy as a driver. Many clients are afraid to try new activities because of past failures or because they do not expect to do well at anything. In addition, individuals with low self-esteem often do not pay sufficient

Figure 10-1
Curative Factors in the REPLAN
system: Efficacy and Self-Esteem

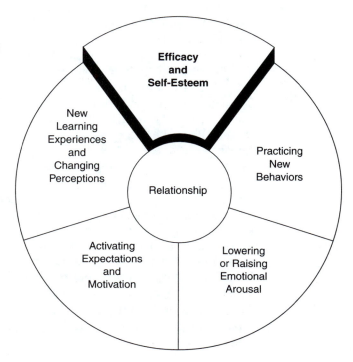

attention to successes and improvements, tending instead to focus on their losses and failures.

In contrast to efficacy, *self-worth* is a global feeling that one has the right to exist, that one is basically good and is worthy to live. It is the sum total of one's attitudes about the self—the fundamental belief that one is "OK" or "not OK" (Berne, 1972). It is possible to feel competent or efficacious at a number of tasks and still experience low self-worth. As helpers, we often meet intelligent, attractive, skilled individuals whose major problems are deeply held negative beliefs about themselves.

Stop and Reflect

Self-esteem can be improved by increasing client self-efficacy. Efficacy is increased when clients recognize their current abilities or learn new skills. The chances that a client will attempt a new activity are increased if he or she engages in warm-up activities including thinking about, talking about, and visualizing the new behavior. To become more familiar with this process, try the following:

1. Make a list of 10 things you cannot do at the present time but would like to be able to do. For example, your list might include the following:

   "I would like to learn to swim."
   "I would like to ask someone out for a date."
   "I would like to be able to use a spreadsheet on the computer."
   "I would like to be able to learn ballroom dancing."

   For this exercise, do not include personal qualities that you would like to develop or global statements about self-worth, such as "I would like to be more patient," or "I would like to be a better person."

2. Once you have developed a list of 10 items, place the letter *T* next to each item if you have talked to a friend or family member about engaging in this activity. Place the letter *V* next to an item if you have *ever* visualized or daydreamed about yourself performing this task. Place the letter *M* for "models" next to an item if you have seen other people perform this task *on several occasions*. Place the letter *A* next to each task that you have attempted to perform in the last year.

3. It is thought that a person is more likely to engage in a new behavior if he or she gets ready by talking about it, visualizing it, and watching others. Conversely, when we have not readied ourselves through these activities, we are further away from actually attempting the behavior. Look at your list and decide whether your answers confirm this "readiness hypothesis." Identify one or two behaviors that have the fewest letters next to them. Which letters are missing? The missing letters should indicate which activities you can initiate if you wish to increase your readiness.

4. Do you think you might experience any change in your self-esteem if you were able to engage in all of the activities on this list?

5. Compare your answers to this exercise and your reactions with others in your training group.

Sources of Low Self-Esteem

Drivers

Messages received during childhood sometimes become internalized images or phrases about the self. In transactional analysis (Berne, 1972), the individual's life plan or script is thought to be transmitted from the parents along with accompanying injunctions, such as "You'll never amount to anything," "Don't trust anyone," etc. Some of these injunctions or themes become preeminent and rule a person's life. These ruling injunctions are called *drivers* because they broadly motivate or drive behavior (Kahler, 1977). The person attempts to maintain self-esteem by attempting to live up to the standards of parents and others. Unfortunately, these internalized sentences may not be relevant to the present, or healthy, or even possible to uphold.

An obvious example of an impossible driver is "Be perfect." For example, a client reported that she never plays the guitar anymore even though she enjoys it because she cannot afford lessons, nor can she stand to make mistakes. She was raised with the injunction that "Anything worth doing is worth doing right." In reality, some things, like playing the guitar, are worth doing sloppily if one enjoys them. Perfectionism keeps people from trying new things and from enjoying activities that they perform less than flawlessly.

Table 10-1 shows physical, psychological, and behavioral manifestations of some common drivers. The author of the table suggests that drivers give rise to physical manifestations, internal discounts or beliefs, and specific word uses and tones, as well as gestures, postures, and facial expressions. The internal discounts or beliefs are silent sentences a person says over and over that maintain low self-esteem. A helper can recognize the manifestations of a driver in a client by the behaviors associated with it.

Irrational Beliefs

Irrational beliefs are self-destructive ideas about ourselves that lead to low self-esteem (Daly & Burton, 1983). They cause us to suffer emotionally, but are so firmly entrenched that they are difficult to challenge and expunge. Albert Ellis (1973) ascribes low self-esteem to a set of "nutty beliefs" about ourselves and the world. It is not our experiences that keep us in a state of low self-esteem, but our ideas that hold us there. For example, Ellis asserts that it is not a black cat that makes us afraid but the belief that a black cat causes bad luck. Similarly, if we rid ourselves of irrational beliefs and develop more realistic ones, we relieve ourselves of emotional turmoil. Although we each probably have something unique about our belief systems, Ellis found that most people's irrational ideas fall into some broad categories; he has identified seven of the most common. These include:

1. The idea that it is a dire necessity for an adult human to be loved or approved of by virtually every significant other person in his or her life.
2. The idea that one should be thoroughly competent, adequate, and achieving in all possible respects to consider oneself worthwhile.

Table 10-1
Drivers: Sources of Negative Self-Image

| Drivers | Compliance (Inner Feelings) | | | Important Behavior | | | |
	Physical	Psychological: Internal Discount	Words	Tones	Gestures	Posture	Facial Expressions
Be perfect	Tense	"You should do better."	"Of course." "Obviously." "Efficacious." "Clearly." "I think."	Clipped, righteous	Counting on fingers, cocked wrist, scratching head	Erect, rigid	Stern
Try hard	Tight stomach, tense shoulders	"You've got to try harder."	"It's hard." "I can't." "I'll try." "I don't know."	Impatient	Clenched, moving fists	Sitting forward, elbows on legs	Slight frown, perplexed look
Please me	Tight stomach	"You're not good enough."	"You know." "Could you." "Can you." "Kinda."	High whine	Hands outstretched	Head nodding	Raised eyebrows, looks away
Hurry up	Antsy	"You'll never get it done."	"We've got to hustle."	Up and down	Squirms, taps fingers	Moving quickly	Frowning, eyes shifty
Be strong	Numb, rigid	"You can't let them know you're weak."	"No comment." "I don't care."	Hard monotone	Hands rigid, arms folded	Rigid, one leg over	Plastic, hard, cold

Source: "Driver Chart" in "The Miniscript" by Taibi Kahler from *Transactional Analysis After Eric Berne.* Copyright © 1977 by Graham Barnes. Reprinted by permission of Harper Collins Publishers.

3. The idea that certain people are bad, wicked, or villainous and that they should be severely blamed or punished for their villainy.

4. The idea that it is awful and catastrophic when things are not the way one would like them to be.

5. The idea that human unhappiness is externally caused and that people have little or no ability to control their terrors and disturbances.

6. The idea that it is easier to avoid life's difficulties and self-responsibilities than to face them.

7. The idea that one's past history is an all-important determinant of one's present behavior, and that because something once strongly affected one's life, it should definitely continue to do so (Ellis, 1973, p. 37).

Body Image

Psychological literature tells us that attractiveness is a valuable social asset (Adams, 1977) and that feeling unattractive is often equated with low self-esteem (Greenspan, 1983). Those with high self-worth generally feel good about their bodies. Those who do not like their bodies tend to be negative about themselves as a whole. An individual may have a negative *body image* because of a physical disability, a difference, or a lack of attractiveness by media standards. On the other hand, a distorted body image is a common symptom of many psychological syndromes, especially eating disorders, resulting in the evaluation that one is fat or unattractive despite evidence to the contrary (Baird & Sights, 1986). The belief that one must be perfect is probably behind this powerful dissatisfaction that propels starvation, causes self-induced vomiting in extreme cases, and engenders low self-esteem, anger, and distress even in those without major emotional problems (Thompson & Thompson, 1986). To deal with the perfectionism associated with body image, helpers have adopted strategies such as the following:

1. Asking the client to describe the perfect body and then to compare his or her own body to this description. The client is confronted with the fact that the self-description is not far from the ideal.

2. Helping the client to focus on aspects or positive qualities of the self that do not require a perfect physical appearance.

3. Having the client describe childhood experiences that involved the importance of appearance, from early memories to parental statements and asking the client to be specific and to identify those individuals from whom this learning took place. If clients realize that their tendency to emphasize physical attractiveness actually comes from early influences of significant others, it may lead them to reevaluate and ask themselves if appearance is really that important.

Stop and Reflect

One way to increase self-esteem is to ask clients to pay more attention to their strengths and abilities. Because helping is a profession in which results are not often immediate, even helpers need to pause and reflect on their accomplishments from time to time. Take this moment to reflect on your own personal assets.

A Self-Esteem Personal Inventory

1. Write down eight personal characteristics that you are proud of—for example, you may be creative, organized, humorous, goal-oriented, and so on.
2. List eight things that you do well.
3. Write down a few compliments about yourself that you hear from friends and family. What are the good things people say about you?
4. List three occasions when you felt that you had truly helped another person.
5. List the top three accomplishments of your life so far.
6. Write down three things that you like about your body.
- When you have completed this exercise, conduct a brief scan of your emotional state. Do you notice any difference in the way you feel?
- Were there any answers you felt reluctant to write down? Were you apprehensive about "bragging"? What are the rules in your own family or culture governing when it is all right to give yourself a compliment?
- If you were given this assignment as a client, how do you think you might react to it?
- Which question was the most difficult to answer? Why? If you had been asked to list your negative qualities, would it have been easier or more difficult?

Defense Mechanisms: Guardians of Self-Esteem

Defense mechanisms are psychological techniques designed to reduce anxiety and protect self-esteem (see Table 10-2). Excessive use of defense mechanisms is considered unhealthy since, by definition, they avoid or distort reality rather than help us cope with it. Defense mechanisms may not be all bad, though. Denial, for instance, has been found to be quite useful in the beginning stages of coping with death and calamities such as hurricanes and floods (Grayson, 1986; Lazarus & Golden, 1981; Lazarus & Folkman, 1984). Defense mechanisms may serve to pace or slow down the experience of anxiety so that individuals are not forced to face more arousal than they can cope with at that time (Epstein, 1983).

Helping Clients Recognize Defense Mechanisms

It is important for helpers to recognize when a client is using defense mechanisms to distort rather than deal with reality. A client who does not accept the death of a spouse, the loss of a job, or the consequences of a divorce is unable to move on and deal with life's new challenges. The major method for confronting clients with defensive reactions is a blend of reflecting meaning and confrontation (that is, to make a suggestion about the reason for the client's behavior and at the same time focus on the unproductive nature of the behavior). Two helper responses that reflect meaning and confront defensive maneuvers are given here:

Helper's Response to Compensation: "Because your sister was so good in school, you decided to excel in sports. (reflection of meaning) Now I'm wondering whether your belief that you are no good at academics is entirely accurate or something you just didn't develop." (confrontation)

Helper's Response to Avoidance/Withdrawal: "It sounds to me as if you have decided to give up on the relationship because you have been hurt before. (reflection of meaning) Even though you don't know what might come of it, you'd rather stop now and avoid the potential pain. Is that right?" (confrontation)

In summary, client defensive responses are designed to preserve self-esteem, but they typically trade growth for safety. The helper must not always insist on growth, but should bring defensiveness into the client's awareness and let the client decide how to proceed. Setting viable goals and examining defended areas is necessary, as the examples illustrate. Defenses serve a purpose, though: to maintain and support self-esteem. They should not be callously exposed to ridicule, but deliberately and respectfully explored.

Other Self-Protective Strategies

Self-handicapping is a strategy involving attributing all failures to one's handicap, such as "I am an alcoholic" or "I have test anxiety," and attributing all successes to the self. Believing that one has a disability, one can avoid labeling himself or herself as stupid or lazy (Smith, Snyder, & Handelman, 1981; Tucker, Vuchinich, & Sobell, 1981). Those using self-handicapping strategies should be encouraged to become aware of strengths and confronted when the helper feels the label is being used to avoid changing.

Learned helplessness refers to an attitude of acceptance, demoralization, and unwillingness to try in what appear to be unalterable circumstances, because of a person's previous experiences, even if change may now be possible (Seligman, 1975).

Table 10-2

Some Common Defense Mechanisms and Their Functions

Defense Mechanism	Function in Maintaining Self-Esteem
Avoidance/withdrawal	Escaping responsibility (No attempt, no failure)
Denial	Refusing to admit to problems
Fantasy	Imagining self as powerful and achieving
Substance abuse	Creating grandiose and powerful self-image
Rationalization	Denying failure by giving excuses
Projection	Denying negative traits and feelings in the self and ascribing them to others
Compensation	Denying inferiority by achieving in other areas.

For example, victims of domestic violence often feel that their situation is hopeless because attempts to change the circumstances have been thwarted for so long. They reach a point where they no longer believe that another kind of life is possible. Helping such individuals may be frustrating for the helper who has not experienced such hopeless circumstances. Out of their own frustration, helpers may try to confront such clients too early. Patience, support, empathy, and exposure to others who have made significant changes are the most important factors in changing people's views of themselves as helpless.

In a similar vein, seeing oneself as a victim is usually the result either of a lifetime of neglect or abuse or of sudden, catastrophic events. This view of the self helps the person survive, but it also keeps the person stuck. Helping those who have suffered tragedies is a long-term project. Beyond initial crisis intervention, the stages of the victim's experience, including feelings of anxiety, depression, and rage, must be taken step by step. For some events, such as the death of a child or sexual assault, no time limit can be assigned to the mourning and recovery period. But certainly a point comes when the client must release the role of victim in order to grow. Instead of blaming others or engaging in self-recrimination, he or she must begin to consider the future. It does not mean that he or she forgets about the event, but instead the client begins to see himself or herself as a survivor and to take responsibility for making personal changes.

Methods for Developing Self-Esteem

Silencing the Internal Critic: The Technique of Countering

Before one can experience self-worth, it is often necessary to silence the internal critic, the "voice in the head" that reproaches and finds fault. This critic is probably created early in life through the learning of irrational beliefs and drivers (McKay & Fanning, 1987). These irrational beliefs and drivers persist later in life as silent sentences that the individual repeats in the mind and sometimes even aloud. These thoughts tend to occur automatically. For example, before giving a speech, the following thought might occur: "I am going to get up and make a fool of myself." These negative thoughts lead to negative emotions of anger, depression, and lowered expectations of the self. Thus, before self-esteem can be built, it is often necessary to reduce the power of the internal critic and to modify these self-statements (Dowd, 1985).

How to Counter

The technique of *countering* is selected as an intervention when the helper and client have determined that the client's emotional turmoil can be lessened by reducing negative self-talk. Countering consists of identifying the discouraging or self-downing statements the client says to himself or herself, and replacing them with equally powerful affirmations. The countering method has several steps:

Step 1: Do a Brief Assessment

Once helper and client have agreed that negative self-talk is a problem, it is critical to determine the frequency of the negative self-statements and their effects on the client. For this purpose, ask the client to engage in self-assessment or self-monitoring activities to determine the frequency and types of self-downing behavior. Typically, the client carries an index card in a pocket, wallet, or purse and notes each time a self-criticism occurs. The client writes down the exact words of each self-criticism and the associated negative emotions.

The self-criticism card serves two functions: it gives client and helper more data about the problem, and it helps the client make the connection between negative self-statements and the feeling states they produce. The client can begin to see that instead of providing valid criticisms, the internal monologue is producing negative emotions.

Step 2: Identify the Negative Thought Patterns and Core Beliefs

Once the client has completed at least a week's worth of self-monitoring, the major negative thought patterns and core beliefs about the self may be identified from the compiled results of the self-monitoring task. Together, helper and client look at the self-monitoring material and choose a few negative patterns to focus on. Often three or four general ideas come to the surface—for example:

> "I am not disciplined and never get anything accomplished."
> "I am disorganized."
> "I'll never be able to reach my goals."

Step 3: Identify Effective Counters

Countering is a term coined by McMullin (1986) to describe the production of a self-statement that is incompatible with the critical thought. The counter can be a phrase, a sentence, or a single word such as "Nonsense." The counter is a way of talking back to oneself and disputing the self-criticism. The best counters are those that fit the client's values and philosophy; hence the need for a good understanding of the client's world view.

Together client and helper brainstorm a number of possible counters, and the client selects several to try. An example of a self-criticism and the list of counters generated by client and helper follows:

Self-Criticism	Counters
"I am stupid."	1. "I have always performed well in school; there's no evidence for this."
	2. "Feeling stupid doesn't mean I am stupid."
	3. "That's something my dad always told me. But it's not true!"
	4. "Not true!"

Step 4: Test Counters and Modify Them

The final stage in the process of eliminating self-criticism is to evaluate the effectiveness of the counters that the individual has practiced since the last helping session. The client will likely need more than one week to feel a sense of effectiveness, since much self-criticism takes place without full awareness. In a short time, the client should be able to identify an effective counter or two for each core belief. It must be emphasized that there is a great deal of individuality as to which counters will be effective.

One method for evaluating the effectiveness of a counter is for the helper to practice the countering technique with the client. First, the client selects a statement from a list of self-criticisms and reads it aloud to the helper. After making the self-criticism, the client rates his or her emotional reaction to the criticism on a 100-point SUDS (subjective units of discomfort scale). On the SUDS, 100 equals high emotional distress and 0 equals no emotional distress. Next, the client reads a counter from the list that was brainstormed earlier and again rates his or her feelings of distress. In the following example below, the client learns that this self-criticism is very disturbing (with a SUDS score of 80) and that the counter is very effective because it reduces the strength of the emotional reaction to about 20.

Self-Criticism	Counter
"I am stupid."	"I have always performed well in school; there's no evidence for this."
SUDS after self-criticism—80	SUDS after counter—20

Problems and Precautions When Teaching Countering

Ineffective counters should be discarded, and the client should be prepared for the fact that some counters are more potent than others. The client can be asked to modify the counter slightly in any way that might refine it or make it more effective. The helper should also suggest any personal words or phrases that might cue more self-confidence. For example, one client found that introducing each counter with "Clearly . . . " gave the counter more power for her.

Counters should be realistic. They should not be simply positive thinking or "affirmations," but should actually dispute the negative ideas. A statement such as "Every day in every way, I'm getting better and better" is a pep talk without real substance; it is not tied to any particular self-criticism. Some negative self-statements are quite persistent, and it may take months to eliminate insidious automatic thoughts. For this reason, helping may have to include follow-up visits to check on progress.

McMullin (1986) suggests that the counter should be in the same mode as the thought it is disputing. Negative visual images should be countered with positive visual images; angry thoughts should be countered with compassionate ones, and "passive thoughts with assertive ones" (p. 5). Also, shorter counters tend to be more effective than longer ones.

A Variation on Countering: Thought Stopping

Sometimes clients are troubled by unwanted thoughts and images that create anxiety and depression and damage self-esteem. Unwanted thoughts and images may be memories of failure or concern about upcoming events. Compared to the developing of counters, *thought stopping* can be considered more of an emergency measure to halt the flow of negative messages. The helper teaches the client the technique in the office, and the client practices it whenever a severely disturbing thought arises. Three steps in the thought-stopping technique have been identified (Davis, Eshelman, & McKay, 1980; Lazarus, 1971; Witmer, 1985):

1. Stating the thought.
2. Creating a startling interruption.
3. Replacing the thought.

Once the thought has been identified, the client is asked to label and state it either mentally or aloud——for example, "I am seeing her laughing at me again." This repetition brings the thought into clearer focus.

The client then creates a startling response strong enough to interrupt the negative thinking pattern. One practical method when practicing thought stopping privately is to yell "Stop!" as loud as possible. In public, it is best to use "the tongue of thought" by saying "Stop!" mentally. Some helpers suggest wearing a rubber band around the wrist, snapping it along with a mental "Stop!" to produce the interruption.

The final step is to insert a positive thought to replace the irrational, self-downing thought. This can be either a spontaneous or a planned counter that the client produces to counteract the negative thought.

Assertiveness Training

Assertiveness training is a term that became popular in the 1970s (Alberti & Emmons, 1974; Rathus, 1975; Smith, 1975). *Assertiveness* refers to a broad set of social skills used to enhance self-esteem. It has been used successfully with a wide variety of client concerns, including marriage problems, depression, sexual dysfunction, aggressive behavior, substance abuse, and dependency, as well as raising low-self esteem (Enns, 1996; Gambrill, 1985; Tanner & Holliman, 1988).

Recently, the term *assertiveness training* has been replaced with *social-skills training*. This change reflects a recognition that assertion is not as simple as standing up for one's rights or saying no; rather, it includes other positive interpersonal skills such as self-disclosure. Today, when we speak about assertiveness training, we are talking about educational programs that include specific combinations of a number of social skills, depending on the needs of the person or group. The training may include the following:

Giving and receiving compliments

Greeting others and initiating conversation

Refusing requests and saying no

Disclosing oneself to others and developing intimacy

Asking for information

Asserting beliefs, preferences, requests, and rights (Witmer, 1985)

Ineffective social behavior can be classified as either submissive (nonassertive) or aggressive (Alberti, 1977). Assertiveness is usually described as falling in the middle of a continuum between these two poles. Although it may be educationally useful to explain assertiveness as a compromise between submission and dominance, and as a counterbalancing of one's own needs and those of others, it has been found that assertiveness is also very situation-specific. A woman who is a very assertive director of a large business may be very nonassertive with her parents. Therefore, clients in assertiveness training should be exposed to some general principles, but they should also have the opportunity to work within specific situations in which they have difficulty. Assertiveness training for individuals and groups includes some common components; which we will discuss next.

Assertive Verbal Behaviors

One of the most basic assertive behaviors you can teach clients is to use the word *I* instead of *you*. When we use *I* at the beginning of a statement such as "I am bothered by your smoking," we take responsibility for the statement and, at the same time, avoid a "you-statement" that might place blame or make the other person defensive. Other examples of "I-statements" include:

"I disagree with you" rather than "You are wrong."

"I get angry when . . . " rather than "You make me angry."

"May I have one of those programs?" rather than "You forgot me."

Help your clients understand also that different levels of assertion are needed for different situations. At the first level, a polite request is attempted: "I'm having trouble hearing the movie; would you mind speaking more quietly?" Notice that the request describes the situation in nonjudgmental terms and specifies what is wanted of the other person. If the assertive request does not have the desired effect, it may be necessary to increase the power of the request. This is done by adding feelings to the polite request, as in the following statement: "I feel very uncomfortable when you tell racist jokes, and I wish you wouldn't." In extreme situations, it may be necessary to indicate the consequences if the behavior continues—for example, "I find this situation with my stereo very frustrating because I have had to bring it back for repairs on three occasions, and I would like you to refund my money. If you don't, I will talk to the manager about this."

A quick way of remembering the components of a verbal assertive response is the DERC system. *D* stands for describing in a nonjudgmental way. *E* stands for expressing your feelings or the way in which the other person's behavior is affecting you. *R* is making a request, and *C* is specifying the consequences if the person does not change the behavior. In the preceding example of the stereo, all four of these components are exemplified. The use of the final step, specifying consequences, is one that should be used mainly as a last resort, since indicating the action you will take will arouse defenses and might be seen only as a bluff. Most assertive responses should describe the situation nonjudgmentally, express feelings or the effects of the situation, and end with a request.

Assertive Nonverbal Behaviors

Remind clients that many body postures reflect assertiveness or nonassertiveness.

Eye Contact   Maintaining direct eye contact is an effective way of expressing sincerity. In the United States, looking away or looking down is most often interpreted as a lack of confidence or deference to the other as the authority.

Body Posture   An assertive body posture involves squarely facing the other person, sitting or standing appropriately close, and perhaps leaning forward slightly with head erect. A side-tilted head is a questioning rather than an assertive position.

Touch   Touch can be used in making a request from a close acquaintance, since it gains the attention of the listener and affirms the relationship. When denying a request, a touch can lessen the feelings of rejection.

Gestures   Gestures add emphasis to the message and can be descriptive and visually communicative. A few strong gestures that accentuate the message can be useful. On the other hand, extensive gesturing can be viewed as indication of confusion and discomfort, and thus nonassertive.

Facial Expression, Voice Tone, Inflection, and Volume   The verbal message and the facial expression should match in an assertive response. Usually, a well-modulated conversational tone accompanies assertion. Speaking softly will water down an assertive message, and a loud dominating tone of voice may seem aggressive, activating the other person's defenses.

Responding to Criticism: Helpful and Unhelpful Reactions

Knowing Your Rights

Smith (1975) states that one way to educate clients about assertiveness is to hold a discussion about "assertive rights." A discussion of this sort may encourage a client to realize that one can be polite and yet be fully justified in standing up for oneself. The following list includes some of Smith's ideas and some additional ones:

1. You have the right to change your mind.
2. You have the right to try something and make mistakes.

3. You have the right to say, "I don't know."

4. You have the right to make a request.

5. You have the right to refuse a request.

6. You have the right to refuse destructive feedback.

7. You have the right to be illogical when making decisions.

Viewing Criticism as Valuable

As a helper, encourage your clients to see criticism as valuable and not just something to tolerate. Help them learn to take a detached attitude and to find the constructive aspects of criticism, even if it is uttered in a most offensive way. In order to do this, clients must be taught to distinguish between destructive and constructive criticism. Destructive criticism tends to be global, using such words as *always* and *never*. Global statements are hard to profit from because exceptions easily leap into mind. Destructive criticism also encompasses situations in which another person tries to make us feel guilty, to manipulate us through outbursts of anger, to engage in lengthy monologues, or to resort to name calling. Finally, destructive criticism may take the form of bringing up irreconcilable issues from the past, rather than focusing on what can be changed in the present. Teach your clients to recognize these destructive forms of criticism, which can be harmful to the self-concept if accepted at face value.

More often than not, criticism contains a germ of truth that an individual may examine and benefit from. According to Egan (1990), constructive criticism:

1. Includes noticing positive as well as negative aspects of performance.

2. Is brief and specific.

3. Does not require the other person to change instantly, but acknowledges that change takes time.

4. Involves an openness to the other person's viewpoint and is stated tentatively to acknowledge this.

5. Includes a commitment to negotiate and take positive action to solve the problem.

While clients cannot expect that they will receive constructive criticism at all times, they can learn to ask for this type of feedback. In the following example, Alicia receives some destructive feedback but handles it well by asking questions, listening non-defensively, making sure her opinion is heard, and obtaining a constructive suggestion:

Boss: "Your attitude has got to change."

Alicia: "Tell me what you mean."

Boss: "You've got a bad attitude."

Alicia: "OK, can you give me an example so I can think about how to change this situation?"

Boss: "Well, yesterday when I gave you that big order to input into the computer, you sighed. You don't seem to like your job."

Alicia: "You're right, I did sigh, but I don't think that reflects my usual attitude."

Boss: "It's just that this job is really important to me and I wish everybody on the team would feel that way."

Alicia: "I understand how you feel, but I also want you to realize that I am excited about this project and I am happy on the job. Your comment was helpful, though; I don't want to appear to have a bad attitude."

Stop and Reflect

Table 10-3 contains the Rathus Assertiveness Schedule (RAS) (Rathus, 1973). The RAS is a well-known self-report inventory designed to measure assertiveness or "social boldness." It is designed to give clients feedback on their frankness. Complete the inventory for yourself and consider the questions that follow.

How to Score the RAS: Add the answers to all of the questions. For questions that have an asterisk next to them, change the valence; that is, change all negatives to positives and all positives to negatives.

Norms: The RAS was tested with undergraduates from about 17–27 years of age. The average score was about .3, with a standard deviation of approximately 29. High scores, say over 40, suggest the possible need for assertiveness training, but the best use of the instrument may be to gauge the change that takes place in assertiveness training.

- After looking at your own scores on the RAS, examine some of the individual items. Do they suggest any specific behaviors that you have difficulty with?
- What situations or behaviors does the inventory seem to neglect?
- Has this inventory changed your ideas about your view of yourself as an assertive person?
- In a small group, discuss the possible uses of an inventory such as this in assertiveness training.

How to Teach a Client to Be More Assertive

The goal of teaching a client to be more assertive—like any therapeutic goal—must be carefully established on the basis of a good working relationship with the client. Assertiveness training is best done in a classroom setting, because participants can obtain support from a group and see others practicing assertiveness. When such groups are not available, assertiveness training can be taught one-to-one in an office setting.

Table 10-3
Rathus Assertiveness Schedule

Directions: Indicate how characteristic or descriptive each of the following statements is of you by using the code given below.

+3 very characteristic of me, extremely descriptive[a]
+2 rather characteristic of me, quite descriptive
+1 somewhat characteristic of me, slightly descriptive
−1 somewhat uncharacteristic of me, slightly nondescriptive
−2 rather uncharacteristic of me, quite nondescriptive
−3 very uncharacteristic of me, extremely nondescriptive

_____ 1. Most people seem to be more aggressive and assertive than I am.*
_____ 2. I have hesitated to make or accept dates because of "shyness."*
_____ 3. When the food served at a restaurant is not done to my satisfaction, I complain about it to the waiter or waitress.
_____ 4. I am careful to avoid hurting other people's feelings, even when I feel that I have been injured.*
_____ 5. If a salesman has gone to considerable trouble to show me merchandise which is not quite suitable, I have a difficult time in saying "No."*
_____ 6. When I am asked to do something, I insist upon knowing why.
_____ 7. There are times when I look for a good, vigorous argument.
_____ 8. I strive to get ahead as well as most people in my position.
_____ 9. To be honest, people often take advantage of me.*
_____ 10. I enjoy starting conversations with new acquaintances and strangers.
_____ 11. I often don't know what to say to attractive persons of the opposite sex.*
_____ 12. I will hesitate to make phone calls to business establishments and institutions.*
_____ 13. I would rather apply for a job or for admission to a college by writing letters than by going through with personal interviews.*

Step 1: Preparing and Educating the Client

Begin by familiarizing the client with the theory behind assertiveness training, which also helps to gain his or her trust and assistance in learning the method. This preparation is based on the client's level of knowledge and the specific goal he or she is trying to accomplish. Information presented earlier in this chapter on assertive behaviors and responding to criticism may be a useful starting point. Preparation can be accomplished by the helper in the office or by homework or reading assignments.

Step 2: Boiling Down the Problem

Move on to specific areas of concern with the client; agree upon the specific assertive behaviors that would help the client feel a greater sense of confidence in a particular situation. Have the client list these behaviors in hierarchical order, based on his or her evaluation about how easy or difficult each behavior would be to perform. The general principle is that clients move from mastery of easy behaviors to more difficult ones. In the following example, a helper and client identify steps to confronting her boss.

_____ 14. I find it embarrassing to return merchandise.*
_____ 15. If a close and respected relative were annoying me, I would smother my feel-ings rather than express my annoyance.*
_____ 16. I have avoided asking questions for fear of sounding stupid.*
_____ 17. During an argument I am sometimes afraid that I will get so upset that I will shake all over.*
_____ 18. If a famed and respected lecturer makes a statement which I think is incor-rect, I will have the audience hear my point of view as well.
_____ 19. I avoid arguing over prices with clerks and salesmen.*
_____ 20. When I have done something important or worthwhile, I manage to let others know about it.
_____ 21. I am open and frank about my feelings.
_____ 22. If someone has been spreading false and bad stories about me, I see him (her) as soon as possible to "have a talk" about it.
_____ 23. I often have a hard time saying "No."*
_____ 24. I tend to bottle up my emotions rather than make a scene.*
_____ 25. I complain about poor service in a restaurant and elsewhere.
_____ 26. When I am given a compliment, I sometimes just don't know what to say.*
_____ 27. If a couple near me in a theatre or at a lecture were conversing loudly, I would ask them to be quiet or to take their conversation elsewhere.
_____ 28. Anyone attempting to push ahead of me in a line is in for a good battle.
_____ 29. I am quick to express an opinion.
_____ 30. There are times when I just can't say anything.*

[a]Total score obtained by adding numerical responses to each item, after changing the signs of re-versed items.
*Reversed item.
Source: From Rathus, S. A. (1973). A 30-item schedule for assessing assertive behavior. Behavior Therapy, 4, 398–406. Reproduced with the permission of Academic Press.

Nadine, a graphic artist, wanted to be more assertive at work. The helper, Pat, asked her to identify a specific situation that, if changed, would help her feel more confident and assertive. Nadine indicated that she would like to be able to respond more assertively to her boss's criticism, which she sees as unjustified. He normally walked by her office every morning, looked over her shoulder, then made negative comments about her work. Nadine usually said nothing, but just listened until the boss was finished. This left her feeling upset and self-critical for at least an hour.

Nadine and Pat explored and listed the kinds of assertive things she would like to do when the boss came by for an inspection. Nadine ordered them from easiest to most difficult as follows:

1. Ask the boss to go into greater detail, then consider later whether any of the boss's criticisms constituted valuable feedback.
2. Remind the boss that the idea he is criticizing is not hers.
3. Remind the boss that the design he is criticizing was approved by him.
4. Disagree with the boss's criticism but agree to change the product.
5. Disagree with the boss's criticism and politely argue for her own viewpoint.

Step 3: Present a Model of Assertive Behavior

If the client is working in a group situation, he or she will undoubtedly have the opportunity to see role-playing situations in which a person demonstrates assertive behavior. This can go a long way in easing the client's fears that assertiveness is destructive. In an individual counseling setting, you, the helper, will need to demonstrate assertive behavior for the client. For example, in working with Nadine, Pat asked Nadine to select a response on the list that she was ready to practice. Nadine selected number 1, and Pat initiated a role-play situation in which Nadine was asked to play the part of the boss and Pat explored the boss's criticism to see what constructive elements it might contain. Nadine felt that Pat's behavior was not aggressive and she said she thought she was ready to try this herself.

Step 4: Rehearsal and Feedback

Once the client has seen a positive model, he or she must rehearse assertive behavior in a role-playing situation, receiving feedback from the helper or other trainees in an assertiveness training class. At this stage, Pat arranged her office to fit Nadine's description of her workplace. Then she and Nadine role-played the morning ritual in which the boss came in and began criticizing Nadine's work. This time, Pat played the role of the boss and Nadine, in her own way, practiced listening nondefensively, searching for the constructive elements (number 1 on her list). Pat then gave her feedback on her performance, mentioning both positive behaviors and ways to improve.

Step 5: Give a Homework Assignment to Be Assertive

Homework assignments are real-life practice sessions. Normally the client and the helper choose an assertive behavior from the client's own list, beginning with the easiest one, and progressing until all behaviors have been displayed.

Pat and Nadine agreed that the next time the boss came by, she would begin to respond assertively by asking him to go into greater detail concerning his criticisms, then politely reminding him that she did not select the design. Pat suggested that the real situation might not go as smoothly as the practice session. She and Nadine talked about the possibility that the boss might not cooperate with her assertive behavior and might even leave the room. They agreed that Nadine was not to concern herself with his behavior, but was simply to begin trying out her assertive skills.

Problems and Precautions of Assertiveness Training

Sometimes clients complain that although they may look assertive (display the appropriate nonverbals), they do not feel assertive and are scared or angry during their practice of assertive behaviors. Explain that, initially, one simply tends to go through the motions before actually feeling the results. Alcoholics Anonymous has the following maxim: "Fake it 'til you make it." The saying implies that acquiring a behavior sometimes precedes positive feelings, and that one must persevere.

Occasionally clients will feel that assertiveness training is inconsistent with their values. Religious clients, in particular, may feel that they should be more selfless. Other clients may wrongly believe that the aim of assertiveness training is to turn them into very aggressive people who are only "looking out for number one." Helpers need to be sensitive to such concerns. Assertiveness can be presented as a social skill designed to ensure that both members in a relationship find satisfaction rather than dominating each other. The education phase of the method is also crucial in eliminating misconceptions that can lessen the client's willingness to participate.

Gambrill (1985) reports that assertive people are not always viewed as positively as are submissive people. This might mean that assertiveness, if aimed only at getting one's needs met or at standing up for one's rights, may have longer-term negative effects. The squeaky wheel may get the grease, as the saying goes, but it may also engender resentment. However, assertiveness training, as it is now practiced, is more likely to emphasize the use of tentativeness, politeness, and a more humble attitude, especially when dealing with longer-term relationships. Reporting a recalcitrant store clerk to the store manager may help a client stand up for his or her rights. On the other hand, placing consequences on family and friends or bosses may be counterproductive, disrupting these relationships and creating adverse consequences.

Other Methods for Assertiveness Training

Broken-Record Technique

This technique is one of the most widely taught assertive behavior sequences. It is especially useful when trying to get a point across to another person who is trying to change the topic. The method involves repeating one's feelings, needs, or major points over and over. The method is effective in situations where the message does not seem to be getting through to the other person. It is not an attempt to bully the other person into submission, but to repeat the message until it is understood. For example, consider this exchange between employee and boss:

Employee: "I think this has been a banner year for me. I have broken the company sales record and I would like a raise."

Boss: "This has not been a good year for the company as a whole. The president says we have to keep raises at 3 percent."

Employee: "I understand, but my case is different. I think I deserve a raise."

Boss: "I would like to give everybody a raise in my department."

Employee: "It would be great if everyone got a raise, but I think I have done better than the average employee and I would like a raise. Can you understand that?"

Boss: "Yes, I hear what you are saying."

Fogging

Fogging, or letting criticism go in one ear and out the other, has been a very effective method for some clients, especially when dealing with family members or others who want to give unsolicited advice or criticism. The client actively listens to the advice giver but is taught to internally dispute the criticism or ignore the suggestion. For example, a client whose family members criticized her was told to silently say the following phrase when the criticism began: "What they are saying is nonsense; I can ignore it and stay calm."

Summary

Self-esteem has two components: self-worth and efficacy. Enhancing both is critical for boosting self-esteem. Clients can learn to enhance efficacy by attempting new behaviors and by paying attention to their present strengths and skills. Low self-worth is a general attitude that the self is "not OK," worthless, or ineffective. Low self-worth is responsible for a number of serious psychological conditions and is responsible in less severe cases for a demoralized attitude toward life. We have explored causes of low self-worth and identified injunctions learned early in life, including drivers, irrational ideas, and negative body image.

In the second half of the chapter we looked at two methods for enhancing self-esteem. The first technique, called *countering*, is aimed at reducing negative self-talk or internal dialogue. The second technique, *assertiveness training*, helps to decrease criticism from others and enables people to feel more efficacious in social situations. These two techniques are fundamental to working with clients who have problems of low self-worth. They are nonetheless dependent on the helper's building an effective therapeutic relationship using the therapeutic building blocks of invitational skills, reflecting skills, advanced reflecting skills, and challenging skills. Unless the helper utilizes these building blocks, clients are unable to explore deeply held beliefs about themselves, to question them, and to consider new ways of behaving.

Group Exercises

Group Exercise 1: Identifying Irrational Beliefs

First, form groups of four with each student in turn taking on the roles of client, helper, and observers. The client discusses one of the following topics with the helper:

- A time when the client was very angry at someone.
- A time when the client was very angry at himself or herself.
- A time when someone disappointed the client.
- Something the client has a difficult time forgiving.

The helper's job is to listen, using all of the skills in the nonjudgmental listening cycle, for 5–10 minutes. He or she is not to make an effort to challenge the client's beliefs, but simply to draw them out.

Observer 1 writes down all of the helper's interventions verbatim. Observer 2 reviews the

Feedback Checklist: Assertiveness Training
Observer Name _____ Helper Name

_____

Preparing
1. Specifically, how did the helper educate and
   prepare the client for assertiveness training?
2. Was the preparation relevant to the client's
   problem?

Boiling Down the Problem
3. Did the helper boil down the problem to a specific situation for the client to work on?

Presenting a Model
4. Did the helper model an appropriate behavior
   for the client or give examples of statements
   that might be assertive alternatives to
   nonassertive client statements? If so, indicate in
   a few words how the helper did this.

Rehearsal
5. Did the client rehearse a specific behavior that
   he or she wants to work on?
   a. Did the helper give the client feedback on the
   rehearsal?
   b. Was this feedback specific and understandable to the client?
   c. How closely did the client's assertive statements mirror the DERC system described earlier in the chapter?

Homework
6. Did the helper suggest homework for the client
   to practice one of the assertive behaviors?
   a. In your estimation, how likely is the client to
   actually practice the assertive behavior?
   b. Do you think the helper should have suggested an easier or more difficult behavior to
   practice?

list of Ellis's seven irrational beliefs, described
earlier in the chapter. Then, during the session,
observer 2 listens carefully to the client's statements and records the gist of those that seem to
indicate an underlying irrational belief.

Take a couple of minutes to allow client,
helper, and observers to share their thoughts
about this exercise. Then, Observer 1 gives the
helper the list of interventions and feedback
about his or her performance on the nonjudgmental listening cycle. The helper can keep the
list of interventions and review them later. At
this point, the list of interventions should include several paraphrases, reflections of feeling,
and perhaps a reflection of meaning or two, depending on the depth of the client's story. If
questions predominate, the helper should return to previous chapters for review, and schedule additional practice sessions with classmates.

Finally, observer 2 indicates any irrational
ideas that he or she identified in the client's
statements. As a group, the helper and the two
observers can identify some counters that
might be used by the client as an antidote to
these beliefs. The client, in turn, can indicate
which counter he or she feels might be the
most effective.

Group Exercise 2: Assertiveness Training

Form groups of three. Members take turns sharing "a time in my life when I was not as assertive
as I wanted to be." In this situation, you may
have been either too passive or too aggressive.
Students take turns as helper, client, and observer. The helper should follow the general
steps for assertiveness training given in this
chapter. In the preparing and educating phase,
be sure to help the client understand the components of an assertive response according to
the DERC system. The observer fills out the
Feedback Checklist for the helper, giving examples of the various steps.

Quick Tips: Assertiveness Training

- When preparing a client, there is no need
  to do a complete overview of the field of
  assertiveness; instead focus on some
  ideas that will help the client with this
  particular problem.
- Preview the technique. Tell the client the
  steps that you are going to go through.

- Emphasize that assertiveness is a skill, not a personality trait. Anyone can learn to be more assertive.
- Show enthusiasm, but indicate that changing to more assertive behavior will be hard work and will feel unnatural at first.
- Feel free to shift gears during the training and return to the nonjudgmental listening cycle if the client needs to talk about the issues, but eventually return to the training sequence.
- Make a hierarchy of the client's assertive behaviors and try to take small steps rather than attack the big issues right away.

Additional Exercises

Exercise 1: Confronting Defense Mechanisms

Form groups of four or five. Review the section on defense mechanisms and the sections on learned helplessness, victimization, and self-handicapping. As a group, devise a role play in which the client uses defensive mechanisms in a self-defeating way or shows other self-protective strategies. Present your role play to the class. The student who plays the helper in this exercise should utilize invitational and reflecting skills initially, but should move very quickly to challenging skills. In the class discussion, make a list of discrepancies in the client's story.

Exercise 2

In small groups, conduct a discussion on the dangers of assertiveness training. From your experience, do you think that during initial training, clients should be warned that they might tend to go overboard and become aggressive when they practice? How important is it for an assertive statement to be polite? Does politeness water down the force of an assertive statement?

Exercise 3

Look at the example in the section on the broken-record technique, in which an employee and a boss are engaged in negotiations over a raise. Was the employee's verbal behavior assertive as judged by the DERC system? If not, how might it be improved? See if you can identify some alternate employee responses that would be too polite or nonassertive and some that represent the other end of the scale—too aggressive.

Homework

Homework 1: Personal Experiments

Think about something you don't do very well, or think about a part of your body that you do not feel is very attractive. Get opinions from eight friends or family members. How accurate is your self-concept? If they do not agree, why do you cling to this belief? In what ways have you distorted your view of the self? Write a half-page reaction to this exercise.

Homework 2: Assertiveness Script Writing

One way that clients can rehearse assertiveness is to write out "scripts" or imaginary conversations with someone with whom they would like to be assertive. Think about a situation in your own life and write out what you would like to say. Write the other person's likely responses, even if you believe the person will not grant your request or appreciate your feelings. Remember that your initial goal is to respond in the way you would like, in a caring but firm way. Next, make a second version of your script, improving your statements to make them clearer. Give a copy of your script to a classmate for feedback on the effectiveness of your assertive responses.

References

Adams, G. R. (1977). Physical attractiveness research: Toward a developmental social psychology of beauty. *Human Development, 20,* 217–239.

Alberti, R. E. (Ed.) (1977). *Assertiveness: Innovations, applications, issues.* San Luis Obispo, CA: Impact.

Alberti, R. E., & Emmons, M. L. (1974). *Your perfect right: A guide to assertive behavior.* San Luis Obispo, CA: Impact.

Baird, P., & Sights, J. R. (1986). Low self-esteem as a treatment issue in the psychology of anorexia and bulimia. *Journal of Counseling and Development, 64,* 449–451.

Bandura, A. (1982). Self-efficacy mechanism in human agency. *American Psychologist, 37,* 122–147.

Berne, E. (1972). *What do you say after you say hello?* New York: Grove Press.

Branden, N. (1969). *The psychology of self-esteem.* Los Angeles, CA: Nash.

Branden, N. (1971). *The disowned self.* New York: Bantam Books.

Brehm, M., & Back, W. (1968). Self image and attitude towards drugs. *Journal of Personality, 36,* 299–314.

Daly, M. J., & Burton, R. L. (1983). Self-esteem and irrational beliefs: An exploratory investigation with implications for counseling. *Journal of Counseling Psychology, 30,* 361–366.

Davis, M., Eshelman, E. R., & McKay, M. (1980). *The relaxation and stress reduction workbook.* Richmond, CA: New Harbinger.

Dowd, E. T. (1985). Self statement modification. In A. S. Bellack & M. Hersen, *Dictionary of behavior therapy techniques* (p. 200). New York: Pergamon.

Egan, G. (1990). *The skilled helper* (4th ed.). Pacific Grove, CA: Brooks/Cole.

Ellis, A. (1973). *Humanistic psychotherapy.* New York: McGraw-Hill.

Enns, C. Z., (1996). Self-esteem groups: A synthesis of consciousness-raising and assertiveness training. *Journal of Counseling and Development, 71,* 7–13.

Epstein, S. (1983). Natural healing processes of the mind: Gradual stress inoculation as an inherent coping mechanism. In D. Meichenbaum & M. S. Jaremko (Eds.), *Stress reduction and prevention* (pp. 39–65). New York: Plenum Press.

Frey, D., & Carlock, C. J. (1989). *Enhancing self-esteem* (2nd ed.). Muncie, IN: Accelerated Development.

Gambrill, E. (1985). Assertiveness training. In A. S. Bellack & M. Hersen (Eds.), *Dictionary of behavior therapy techniques* (pp. 7–9). New York: Pergamon.

Grayson, P. A. (1986). Disavowing the past: A maneuver to protect self-esteem. *Individual Psychology: Adlerian Theory, Research and Practice, 42,* 330–338.

Greenspan, M. (1983). *A new approach to women and therapy.* New York: McGraw-Hill.

Ingham, J. G., Kreitman, N. B., Miller, P. M., & Sasidharan, S. P. (1986). Self-esteem, vulnerability and psychiatric disorder in the community. *British Journal of Psychiatry, 148,* 373–385.

Kahler, T. (1977). The miniscript. In G. Barnes (Ed.), *Transactional analysis after Eric Berne* (pp. 220–241). New York: Harpers College Press.

Kurpius, D., Rockwood, G. F., & Corbett, M. O. (1989). Attributional styles and self-esteem:

Implications for counseling. *Counseling and Human Development, 21,* (8), 1–12.

Lazarus, A. A. (1971). *Behavior therapy and beyond.* New York: McGraw-Hill.

Lazarus, R. S., & Folkman, S. (1984). *Stress, appraisal, and coping.* New York: Springer.

Lazarus, R. S., & Golden, G. (1981). The function of denial in stress, coping and aging. In E. McGarraugh & S. Kiessler (Eds.), *Biology, behavior and aging.* New York: Academic Press.

McKay, M., & Fanning, P. (1987). *Self-esteem.* Oakland, CA: New Harbinger.

McMullin, R. E. (1986). *Handbook of cognitive therapy techniques.* New York: W. W. Norton.

Rathus, S. A. (1973). A 30-item schedule for assessing assertive behavior. *Behavior Therapy, 4,* 398–406.

Rathus, S. A. (1975). Principles and practices of assertiveness training: An eclectic overview. *The Counseling Psychologist, 5,* 9–20.

Rosenberg, M. (1962). The association between self-esteem and anxiety. *Journal of Psychiatric Research, 1,* 135–152.

Seligman, M. E. P. (1975). *Helplessness: On depression, development, and death.* New York: W. H. Freeman.

Smith, M. J. (1975). *When I say no, I feel guilty.* New York: Bantam.

Smith, T. W., Snyder, C. R., & Handelman, M. M. (1981). On the self-serving function of an academic wooden leg: Test anxiety as a self-handicapping strategy. *Journal of Personality and Social Psychology, 42,* 314–321.

Tanner, V. L., & Holliman, W. B. (1988). Effectiveness of assertiveness training in modifying aggressive behaviors in young children. *Psychological Reports, 62,* 39–46.

Thompson, J. K., & Thompson, C. M. (1986). Body size distortion and self-esteem in asymptomatic, normal weight males and females. *International Journal of Eating Disorders, 5,* 1061–1068.

Tucker, J. A., Vuchinich, R. E., & Sobell, M. B. (1981). Alcohol consumption as a self-handicapping strategy. *Journal of Abnormal Psychology, 90,* 220–230.

Walz, G. (1990). *Counseling for self-esteem.* Alexandria, VA: American Association for Counseling and Development.

Wilson, A., & Krane, R. (1980). Change in self-esteem and its effect on symptoms of depression. *Cognitive Therapy and Research, 4,* 419–421.

Witmer, J. M. (1985). *Pathways to personal growth: Developing a sense of worth and competence.* Muncie, IN: Accelerated Development.

Practicing New Behaviors

Introduction

T he third curative factor in the REPLAN system is practicing new behaviors (see Figure 11-1). Anyone who has ever learned to play a musical instrument or gained proficiency in a sport knows the value of practice. Practice is also an integral part of any educational curriculum. Besides the fact that practice helps to perfect a skill, it is also the key to success in making a change permanent. What is uncomfortable at first becomes second nature through practice.

Helping can also be conceived of as a learning process (Guerney, Stollack, & Guerney, 1971; Schutz, 1981; Young & Rosen, 1985). Clients often need to learn behaviors such as better parenting, communication skills, facing fearful situations, or developing effective thinking skills. As an educator, the helper cannot be content with helping the client to eliminate a problem behavior or merely to gain insight into the fact that he or she is operating in a self-defeating manner. Clients must overcome the force of old habits by establishing a new pattern of behaviors through practice.

The best instruction for any skill includes the following sequence: (1) some theory is explained that provides a rationale for learning the new skill; (2) the learner is exposed to a model who correctly demonstrates the skill; and (3) in-class practice and homework assignments promote acquisition of the new skill. For example, if you were learning to play the guitar, the instructor might explain the fingering using a

Figure 11-1
Curative factors in the REPLAN system: Practicing new behaviors

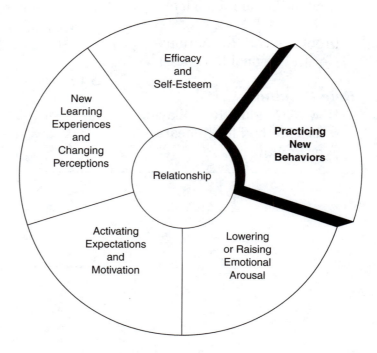

chart or graph. Then the instructor would probably demonstrate how the piece is to be played, or you might listen to a recording of the selection. You would then attempt the music with the instructor present and later you would be sent home to practice. The process of acquiring a new behavior or a new thinking pattern with a helper takes place in much the same way.

In taking these steps during instruction, helpers use special techniques to help clients practice skills learned in the helping process. In this chapter we will look at three of these special techniques: imaginal rehearsal, role playing, and homework. These three techniques exist on a continuum, with imaginal rehearsal being an exclusively mental practice, role playing being closer to real life, and homework or independent practice being the final step. The helper must select the level of practice that the client needs, based on the client's readiness. Clients who cannot see themselves attempting a new behavior will benefit from imagining a successful performance first. Then they can move to the next level of practice, role playing, with the helper present. Finally, they are ready to try out a new behavior in a natural situation as a homework assignment.

Imagery

Images are "pictures in the head" that we produce as we remember or imagine the future. We use images every day to give directions, to rearrange the furniture, or to think about someone we love. Imagery in the helping professions has become more popular in recent years. After a long period of neglect it is now used for a variety of purposes (Gladding, 1986).

In this section, we will discuss the use of imagery as a means of rehearsal. If imagery as rehearsal or practice seems strange to you, think about how Olympic divers on the 3-meter board go through the preparation for a dive. Typically they close their eyes and imagine the twists and turns they must make. Sometimes they even display minor muscle movements that mimic the dive they are imagining. When practiced regularly, imagery has been found to enhance performance in a variety of situations, from shooting foul shots in basketball to learning how to give a public talk (Fezler, 1989).

Mental, or *imaginal,* rehearsal has sometimes been termed "covert rehearsal" (Bellack, 1986; Kazdin, 1978). The term *covert* in this context means "hidden" or "invisible," as contrasted with the term *in vivo,* which means "behaviorally" or "in real life." Imaginal rehearsal allows a client to practice a skill when live practice is not feasible (Cautela & Bennet, 1981). Live practice may not be possible because the client's emotional state is such that confronting the real-life situation would be too stressful or the opportunity for practice in a real situation is not available on a regular basis. Imaginal rehearsal can be accomplished in minutes, may be repeated several times in a therapeutic session, and can also be assigned as homework.

Besides practicing new behaviors, imagery techniques have been used to help clients plan for the future, enhance career development, gain control over undesirable behavior, treat physical illness, improve memory, reduce stress, and increase creativity and problem solving in everyday living (Pope, 1982; Sheikh, 1983; Witmer & Young, 1985, 1987). A few examples of client problems currently treated with imagery show its range. These include bulimia (Gunnison & Renick, 1985), career indecision (Sarnoff & Remer, 1982; Skovholt, Morgan, & Negron-Cunningham, 1989), post-traumatic stress disorder (Grigsby, 1987), and parenting decision making (Skovholt & Thoen, 1987).

Stop and Reflect

Take a few minutes to close your eyes and imagine the following scenes, one by one:

Group A

1. A bowl of fruit that has just been taken out of the refrigerator, with moisture condensing on the surface, on a table
2. The place where you live, starting with the front door and moving through all of the rooms

Group B

1. The sound of an engine starting
2. The cry of seagulls or the sounds birds make in the morning

Group C

1. The smell of food frying
2. Leaning over and smelling a rose

Group D

1. The feel of a warm shower
2. A pin prick on your finger

Group E

1. The taste of a lemon being squeezed into your mouth
2. The taste of dark chocolate

- People differ in their visualizing ability. Some of us cannot imagine or sustain an image in our minds. This is not a handicap, but an individual difference. Clients who have little ability to imagine will not benefit much from imaginal rehearsal. Of the 10 preceding scenes, how many were you able to imagine clearly?

- Each group in the preceding list represents a different sense modality: A, sight; B, hearing; C, smell; D, touch; and E, taste. Go back and rate each image on a 10-point scale indicating how vivid it was for you. A 1 indicates very fuzzy imagery and a 10 indicates very clear and vivid imagery. Do you find any differences among the groups A through E in terms of what you can imagine? If you were a client, which sensory modality could a helper use most effectively with you?

How to Conduct Imaginal Rehearsal

Step 1: Identify the Target Behaviors

The first task of the client and the helper is to cooperatively transform the client's goal into a list of skills (target behaviors) that are required to perform the desired task successfully. For example, Danielle would like to be able to ask someone out for a date, but she is uncomfortable since she is recently divorced and has not dated for several years. She and the helper, Ben, break the skill into the following components:

1. Dialing the phone.
2. Greeting Tom (a co-worker she has become interested in)
3. Describing an outdoor jazz concert she would like him to attend with her
4. Asking Tom to join her at the concert
5. Politely ending the call

Those who are adept at social skills might find the preceeding list simplistic and rather clinical. It may come as a surprise to know that helpers are commonly asked by clients to help them acquire elementary social skills such as making small talk, telling friends how they feel about them, or asking for a raise. Having a script like Danielle's can significantly reduce anxiety for someone who is trying an unfamiliar activity. It prepares him or her for various consequences and instills confidence.

Step 2: Prepare the Client for Imagery

Imaginal rehearsal is ideally performed in a quiet environment, away from glaring lights, with eyes closed. The helper may reassure the client that the technique is not hypnosis but an active rehearsal process. The purpose is explained as a method of learning to avoid or eliminate negative images of failure and to develop positive, successful ones. Talking with Danielle, for example, Ben explains that she is not simply trying to get a date. The real goal is to develop the social skills that will make her more comfortable and effective in similar situations in the future.

Step 3: Help the Client Imagine Each of the Target Behaviors

Remind the client of the first target behavior on the list and instruct him or her to visualize performing it in a specific situation where it is likely to be needed. Then ask the client to visualize each successive target behavior in turn, moving ahead only when the client can produce a vivid image. For example, in the preceding list, Ben asks Danielle if she can imagine sitting on her bed dialing Tom's number. When she is able to clearly imagine this scene, Ben directs her to imagine greeting Tom on the phone. Client and helper move through the whole scenario step by step. During this process, it is important to carry on a dialogue with the client to make certain that the client has a clear understanding of target behavior and can vividly imagine it. This is a stop-and-go procedure, during which the helper is testing to make sure the client can imagine successfully completing each individual skill.

Step 4: Guide the Client in Imagining a Successful Sequence of Behaviors

Once the steps for performing all of the target behaviors have been visualized, guide the client through the entire sequence again, this time without stopping. Describe the sequence in the present tense as if telling a story. For example, Ben says to Danielle, "It is late afternoon on Saturday and you decide to call Tom. You go to your bedroom with a glass of water in case your mouth gets dry. You look up Tom's number and dial it. When he answers, you say, 'Hi, Tom, this is Danielle, how are you?' When he responds, you tell him a little bit about the jazz concert next Friday night. You tell him it is outdoors and you thought it might be fun. You say you are wondering if he is free to come along." At this point, Ben asks Danielle to rehearse two different endings. In the first scenario, Ben suggests she imagine the following: "Tom apologizes and says he can't come. You say, 'Oh, too bad, maybe another time. I'll see you at work next week, okay?' " In a second scenario, Ben instructs her to imagine that Tom says yes. In that case, Danielle arranges a time and a place for their meeting.

Step 5: Provide the Client with an Imagined Reward

At the end of the first complete visualization, give the client a covert reinforcement, or imagined reward, to reinforce the sequence of behaviors. For example, in both scenarios, Ben instructs Danielle to imagine herself sitting on the bed after hanging up, congratulating herself for having made the call, and feeling good about having practiced a difficult new skill.

Problems and Precautions with Imaginal Rehearsal

1. While the focus of the imagery technique is on positive future performance, memories of past failures occasionally intrude. Imagery tends to evoke a much fuller experience of remembered events than simply talking about them. Some clients may be overwhelmed by these feelings and may require support from the helper if the imagery involves painful events from the past. This is your cue to ask the client to open his or her eyes, and then to shift gears and return to the nonjudgmental listening cycle.

2. Clients differ in their capacity to produce imagery. The ability of individuals to produce vivid images can be tested and improved by methods described by Lazarus (1977). In our experience, about 10% of clients in group settings report an inability to sustain mental imagery long enough for helping purposes. Some clients feel inadequate because of this, and it is important to explain that the technique is not essential for helping to take place. Other rehearsal methods are available.

3. Some clients resist imagery because of anxiety, embarrassment, or fear of losing control. They may feel that they are being hypnotized and object to it. Sometimes lack of vividness or the inability to imagine may be a form of re-

sistance. Clients can be reassured that learning to develop imagery will actually lead to greater control.

4. Imagery techniques are not appropriate for individuals reporting hallucinations or delusions.

5. Some children may overuse fantasy and storytelling as an escape. They may wish to use magical images rather than acquiring social tools to deal with problems.

Role Playing

Role playing in psychotherapy is a technique commonly used by helpers in social-skills training and for helping clients face situations they are avoiding. Role playing is one of the most effective ways of establishing and maintaining a new behavior. The immediate observation and feedback allow for actual practice, not simply talking about problems (see Blatner, 1973).

Although its origins lie in psychodrama, role playing has been used by practitioners from many theoretical backgrounds (Kipper, 1986; Yablonsky, 1976). In psychodrama, the method is used to help the client explore troubling situations from the past; a classical psychodrama may take several hours. Gestalt therapists have utilized role playing to help clients explore disowned parts of themselves and to analyze dreams. In this section, we will look at role playing strictly as it is used to practice new behaviors.

Role playing can be performed by a single client who plays all of the roles in the drama, or with the help of other individuals who play roles of significant others. In an individual counseling setting, the helper may take on the role of other important individuals to facilitate the role play.

The helper may also use *role reversal* to allow the client to experience the viewpoint of one of the important people in the drama. In role reversal, the helper instructs the client to pretend to be the other person and respond as he or she might—for example, the client changes places and sits on the empty chair that previously represented his mother. He responds as his mother might respond in a given circumstance. Role reversal is one of the most effective ways of getting the client involved in the role play. In addition, role reversal makes the situation more real. The client is able to anticipate the responses of a significant other and strategies can be devised to cope with them.

How to Conduct Role Playing as a Method for Rehearsal or Practice

The method described here is a generic role-playing technique for practicing new behavior. To make the method easier to understand, the explanation follows a case example. The client, Martin, is anxious because he has to give a presentation to his board of directors concerning progress on his yearly goals. The helper, Andrea, suggests that they role-play the situation to rehearse his talk.

Step 1: Warm-up

In the warm-up, Andrea previews and explains the purpose and the elements of role playing. She begins by asking Martin to discuss aspects of his job that he will be presenting, details of the work place, and other tangential topics. The most important aspect of the warm-up is for Andrea to get Martin to describe his target behaviors very specifically. He wants to:

1. Maintain eye contact with his audience.
2. Speak from his notes in a loud, clear voice.
3. Smile when questions are asked.
4. End the session by thanking the audience.

Step 2: Scene Setting

After Martin has discussed the situation, he appears more relaxed. Andrea invites him to describe his own office (peripheral) and then the boardroom (central). She lets Martin literally set the scene, rearranging her office furnishings to approximate the setup of the boardroom. Andrea encourages Martin to point out various features such as the color of the walls and the furniture to establish the scene in their minds.

Step 3: Selecting Roles and Role Reversal

In this step, the client identifies important people in the scene and briefly describes them. In a group setting, other members of the group are assigned these roles. In an individual session, empty chairs represent these significant people. Andrea asks Martin to reverse roles and pretend to be his boss to get a sense of his demeanor and attitude. She also requests that he point out the chairs of some of the other board members and briefly describe them.

Step 4: Enactment

At this point, the helper asks the client to portray briefly the target behaviors as described during the warm-up. In Martin's case, the scene begins in his office and culminates with his entrance into the "boardroom." Andrea acts as a coach during the first run-through, prompting Martin to display each identified behavior. Because she is dissatisfied with his portrayal of the final behavior, thanking the audience, she stops the action and takes on Martin's role to model an effective closing statement. Following the modeling, Andrea asks Martin to try the closing a second time in his own way, using whatever parts of her own closing that he liked.

Step 5: Sharing and Feedback

After enactment, the helper shares feedback with the client on the client's performance. The feedback should be specific, simple, observable, and understandable to the client. It should mainly reinforce positive aspects of the behavior. For example, Andrea tells Martin, "Your voice was very strong and clear. I think you got your points across very well. I would like to see even more eye contact with the board members during the next run-through."

Step 6: Reenactment

Reenactment is a repetition of the target behavior from entrance to exit. Martin repeats the sequence until he is confident that he has mastered each of the behaviors in the target list.

Step 7: Homework and Follow-Up

At the next session, the client is asked to report practice results. Martin has practiced the behavior by giving his presentation to family members, and he describes this to Andrea. If she feels it is necessary, Andrea will give further role-playing practice during the session. When she feels that Martin has consistently demonstrated the target behaviors, she will urge him to display the behaviors in the actual meeting with board members.

Stop and Reflect

Think about a particular behavior that you find difficult to accomplish. It might be asking someone a difficult question, returning an item to a store, or dealing with an unpleasant person you know. Now, break down the behavior into a set of smaller units. Imagine each of the target behaviors individually and then imagine them sequentially as you complete the rehearsal successfully. Imagine a reward and compliment yourself for a job well done.

- After completing this activity, do you find yourself nearer to actually attempting this behavior?
- Can you think of any other ways you might increase your readiness to engage in this behavior?
- Discuss the behavior with two friends and ask how they would handle it.
- If you were asked to role-play this situation in front of a group, how do you think you would feel?

Homework

Homework has been identified as a crucial tool in effective helping (Beck, Rush, Shaw, & Emery, 1979; Ellis, 1962; Shelton & Ackerman, 1974). *Homework* refers to any tasks or assignments given to clients to be completed between sessions (Last, 1985). Some tasks are used for assessment purposes; others are used to increase client awareness of the behavior (Martin & Worthington, 1982), and still other homework assignments are designed as independent practice sessions.

Our main emphasis will be on homework that is used to practice new behaviors. These new behaviors are normally learned during the therapeutic session and may be modeled or rehearsed in the office before they are assigned as homework. Review of homework provides a starting point for each new session with a review of progress made and problems encountered in the assignment.

Reasons for Using Homework

A major advantage of using homework assignments is that it provides follow-up or treatment continuance between sessions. When one realizes that a client spends 1 hour out of 112 waking hours per week in counseling, it is easy to see how helping can be diluted by other activities. Homework assignments, especially if they require some daily work, can enhance treatment considerably (Shelton & Ackerman, 1974; Shelton & Levy, 1981). Second, homework assignments turn insights and awareness into tangible behaviors and prevent the helping sessions from being only a place to unload one's feelings. Transfer of training or generalization of learning is facilitated by applying descriptions and models of behavior to real-life situations as soon as possible. Homework practice also begins the shift of control from the helper to the client. If the client attributes progress to his or her own effort in outside assignments, greater efficacy and self-esteem will result.

Examples of Homework Assignments

Bibliotherapy

Bibliotherapy means assigning readings to clients to help them achieve their goals. The plethora of self-help books now on the market is evidence of a growing awareness that psychological literature can bring about change; however, many trade books are oversimplified, based on opinion or a few anecdotes. Before recommending a book to a client, the helper should have read the book and should think carefully about whether the book will be acceptable to the client's present frame of reference and assist with the client's goals. At each session, the helper should discuss the client's reading and go over important points, perhaps even asking a few relevant questions as to how the assignment fits the client's current dilemma.

Although it is not possible to provide an exhaustive list of good bibliographic materials here, resources for selecting books and manuals are available (see Glasgow & Rosen, 1978). A very good stress management workbook-and-tape set, "Kicking Your Stress Habits" (Tubesing, 1979), is available. Many clients with marital problems have benefited from *Divorce-Busting,* Michele Weiner-Davis (1992), while *Feeling Good,* by David Burns (1980), contains an excellent cognitive approach to depression that the average person can easily grasp. A number of other books, such as *Personal Enrichment through Imagery,* by Arnold Lazarus (1982), are now available on audiotape and can be listened to while driving or relaxing.

Besides informing the client, bibliotherapy can provide covert practice by exposing the client to a fictional or historical model of a desired behavior. Clients may identify with case studies or with fictional characters who face similar problems. The "Big Book" of Alcoholics Anonymous, for example, contains a number of true accounts of individuals who have successfully overcome drinking problems.

Aides

One way to increase the efficacy of homework practice is to enlist the help of a client's friend, spouse, or family member as an aide who provides either feedback or support for completing assignments. Generally, an aide comes to sessions with the client. The helper specifically identifies the aide's role as either support or feedback. Let us say that the client is attempting to become more assertive. The aide would be given specific verbal and nonverbal behaviors to observe and would report observations to the client. Alternatively, the aide might be enlisted simply to provide support or to accompany the client while he or she completes assignments. A client who is attempting to exercise regularly may use an aide as a regular walking partner. The aide would help the client increase regularity and provide encouragement from session to session. The major pitfall of using aides is that they must be supervised by the helper. Sometimes aides are too helpful and wish to take excessive responsibility for the client. If this behavior cannot be modified, the client should proceed alone.

Journaling and Record Keeping

Journaling is a daily writing assignment given to the client by the helper. Ordinarily the client brings these journals to the next session for the helper's reaction. Journals usually serve one of two purposes. Sometimes a journal is assigned as an open-ended writing assignment to help the client do more in-depth examination of his or her thoughts, feelings, and behaviors. Alternatively, the helper may use journaling to record practice sessions. These might include keeping track of countering skills (cognitive), recording emotional discomfort (affective), or noting the number of times a new behavior was actually practiced (behavioral).

Consider the case of Joe, a 29-year-old administrator for an insurance company who has come for help to deal with problems associated with "stress." He has borderline high blood pressure and is often tense and angry after work, and as a result sometimes speaks rudely to his fiancée, alienating her. He plays racquetball competitively and last week, he purposely broke an expensive racquet after a bad shot. He wishes to control his anger and feel less "stressed" at work.

During the assessment, the counselor identified negative self-statements as a major cause of Joe's stress and felt that, in general, the most useful path for him was to increase his self-esteem. Joe agreed, but also felt he needed better organizational skills. The initial plan was negotiated as a two-pronged attack: to decrease self-criticism and to develop better time-management and organization skills. Joe enrolled in a 3-day time-management workshop sponsored by his company and at the same time began keeping a journal, as shown in Table 11-1. Figure 11-2 is a graph of Joe's SUDS levels and negative self-statements over the first 10 days. In this case, 0 represents no discomfort and 100 represents extreme distress. Using a homework card, Joe found that he was generating anger with his self-statements, which were first aimed at himself, and that sometimes he discharged his emotions on innocent bystanders. Joe agreed to continue to monitor his self-statements for two more weeks and noticed a marked diminishing of his self-criticism. Although the major purpose of keeping a journal was to encourage practice, the client also became aware of the ways he fueled his anger with negative thoughts. In Joe's case, there seemed to be a correspondence between his self-criticism and his emotional discomfort, as shown in Figure 11-2. Graphing these results helped him see the correlation and encouraged him that he was making progress.

Table 11-1

Self-Criticism Homework Card for Joe

No.	Time	Self-Statement	Feeling	SUDS
1.	8:15	I'll never get all this work done.	Discouraged	85
2.	9:00	I didn't do a good job on that report.	Disgust	50
3.	10:00	I'll never be good at this job. I'm just average and that's all.	Self-Pity	60
4.	10:35	I'm daydreaming again. Why am I so lazy?	Anger	35
5.	12:00	I offended the secretary again. Why can't I just keep my mouth shut?	Anger	45
6.	1:00	I feel fat after eating so much. I'm turning into a blimp.	Disgust	35
7.	2:40	Another day almost done, and I've completed nothing.	Anger	40
8.	3:30	My desk is a mess. What a slob!	Discouraged	50
9.	5:15	Even my car is full of trash. I wish I were more organized.	Anger	25

SUDS = subjective units of distress

0 100

No emotional distress   Extreme emotional distress

Emotions = fear, anger, sadness, guilt, interest-excitement/(boredom), joy, disgust, surprise

Summary

9 = negative self-statements; average SUDS = 47 (approx.)

Most prevalent emotion = self-anger/disgust

Problems and Precautions of Homework Assignments

1. Homework assignments that have a high probability of success should be chosen (Dyer & Vriend, 1977). This is especially true early in the helping relationship in order to keep the client's hope alive. Also, when the helper promotes small, easily completed goals, the client begins to learn that most change is gradual, not an overnight phenomenon.

2. Homework strategies should be individually tailored for each client (Haley, 1978, 1989). Too often the helper uses a standard homework assignment that, to the discouraged client, may seem impersonal. Creatively conceived, some assignments can incorporate more than one of the client's goals. If the client likes to read, recommending self-help books as homework might work well. If the client enjoys writing, assign a journal.

3. Regularity of practice is important. It would be better, for example, to ask a client to perform an imaginal rehearsal for 10 minutes, once per day, rather than to practice for an hour one time per week.

4. Homework should be simple and fit easily into the client's lifestyle. Complicated homework involving extensive record keeping may not be completed.

5. As the client progresses, homework should increase in difficulty or discomfort. Clients usually have a feel for when they are ready for more challenging tasks that were once beyond them.

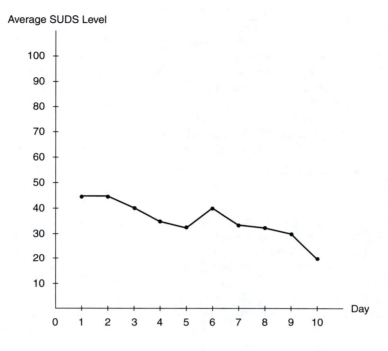

Average SUDS Level

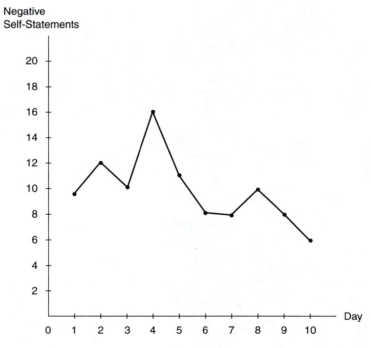

Negative
Self-Statements

Stop and Reflect

Think back on homework assignments that you have been given as a student. Of these, which did you enjoy most? Which did you learn the most from? Can you apply any of this experience to homework assignments that you might give to clients?

If you ever failed to turn in a homework assignment on time, what excuses did you use? What really stopped you from completing the assignment? Did the assignment seem irrelevant to you or did you just forget? Based on your experience, what might you do as a helper to encourage clients to complete their homework assignments?

Summary

Practice is used to put insights into action and to help clients try out new behaviors in a protected environment. Three levels of practice have been described in this chapter: imaginal practice, role playing, and homework. Each has its appropriate use, but imaginal and role-playing practice may be considered initial steps that eventually lead to homework (*in vivo*) practice.

Imagery as a helping method has become popular in recent years as a means of self-exploration, but it can also be used to rehearse desired behaviors. Imagery can provide initial practice of a new behavior in a non-threatening way.

Role playing is a practice technique that involves recreating the context of a desired behavior right in the helper's office. Major contributions to this technique have come from psychodrama and the behaviorists (Lazarus, 1985). This technique allows the helper to obtain firsthand knowledge about the client's behavioral style, while the client benefits from rehearsal and feedback.

Homework assignments are given to clients to prolong treatment between sessions as well as to establish the new behavior as a habit. Assignments should be individually tailored to the client and may involve journaling activities, lay helpers as aides, and bibliotherapy. Helpers who regularly utilize practice in the office or as homework are more likely to increase the transfer of training to real-life situations.

Group Exercises

Group Exercise 1

For this exercise, which involves practicing an assertive response, students form groups of four with roles of helper, client, observer 1, and observer 2. Observer 1 gives the client feedback and observer 2 gives the helper feedback on his or her ability to demonstrate the skill of role playing. The client chooses a situation to role-play that involves someone with whom he or she would have liked to have been more assertive. For example:

"My boyfriend criticized me in front of his mother but I did not mention it."
"A teacher treated me unfairly."
"I was attracted to or liked someone but I never told him or her."

For this exercise, take the following steps:

1. The helper directs the client through the first five steps of role playing.
2. Observer 1 and the helper give the client feedback, and the client reenacts the role play if more practice seems advisable.

3. Observer 2 and the training group give the helper feedback and discuss the exercise.

Quick Tips: Role Playing

- If the client appears to have difficulty getting into the role play, spend some time discussing the issue first as a "warm-up."
- If clients resist the role play technique, you may have to abandon it until trust is better developed. On the other hand, your confidence in the procedure will encourage them, and reassurance that "you'll get into it" may help them to bypass initial reluctance.
- If the client has trouble displaying a target behavior, stop the action and model the behavior for the client.
- Make sure that you bring a role play to a successful conclusion. Continue to reenact until the client feels that he or she has come to a positive ending.

Group Exercise 2

Consider the following case studies.

a. Carol is a 37-year-old married woman with one child. She and her counselor agree to work on her extreme reluctance to leave home even for a few hours to go to the grocery store. She experiences fear and panic attacks in public situations. She has not been shopping in 2 years and has lost respect for herself as a contributing member of her family. Following two sessions of history taking and a medical evaluation (the client in- correctly believes that she has a heart condition), the counselor and client, following a complete assessment, agree that she needs assistance in dealing with low self-esteem and that she needs to practice going out in public. The client has a number of dysfunctional beliefs, including "I am weak," that seem to contribute to her inability to attempt new behaviors.

b. Maureen is a 20-year-old college student and only child whose parents appear to be on the verge of divorce. She comes to the college counseling center complaining that she is always in the middle and that each parent calls to tell her about the other's failings. In her attempts to placate both sides, Maureen has become anxious and depressed and has trouble studying. She experiences periods of crying and expresses sympathy for both parents. Maureen initially frames her problem as "how to help my parents cope with their divorce." In the second session, Maureen agrees that what she wants is to maintain a relationship with both parents, be supportive of both, and not to listen to their complaints about each other.

What does each client need to practice? Which issues would you address first? What level of rehearsal seems best suited to each of these clients' problems? In a small group, brainstorm two or three creative homework assignments for each client. Role-play one of these situations, with one student playing the client and the other, the helper, making a homework assignment.

Homework

Homework 1: Diary

Select a personal growth goal for yourself that involves practicing a new behavior—For example:

"I would like to play my guitar every day."

"I would like to cook regular meals to combat my tendency to snack throughout the day."

"I would like to take time every day to improve my relationship with people at work."

  a. At the end of each day, for one week, write down the number of times you engaged in practice of the behavior, or indicate if you did not practice during the day. Write down as well any ideas you have about why you did or did not practice the behavior during the day.

  b. At the end of the week, summarize your conclusions in a half-page reaction. Do you think that self-monitoring by keeping a journal was helpful to you? What kind of clients might benefit from this approach? What kinds of problems are best suited to keeping a diary such as this?

Homework 2

Select a building-block skill from this book that you would like to improve.

  a. Write down the name of the skill: _____

  _____

  b. Does the skill need to be broken down into small components?

  If so, list them here:_____

  _____

  c. Spend 5 minutes imagining yourself successfully demonstrating each part of the skill.

  d. Ask a fellow student who is proficient in the skill to model it for you.

  e. Ask a student partner to act as an observer and practice the skill with a third student, who will serve as the client.

  f. Get feedback and rehearse again, incorporating the suggestions you received.

  g. With help from your training group, select several situations in real life where you might practice this skill.

  h. Make an appointment with a fellow student to call him or her and report on your progress in a week.

References

Beck, A. T., Rush, A. J., Shaw, B. F., & Emery, G. (1979). Integration of homework into therapy. In A. T. Beck, A. J. Rush, B. F. Shaw, & G. Emery, *Cognitive therapy of depression* (pp. 272–294). New York: Guilford.

Bellack, A. S. (1986). Covert rehearsal. In A. S. Bellack & M. Hersen (Eds.), *Dictionary of behavior therapy techniques.* New York: Pergamon.

Blatner, H. A. (1973). Acting-in: Practical applications of psychodramatic methods. New York: Springer.

Burns, D. D. (1980). *Feeling good.* New York: Morrow.

Cautela, J. R., & Bennet, A. K. (1981). Covert conditioning. In R. J. Corsini (Ed.), *Handbook of innovative psychotherapies.* New York: Wiley.

Dyer, W., & Vriend, J. (1977). *Counseling techniques that work.* New York: Funk & Wagnalls.

Ellis, A. (1962). *Reason and emotion in psychotherapy.* New York: Lyle Stuart.

Fezler, W. F. (1989). *Creative imagery: How to visualize in all five senses.* New York: Simon & Schuster.

Gladding, S. T. (1986). Imagery and metaphor in counseling: A humanistic course. *Journal of Humanistic Education and Development, 25,* 38–47.

Glasgow, R. E., & Rosen, G. M. (1978). Behavioral bibliotherapy: A review of self-help behavior therapy manuals. *Psychological Bulletin, 85,* 1–23.

Grigsby, J. P. (1987). The use of imagery in the treatment of posttraumatic stress disorder. *Journal of Nervous and Mental Disease, 175,* 55–59.

Guerney, B., Stollack, G., & Guerney, L. (1971). The practicing psychologist as educator: An alternative to the medical practitioner's model. *Professional Psychology, 11,* 276–282.

Gunnison, H., & Renick, T. F. (1985). Bulimia: Using fantasy-imagery and relaxation techniques. *Journal of Counseling and Development, 64,* 79–80.

Haley, J. (1978). Ideas which handicap therapists. In M. Berger (Ed.), *Beyond the double blind: Communication and family systems, theories, techniques with schizophrenics* (pp. 24–36). New York: Brunner/Mazel.

Haley, J. (1989, April). Strategic family therapy. Symposium conducted at Stetson University, DeLand, FL.

Kazdin, A. E. (1978). Covert modeling: The therapeutic application of imagined rehearsal. In J. L. Singer & K. S. Pope (Eds.), *The power of human imagination.* New York: Plenum Press.

Kipper, D. A. (1986). *Psychotherapy through clinical role-playing.* New York: Brunner/Mazel.

Last, C. G. (1985). Homework. In A. S. Bellack & M. Hersen (Eds.), *Dictionary of behavior therapy techniques* (pp. 140–141). New York: Pergamon.

Lazarus, A. (1977). *In the mind's eye: The power of imagery for personal enrichment.* New York: Rawson.

Lazarus, A. A. (1982). *Personal enrichment through imagery* [Cassette recording]. New York: BMA Audio Cassettes/Guilford Publications.

Lazarus, A. A. (1985). Behavior rehearsal. In A. S. Bellack & M. Hersen (Eds.), *Dictionary of behavior therapy techniques* (p. 22). New York: Pergamon.

Martin, G. A., & Worthington, E. L. (1982). Behavioral homework. In M. Hersen, R. Eisler, & P. M. Miller (Eds.), *Progress in behavior modification* (Vol. 13, pp. 197–226). New York: Academic Press.

Pope, K. S. (1982). A primer on therapeutic imagery techniques. In P. A. Kellar & L. G. Ritt (Eds.), *Innovations in clinical practice: A sourcebook* (Vol. 1, pp. 67–77). Sarasota, FL: Professional Resource Exchange.

Sarnoff, D., & Remer, P. A. (1982). The effects of guided imagery on the generation of career alternatives. *Journal of Vocational Behavior, 21,* 299–308.

Schutz, W. (1981). Holistic education. In R. J. Corsini (Ed.), *Handbook of innovative psychotherapies* (pp. 378–388). New York: Wiley.

Sheikh, A. (Ed.) (1983). *Imagery: Current theory, research and application.* New York: Wiley.

Shelton, J. L., & Ackerman, J. M. (1974). *Homework in counseling and psychotherapy.* Springfield, IL: Thomas.

Shelton, J. L., & Levy, R. L. (1981). *Behavioral assignments and treatment compliance.* Champaign, IL: Research Press.

Skovholt, T., & Thoen, G. A. (1987). Mental imagery in parenthood decision making. *Journal of Counseling and Development, 65,* 315–316.

Skovholt, T. M., Morgan, J. I., & Negron-Cunningham, H. (1989). Mental imagery in career counseling and life planning: A review of research and intervention methods. *Journal of Counseling and Development, 67,* 287–292.

Tubesing, D. (1979). *Kicking your stress habits.* Duluth, MN: Whole Person Press.

Weiner-Davis, M. (1992). *Divorce busting.* New York: Summit Books.

Witmer, J. M., & Young, M. E. (1985). The silent partner: Uses of imagery in counseling. *Journal of Counseling and Development, 64,* 187–190.

Witmer, J. M., & Young, M. E. (1987). Imagery in counseling. *Elementary School Guidance and Counseling, 22,* 5–16.

Yablonsky, L. (1976). *Psychodrama: Resolving emotional problems through role-playing.* New York: Basic Books.

Young, M. E., & Rosen, L. S. (1985). The retreat: An educational growth group. *Journal for Specialists in Group Work, 10,* 157–163.

Lowering and Raising Emotional Arousal

Introduction

The fourth curative factor in the REPLAN system is lowering and raising emotional arousal (see Figure 12-1). In this chapter, we discuss ways of helping clients deal with overpowering feelings of anger, stress, and fear, primarily through methods of relaxation. In addition, we will look at methods that arouse emotions to act as catalysts for change and encourage clients to express deep feelings within the therapeutic relationship.

These two methodologies, quieting and arousing, are at each end of a continuum and their use is determined by the individual circumstances of each client. Many clients benefit from relaxation training, meditation, and other quieting techniques. "Hurry sickness," or high levels of stress, are common symptoms in this increasingly hectic world. On the other hand, methods that encourage clients to experience and then express deeply held feelings are helpful for clients who have not dealt with painful or traumatic events, who are underexpressive, or who are using defense mechanisms rather than dealing with important emotional problems.

While quieting methods are safe and quickly lead to positive experiences by clients, arousing emotions in clients is risky without a long period of training and close supervision. Most of these methods, such as the empty-chair technique of Gestalt therapy and several psychodramatic methods, are too advanced for the scope of this book;

Figure 12-1
Curative factors in the REPLAN system: Lowering or raising emotional arousal

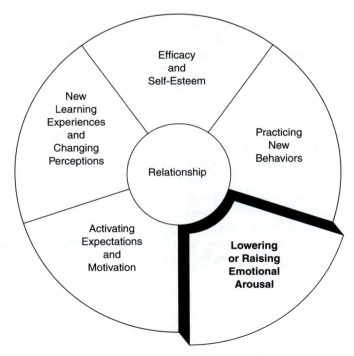

this does not mean that the beginning helper must shy away from exploring unexpressed emotions. In this chapter, you will learn the technique of increasing emotional awareness to prevent the client from ignoring emotionally charged issues. On the other hand, you will also learn to help clients reduce emotions through relaxation when emotions become overwhelming or interfere with the enjoyment of life.

Reducing Emotional Arousal

While a little anxiety may actually enhance performance at times, and anger may motivate us to act assertively, these emotions can easily run out of control, causing distress and interfering with relationships and job performance. Modern life, with more crowding, more work pressure, and more choices, has led to greater stress levels in just about everyone. The emotional arousal associated with anger and fear (fight or flight) may have been useful in more primitive times. Today, however, these emotions can be destructive as they are experienced by more and more people sitting behind desks. What once may have increased the chances for survival now threatens our health, because the physiological by-products of stress can not be easily dissipated in a sedentary lifestyle.

Today's helper is frequently called upon to help clients learn to reduce the causes of stress by acquiring time-management skills; developing a capacity for self-care, including exercise and good nutrition; and gaining a more healthy outlook on life. In addition, helpers assist clients in lowering stress by reducing emotional arousal through quieting techniques.

Some of the better known methods for reducing emotional arousal are systematic desensitization for phobic anxiety (Wolpe, 1958), progressive relaxation (Jacobson, 1938), coping skills training (Tubesing, 1981), guided imagery (Overholser, 1991), confession/ventilation (Menninger, 1958), emotional support (Gilliland, James, & Bowman, 1989), stress inoculation (Novaco, 1977, 1983), biofeedback training (Fair, 1989), and meditation (Bogart, 1991; Carrington, 1978; Shapiro, 1994; Singh, 1996). These techniques are often combined and offered in a psychoeducational format as stress-reduction or coping-skills training courses. In a group setting, moreover, participants can benefit from the support of fellow participants, which also helps to reduce stress.

The most fundamental method for helping clients reduce arousal is muscle relaxation. Muscle relaxation training brings about immediate relief from troubling symptoms of anxiety and lets clients experience the positive sensations associated with reduced muscle tension. This technique is explained in detail here, since it is part of most stress-reduction courses and forms the basis of systematic desensitization and biofeedback training.

Relaxation Training

Edmund Jacobson's progressive relaxation technique (1938) was for many years the favored method for teaching clients deep muscle relaxation, which in turn reduces emotional arousal. Jacobson's method, if faithfully followed, enables the client to identify and relax every major muscle group in the body. The training may actually take several months in weekly sessions. Although abbreviated versions have been used successfully (Gatchel & Baum, 1983; McKay, Davis, & Fanning, 1981), the following is a simple format developed by Witmer (1985) that can be learned in three or four sessions, each lasting about 20 minutes. Each session is identical and provides a complete run-through of all the muscle groups (see Table 12-1).

Clients with symptoms of anxiety or stress are most likely to benefit from relaxation training; however, relaxation training alone is not a sufficient treatment for phobias. Phobic clients must also confront their fears *in vivo* through some sort of gradual exposure to the feared object. Relaxation training does help these clients learn to relax in such situations, though, and may bring about greater feelings of self-control.

A typical case of a person who benefited from relaxation training was Terrence, a 45-year-old owner of a small factory, who was referred for help by his family doctor. The physician had found high levels of back and neck tension that were causing headaches. Terrence had started out working at a small machine shop and had eventually purchased it with a partner. The shop had grown into a good-sized business, and many of the personnel and production problems fell on Terrence. In the initial session, the counselor interviewed Terrence and determined that the client would benefit from lowering emotional arousal to decrease back and neck tension. Terrence began to learn the technique of deep muscle relaxation, and at the same time the counselor encouraged him to build in regular exercise, better nutrition, and regular days off from work. Along with the relaxation training, Terrence needed a change in outlook (new learning experiences—see Chapter 14) about his unwillingness to take care of himself and a self-critical attitude that drove him to neglect his physical warning signs. Relaxation training helped reduce the client's headaches, but it took some time before Terrence was able to make lifestyle changes. Eventually, Terrence's wife was able to get him to build in regular vacations, and Terrence agreed to hire a human resources consultant to deal with stressful personnel issues. Together, the two curative factors of lowering emotional arousal and new learning created both a reduction of tension and a lifestyle that supported the change.

The Technique of Deep Muscle Relaxation

Step 1: Preparation

Ask the client to find the most comfortable position with eyes closed. This may be sitting or lying down, but in either case there should be support for the head. The procedure is best practiced without the distractions of noise or glaring lights. Instruct the client to speak as little as possible and to avoid moving except as necessary to achieve a more comfortable position. The legs and arms should not be crossed.

Step 2: Tighten and Relax

Ask the client to progressively tighten and then relax each muscle group, using the instructions in Table 12-1. Encourage the client to hold each tensed muscle 6 or 7 seconds until the experience of tightness is fully felt. On the other hand, if the posture is

Table 12-1
Instructions to the Client for Tensing and Relaxing Muscle Groups

Major Muscle Group and Area of Tension	Tensing and Relaxing Instructions
1. Hands and Arms	
Hand: The back of your hand, fingers, and the wrist	Tense the muscles in the right hand and lower right arm by making a tight fist. Hold for at least five seconds. Feel the tension. Now relax. Notice the difference between the tensing and relaxing. Repeat the same procedure. Now do the same thing with your left hand. Finish by tensing and relaxing both hands together.
Lower Arm: The forearm and the wrist	Hold both arms out in front of you with palms up, bend the hands down. Feel the tension in the hand, wrist, and forearm. Then relax. Repeat the same procedure. Now extend your arms out in front of you but with palms down. Bend your hands up. Feel the tension. Relax. Repeat the same procedure. Now let both arms hang loosely at your side.
Upper Arm: The bicep muscles	Start with your right arm. Bend the elbow, touch your shoulder with your fingers, and tense the bicep just like you want to show off your muscles. Feel the tension, then relax and notice the contrast. Repeat the same procedure. Now do the same thing with your left arm. Finish by tensing, then relaxing both arms together. Now let both arms hang loosely at your side.
2. Head, Face, and Throat	
Forehead and Scalp: The entire forehead and scalp area	Wrinkle your forehead by raising your eyebrows as high as you can. Feel the tension in the forehead and scalp area. Now relax, notice the difference between tension and relaxation. Repeat the procedure. Next frown by pulling your eyebrows down as far as you can. Feel the tension, then relax. Repeat the same procedure. Let go of all tension, then relax. Repeat the same procedure. Let go of all tension in the forehead and scalp area. Feel the smoothness of the muscles.
Eyes and Nose: The eyelids and muscles around the eyes, nose, and upper cheeks	Squeeze your eyes shut and at the same time wrinkle up your nose. Feel the tension, then relax. Repeat the procedure. Next roll your eyes left and right, up and down or rotate them in both directions. Finish by opening your eyes as widely as you can, then relaxing them. Now feel the relaxation of muscles around your eyes.
Mouth and Jaw: The area around the mouth and the lower face	Bite your teeth together and pull the corners of your mouth back. Feel the tension, then let go. Now press your lips tightly together and extend them as though you are sucking a straw. Feel the tension and relax. Next open your mouth widely, then relax. Now pull

Throat and Jaw: Muscles inside the mouth and throat

your mouth to the left side of your face, then to the right. Repeat any of the above exercises until this part of your face is deeply relaxed.
Push your tongue against the roof of your mouth. Feel the tension, then relax. Clench your jaw tightly, then relax.

Entire Head and Facial Area

Try a final tensing and relaxing by making a face. Scrunch up your face so your eyes squint, your nose is wrinkled up and your mouth is pulled back. Now your face feels smooth and relaxed as you let go of any tension left over.

3. Neck and Shoulders

Neck: The muscles in the back of the neck, at the base of the scalp, and across the shoulders

Drop your chin down against your chest. Press down hard enough so you feel tension under your chin and at the back of your neck. Now lift your head and press it backward. Roll your head to the right, then forward to your chest, then to the left and back to where you started. Go slowly and gently. Repeat this at least twice in the same direction. Next, do the same exercise in the other direction. Relax with your head in a normal position, stretching it in whatever way you need for working out remaining tension spots.

4. Chest, Shoulders, and Upper Back

Muscles in the Chest, Shoulders, and Upper Back Area

Take a deep breath, hold it and at the same time pull the shoulders back, trying to make the shoulder blades touch. Feel the tension around your ribs, shoulders, and the upper back. Exhale slowly and feel the relaxation as you return to a natural position. Now pull your shoulders as far forward as you can, then as far up, as far back, and as far down as you can, making a kind of circular motion. Repeat this at least twice. Feel the tension and relaxation. Next go in the opposite direction in your rotation of the shoulders. Sense the looseness and relaxed feeling in this part of your body.

5. Lower Back, Stomach, and Hips

Lower Back: The muscles across the lower back area

Begin by taking a deep breath and sitting up straight. Pull the shoulders back and arch your back so your stomach sticks out. Exhale and let all the air and tension flow out. Repeat this procedure. Next bend forward arching your back the other way with your head down to your knees and your hands touching the floor. Feel the muscles stretching. Return to a normal sitting position and feel the relaxation. Repeat the procedure.

Stomach and Hips: The muscles in the abdominal area and hips

Take a deep breath and hold it as you make your stomach muscles hard. Just tighten them up as though you were going to hit yourself in the stomach. You should feel a good deal of tightness in the stomach area. Breathe out and feel the relaxation as you do let go of this tension. Repeat the procedure. Next breathe out as far as you can, feeling the tension in your stomach area as you hold your breath. Now let go and allow yourself to breathe naturally, noticing the difference between tension and relaxation.

Table 12-1, continued

Major Muscle Group and Area of Tension	Tensing and Relaxing Instructions
6. Hips, Legs, and Feet *Hips and Upper Legs:* The muscles in the upper and lower parts of the thighs *Lower Legs:* The muscles from the knees to the ankles	Gently hold fast to the bottom of your chair. Press your heels down hard on the floor. Feel the tension around your hips and the hardness of the large upper leg muscles. Relax and notice the difference between tension and relaxation. Repeat the procedure. Hold both legs straight out in front of you. Point your feet and toes away from your head. Feel the tension in your legs and on top of your feet. Relax and drop both feet on the floor. Now extend your legs again, but point your feet and toes toward your head. Feel the tension in the calf muscles and around your ankles. Relax and drop both feet. Notice the relaxed feeling.
Feet: The muscles around the ankles, over the top of the feet, the arch and ball of the feet, and the toes	Extend both toes pointed away from you. Then turn both feet inward and at the same time curl your toes. Gently tense the muscles just enough to feel the tension and relax. Now try moving each foot in a circular motion, feeling the stretching and tensing. Relax. Repeat but reverse the direction and relax! Try spreading your toes, then relaxing, letting all the tension go out of your feet. Now put both feet flat on the floor, take a deep breath and relax.
7. Body Review	Scan your whole body and recognize how it now feels more relaxed. Let the muscles of your body relax even more as you do a body scan from head to toe. Muscles that still feel a bit tight can be tensed, then relaxed. Next, try tensing your whole body at one time. Take a deep breath and feel the tension all over your body. Hold for several seconds, then let go. Let all the air out and feel the deep relaxation over your entire body. The tension is flowing out like the air escaping from a balloon. Enjoy the relaxed feeling.

held too long, cramps and spasms may result. While a muscle group is tensed, ask the client to focus on that area, simultaneously relaxing other parts of the body and holding the breath.

Step 3: Relax Fully and Breathe

Following the tensing of a muscle group, instruct the client to exhale and relax fully and completely. This relaxation is to be accompanied by slow, deep, diaphragmatic breathing and should last 20 seconds or so. The tension and relaxation of the same muscle group is then repeated before moving on.

Diaphragmatic breathing consists of inhaling and exhaling below the ribs rather than in the upper chest. It is the relaxed breathing demonstrated by sleeping babies and practiced by singers. Help clients learn diaphragmatic breathing by placing one hand on the chest and the other on the diaphragm/stomach area. Breathing is diaphragmatic when the stomach hand goes up and down but the chest hand remains largely immobile.

Step 4: The Body Scan

The most important phase of the lesson is the body review or *body scan*. The client is asked to return to specific, discrete areas of tension and to relax them. The client is instructed that the final part of the body scan, tensing the whole body, is also a simple way of achieving relaxation at times when the full process cannot be implemented.

Step 5: Assign Practice

The first administration of the relaxation technique should be recorded on audio cassette for the client, or a standardized commercially available version of the technique should be provided. Ask the client to practice the relaxation technique twice daily, usually once upon arising and once in bed before falling asleep. Have the client note which of the six target areas shown in Table 12-1 are the greatest sources of tension and report this information to you at the next session.

Meditation

Meditation is one of the most effective means for decreasing anxiety and persistent anger. The practice is often associated with religious groups such as the Quakers or practitioners of Zen, but it is also possible to practice meditation without belonging to any religion. Unlike relaxation techniques, meditation has the effect of producing mental quietude, not just physical rest. Meditation is not merely a method for reducing tension; it actually produces positive states of alertness, optimism, and joy as well as feelings of well-being. Meditation is a good alternative to tranquilizers and other medications.

Like relaxation, meditation must be practiced on a regular basis for at least 15 minutes per day for several weeks, before real benefits can be realized (Benson, 1984). As with any skill, a teacher is helpful at all stages of training (Singh, 1996).

An immediate benefit of meditation is that it stops the chattering of the mind and eliminates the mental images that produce anxiety. For example, have you ever tried to sleep and found plans for the next day going around in your head? Meditation is a means of putting such thoughts to rest for a while. To keep the mind occupied, meditation practitioners have found that a "mental device" (Benson, 1984) or *mantra* is an effective way of reducing the stressful thoughts coming from the mind. A mantra gives the mind something to occupy itself. A word or phrase is repeated slowly and at intervals, mentally, not aloud but with the "tongue of thought" (Singh, 1996). For those who are spiritually inclined, any name of God can be used. Others have found it effective to repeat a word such as "one" or "calm."

Learning to quiet the mind is a challenge, but the benefits make the investment of time worth the effort. If you are interested in learning more about meditation, read Rajinder Singh's book entitled *Inner and Outer Peace through Meditation.* It contains complete and simple instructions for nondenominational spiritual meditation and exercises to get started. For clients or helpers who are not attracted to a spiritual meditation procedure, Patricia Carrington's clinically standardized meditation (1978) may be of interest.

Raising Emotional Arousal

The patient only gets free from the hysterical symptom by reproducing the pathogenic impressions that caused it and by giving utterance to them with the expression of affect and thus the therapeutic task consists solely in inducing him to do so (p. 283).

Breuer and Freud (1895/1955)

The earliest records of cathartic methods are found in ancient Greek drama. The word *katharsis* indicates a purging or purification experienced after the expression of emotions. The effectiveness of traditional uses of cathartic methods is documented in the history of religious rituals, confession of sins, mesmerism, drug-induced emotional states, and rituals of mourning.

The quotation that opens this section is from the classic book *Studies on Hysteria* (1895/1955). In this publication, Breuer and Freud presented their discovery that reliving past traumas by provoking emotional reactions and getting clients to express their feelings had healing power. Freud's idea was that relief from emotional suffering can be obtained by releasing pools of stored emotions that are held in the unconscious. When freed, these stored emotions dissipate like water running down a drain. In all fairness to Freud, he modified his ideas about emotions later in his life, but this idea of releasing stockpiled emotions became popular and took root in many other therapeutic systems. Since Freud's time, the terms *catharsis, abreaction, emotional insight, corrective emotional experience, releasing blocked emotion,* and *experiencing* have all been used to describe the release of emotions in the helping relationship (Nichols & Efran, 1985; Nichols & Zax, 1977).

Not all helping professionals believe that the effectiveness of cathartic techniques is explained by Freud's "hydraulic" metaphor, but they still embrace arousal and expression of emotions as a major technique. This group includes practitioners of Gestalt therapy (Perls, 1977; Prochaska & Norcross, 1994), psychodrama (Moreno, 1958), and a number of group approaches including encounter groups and marathon groups. Emotional arousal has been activated through hypnosis and drugs (Wolberg, 1977), psychodramatic methods (Moreno, 1958), guided imagery (Witmer & Young, 1985), reflective listening in client-centered therapy, confrontation, deprecating and devaluating feedback in Synanon groups, free association in psychoanalysis, the empty-chair technique of Gestalt therapy (Polster & Polster, 1973), focusing (Gendlin, 1969), flooding, implosive therapy (Stampfl & Levis, 1967), bioenergetics (Lowen, 1967), primal therapy (Janov, 1970), reevaluation counseling (Jackins, 1962), provocative therapy (Farelly & Brandsma, 1974), and many others.

Arousal and Expression

The term *catharsis* is the most commonly used term in the context of arousal and expression, but it has become a catch-all that actually encompasses two separate activities: (1) stimulating emotional arousal of the client, and (2) the encouragement of emotional expression by the client (Young & Bemak, 1996). *Arousing techniques* frustrate, shock, anger, or evoke some other state of emotional arousal for the purpose of motivating change. *Expressive techniques,* on the other hand, help clients fully experience their feelings and allow them to communicate these emotions to the helper. Clients report cathartic events as extremely significant; several studies indicate that emotional arousal should be accompanied by a cognitive change or perspective shift to achieve maximum therapeutic effectiveness. There is some indication that individuals who are underexpressive will benefit most from highly arousing and expressive therapies (Young & Bemak, 1996).

It is extremely important to be aware right from the start that methods that arouse emotions can be traumatic and hurtful to clients. Arousing techniques, in their simplest and most benign form, can push clients to talk about troubling experiences and feelings and not to avoid them. At the most harmful level, helpers applying these techniques can force clients to face powerful emotions that make them feel out of control. Because some arousing techniques can lead to such harmful reactions, we will discuss methods that focus clients on their emotions but do not pressure them to do so. The more confrontational and cathartic methods are very advanced skills to be used only by experienced practitioners within strict ethical guidelines and in conjunction with close supervision (Young & Bemak, 1996). We mention them here because, sooner or later, every helper will see these methods on films or at conference workshops. Like a knife that cuts both ways, it is important to keep in mind that while these methods can produce powerful reactions, the risks are substantial.

Why Do Emotional Arousal and Expression Stimulate Change?

1. They promote greater self-understanding. Besides Freud's psychodynamic explanation that emotional arousal and expression release stored emotions, there have been several other hypotheses. For example, in Chapter 3, we mentioned the work of Pennebaker (1989), who asked college students to

write about traumatic events in their lives. These students experienced better mental and physical health compared to control subjects. When the students were asked why they found the exercise helpful, they did not think that
positive changes were simply due to the release of pent-up emotions.
Participants did not feel better after the writing experience. Eighty percent
of them explained the benefits as due to greater self-understanding, as opposed to getting negative emotions "off their chests." The following are some
examples of client statements (Pennebaker, 1990, pp. 48–49):

"It helped me think about what I felt during those times."
"I never realized how it affected me before."
"I had to think and resolve past experiences. . . . One result of the experiment
is peace of mind, and a method to relieve emotional experiences. To have to
write emotions and feelings helped me to understand how I felt and why."

2. They convince the client that help is needed when it becomes apparent that
   powerful emotions have been denied or repressed. Emotions have been called
   "hot cognitions" (Greenberg & Safran, 1988). In other words, the emotional
   aspects of a problem are the most pronounced to the client. Dealing directly
   with the emotions is persuasive since it brings about an immediate sense that
   core issues are being dealt with. It is a confirmation, by direct knowledge, of
   the power of the helping relationship—a real experience versus an intellectual insight. When helpers use listening techniques or ask clients to focus on
   emotional pain, the client becomes aware that strong emotions are lurking beneath the surface. This gives the client hope that the helping relationship is
   working on a deeper level (Greenberg, Rice, & Ailed, 1993; Greenberg &
   Safran, 1988).

   An example of this occurred in the case of a physician and his wife, a
   nurse, who came for help to deal with a 25-year-old son who was a drug ad-
   dict and who lied to and stole from his parents. At first, the father was skeptical about how counseling would help and he was only minimally involved. In
   the third session, as he discussed the effects of the son's behavior on their
   lives, he became aware of a deep and troubling experience. He hated his own
   son. He broke into tears and was inconsolable for over an hour. He later reported that he knew he was angry at his child, but had never come face to face
   with his own feelings of failure and rage at the situation he and his wife were
   forced to deal with. This incident, among other things, helped to convince him
   that counseling was a potent tool. He became more involved in counseling,
   and he and his wife were able to begin to deal with the problem of their son
   more cooperatively.

3. Expressing deeply felt emotions to the helper cements the helping relationship. When a client finds acceptance after revealing deeply held emotions,
   trust increases. As Yalom (1975) said, "Catharsis is part of an interpersonal
   process; no one ever claimed enduring benefit from ventilating feelings in an
   empty closet" (p. 84).

   When clients express their feelings of anger, attraction, or dependency in
   a group, they fear rejection and feel guilty. Instead, they are most often met
   with understanding and acceptance. Other people in the group identify with

the client's experience. This creates a cohesive bond in a group and between a helper and client.

4. Arousal melts down old attitudes. Kurt Lewin (1935) talked about therapeutic change being an "unfreezing and refreezing" process, meaning that the client's world view can be catalyzed by emotional arousal. During periods of intense emotion, client attitudes are most susceptible to modification by the helper (Frank & Frank, 1991). For example, a client once relived her experiences of physical abuse in therapy. Previously, she could not accept the fact that the abuse was not her fault. During the emotional peak of the session, the helper confronted the client with this issue again. When her defenses were down, the client was able to more readily accept this interpretation.

When emotional arousal subsides, the insights that have been gained "refreeze" or solidify into a new and stable viewpoint. McMullin (1986) calls this phenomenon the "melted wax theory." Emotional arousal can be used to provide the heat needed to melt down old beliefs so that they may be reformed.

Techniques that Stimulate Emotional Arousal and Expression

One does not destroy an emotion by refusing to feel it or acknowledge it; one merely disowns a part of one's self.

Nathaniel Branden, 1971, p. 28

Stimulus Techniques

Several methods for emotional arousal and expression can be grouped together as *stimulus techniques*. Helpers supply clients with media such as music, films, or books that relate to their personal problems. The ability of the client to identify with the protagonist of the story enhances the emotional arousal and subsequent expression. For example, a helper might suggest the movie *The Great Santini* to a client from a military family. Later, helper and client discuss the film in terms of what feelings and thoughts were aroused.

Creative Arts

A second set of techniques is associated with the use of the creative arts in counseling (Gladding, 1992). Helpers encourage clients to express themselves and release emotions through artistic media. Arts as emotional catalysts differ from stimulus methods in that clients are not passive, but actively create an artistic work. These works may include dance and movement, music performance, expressive writing of poetry, journaling, painting, drawing, sculpting, making collages, sandtray work, and dramatic use of puppets and dolls. For example, a client who has trouble expressing his feelings about a past relationship could be asked to paint a picture or write a poem about the experience to be shared during the next session.

Stop and Reflect

Journal writing can be used in the helping relationship for the expression and release of emotions. Writing down our inner thoughts is a different activity from merely thinking about them or talking about them. In writing, we have the opportunity to examine thoughts in detail, think about them, and challenge them. We may record dreams, daily feelings, reflections on self-concept, or spiritual progress, or we may write about particularly troubling or significant periods of change in our lives. All of these activities may help us become more deeply aware of emotional issues behind these events.

In this activity, called a "period log" (Gladding, 1992), you are asked to indicate a particular interval of your life during which you experienced a number of changes or personal growth and to reflect on your experiences during that time. Once you have identified a particular time period, begin writing and do not stop to edit your thoughts. Since you need not show this work to anyone, turn off your internal censor and write whatever comes up or emerges without editing your thoughts or feelings. This is a free association or stream-of-consciousness method that psychodynamic therapists have found effective for uncovering underlying issues. Some practice is required before you can really let go and let your thoughts and feelings flow. One way to do this is to place your pen on a blank sheet of paper with a headline indicating the particular time period and write without lifting the pen from the paper for about 5 minutes. Start with the words, "I felt . . .," and continue writing for the allotted time. When you have finished, answer the following questions.

1. What were the major feelings you experienced during this period in your life? Did you reexperience any of them while writing?
2. Did you find it hard to write in a stream-of-consciousness style?
3. How did you block yourself from letting the ideas flow out?
4. Do you think clients censor their true feelings about issues or a particular period in their lives?
5. Did you encounter any personal reluctance to look at this period in your life?
6. Do you see any value in reviewing the past, or would it be best to let these issues lie?
7. What does your writing indicate about how comfortable you are now with this important period in your life?
8. What other artistic media would you personally be most likely to use if suggested by a helper?
9. How could you determine which methods would be best for a specific client?

Psychodrama

In our earlier discussion on role playing, we discussed the basic elements of psychodrama. Some of the most intensely emotional methods are those elicited in psychodrama. Psychodrama was conceived by Moreno (1958) as a method of emotional expression similar to dance and visual art; it is the re-creation of an individual's joys and sorrows on a therapy stage. Typically, in a group, the protagonist is asked to recreate a scene from the past and to explore his or her thoughts and emotions in as much depth as possible. Considerable training and experience are required before a helper can responsibly use psychodramatic methods for arousing emotions.

The Technique of Increasing Emotional Awareness

As we mentioned at the beginning of this chapter, many of the techniques for arousing client emotions and encouraging the client to express them are quite advanced and can be harmful if misused. However, the technique of increasing the client's emotional awareness flows directly from what you have already learned in the nonjudgmental listening cycle. You have learned to reflect feelings and to relate these to deeper meanings in a client's life. As we have seen, clients use defense mechanisms at times to pull away from these feelings and to avoid looking at underlying issues. The technique of increasing emotional awareness is, in essence, asking the client's permission to stay with these emotions, even if they are painful, in order to fully explore the problem and to help the client communicate these feelings within the therapeutic relationship. The technique of increasing emotional awareness rests on the building blocks of reflecting feelings, reflecting meaning, summarizing, and giving clients directives to focus on these issues and not move away from them.

The steps for increasing a client's emotional awareness can be summarized as follows:

Step 1 *Observe and note the client's attempts to move away from the emotion.* The client's avoidance of emotion may take various forms, including changing the subject, blocking of speech, stuttering, fidgeting, and other nonverbal changes such as facial sagging or tightening, or the presence of tears hidden by downcast eyes. The helper brings awareness to nonverbal expression of emotions, such as voice tone, gestures, eye movement, bodily tension, or movement. For example, the helper may simply encourage the client to pay attention to a particular area by saying, "Are you aware that you are clenching your jaw?"

Client: "Well, um, I love them to death. They're great kids. But. . ."

Helper: "You keep mentioning your positive feelings for the kids, but I can tell by your voice that you get really angry sometimes as well."

Step 2 *Stop the client's movement away from the emotion and direct the client to focus on the emotional content.* The helper interrupts the conversation and asks the client to express how he or she feels about the problem right now.

Client: "I do. I get really angry at them. Sometimes I feel like hitting them. But that's OK, I know I won't. I'm not a child beater, you know. Besides, school is about to begin again and they'll be out of my hair soon."

Helper: "Let's go back to your feelings of anger toward the kids for a moment. Can you help me understand a little more about how you feel?"

Step 3   *Invite the client to become aware of the emotion.* The helper asks the client to focus on the emotion underlying the story the client is telling, explore the meaning of that emotion, and express it as fully as possible. As the client responds, other emotions often come to the surface as well. For example, the helper might observe that the client has brushed by or glossed over the feeling aspects of a problem and ask, "What are you experiencing now?" "What are you aware of right now?" "How does that statement feel to you?"

Helper: "For a moment, just try to stay with the emotion you feel when you are really frustrated with the kids. What is that like?"

Client: "I'm angry. Why can't we have a happy family? Why is there so much fighting? I've done everything I can."

Helper: "You feel guilty because there is so much conflict."

Step 4   *In a summary, challenge the client to follow through and act on the discoveries made through awareness of the emotion.* When it seems that the client is in touch with underlying feelings, the helper attempts to focus on what the client wants to do next. The motive power of the emotion has been released and needs a direction. Helpers encourage this tendency by challenging clients to develop plans and goals with the following kinds of interventions: "What do you need?" "What do you want?" "Where do you go from here?"

Helper: "From what I've gathered in this session, despite your best efforts, your teenage kids argue a lot, creating a difficult climate in the home. In the past this has made you angry, and you feel guilty because you see it as your job to create a happy family. Is this about right?"

Client: "Yes, that's mainly it. What I really need to do is stay out of their fights and remove myself from that situation rather than feeling guilty. They are not going to hurt each other physically, and my involvement does not seem to stop their fighting. I just get upset."

Helper: "Your plan to stay out of their disagreements sounds like a good one. I think that would be a good homework assignment for next week. Would you be willing to try your new approach and report back to me then?"

Stop and Reflect

Eugene Gendlin has developed a technique called *focusing*. It is a way of becoming more aware of troubling issues in one's life. Central to this method is the idea of a *felt sense*. A felt sense is a physical sensation or a bodily awareness that can help us get to the heart of a problem (Gendlin, 1978). Try Gendlin's technique yourself in the following adaptation, then answer the questions.

Step 1: Preparation

Find a quiet time and place and sit quietly and comfortably. Close your eyes if you wish. You may read the instructions yourself or ask a friend to read them to you.

Step 2: Clearing a Space

Ask yourself, "How do I feel?" "What is keeping me from feeling good?" "What is bothering me right now?" Then stop and quietly listen. A number of problems might start to arise, some important and others trivial. Let them all emerge. Don't let your mind focus too long on any one problem. Let go. Take on an air of detachment as these problems surface. Let them pile up and then observe them as if at a distance.

Step 3: Feeling for the Problem

As you survey your problems, ask yourself which problem *feels* the most pressing right now. Can you sense one that is heavier than the others? Ask yourself how the problem feels. Get a sense of the whole thing, but do not analyze it with your mind. Use your bodily sensations to get a grasp of what the entire issue feels like. It may take some time and concentration to experience this feeling that encompasses the entire issue. Don't try to solve the problem or dissect it; just let it be and experience your feelings about it.

Step 4: Finding the Crux

In this step, focus on the problem and see if you can find one aspect of it that feels the worst—the crux of it. But instead of coming up with an answer, just wait quietly and see if something emerges. The response may be only a special feeling or sensation, such as tension or fear. Don't attach any words to your experience; just let the feeling come forth.

Step 5: Labeling

Allow words and pictures to flow from the feeling you are experiencing. Keep your concentration on the crux of the problem and see what words or images you experience.

Step 6: Checking Back with the Feeling

Place the words you have come up with next to your feeling or bodily sensations about the problem. Do they match? Make sure they fit precisely. If they are correct, you will have a physical experience of completeness or a "confirming sensation." Get in touch with your feeling about the problem again to make sure the words you have found really fit for you. Spend a moment or two in silence as you experience this.

When you are finished, open your eyes. You may wish to record your experience in a journal.

- What insights did you have about the problem that came to the surface in this exercise?

- Were you surprised by the problems that came to the surface?
- How did you feel about getting in touch with this issue? Was it uncomfortable, or was it a pleasant experience?
- Which clients might have difficulty with a technique like this? Which clients might respond well?
- Gendlin suggests that you can also get in touch with positive feeling and experiences through focusing. Try this exercise again and this time ask yourself, "Why do I love _____?" in step 2 and move through the cycle.

Summary

Some clients come for help because they are experiencing excessive emotional arousal; they are suffering from intense fear or anger. Relaxation techniques and meditation are simple but effective ways of beginning to help such clients. Teaching deep muscle relaxation is not a very complicated procedure. It involves training the client individually or in a group to tense and relax the major muscle groups of the body. The client is assigned practice sessions as homework; the main task of the helper is to encourage practice and to help the client stick with the technique until he or she begins to benefit from it.

Increasing emotional arousal and expression is another time-honored method in the helping professions. It is not written about frequently because of the potential negative results that may occur if a client becomes highly aroused. With clients who are underexpressive or not in touch with the emotional side of their problems, stimulating arousal and expression can be very useful. The viewpoint expressed in this chapter is that experiencing and expressing emotions is not suf-

ficient to produce real change. When clients become more aware of deeply held emotions, they must place their experience in a new cognitive framework and act on their insights.

Some of the methods used to produce cathartic experiences can be dangerous if practiced by inexperienced helpers. Still, even a beginner can learn to help clients face the emotional content of their problems by using the technique of increasing emotional awareness. This technique involves asking the client to focus on emotions and inviting the client to fully experience and express this aspect of the story.

Although the techniques of relaxation and arousal may seem antagonistic, in reality both may be taught to a single client. On the one hand, the client may wish to become aware of the angry feelings that he or she keeps inside, search out the roots of the problem, and develop a better outlook. At times when expression of anger is inappropriate and counterproductive, a client may wish to reduce emotional arousal through relaxation methods.

Group Exercises

Group Exercise 1: Relaxation Training

For this exercise the training group divides into dyads. Each person has a turn as either client or helper. Each dyad finds as quiet a spot as possi-

ble to practice the training. The helper takes the client through an abbreviated version of deep muscle relaxation, given in Table 12-1. In this shorter variant, steps 2 and 5 are eliminated and the helper reads the instructions for steps 1, 3,

4, 6, and 7 only. For time considerations, each muscle group is to be tightened and relaxed only once rather than twice, as one would do in normal practice.

Following the relaxation sequence, take 5 minutes to discuss the effectiveness of the procedure. The client should answer the following questions.

a. Using a 100-point scale (with 100 being the most relaxed you've ever been and 0 being very tense), how deeply were you able to relax in this exercise?

b. Were the helper's instructions presented in a calm and methodical way?

c. Did the helper allow sufficient time for relaxation before proceeding to a new muscle group?

d. What might the helper have done to deepen your relaxation?

Following this feedback, client and helper switch roles and repeat the exercise.

Quick Tips: Relaxation Training

- Ask the client to move around slightly and find the most comfortable seating position before you begin the relaxation instructions.

- Keep your voice tone modulated and soothing.

- Watch the client for signs of tension or discomfort. When the procedure is complete, return to those areas where the client has difficulty relaxing, and ask the client to tense and relax those areas again.

- Make sure that you pause regularly in the process and suggest deep diaphragmatic breathing as a transition between tensing and relaxing muscle groups.

Group Exercise 2: Relaxing with Imagery

You can apply what you have already learned about imagery in Chapter 11 to relaxation training. Form groups of four, with three clients and one helper. The helper asks the other three members to find a comfortable position and then reads the instructions for the body scan in Table 12-1. This quick tensing and relaxation of the body provides a beginning point for the exercise, but participants should be instructed to notice any areas where tension lingers and to attend to that area by tensing and then relaxing those areas. If time permits, participants may practice diaphragmatic breathing to finish the first part of the exercise. Each member is to mentally note on a 100-point scale how tense he or she feels. A score of 100 represents extreme tension; a score of 0 represents the most relaxed he or she has ever felt.

In the second phase of the exercise, the helper reads the following material to the group:

Imagine that you are lying on a beach in a very comfortable lounge chair. It is a bright and sparkling day. You can hear the sounds of waves brushing the shoreline as you relax. In the distance you can also hear the cries of seagulls. The sun is beating down and it feels almost like a weight as your body becomes relaxed and heavy. Stay with this scene and imagine it in as much detail as you possibly can, letting your relaxation deepen.

For 3 minutes, participants continue to imagine this scene. End by saying, "This concludes the exercise. When you feel ready, slowly bring yourself back and open your eyes." Finally, the helper leads a discussion with the following questions:

a. Comparing your level of relaxation from beginning to end, would you rate your relaxation as deeper following the imagery exercise?

b. Can you think of some scene other than the beach that is more relaxing for you?

c. What elements of the relaxation image were the most relaxing? Did any part of the image increase your tension rather than relax you?

Homework

Homework 1

Listen to a piece of classical music for about 15–20 minutes—for example, orchestral pieces by Beethoven, Wagner, or Bach. Close your eyes and relax. As you listen, note any feelings that you are experiencing. If you can, draw a picture associated with the music. Do you notice an overall emotional theme in the music? How could music be effective in helping clients get in touch with emotions? For more information, see Gladding's book entitled *Counseling as an Art: The Creative Arts in Counseling* (1992). For contrast, listen to another, more relaxing kind of music, or environmental sounds, ocean waves, and the like. How might listening to relaxing music and sounds be a helpful activity for clients who want to learn relaxation?

Homework 2

Make two separate collages using photos, drawings, and words from newspapers, magazines, and other print media. The first collage should represent a time in your life when you were experiencing troubling or conflicting emotions. Prepare a second collage that represents your feelings and experiences during one of the best times of your life. Identify these feelings in writing beneath each picture. As you look back at each period of your life, does it reawaken any of these feelings in you? Which of these periods do you think about the most in your daily life? How might a collage such as this be useful for a client who is trying to deal with conflicting emotions from the past? How would you develop a conversation with a client, using the collage as a stimulus?

Homework 3

The skill of relaxation requires the therapeutic factor of practice to make it a part of one's life. Find a way of building relaxation practice into your daily life. Consider the following suggestions and then implement one in your own daily life. Report on your attempts in a paragraph or two.

- Every time you stop at a traffic light, do deep diaphragmatic breathing to lower your tension.

- Use small colored dots, available in office supply stores, to remind you to do a body scan. Place these dots on your computer screen, watch, or appointment book. Whenever you see one, tense and relax those muscles that seem the most tense.

- Before going to sleep each night, do a complete body scan and note the areas where the most tension resides. Keep a diary for a week and see if the same areas tend to hold much of your tension.

- Meditate for 10–15 minutes each morning. What effects does it have on your level of tension and your mental attitude?

References

Benson, H. (1984). *Beyond the relaxation response*. New York: Berkley Books.

Bogart, G. (1991). The use of meditation in psychotherapy: A review of the literature. *American Journal of Psychotherapy, 45,* 383–412.

Branden, N. (1971). *The disowned self.* New York: Bantam.

Breuer, J., & Freud, S. (1895/1955). *Studies on hysteria*. In J. Strachey (Ed.), *The complete works of Sigmund Freud, Standard Edition* (Vol. 2). London: Hogarth.

Carrington, P. (1978). *Learning to meditate: Clinically standardized meditation* (Instructor's manual). Kendall Park, NJ: Pace Educational Systems.

Fair, P. L. (1989). Biofeedback-assisted relaxation strategies in psychotherapy. In J. V. Basmajian (Ed.), *Biofeedback: Principles and practice for clinicians* (3rd ed.) (pp. 187–196). Baltimore: Williams & Wilkins.

Farelly, F., & Brandsma, J. (1974). *Provocative therapy.* Cupertino, CA: Meta.

Frank, J. D., & Frank, J. B. (1991). *Persuasion and healing: A comparative study of psychotherapy.* (3rd ed.). Baltimore: Johns Hopkins University Press.

Gatchel, R. J., & Baum, A. (1983). *An introduction to health psychology.* Reading, MA: Addison-Wesley.

Gendlin, E. T. (1969). Focusing. *Psychotherapy: Theory, Research and Practice, 6,* 4–15.

Gendlin, E. T. (1978). *Focusing.* New York: Everest House.

Gilliland, B. E., James, R. K., & Bowman, J. T. (1989). *Theories and strategies in counseling and psychotherapy.* Upper Saddle River, NJ: Prentice-Hall.

Gladding, S. T. (1992). *Counseling as an art: The creative arts in counseling.* Alexandria, VA: American Counseling Association.

Greenberg, L. S., Rice, L. N., & Ailed, R. (1993). *Facilitating emotional change.* New York: Guilford.

Greenberg, L. S., & Safran, J. D. (1988). *Emotion in psychotherapy.* New York: Guilford.

Jackins, H. (1962). *Elementary counselor's manual.* Seattle, WA: Rational Island.

Jacobson, E. (1938). *Progressive relaxation* (2nd ed.). Chicago: University of Chicago Press.

Janov, A. (1970). *The primal scream.* New York: Dell.

Lewin, K. (1935). *A dynamic theory of personality.* New York: McGraw-Hill.

Lowen, A. (1967). *The betrayal of the body.* New York: Collier.

McKay, M., Davis, M., & Fanning, P. (1981). *Thoughts and feelings: The art of cognitive stress intervention.* Richmond, CA: New Harbinger.

McMullin, R. (1986). *Handbook of cognitive therapy techniques.* New York: W. W. Norton.

Menninger, K. (1958). *Theory of psychoanalytic technique.* New York: Harper & Row.

Moreno, J. L. (1958). *Psychodrama* (Vol. 2). New York: Beacon House.

Nichols, M. P., & Efran, J. S. (1985). Catharsis in psychotherapy: A new perspective. *Psychotherapy, 22,* 46–58.

Nichols, M. P., & Zax, M. (1977). *Catharsis in psychotherapy.* New York: Gardener Press.

Novaco, R. W. (1977). Stress inoculation: A cognitive therapy for anger and its application to a case of depression. *Journal of Consulting and Clinical Psychology, 45,* 600–608.

Novaco, R. W. (1983). Stress inoculation therapy for anger control. In P. A. Keeler & L. G. Rift (Eds.), *Innovations in clinical practice: A source book* (Vol. 2, pp. 181–201). Sarasota, FL: Professional Resource Exchange.

Overholser, J. C. (1991). The use of guided imagery in psychotherapy: Modules for use with passive relaxation training. *Journal of Contemporary Psychotherapy, 21,* 159–172.

Pennebaker, J. W. (1989). Confession, inhibition, and disease. In L. Berkowitz (Ed.), *Advances in experimental social psychology* (Vol. 22, pp. 211–214). New York: Academic Press.

Pennebaker, J. W. (1990). *Opening up: The healing power of confiding in others.* New York: Morrow.

Perls, F. S. (1977). *The Gestalt approach: An eye witness to therapy.* Palo Alto, CA: Science and Behavior Books.

Polster, E., & Polster, M. (1973). *Gestalt therapy integrated.* New York: Brunner/Mazel.

Prochaska, J., & Norcross, J. C. (1994). *Systems of psychotherapy: A transtheoretical analysis* (3rd ed.). Pacific Grove, CA: Brooks/Cole.

Shapiro, D. H. (1994). Examining the content and context of meditation: A challenge for psychology in the areas of stress management, psychotherapy and religion/values. *Journal of Humanistic Psychology, 34,* 101–135.

Singh, R. (1996). *Inner and outer peace through meditation.* New York: Element Books.

Stampfl, T. G., & Levis, D. J. (1967). Essentials of implosive therapy: A learning-theory-based psychodynamic behavioral therapy. *Journal of Abnormal Psychology, 72,* 496–503.

Tubesing, D. (1981). *Kicking your stress habits.* Duluth, MN: Whole Person Press.

Witmer, J. M. (1985). *Pathways to personal growth: Developing a sense of worth and competence.* Muncie, IN: Accelerated Development.

Witmer, J. M., & Young, M. E. (1985). The silent partner: Uses of imagery in counseling. *Journal of Counseling and Development, 64,* 187–189.

Wolberg, L. R. (1977). *The technique of psychotherapy.* New York: Grune & Stratton.

Wolpe, J. (1958). *Psychotherapy by reciprocal inhibition.* Stanford, CA: Stanford University Press.

Yalom, I. (1975). *Theory and practice of group psychotherapy.* New York: Basic Books.

Young, M. E., & Bemak, F. (1996). Emotional arousal and expression in mental health counseling. *Journal of Mental Health Counseling, 25,* 1–16.

Activating Client Expectations, Hope, and Motivation

Introduction

In this chapter, we will take a closer look at the curative factor involved in instilling hope, increasing expectations, and overcoming client resistance to change. Figure 13-1 shows this factor highlighted among the six curative factors. Before learning the techniques for increasing hope and expectations, it is important first to understand the problems that they attempt to address: the discouragement, lack of confidence, and demoralization that most clients are experiencing when they come for help.

The Demoralization Hypothesis

According to Jerome Frank (Frank & Frank, 1991), those who seek counseling are demoralized. *Demoralization* is described by Frank as a "state of mind characterized by one or more of the following: subjective incompetence, loss of self-esteem, alienation, hopelessness (feeling that no one can help), or helplessness (feeling that other people could help but will not)" (p. 56). According to this view, when clients seek help they are looking not only to alleviate problems and symptoms of distress, but also to decrease feelings of discouragement.

Figure 13-1
Curative factors in the
REPLAN system: Activating
expectations and motivation

Demoralization is well known among professional helpers. Adlerians call it *dis-courangement*. Seligman (1975) identified an aspect of demoralization called *learned helplessness,* a state in many ways analogous to depression. Learned help-lessness was discovered in animal research and later in humans. Seligman found that people exposed to unsolvable problems became so discouraged that their later per-formance on solvable problems was negatively affected.

Frank believes that anxiety, depression, and loss of self-esteem (the most com-mon presenting symptoms) are the result of demoralization. Frank also proposes that symptoms and mental demoralization interact. Client problems or symptoms are worsened by a sense of discouragement and isolation. For example, a minor physical problem may be seen as inconsequential by one person, whereas a demoralized indi-vidual takes it as a further indication of the hopelessness of his or her situation.

Many clients improve radically early in the helping process. This has been at-tributed to the *placebo effect,* a medical analogy that has been unfortunately applied to the psychological realm. The placebo effect implies that the client can be fooled by the helper and that client symptoms are imaginary. According to the placebo ef-fect, well-established factors (Patterson, 1973) in social influence—attractiveness and trustworthiness of the helper, high expectations for treatment—are akin to sugar pills. Another, perhaps better way of understanding this kind of improvement is to see it as the ending of demoralization and the activation of hope and expectations for change (Frank, Nash, Stone, & Imber, 1963). It is the expectation itself that is heal-ing. Faith is powerful medicine (Siegel, 1986).

Encouragement

Witmer (1985) points out that a close analysis of the word *encouragement* shows that it means "to cause to have heart." Encouragement is closely aligned with Alfred Adler's school of individual psychology. Encouragement, in the Adlerian sense, is the major method by which the helper helps the client overcome demoralization or discourage-ment. Rather than being a specific method, it is a set of techniques that the helper uses throughout the helping process to coax the client away from discouraging beliefs and a self-centered world built on private logic. *Private logic* is another name for a world view that is unrealistic and based on premises that have never really been tested. Private logic sometimes derives from a person's upbringing, family constellation, cul-ture, or one-time learning that may not be appropriate to current challenges.

In a national survey conducted by the author (Young & Feiler, 1993), encour-agement was the second most frequently used counseling technique. It was utilized by 90% of the mental health counselors and counselor educators surveyed. We can-not be certain from these data that all respondents were operating under the same definition of encouragement; however, the survey is supportive of the notion that client encouragement is essential to most helpers.

To get a clearer idea about encouragement, look at Table 13-1, which compares the concepts of reinforcement from the behavioral tradition and the Adlerian concept

Table 13-1
Comparison of Encouragement and Praise/Reinforcement

Dimension	Encouragement	Reinforcement
Purpose	To motivate, inspire, hearten, instill confidence	To maintain or strengthen a specific behavior
Nature	Focuses on inner direction and internal control; emphasizes personal appreciation and effort more than outcome	Focuses on outer direction and external control; tends to emphasize material appreciation; emphasizes outcome
Population	All ages and groups	Seems most appropriate for children, situations with limited self-control and development, and conditions of specific problem behavior
Thoughts/Feelings/ Actions	A balance of thinking, feeling, and actions with feeling underlying the responses; i.e., satisfaction, enjoyment, challenge	Attending primarily to an action (behavioral) response that is observable
Creativeness	Spontaneity and variation in how encourager responds; encouragee has freedom to respond in spontaneous and creative ways; however, it may be difficult to understand the expectations of the encourager	Reinforcer responds to very specific behavior in a specific way; reinforcee is expected to respond in a specific and prescribed way; little doubt about the expectations of the reinforcer; helpful in establishing goals
Autonomy	Promotes independence, less likelihood of dependency upon a specific person or thing; more likely to generalize to other life situations	Tends to develop a strong association, perhaps dependence, between a specific reinforcer and a behavior; less likely to generalize to other life situations

of encouragement. As the table shows, praise (positive reinforcement) and encouragement have important but distinct uses. In general, encouragement is designed to inspire, to foster hope, to stimulate, and to support (Pitsounis & Dixon, 1988), whereas praise is designed to increase the likelihood that a specific behavior will be repeated. Encouragement focuses on developing autonomy, self-reliance, cooperation rather than competition (it avoids comparisons), and an internal locus of control (Hitz & Driscoll, 1988). Praise is a reward that strengthens a behavior when it occurs. Praise has some drawbacks in the helping relationship: it recognizes only success, not intentions, and it places the helper in a position of superiority. For these reasons, we will focus on methods of encouragement in our discussion.

Who Benefits Most from Encouragement?

According to Losoncy (1977), people who are dependent, depressed, cut off from social support systems, or suffering from low self-esteem respond to encouragement.

Encouragement also helps clients who show an excessive need for attention, for power, for control of situations and people, and for revenge. It is useful as well with clients who avoid participation and responsibility, are perfectionistic, or tend to be closed-minded (Losoncy, 1977).

Types of Encouraging Responses

In a review of the literature, we identified in the writings of Dinkmeyer and Losoncy (1980), Losoncy (1977), Sweeney (1989), and Witmer (1985) 14 types of encouraging behaviors that are effective therapeutic interventions:

1. Acknowledging the client's efforts and improvement.
2. Concentrating on the client's present capacities, possibilities, and conditions rather than on past failures.
3. Focusing on the client's strengths.
4. Showing faith in the client's competency and capabilities.
5. Showing an interest in the progress and welfare of the client.
6. Focusing on those things that interest or excite the client.
7. Asking the client to evaluate his or her own performance rather than comparing it to another standard.
8. Showing respect for the client and the client's individuality and uniqueness.
9. Becoming involved with clients through honest self-disclosure.
10. Offering assistance as an equal partner in the counseling process.
11. Using humor.
12. Providing accurate feedback on deeds rather than on personality.
13. Confronting discouraging beliefs.
14. Lending enthusiasm and asking for commitment toward goals.

Summarizing these 14 interventions may oversimplify the Adlerian concept, but it may give some general direction to helpers and improve the understanding of the method. I have divided these interventions into three major helper activities: focusing on the positive and the changeable, emphasizing equality and individuality, and pushing with enthusiasm.

Focusing on the Positive and the Changeable

Optimism is the tendency to view the world as a benign, friendly source of support. Not everyone has this point of view, but optimism can be learned. The work of Simonton and Mathews-Simonton (1978) with cancer patients has pointed to the potential health benefits of optimism. More recently, the work of Bernard Siegel (1986) has interested millions in the power of optimistic attitudes in dealing with medical crises. An optimistic point of view is also associated with good mental health and freedom from stress (Witmer, 1985).

In the preceding list, interventions 1 through 4 are grouped together into the encouraging helper behavior of focusing on the positive and the changeable. All of these interventions foster development of an optimistic attitude by helping to shift the client's attention from the deficits to the strengths in his or her life. Such encouragement entails noticing the client's successes as well as showing faith in the client's ability to succeed. Focusing on the positive and the changeable also includes redirecting the client's discussions from the past to the present. Interventions of this nature are apparent in the following client/helper dialogue:

Client: "I feel like I've totally messed up my future."

Helper: "Tell me what you really enjoy doing."

Client: "What? . . . Oh, well, I really enjoy working in the garden." (The client goes on to describe the feelings he enjoys and the helper encourages him.)

Helper: "How do you feel now?"

Client: "Better. But I always feel better when I think about good things like that."

Helper: "Yes, so do I. I prefer to feel good."

Client: (laughing) "So do I. But it isn't always easy."

Encouragement should not be seen as trying to get the client to ignore difficult issues; instead, it asks the client to develop a balanced view which includes the positives. In addition, it helps the client focus on the parts of the problem that can be changed, rather than ruminating over the unchangeable. Here is an example:

Client: "We went to the picnic and it was a total disaster just like I said it would be. Her mom started criticizing us again, so my wife and I ended up spending most of the time playing with the kids and talking to each other."

Helper: "It sounds like there were some uncomfortable moments, but it also sounds like you did something positive to deal with her mother's criticism."

Client: "What?"

Helper: "Well, instead of getting involved in the argument, you got away from it and spent some time with each other and with some of the kids. It sounds like you hit on a good strategy. Do you agree?"

Communicating Equality and Respect for the Individuality of the Client

The essence of interventions 5 through 10 on the list of encouraging responses is to communicate to the client that the helper and client are on equal footing and that each is unique. By self-disclosing, the helper takes away some of the artificiality of the helper role and connects with the client in a more genuine way. Finally, the helper teaches the client to challenge the idea that the worth of a person is judged by external standards. The client must come to evaluate performance against internal standards and to appreciate his or her personal strengths and unique approach to life, as in the following client/helper exchange:

Client: "I finally got off drugs, got a job and an apartment. My life is back on track, but it's still not good enough."

Helper: "What do you mean?"

Client: "My mom won't let up about how I disappointed her, how I was supposed to finish college two years ago. Even though I'm back in school in the fall, all she can say is 'Two years too late.' "

Helper: "What about you—how do you look at it? Are you proud of what you've accomplished in the last eight months?"

Client: "Well, don't you think I've done a lot?"

Helper: "You tell me."

Client: "I have. I have come a long way. It was hard, too."

Pushing with Enthusiasm

Interventions 11 through 14 demonstrate that encouragement is not merely support; it does not mean accepting the status quo. There is an element of confrontation and a sincere effort to produce movement in the client. Discouragement is actually a defensive maneuver that maintains the status quo through inaction. Encouragement pushes the client by giving feedback, confronting the private logic of the client, asking for a commitment, and using humor to turn the client around (Mosak, 1987). The following example continues the client/helper dialogue from the preceding section. Notice the confrontation and the helper pushing the client to make a commitment:

Helper: "So although you know you've overcome a lot, sometimes you still use your mother's yardstick on your life rather than your own. Would you agree?"

Client: "That's when I get depressed. I'm not sure I can ever please her, but that's not going to stop my recovery."

Helper: "So how are you going to stop doing that?"

Client: "Well, first of all, I will try to let it go in one ear and out the other. But really, I think I'll just spend less time over there."

Helper: "That sounds like a good start. Let's consider that as a plan for this week and when we get back together, you'll let me know, right?"

Client: "Right."

How to Encourage

Following are general guidelines that can assist the helper in dealing with discouragement. Encouragement is typically employed at the beginning of a session so that a client will open up, and at the end of a session to inspire the client to practice. The steps to take in encouraging a client are shown in conjunction with a case example that includes client statements and helper responses. Notice that the technique of encouragement consists of giving the client directives to pay attention to his or her own strengths and to focus on what can be changed; it includes the building blocks in the nonjudgmental listening cycle as well as confrontation and feedback.

Step 1   *Use the nonjudgmental listening cycle to gain rapport and understand the problem.* Encouraging responses will not be taken seriously if the helper does not fully understand the client. The nonjudgmental listening cycle is encouraging to the client because it promotes a relationship based on equality and respect.

    Herb was a furniture salesman out of a job. He was very pessimistic about getting hired. Although he had initially been rather active, recently he had spent more time driving around in his car than actually looking for a position. His wife accompanied him to the first counseling session but refused to return. She was angry and frustrated. According to Herb, he had lost all ambition, and he feared he would never be able to locate a new job.

Helper: "So tell me what it is like to be out of a job."

Herb: "It is hell! Everyone blames me. I get depressed and resentful, but mostly I am angry."

Helper: "You're mad at yourself for being in this situation."

Herb: "Exactly. What kind of man am I? My father never lost a job. Neither did my father-in-law."

Helper: "You mention your father and father-in-law. You seem to be saying that working is an important part of being a man."

Herb: "Of course—I am supposed to be the provider. Now my wife is taking care of me."

    In this part of the dialogue, the helper begins with an open question, reflects feelings, and finally reflects meaning. These responses convince the client that the helper understands the situation at a fairly deep level.

Step 2   *Offer to be an ally.*

Helper: "Herb, my feeling is that what you really need right now is a coach. You seem to have job-seeking skills, a good work history, and a positive attitude about your chosen profession. You've shown a lot of success in sales previously. Perhaps together we can help you find your enthusiasm again."

Herb: "Yes, I've had success in the past but I'm at a dead end now. Sometimes I think it is hopeless."

Helper: "My thought is that we begin to look at this thing from a different angle. Perhaps if we put our heads together, we might be able to find a solution."

Step 3 *Focus on the positive and note client attempts, however small, to accomplish the goal.*

Herb: "I still get up at 6:30 A.M. like I did when I was working. I get dressed and start out all right. First, I read the paper and start to make a call or two. That's when I start getting down. I end up driving around town, killing time until dinner, making my wife think that I am out looking for a job. Why am I doing this?"

Helper: "Well, one of the things I notice is that the rhythm is still there. You are set to get back into a work routine, and you seem to like that. Even though you are not making the contacts, you are going through the motions, rehearsing for that day when you are back to work. That is a good sign and something we can build on."

Step 4 *Offer feedback or confrontation and ask for commitment.*

Helper: "I've got some feedback for you if you want it."

Herb: "OK."

Helper: "It seems like one of the problems is that you are not being honest with yourself or your wife about what you do all day. I would like you to keep track of your activities a little better. I think this would help you feel better about yourself and it might help the relationship, too."

Herb: "It's hard to do when I get nothing back."

Helper: "I agree, it *is* difficult. But I am only asking that you begin to keep a log of what you're doing toward finding a job each day, and we will see if we can increase that or make some changes in the direction of your search."

Herb: "All right. I can do that."

Step 5 *Show continued enthusiasm for the client's goals and interest in the client's feelings and progress.*

Herb: (one week later) "Since the last time we talked, I didn't do what we decided. I didn't make two calls a day looking for a job. I guess I averaged about one call per day. The first day I did three, then one, then one again, and I took the weekend off. I got no response."

Helper: "I am very glad to hear about this. That kind of progress is what we've been looking for. It seems that getting off dead center is the hardest part, and you've gotten through that. Besides, by being honest about it, you've now included me in what's going on. Now what is needed is keeping up your efforts. Right?"

Client: "I guess so. I'm afraid that this won't work, that it will be just like last time and fizzle out."

Helper: "Yes, it can be scary, but let's try to focus on the present if we can, rather than look back. I have been hoping that you'd make this beginning and then hang in there until something breaks. Let's continue with this plan. I'll call you about Wednesday to see how things are going. Again, I feel good about these first steps. Keep up the good work."

What Is Resistance?

Traditional Definitions

Resistance is antitherapeutic behavior by the client. Freud (1900/1952) first identified the concept as a defensive reaction against anxiety when unacceptable thoughts, feelings, and impulses are driven into conscious awareness through the uncovering process of the therapeutic relationship. Resistance has always been a topic of great interest to helpers because at some point nearly all clients seem to waver or resist change just when it seems to be within reach.

Resistance remains a hot topic in the helping professions because it is connected with the notion of the reluctant client (Dowd & Milne, 1986; Harris & Watkins, 1987). The reluctant client is one who does not wish to come for help in the first place but who has been forced or pressured to do so. It is estimated that 50–75% of clients could be described as reluctant (Dyer & Vriend, 1977; Haley, 1989; Ritchie, 1986). They are coerced by the courts or by the corrections system, are brought for help by a spouse or a family member, or are being disciplined by a school or college. There has been a great interest in techniques for engaging reluctant clients, probably because they represent such a large proportion of clients (Amatea, 1988; Larke, 1985; Larrabee, 1982).

Do Clients Want to Change?

Resistance has been described as present in every therapeutic situation (Brammer, Shostrom, & Abrego, 1989) and as the cause of most therapeutic failures (Redl, 1966). Hart (1986) says, "Therapy is difficult because clients are resistant to change and defensive about revealing their urges" (p. 211). This definition focuses primarily on the seeming unwillingness of clients to give up self-defeating behavior. Sometimes claiming that the client is resistant is merely a way of focusing attention away from the fact that the helper is having a difficult time.

This tendency to place the entire blame on the client is found in other therapies besides the psychodynamic approach. Perls (1971), the Gestalt therapy founder, saw resistance as an attempt to decline responsibility for change. He felt that clients were consistently avoiding their problems in the helping relationship (Brammer et al., 1989). Rational-emotive therapy practitioners have thought of resistance as either laziness or fear (Mahoney, 1988a), and transactional analysts have accused clients of playing games.

Family therapists, in contrast, have traditionally seen resistance as attempts by the family to maintain a homeostatic balance. Jackson (1968) pointed out that most families come to the helping process as a result of a change and are looking for security. They are seeking stability rather than disruption. Families who resist change have even been described as "barracudas" (Bergman, 1985), presumably because they can be aggressive when asked to change.

A different definition is that resistance is any behavior by client *or* helper that moves the client away from therapeutic goals (Cormier & Cormier, 1991) or that leads to anything less than full commitment to the goals (Cormier & Hackney, 1987). Thinking about resistance in this way makes it a problem affecting the helping process rather than an avoidance by the client. In addition, helper behaviors that delay progress may also be termed resistance.

Another viewpoint is that resistance can be perceived as communication. The client is telling the helper about his or her defenses and coping patterns. It signals the helper that the helping process is slowing down and may be headed for termination (Brammer et al., 1989). Blocks in the helping relationship probably are a clue to similar difficulties in the client's other relationships.

A new idea has been advanced by some cognitive therapists who point out that resistance is a natural reaction to changing one's *schemata,* or mental constructs about the world (Dowd & Seibel, 1990; Mahoney, 1988b). The client naturally clings to his or her habitual ways of thinking about life, no matter how dysfunctional. When the helper begins to disrupt long-held and cherished beliefs about the world, the client tries to protect his or her core beliefs from sweeping changes that may bring chaos. Cognitive therapists believe that change should be a gradual process of modifying the client's world view so as to limit the amount of resistant behavior.

Finally, a new viewpoint about resistance is developing in the strategic-therapy and solution-focused schools (de Shazer, 1985, 1988; Haley, 1976; Lawson, 1986; Otani, 1989). One way of expressing their ideas is to say that for them, resistance does not exist. In fact, a funeral for resistance was apparently held at one training center. A client's failure to comply with directives is interpreted as an attempt to improve on or to individualize assignments. Rather than being seen as uncooperative behavior, it is perceived as the client's best attempt to change. According to traditional interpretation, resistance implies that the client does not want to change and thus resistance becomes a self-fulfilling prophecy; if the helper searches for resistance, he or she will surely find it (O'Hanlon & Weiner-Davis, 1989). Conse-quently, strategic and solution-focused therapists interpret signs of resistance not as uncooperative client behavior, but as a signal that techniques are missing the mark and need to be modified or eliminated.

What Does Resistance Look Like?

The following is a list of common symptoms of resistance reported by various writ-ers (Blanck, 1976; Brammer et al., 1989; Lerner & Lerner, 1983; Sack, 1988; Wolberg, 1954).

1. The client criticizes the helper or the counseling process.
2. The client comes late to sessions, fails to keep appointments, or forgets to pay fees.
3. The client is silent.
4. The client intellectualizes and philosophizes.
5. The client terminates prematurely or reports a sudden improvement that is actually a protection against further change.
6. The client uses excessive humor, silliness, or facetiousness.
7. The client persistently says "I don't know."
8. The client does not wish to terminate and wants to extend session length.
9. The client delves into the helper's personal life.
10. The client presents irrelevant material designed to intrigue the helper.
11. The client develops insights but does not apply them, dissociating the help-ing process from everyday life.
12. The client fails to complete homework and directives or to follow advice.

What Causes Resistance?

While different theorists explain resistance in varying ways, a number of common factors seem to surface (Bugental & Bugental, 1986; McMullin, 1986; Ritchie, 1986). The explanations are sometimes divided into client, helper, and environmental sources (Cormier & Cormier, 1991). Remember that resistance is defined here as anything that interferes with a client's progress toward the goals, whether it is in-tentional or not.

Client Sources of Resistance

Sometimes clients lack the skills to comply with the helper's suggestions. For exam-ple, clients may not possess certain social skills needed to overcome a fear of public speaking. A client's inability to follow homework assignments may be due to lack of skill in self-expression rather than an oppositional attitude.

A second area of resistance involves client fears. Clients fear the helping process because they find self-disclosure with a stranger uncomfortable. They fear the in-tensity of emotions that might be unleashed. They lack trust and fear exposure. They are afraid that the helping process will cause disequilibrium. They may fear change most of all (Bugental & Bugental, 1986).

Another major source of resistance is *involuntary status,* the feeling of being coerced into the helping process by some third party: an employer, a spouse, or the court (Driscoll, 1984). Some people are rebels. Others resist the system and see the helper as an extension of government control.

Other clients resist the helping process because of a conflict between their own values and those of the helper or the community. Some religious groups feel that the helping process attempts to shift their values toward those of an unhealthy society. Others feel that exposing problems to a professional is shameful to their families. Still others reject the helping process because of cultural injunctions against being dependent on strangers when one should rely on the family or on one's own resources.

Dislike of the helper can be a reason for slowed progress in the helping relationship. The client may not like the helper because of the helper's gender, religion, appearance, class, race, or cultural background. The helper's personal style and even the school of therapy to which the helper belongs can be aversive to the client (Stream, 1985).

McMullin (1986) reminds us that clients come to the helping process for a variety of reasons and that acceptance of initial goals may not be genuine. The real goal may be hidden behind a "calling card" or superficial goal. If a client does not seem committed to the agreed-upon goals, there may be some other, undisclosed reason for coming to the helping process. One reason may be that the client is lonely and wants the companionship of an intelligent and sensitive friend. Other clients may only be seeking the temporary relief that accompanies unloading their feelings and frustrations, or they may simply be sampling the helping process as some people go for a massage.

Helper Sources of Resistance

Helper frustration often leads to a further slowdown in progress. The client may view the helper's frustration as punitive (Martin, 1983) or as a sign that the client's situation is hopeless. The root of frustration may be that the helper wants more for the client than the client wants for himself or herself (Cormier & Hackney, 1987). When helpers become frustrated, they may respond by putting less effort and energy into the session or by becoming aloof. Sometimes this is due to the fact that the helper takes the client's lack of progress personally. It makes the helper feel ineffective and impotent. In a worst-case scenario, a helper's frustration may tempt him or her to criticize or blame the client for the lack of progress or may prompt the helper to make an inappropriate referral just to get rid of the client.

Environmental Sources of Resistance.

Engaging a professional helper can be expensive. It is common for clients to drop out simply because they cannot afford to continue. Another environmental obstacle is that gains made by the client may not be supported by family and friends. A client attempting to lose weight may find family members encouraging him or her to go off the diet. Clients also feel that some changes, such as increased assertiveness, may not be accepted by others and that they will be personally rejected. If we accept the concept that a family system attempts to maintain equilibrium, any member who tries to upset the rules and roles of a family will meet stiff opposition.

How to Deal with Resistance

Preventing Resistance

Before dealing directly with this subject, let us think about some ways to prevent resistance in the first place. For example, when it appears that a client is fearful or reluctant to change, before giving a homework assignment, ask the client to brainstorm all of the excuses he or she might give for not completing assignments or for accomplishing goals.

Meichenbaum and Turk (1987) studied noncompliance with medical treatment. They found that as much as 50% of the medication prescribed is never taken. In looking at how to increase client adherence to treatment, they identified a number of methods that can apply to any kind of helping. First of all, they suggest that the helper not overemphasize the client's resistant behavior. Here are nine of their suggestions for dealing with noncompliance:

1. Expect noncompliance and do not react negatively.
2. Consider the homework assignments and treatment plan from the client's point of view. Would you be willing to undergo this kind of treatment yourself?
3. Develop a collaborative relationship and negotiate the goals with the client.
4. Be client-oriented.
5. Customize treatment.
6. Enlist family support.
7. Provide the client with a system of continuity and accessibility to the helper.
8. Make use of community resources (such as support groups).
9. Don't give up.

Identifying Levels of Motivation

One way to deal with resistance is to understand that clients have different levels of motivation. Some are merely considering change, while others are ready to act. Two different groups of writers have begun to look at levels of motivation. One view is promoted by the eclectic thinkers Norcross, Prochaska, and DiClemente (Prochaska & DiClemente, 1983, 1986; Prochaska & Norcross, 1994; Prochaska, Norcross, & DiClemente, 1994). Another comes from the brief family therapy training center (de Shazer, 1988). Both see the client's level of readiness for the helping process as an important aspect of planning treatment.

The eclectic model of Prochaska and DiClemente (1983, 1986) proposes that clients move through four stages in the process of change. Each stage represents a period of time and a set of tasks needed for movement to the next stage. This model is particularly applicable to the addictions field, since it mirrors the process that individuals undergo in the decision to receive treatment and in their relapse or recovery (Marlatt, 1988). The model also indicates that a helper can select the most effective interventions depending on the client's level of motivation (see Table 13-2).

Clients who are unaware of a problem are in the stage of *precontemplation*. At this point, they are not even considering a change and are surprised when friends and family suggest that they have a problem. Many such people are referred for help each year by courts, family, and friends. The best treatments for clients at this level are primarily educational. The helper avoids moralizing and instead invites the client to think more and more about the problem.

When a person becomes aware that a problem might exist, he or she has entered the stage of *contemplation*. A client at this stage may admit that a problem exists, but he or she denies that it is a serious problem or that professional help is needed. Many who suffer from alcoholism cannot cross the threshold of the Alcoholics Anonymous 12-step program because the first steps begin with the admission that one's life has become unmanageable because of alcohol. People may remain in this "I'll quit tomorrow" stage for years until they experience enough pain to motivate further movement.

Action or *determination* is the phase of treatment in which the individual is ready to change behavior patterns or begins to seek outside help. The balance may shift suddenly toward the action phase, or it may be a gradual process. Normally the decision to take action is made when the client experiences so much discomfort that "something has to change." Clients at this stage benefit from directives, treatment

Table 13-2
Stages of Motivation and Change

Prochaska and Di Clemente	de Shazer	Possible Interventions
Precontemplation	Visitor	Awareness exercises Education Feedback Relationship enhancement Observations/confrontation
Contemplation	Complainant	Encouraging commitment Noting rewards and drawbacks Promoting ownership/responsibility
Action	Customer	Action strategies Rehearsal/practice Tasks, ordeals, and homework
Maintenance		Follow-up contacts Support groups Self-control strategies Relapse prevention

programs, and homework assignments that involve experimenting with different behaviors.

Once a client seeks help and receives treatment, the *maintenance* stage begins.
When the problem has come under control, the client attempts to change his or her
lifestyle to accommodate the changes made. This is a crucial period in the process of
change and one that is often neglected in treatment programs. The maintenance
stage may lead to stable change or relapse, depending on how well the helper is able
to extend treatment through follow-up and the degree to which the client can develop personal and environmental supports for new behaviors. Clients at the maintenance stage need continuing support from peers and family and need to practice
self-care and self-control strategies.

De Shazer's Model

Another way of looking at levels of motivation is in a model suggested by Steve de
Shazer (1989). His model divides clients into three categories: visitors, complainants,
and customers. At the lowest level of motivating, *visitors* are individuals who seemingly have no complaints. They may be forced or coerced into the helping process by
some third party who does have a complaint. Visitors can be helped by giving them
information, suggesting educational programs, and getting them to think about their
problems. The helper may be able to help the client recognize that a problem exists
or at least prepare the client to get help later by helping the client become aware of
available resources when help is needed.

Complainants are those clients who are uncomfortable and are seeking solutions. They clearly wish to consider a change of some kind but they may not be ready
to do much about it.

On the other hand, clients who are ready, willing, and able to take action are labeled *customers*. Helpers frequently become frustrated because they confuse complainants with customers. With complainants, the helper's job is to tip the balance and
make the client aware of the need to change. Complainants will not follow through
with action-oriented directives or homework, so it is best to avoid these. Only customers should be given homework or other behavioral tasks. Table 13-2 shows a comparison of the viewpoints of de Shazer and of Prochaska and DiClemente, showing
their similarities and some possible interventions associated with each level of motivation. A helper can refer to this chart to think about possible interventions when it
appears that the client is not ready to change. Thinking about motivation in its various levels can stimulate us to devise appropriate interventions and accept the client's
current state of readiness without becoming frustrated.

Tipping the Balance

Tipping the balance is a name for helper activities that motivate clients to change by
focusing them on the rewards of change or emphasizing the negative aspects of the current situation. Tipping the balance works when clients are stuck. The situations or
problems that bring clients for help can be thought of as a temporary balance of driving

and restraining forces (Lewin, 1951). For example, take the situation of Janice, a young accountant who is considering a move from Ohio to Seattle. Janice has a problem and is stymied because she must consider both the forces pushing her to move and others that urge her to stay. She might list the pros and cons of moving. It is difficult to make a decision this way, however, because it cannot be made simply by seeing which list is longer. Reasons for staying or leaving carry different weights—for example, being close to family might be more important than a salary increase.

Like two sides of a scale, movement occurs only when one side outweighs the other. For example, being satisfied and remaining in Ohio is a condition of *homeostasis* or balance. It can be modified by diminishing the ties that hold her to Ohio or by increasing her incentives to move on. A person may stay put because of loyalty, high pay, supportive friends, and so on, but he or she may move either when a better offer (a *driving force*) comes along or when a *restraining force,* such as fringe benefits or opportunities for advancement, is reduced. By the same token, a client who wishes to lose weight could decrease the pleasure of eating (a restraining force) by eating quickly. Conversely, the desire to feel more attractive (a driving force) can be increased by incentives, such as buying clothes in a smaller size or obtaining positive feedback on attractiveness from supportive friends. Helpers assist clients in tipping the balance toward change when it appears that the client is in the doldrums, caught between opposing forces.

One set of methods for tipping the balance involves rewarding change and taking away rewards for behaviors that are maintaining the status quo. It is important to ascertain which aspects of the client's environment promote maintenance of the status quo and then to remove them. The family of a patient in chronic pain, for example, might be asked to discontinue expressions of sympathy and to stop doing things for the client that he or she can do independently. Using methods of self-control (Kanfer, 1986), clients can also learn to increase the positive consequences associated with their own behavior and to build in rewards for change. In short, the client's resistance to change is sometimes due to the fact that the rewards for giving up the behavior are not as powerful as those for retaining it. Helpers encourage clients to use powerful rewards to tip the balance. For example, a client who wishes to lose 25 pounds may be more motivated to lose weight if the client promises himself or herself a trip to Europe rather than merely a new outfit.

Contingency Contracting: A Method for Tipping the Balance

Negotiating contracts for change has become widespread in schools and counseling centers (Kanfer, 1980). *Contingency contracts* are agreements between individuals who desire behavior change and those whose behavior needs changing, such as between parents and their children. Individuals can make formal contracts with themselves, their spouses, or others. All contracts specify the positive consequences of adhering to the contract and the negative consequences of noncompliance. They also specify contingencies or "if-then" statements, such as "If you take out the trash without being told, then I will give you your allowance regularly." Such contracts have been effective with academic problems, social skills, bad habits, marital problems, and delinquent behaviors (Dowd & Olson, 1985).

Based on Dowd and Olson's recommendations (1985), the following guidelines for effective contracts are suggested:

1. All aspects of the contract should be understood and agreed to by both partners.

2. The contract should be in written form with a solemn signing indicating commitment to the agreement.

3. The contract should stress rewarding accomplishments rather than merely reinforcing obedience.

4. The contract should be considered the first of a series of steps if the behavior to be changed is complex.

5. The contract is not a legal document and can be renegotiated at any time by any of the signers.

6. The behaviors to be achieved should be clearly and objectively defined. They should be relatively short-range goals.

7. If possible, behavioral goals should be quantified and specified (who, what, where, when, and how often) so that it is clear when the contract is being honored.

8. The contract should not contain goals that either of the parties is incapable of reaching. Success should be simple to understand and achieve.

9. The rewards and privileges for displaying each behavior should be specified.

10. The reward for each behavior should be commensurate with the behavior needed to earn it.

11. The reward should be timed to be delivered as soon as possible after the behavior is displayed.

12. The contract should specify small penalties for each person's failure to abide by the contract.

13. Bonuses should be given if goals are exceeded or if they are accomplished more quickly than expected.

Stop and Reflect

Often, a problem is not merely a hurdle that must be jumped or a puzzle to be solved. It may be something like a tug-of-war where each side is equally strong and there is no movement. A problem can be seen as a temporary state in which forces that propel or drive change are balanced by forces that restrain or motivate against change. To understand this better, answer the following questions and then complete Figure 13-2. Also look over Figure 13-3, an example of a completed worksheet.

1. Describe a problem or decision you have to make that is important to you. Describe it as simply and specifically as possible.

2. Who is involved? What other people influence this problem or will be affected if you change?

3. If it were in your power to change one part of the problem, what would you change?

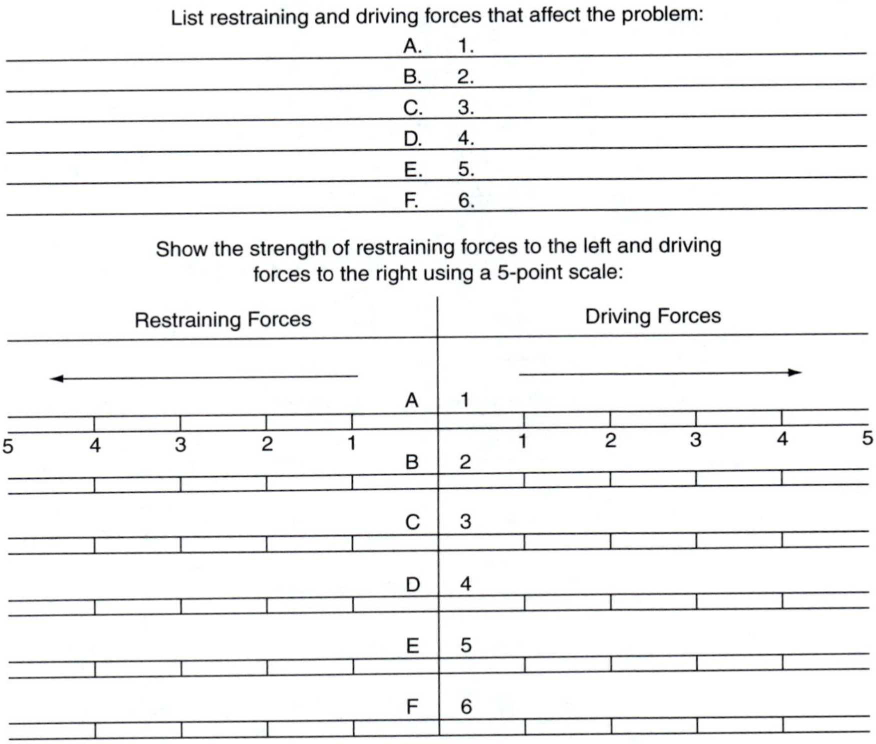

Figure 13-2
Driving and
restraining forces
worksheet

List restraining and driving forces that affect the problem:

A.	1.
B.	2.
C.	3.
D.	4.
E.	5.
F.	6.

Show the strength of restraining forces to the left and driving
forces to the right using a 5-point scale:

Restraining Forces   Driving Forces

	5	4	3	2	1			1	2	3	4	5
						A	1					
						B	2					
						C	3					
						D	4					
						E	5					
						F	6					

4. List up to six forces that are restraining you from changing (see the example in Figure 13-3) and place a number from 1 to 5 next to each, indicating the strength of that force as shown:

   1 = the force is unimportant
   2 = the force has a little impact
   3 = moderate importance
   4 = an important factor
   5 = major factor

5. List up to six forces that are driving you to change. Place a number from 1 to 5 indicating the strength of each of these forces that are pushing you to change, using the scale described in step 4.

6. Chart your answers in Figure 13-2, in the manner shown in the example in Figure 13-3.

7. When you have completed the exercise, consider the following questions individually or share them with some classmates.

   a. Review your answer to step 2. Did you include your feelings of obligation to others as factors?

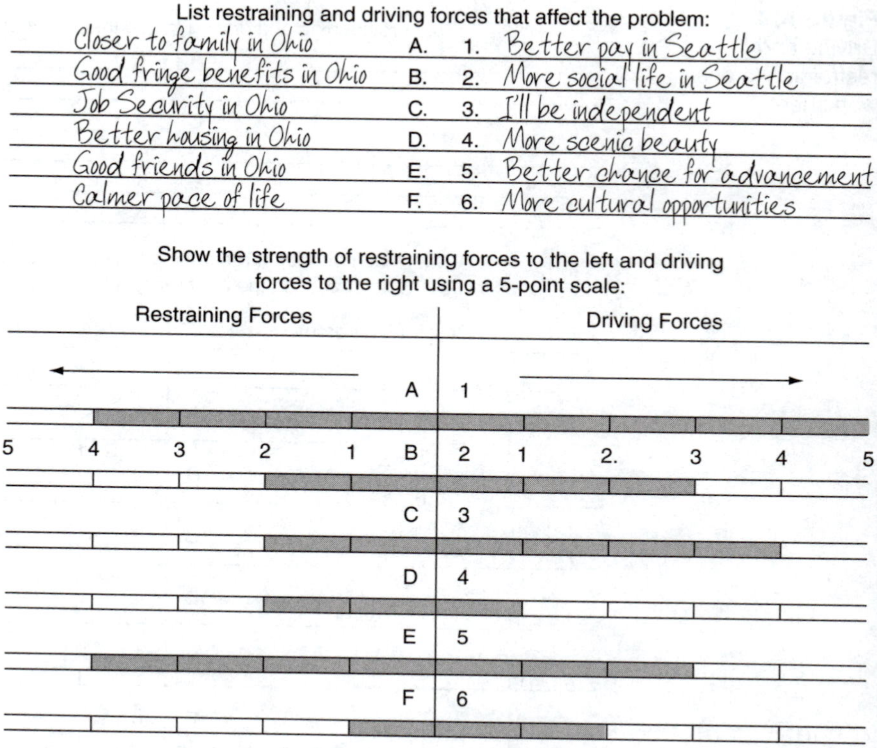

Figure 13-3
A completed driving
and restraining forces
worksheet

List restraining and driving forces that affect the problem:

Restraining		Driving
Closer to family in Ohio	A.	1. Better pay in Seattle
Good fringe benefits in Ohio	B.	2. More social life in Seattle
Job Security in Ohio	C.	3. I'll be independent
Better housing in Ohio	D.	4. More scenic beauty
Good friends in Ohio	E.	5. Better chance for advancement
Calmer pace of life	F.	6. More cultural opportunities

Show the strength of restraining forces to the left and driving
forces to the right using a 5-point scale:

Restraining Forces   Driving Forces

5   4   3   2   1   A   1
                                 B   2   1   2.   3   4   5
                                 C   3
                                 D   4
                                 E   5
                                 F   6

b. Does your answer to step 3 give you any ideas about what would really motivate you to change?

c. Look at the items in your list of restraining forces. Can any of these items
   be reduced? For example, in Janice's case, she enjoys her garden and hates
   to leave it. In Seattle, she would live in an apartment. Could Janice decrease this restraining force by looking into community garden efforts or
   window-box gardening to decrease the power of this restraining force?
   Again, consider your list of restraining forces. Which could be reduced?

d. Now take a look at your list of driving forces. Can any of these be strength-
   ened? For example, Janice might increase the force of "more social opportunities," which she labeled as a 3, by taking one or two trips to Seattle,
   getting to know her co-workers better, or even investigating a dating service. Now take a look at your list. How might you strengthen any of your
   driving forces to propel change?

Confronting Resistance Directly

The language of war has been used to describe the friction in the helper/client relationship when resistance crops up. Helpers have traditionally explained to clients
that they are resisting improvement because they are afraid to change. This is called
interpretation of resistance. The helper continually confronts clients with their un-

willingness to take their medicine. As Sifenos says, "Pounding patients with a truth produces good results" (Davanloo, 1978, p. 241). A gentler version is to confront the client's resistant behavior directly and then ask the client to explore why he or she might be reluctant to change, as in this dialogue between helper and client:

Jonathan: "I didn't do that assignment we talked about last week. To tell you the truth, I was so busy that I forgot about it. I also didn't do any writing."

Kristi: "Interesting. On the one hand, you come to therapy to get over the writer's block and yet you don't do the things that might help you overcome it. Can you explain this to me?" (confronting)

Jonathan: "Well, I do want to get over it, but I just don't have the motivation."

Kristi: "I think this idea of motivation is more of an excuse for not doing the assignment. How much motivation would it have taken to do the homework assignment?" (confronting)

Jonathan: "Not much, I guess."

Kristi: "Let's talk some more about your reluctance to change. Can you think of any reasons why you might not want to write again?" (inviting exploration)

The Technique of Traveling with the Resistance

Adler, Rogers, Sullivan, and Maslow all assert that a hostile, competitive view of resistance with the rhetoric of warfare is counterproductive (Lauver, Holiman, & Kazama, 1982). These helpers and a host of others have developed methods in response to client resistance that "travel with the resistance." *Traveling with the resistance* refers to helper behaviors that attempt to normalize and accept the oppositional behavior (see Brammer et al., 1989; Dyer & Vriend, 1977; Egan, 1990; Guidano, 1988; Walker & Aycock, 1986). When the helper accepts and normalizes the client's resistance, the client does not become defensive and the therapeutic relationship is not damaged. In addition, this reaction helps the client become more aware of his or her resistant behavior. The following suggestions are all ways of accepting the client's resistance and finding a new way of achieving compliance without using strong confrontation:

1. Remind the client that resistance is a normal part of the helping process and that avoidance is an important coping mechanism.
2. Describe the client's resistant response as a positive step forward rather than as a failure. The helper may even ascribe noble intentions to the client's deviations from therapeutic goals (Palazzoli, Boscolo, Cecchin, & Prata, 1978).
3. Use group counseling procedures to provide peer encouragement and support for change.
4. Invite the cooperation and participation of the client in setting goals.
5. Tap the client's social support systems, including family, friends, and significant others, to help encourage or maintain change.

6. Get a foot in the door (Roloff & Miller, 1980). This technique involves asking the client to complete a very minor homework assignment and then following it with a request for a more significant change.

7. Ask the client to change for one week only, as an experiment.

8. Decrease frequency and length of sessions when conflict arises. Slow down the pace of the helping process. There is nothing sacred about weekly counseling sessions. When resistance surfaces, consider reducing sessions to once per month.

How to Travel with the Resistance

The technique of traveling with resistant behavior rests on the assumption that when a client does not follow directives or homework assignments, the helper should shift gears and look for a new angle. Traveling with the resistance involves three steps: (1) using the nonjudgmental listening cycle to convey understanding, (2) communicating acceptance of the client's unwillingness to change, and (3) devising a new strategy based on the client's level of motivation. This technique is demonstrated in Kristi's response to Jonathan, a professional writer with writer's block. In our example, Kristi confronted Jonathan and encouraged him to explore the reasons for his resistance. Here let us examine how she might instead travel with the resistance. In this case, Jonathan returns to the second session, not having done the homework assigned by the helper, Kristi. As a beginning exercise, Kristi had asked him to sit at his desk and write anything for 15 minutes per day.

Step 1 *Use the nonjudgmental listening cycle to convey understanding.* The helper spends a few minutes trying to understand and reflect the client's feelings and the underlying meanings behind the client's noncompliance.

Jonathan: "I didn't do that assignment we talked about last week. To tell you the truth, I was so busy that I forgot about it. I didn't do any writing either."

Kristi: "You sound sort of disappointed in yourself."

Jonathan: "I am. I'm just avoiding it. Like that desk was deadly or something. Why can't I get started?"

Kristi: "You're angry at yourself for avoiding your writing. It sounds like you're almost afraid to begin."

Jonathan: "I get really nervous when I sit down at the desk."

Step 2 *Communicate acceptance of the client's resistant behavior.* The helper surprises the client by accepting the client's resistant behavior and normalizing it.

Jonathan: "For some reason, I just blocked that homework out of my mind."

Kristi: "If you get really anxious when you sit down, I can understand why you did not want to complete this homework assignment. Still, I think this assignment was very helpful because I understand the problem much better."

Step 3 *Determine the client's level of motivation and develop a new strategy that matches it.* The helper shifts gears at this point and develops a different assignment that the client is more likely to complete. It may be useful to refer to the levels of motivation in Table 13-2. In the case of Jonathan, Kristi had asked Jonathan to engage in an action strategy. In the following interchange, she changes direction:

Jonathan: "Now that you know that I can't even write for 15 minutes, what are we going to do?"

Kristi: "After hearing this, I realize that solitary homework isn't going to work. I think you instinctively knew this and that is why you didn't follow through. Instead, let's work on the writing here together. How does that sound?"

Summary

Demoralization, discouragement, and learned helplessness all refer to a condition that indicates lowered expectations, loss of hope, and a lack of motivation for change. At some point in the therapeutic relationship, helpers encounter these feelings in nearly everyone who comes for help. From the outset, one of the major tasks of helping is to help the client overcome demoralization that can interfere with the client's willingness to enter into the therapeutic relationship.

The Adlerian concept of encouragement involves attitudes and behaviors that include a positive focus, a belief in equality, respect for the client, and enthusiastically challenging the client. Encouragement is an attitude, as well as a set of skills, that can be especially helpful with demoralized clients.

Resistance has traditionally been defined as any client behavior that interferes with the agreed-upon goals. Many experts now recognize that resistance is a natural part of any change process and that helpers must also look for sources of resistance in their own behavior and in the environment, including the client's family and friends. Traveling with the resistance is a simple method of accepting and defusing noncompliance by the client by accepting and normalizing the resistant behavior. Other methods for dealing with resistance include direct confrontation, contingency contracting, and finding ways to tip the balance by focusing on driving or restraining forces.

Group Exercise

In this role-play exercise in managing resistance, students form groups of three consisting of client, helper, and observer. The client chooses to enact one of the following scenarios.

He or she may expand on the basic story to give it some scope for the helper to explore. The client should be slightly uncooperative at first to give the helper practice in dealing with a resistant client.

The helper's job is to follow this basic outline: (1) use the nonjudgmental listening cycle to explore the client's resistant behavior, (2) convey acceptance of the resistant behavior, and (3) devise a new strategy to accomplish the goal.

The observer writes down all helper statements in order.

Scenario 1   The client has been coming to the helper over the last few months for career counseling. The client has begun to make some progress and appears to be on the verge of identifying a new career field. Suddenly he or she has begun missing appointments. The client has shown some evidence about being fearful of impending change. When asked about the missed appointments, at first, the client says, "I just got busy."

Scenario 2   The client has been through an assertiveness training group to deal with an inability to say no. The client habitually becomes overloaded with extra responsibilities at work, at church, and with family duties because of a tendency to agree to whatever is asked. During this session, the client tells the helper about a recent episode at work in which the client reverted back to nonassertive behavior. The client understands the problem, and the helper and client have covered this ground before. Still, the

client cannot seem to apply the insights learned in assertiveness training or in the helping relationship.

Following the role play, both observer and client give the helper feedback on the following issues:

- Did the helper show frustration or disappointment in the client?
- Which statements by the helper conveyed acceptance of the resistant behavior?
- Was the helper able to devise a new strategy to accomplish the goal that was acceptable to the client?

The client, helper, and observer then exchange roles so each has an opportunity to practice this technique.

Quick Tips: Traveling with the Resistance

- Be sure that you do not communicate disapproval nonverbally. As you are listening, stay nonjudgmental.
- Try to identify the positive aspects of the client's behavior. If a small step has been made, notice it.
- If the client mentions a favorite activity such as reading, journaling, or watching movies, see if you can use one of these interests when you devise a new strategy.
- If the client appears discouraged, use encouraging techniques.
- If the client appears angry or defensive, return to the nonjudgmental listening cycle.

Additional Exercises

Exercise 1

The following are three client statements. Indicate whether they are visitors, complainants, or customers, according to Table 13-2. What interventions might you use to help each client address goals at his or her current

level of motivation? Exchange your ideas with your classmates.

   a. "You may be right, I do need to do something about my job. I am spending very little time with my wife and kids. She's upset. But at work, we are just about to start a very exciting project. It'll probably mean more time away, but what can I do?"

b. "My ex-girlfriend Verna keeps stopping at the house. I am starting to think it might be a problem. My present girlfriend gets a little annoyed, even though she knows I would never go back to Verna. Maybe I should do something about it because, to tell the truth, I don't really know why she keeps coming around. I guess we're just friends."

c. "Last night, my boyfriend got drunk again. It wasn't just that it happened in front of my parents; it's just that I am always worried. I can't relax when we go out anymore. It used to be fun, but now it's boring and it makes me angry. The relationship is not worth what I have to go through every weekend."

Exercise 2: Practicing Encouragement

Listed here are a number of client responses that suggest pessimism and discouragement. Review the list of encouraging responses and make a statement that reflects feelings or meanings. Then write down one or more encouraging responses that (1) focus on the positive and the changeable, (2) communicate equality in the helping relationship and respect the individuality of the client, or (3) push or confront the client, adding energy and enthusiasm for the goal.

Example: "Our marriage is on the rocks. We just can't talk anymore. Anytime I try, she just starts an argument. I need some freedom to be alone once in a while, to work in my shop or on the computer, to read, or go over to Jeff's house and watch the game. It wasn't like this when we were living together, but now she thinks she owns my time. Before, she would have her interests, I would have mine, and then we would spend some time together. I wish she

had some hobbies or something. It's just too much pressure."

Reflecting: "You feel trapped and you don't know how to improve the situation."

Encouraging: (focusing on the positive and the changeable) "You say that you used to manage this issue pretty well before you were married. You were able to balance alone time and together time. It sounds like you two have the ability to communicate well at times. Is that something you might be able to do again?"

Now give both a reflecting and an encouraging response to the following client statements:

a. "I don't like talking about myself very much. For one thing, how will it really help? You just throw things out. That doesn't change them and besides, I was taught never to air dirty laundry in public."

b. "My wife feels I have problems with drinking. But I don't. She says she's at the end of her rope and is going to leave me unless I get help. I'm working every day, I bring home my paycheck. Lots of people drink more than I do."

c. "I've tried everything to quit smoking in the past. Why, two years ago, I went to hypnosis. Once when I was younger, I went to a seminar. Somebody said I should try nicotine gum or patches. But I've tried before. I know it's bad for my health and the kids are always nagging me, but some people just can't quit."

d. "I'm in a dead-end job. I know I should look for a new job. But maybe I'm too old to go back to school and learn a whole new way of doing things. When I see these young people on computers, they already know so much. Could I really keep up?"

In a small group, discuss your answers to these exercises. Note that these helping responses are designed to increase the client's sense of optimism and hope, not to solve the client's problem for him or her. Evaluate both your reflecting and encouraging responses. When looking at your encouraging responses, think about whether the client might perceive these as patronizing, or not genuine, or whether the client might get the impression that you are ignoring the seriousness of the problem.

Homework

Homework 1: Functional Analysis

One obstacle to change is overcoming the force of habit. A bad habit can be frustrating because we seem to persist in it even when we don't want to. One way of attacking bad habits is to scientifically identify what factors are supporting the behavior. This process is called *functional analysis*. Clients can learn functional analysis and then devise self-management strategies to eliminate bad habits by building in rewards (positive reinforcement) for new behaviors. To understand this process better, select a behavior of your own that you would like to change and follow the instructions:

a. Begin by identifying the behavior or bad habit you would like to change with as much objectivity, simplicity, and specificity as you can—for example, "I bite my fingernails."

_____

_____

_____

b. Indicate things that occur simultaneously with or around the same time as the problem behavior. Example: "I bite my fingernails when I am watching television or when I am reading a good book."

_____

_____

_____

c. List things that are consistently *not* associated with the bad habit. Example: "When I am biting my nails, I am not with anyone else."

_____

_____

_____

d. What happens right before the problem behavior? Example: "I am nervous."

_____

_____

_____

e. What are you experiencing when you are doing the problem behavior? Example: "When I am biting my nails, it seems to distract me and I feel less nervous."

_____

_____

_____

f. What happens right after the problem behavior? Do you get a reward or is something negative eliminated? Example: "I am angry at myself for biting my nails and I call myself an idiot." (no reinforcer found)

_____

_____

_____

g. Based on this exercise, what do you think is maintaining the problem behavior? Example: "Biting my nails makes me feel less anxious when I am alone watching television or reading a book."

_____

_____

h. How could you manipulate the environment to reduce the problem behavior? Example: "I could make an agreement with myself not to watch television by myself for a while. When I am reading, I could wear gloves. That way, I won't bite my nails without thinking."

_____

_____

i. How could you use rewards to change the behavior? Example: "If I can make it through one day without biting my nails, I will treat myself to an ice cream cone. If I can make it through a week, I will get a manicure."

_____

_____

j. Devise a plan to manipulate the environment and to reward alternative behavior. Practice your plan on two occasions and note the results:

Trial Number 1: _____

_____

_____

Trial Number 2: _____

_____

_____

- If you feel comfortable discussing your plan with others, involve someone else in your plan so he or she knows what you are trying to accomplish and can support and encourage you (social reinforcement).
- Discuss this homework with your instructor if you are having trouble devising techniques to manipulate the environment or you can't seem to identify suitable rewards. Refer to Bellack and Hersen's book, *Dictionary of Behavior Therapy Techniques* (1986) for other ideas.
- When applying these techniques with clients, how will you know which rewards will be the most effective? What kinds of clients and client problems might work best with a functional analysis and positive reinforcement?

Homework 2: Contracting

Use the guidelines given in this chapter and draw up a mock contract between a teenager and his or her parents. The parents want the client to improve grades, get a job, and join the basketball team. The teenager wants to spend time with friends, listen to music, watch television, and talk on the phone. Keep in mind that it is not necessary to accomplish everything in a contingency contract, but that greater successes can be built from a small accomplishment.

Homework 3

Recall the dialogue of Jonathan and Kristi. Suppose that Kristi suggests a method for tipping the balance to motivate Jonathan. List five or six questions that you would use to get pertinent information from Jonathan that would help you implement this technique. Next, write a dialogue between Kristi and Jonathan in which Kristi confronts Jonathan's behavior. Of these two methods, which do you think would be the most effective for this client? Defend your answer.

References

Amatea, E. S. (1988). Engaging the reluctant client: Some new strategies for the school counselor. *The School Counselor, 36,* 34–40.

Bellack, A. S., & Hersen, M. (1986). *Dictionary of behavior therapy techniques.* New York: Pergamon.

Bergman, J. S. (1985). *Fishing for barracudas*. New York: W. W. Norton.

Blanck, G. (1976). Psychoanalytic technique. In B. B. Wolman (Ed.), *The therapist's handbook: Treatment methods of mental disorders* (pp. 61–86). New York: Van Nostrand Reinhold.

Brammer, L. M., Shostrom, E. L., & Abrego, P. J. (1989). *Therapeutic psychology: Fundamentals of counseling and psychotherapy*. Upper Saddle River, NJ: Prentice-Hall.

Bugental, J. F. T., & Bugental, E. K. (1986). A fate worse than death: The fear of changing. *Psychotherapy, 21,* 543–549.

Cormier, L. S., & Hackney, H. (1987). *The professional counselor: A professional guide to helping*. Upper Saddle River, NJ: Prentice-Hall.

Cormier, W. H., & Cormier, L. S. (1991). *Interviewing strategies for helpers: Fundamental skills and cognitive behavioral interventions* (3rd ed.). Pacific Grove, CA: Brooks/Cole.

Davanloo, H. (Ed.). (1978). *Basic principles and techniques in short-term dynamic psychotherapy*. New York: SP Medical and Scientific Books.

de Shazer, S. (1985). *Keys to solution in brief therapy*. New York: W. W. Norton.

de Shazer, S. (1988). *Clues: Investigating solutions in brief therapy*. New York: W. W. Norton.

de Shazer, S. (1989, October). Brief therapy. Symposium conducted at Stetson University, De Land, FL.

Dinkmeyer, D., & Losoncy, L. E. (1980). *The encouragement book*. Upper Saddle River, NJ: Prentice-Hall.

Dowd, E. T., & Milne, C. R. (1986). Paradoxical interventions in counseling psychology. *Counseling Psychologist, 14,* 237–282.

Dowd, E. T., & Olson, D. H. (1985). Contingency contracting. In A. S. Bellack & M. Hersen (Eds.), *Dictionary of behavior therapy techniques* (pp. 70–73). New York: Pergamon.

Dowd, E. T., & Seibel, C. A. (1990). A cognitive theory of resistance and reactance: Implications for treatment. *Journal of Mental Health Counseling, 12,* 458–469.

Driscoll, R. (1984). *Pragmatic psychotherapy*. New York: Van Nostrand Reinhold.

Dyer, W. W., & Vriend, J. (1977). *Counseling techniques that work*. New York: Funk & Wagnalls.

Egan, G. (1990). *The skilled helper: A systematic approach to effective helping*. Pacific Grove, CA: Brooks/Cole.

Frank, J. D., & Frank, J. B. (1991). *Persuasion and healing*. Baltimore: Johns Hopkins University Press.

Frank, J. D., Nash, E. H., Stone, A. R., & Imber, S. D. (1963). Immediate and long-term symptomatic course of psychiatric outpatients. *American Journal of Psychiatry, 120,* 429–439.

Freud, S. (1900/1952). *A general introduction to psychoanalysis*. New York: Washington Square Press.

Guidano, V. F. (1988). A systems, process-oriented approach to cognitive therapy. In K. S. Dobson (Ed.), *Handbook of cognitive-behavioral therapies* (pp. 307–355). New York: Guilford.

Haley, J. (1976). *Problem-solving therapy*. San Francisco: Jossey-Bass.

Haley, J. (1989, May). Strategic family therapy. Symposium conducted at Stetson University, De Land, FL.

Harris, G. A., & Watkins, D. (1987). *Counseling the involuntary and resistant client*. Alexandria, VA: American Association for Counseling and Development.

Hart, J. T. (1986). Functional eclectic therapy. In J. C. Norcross (Ed.), *Handbook of eclectic psychotherapy* (pp. 221–225). New York: Brunner/Mazel.

Hitz, R., & Driscoll, A. (1988). Praise or encouragement? New insights into praise: Implications for early childhood teachers. *Individual Psychology: Journal of Adlerian Theory, Research and Practice, 43,* 138–141.

Jackson, D. (1968). *Therapy, communication and change*. Palo Alto, CA: Science and Behavior Books.

Kanfer, F. H. (1986). Implications of a self-regulation model of therapy for treatment of addictive behaviors. In W. R. Miller & N. Heather (Eds.), *Treating addictive behaviors: Processes of change* (pp. 29–47). New York: Plenum Press.

Kanfer, F. H. (1980). Self-management methods. In F. H. Kanfer & A. P. Goldstein (Eds.), *Helping people change*. New York: Pergamon.

Larke, J. (1985). Compulsory treatment: Some practical methods of treating the mandated client. *Psychotherapy, 22,* 262–268.

Larrabee, M. J. (1982). Working with reluctant clients through affirmation techniques. *Personnel and Guidance Journal, 6,* 105–109.

Lauver, P. J., Holiman, M. A., & Kazama, S. W. (1982). Counseling as battleground: Client as enemy. *Personnel and Guidance Journal, 61,* 105–109.

Lawson, D. M. (1986). Strategic directives with resistant clients. *American Mental Health Counselors Journal, 8,* 87–93.

Lerner, S., & Lerner, H. (1983). A systematic approach to resistance: Theoretical and technical considerations. *American Journal of Psychotherapy, 37,* 387–399.

Lewin, K. (1951). *Field theory in social science.* New York: Harper & Row.

Losoncy, L. E. (1977). *Turning people on: How to be an encouraging person.* Upper Saddle River, NJ: Prentice-Hall.

Mahoney, M. J. (1988a). The cognitive sciences and psychotherapy: Patterns in a developing relationship. In K. S. Dobson (Ed.), *Handbook of cognitive-behavioral therapies* (pp. 358–386). New York: Guilford.

Mahoney, M. J. (1988b). Constructive meta-theory II: Implications for psychotherapy. *International Journal of Personal Construct Psychology, 1,* 299–316.

Marlatt, G. A. (1988). Matching clients to treatment: Treatment models and stages of change. In D. M. Donovan & G. A. Marlatt (Eds.), *Assessment of addictive behaviors* (pp. 474–483). New York: Guilford.

Martin, D. G. (1983). *Counseling and therapy skills.* Prospect Heights, IL: Waveland Press.

McMullin, R. E. (1986). *Handbook of cognitive therapy techniques.* New York: W. W. Norton.

Meichenbaum, D., & Turk, D. C. (1987). *Facilitating treatment adherence: A practitioner's guidebook.* New York: Plenum Press.

Mosak, H. H. (1987). *Ha ha and aha.* Muncie, IN: Accelerated Development.

O'Hanlon, W. H., & Weiner-Davis, M. (1989). *In search of solutions: A new direction in psychotherapy.* New York: W. W. Norton.

Otani, A. (1989). Resistance management techniques of Milton H. Erickson, M.D.: An application to nonhypnotic mental health counseling. *Journal of Mental Health Counseling, 11,* 325–333.

Palazzoli, M. S., Boscolo, L., Cecchin, G., & Prata, G. (1978). *Paradox and counterparadox: A new model in the therapy of the family in schizophrenic transaction.* New York: Jason Aronson.

Patterson, C. H. (1973). *Theories of counseling and psychotherapy* (2nd ed.). New York: Harper & Row.

Perls, F. S. (1971). *Gestalt therapy verbatim.* New York: Bantam.

Pitsounis, N. D., & Dixon, P. N. (1988). Encouragement versus praise: Improving productivity of the mentally retarded. *Individual Psychology: Journal of Adlerian Theory, Research and Practice, 44,* 507–512.

Prochaska, J. O., & DiClemente, C. C. (1983). Stages and processes of self-change in smoking: Toward an integrative model of change. *Journal of Consulting and Clinical Psychology, 51,* 390–395.

Prochaska, J. O., & DiClemente, C. C. (1986). The transtheoretical approach. In J. C. Norcross (Ed.), *Handbook of eclectic psychotherapy* (pp. 163–200). New York: Brunner/Mazel.

Prochaska, J. O., & Norcross, J. C. (1994). *Systems of psychotherapy.* Pacific Grove, CA: Brooks/Cole.

Prochaska, J. O., Norcross, J. C., & DiClemente, C. C. (1994). *Changing for good.* New York: Morrow.

Redl, F. (1966). *When we deal with children.* New York: Free Press.

Ritchie, M. H. (1986). Couseling involuntary clients. *Journal of Counseling and Development, 64,* 516–518.

Roloff, M. E., & Miller, G. R. (Eds.) (1980). *Persuasion: New directions in theory and research.* Beverly Hills, CA: Sage.

Sack, T. (1988). Counseling responses when the client says, "I don't know." *Journal of Mental Health Counseling, 10,* 179–187.

Seligman, M. E. P. (1975). *Helplessness.* San Francisco: W. H. Freeman.

Siegel, B. S. (1986). *Love, medicine and miracles.* New York: Harper & Row.

Simonton, O. C., & Mathews-Simonton, S. (1978). *Getting well again.* Los Angeles, CA: J. P. Tarcher.

Stream, H. S. (1985). *Resolving resistance in psychotherapy.* New York: Wiley.

Sweeney, T. J. (1989). *Adlerian counseling: A practical approach for a new decade.* Muncie, IN: Accelerated Development.

Walker, J. E., & Aycock, L. (1986). The counselor as "chicken." In W. P. Anderson (Ed.), *Innovative counseling: A handbook of readings* (pp. 22–23). Alexandria, VA: American Association for Counseling and Development.

Witmer, J. M. (1985). *Pathways to personal growth.* Muncie, IN: Accelerated Development.

Wolberg, L. R. (1954). *The technique of psychotherapy.* New York: Grune & Stratton.

Young, M. E., & Feiler, F. (1993). Trends in counseling: A national survey. *Guidance and Counselling, 9,* 4-11.

New Learning Experiences and Termination

Introduction

The final curative factor in the six-part REPLAN system is new learning experiences (see Figure 14-1). This factor refers to ways of teaching the client new skills or helping the client develop a new outlook. New learning can take place directly, through instruction or modeling, and also indirectly, through varied techniques such as humor, the use of metaphors, interpretation, and reframing.

According to research, gaining a new perspective is one of the most frequently mentioned helpful experiences cited by therapy clients (Elliott, 1985). Clients have been able to recall insights and learning up to 6 months following therapy (Martin & Stelmaczonek, 1988). Yalom (1995) has also identified learning as a significant therapeutic factor consistently identified by group therapy participants.

Definitions of New Learning

A number of different terms have been used to describe new learning experiences: changing the world view, redefining personal mythology, developing insight, developing outlook skills, perception transformation, cognitive restructuring, reframing,

Figure 14-1
Curative factors in the REPLAN system: New learning experiences and changing perceptions

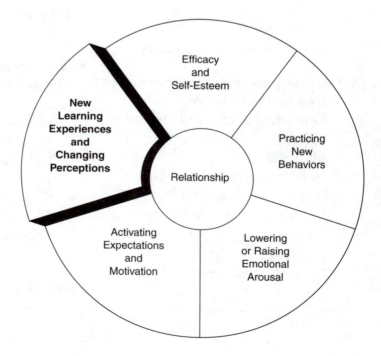

meaning attribution, perception shifts, the "aha!" experience, relabeling, redecision, and so on. All of these terms seem to involve two basic techniques: (1) imparting to clients new information or skills, and (2) persuading clients to change inappropriate beliefs, perceptions, and outlook. These two basic techniques led to new learning experiences for clients in the following two cases.

- Rhonda is a 23-year-old woman who has gone to an alcohol treatment facility following her arrest on a charge of driving while intoxicated. On her first day, the goal of the staff is to introduce clients to a "disease concept" model of alcoholism. She attends a class in which she learns that she is genetically predisposed to addiction based on her family history, and that she cannot help the effect alcohol has on her. The result of this information is that Rhonda begins to stop thinking of herself as "weak" or morally unworthy because of her behavior. This new perspective has been stimulated by learning. It changes her attitude about herself and increases her hope for recovery.

- Don is a 30-year-old man referred for help with panic attacks. During moments of high anxiety, he has been experiencing shortness of breath, a rapid heart rate, and intense fear. At their first session, the helper identifies a core belief that seems to increase his anxiety: "I could lose control over myself and go crazy." During the next three weeks, the helper encourages Don to examine and modify this core belief. The goal is to help him to focus on the evidence for and against this belief and to develop a more reasonable point of view. After a month, Don is able to say, "Watching for danger actually increases my fear rather than reducing it. It is better to have a panic attack once a month than to spend every day worrying about it." Six months later, Don claims that he rarely finds himself falling into his old way of thinking. He feels that he has modified a core belief.

What Client Problems Are Helped through New Learning?

A number of client problems are the result of inadequate training or lack of knowledge about available resources. These include feelings of stress, career indecision, and addictive behavior as well as poor interpersonal communication, marital communication, and parenting skills. Through new learning and gaining new perspectives, clients can change their thinking about painful remembered events and their sense of guilt and responsibility for them. They can see themselves and others in a new light, and they discover that many situations that they have feared and avoided are not really harmful.

Resistance to New Learning

"The truth will set you free, but *first,* it will make you miserable." This saying from a humorous poster summarizes the experience of a person who is undergoing a significant change. Change brought about by new information may ultimately bring about enlightenment, but it can be extremely unsettling at first. The story of Copernicus is a good example. He taught that the earth revolved around the sun and not the other way around. This upset the existing world view so much that he was forced to recant, and his student Bruno was put to death 50 years later for spreading the news (Bernard & Young, 1996). On a much smaller scale, a helper tries to persuade a client to leave behind self-defeating ideas and teaches the client new skills and a new way of looking at the world. The result is that both the client and those close to the client experience discomfort and may actually try to resist or slow down change. For example, a social worker at a hospice had a client, a 65-year-old Italian woman whose husband had died one year ago. The client was lonely but refused to go to social functions in her retirement community because going unaccompanied to such an event was, in her view, undignified and a sign to the world that she was looking for a new partner. She had grown up in a strictly religious, Italian community where such behavior was frowned upon. No external force prevented her from enjoying the company and support of others, only her outdated ideas of propriety. The social worker's attempts to get this client to change her behavior or think about this in a different way met stiff resistance bolstered by years of experience and cultural reinforcement.

The flip side of the coin is that when clients change their unexamined prejudices, outmoded concepts, and self-imprisoning ideas, enormous growth can occur. Among the helper's tools are the methods whereby he or she assists clients in seeing things in a different way and creating new visions of the future.

Common Methods Helpers Use to Provide New Learning Experiences for Clients

Interpretation

Interpretation, next to free association, is one of the oldest therapeutic techniques (Clark, 1995). Interpretation consists of encouraging the client to look at the problem in the context of the theoretical orientation of the practitioner. Once the helper explains the reason for the problem, a client develops insight and is then better able to change. For example, from a psychodynamic perspective, a client's reaction to his boss may be a carryover from his lifelong issues with his own father. Once this reaction is interpreted, confronted, and clarified, the client may start to see the unconscious motives behind his actions. Insight may occur suddenly ("aha!"), or it may dawn gradually. Once insight occurs, that learning may be applied to other situations. In this example, the client may become aware of similar tendencies in his relationships with other authority figures.

The psychodynamic perspective is not the only theory that uses interpretation. The case of Marlene, who works at a grocery store, is described here. Her problem is interpreted according to four different theoretical orientations. Each has a different way of explaining the cause of the problem to her:

Marlene: "I'm the assistant manager at work, and my boss is my main problem. The only thing he can do is find fault. He never gives me a pat on the back. I stay late, I do a good job, and I'm always trying to anticipate what he wants. Every time, I am disappointed because he just ignores my efforts. Sometimes I get so mad, I want to break something. When I get home, I am a bear to live with."

Interpretation from a Psychodynamic Viewpoint:

Helper: "Based on what we know about your family history, it seems to me that you are reliving the same kind of pattern you have with your father. You are always seeking approval that never comes, then you get angry and take this out on others around you."

Cause of Marlene's Unhappiness: "You are trying to get from your boss what you did not get from your father. You are barking up the wrong tree."

Interpretation from a Rational-Emotive Therapy (RET) Perspective:

Helper: "Marlene, can you see that once again, you are saying to yourself that unless this guy approves of you, you are not worthwhile? Doesn't it sound to you like you are letting this guy determine how you are going to feel about yourself? Beyond this, you are saying something else, that it is 'terrible' or 'the end of the world' if your manager doesn't appreciate you."

Cause of Marlene's Unhappiness: "You are berating yourself with an irrational belief: 'I am unworthy unless some significant person approves of me and it would be terrible if he or she didn't.' "

Interpretation from a Behavioral Orientation:

Helper: "Marlene, it sounds like the main problem here is that you need more rewards or recognition for your hard work. First, let's look at some of the ways you might obtain more reinforcement from your job, or alternatively find a new job situation where there are more rewards."

Cause of Marlene's Unhappiness: "You are not getting enough positive reinforcers at work."

Interpretation from a Solution-Focused Position:

Helper: "Marlene, thinking back on this problem from our previous sessions, you have said that there are days when you are not frustrated and angry and times when you go home and don't take it out on the family. Those days are when you take the time to chat with colleagues, take a lunch break, and focus more on doing a good job rather than looking over your shoulder to see if the boss notices. It seems to me that you already have the solution to your problem, which is to do more of those activities."

Cause of Marlene's Unhappiness: "You already have the solution to your problem, but you are not using it."

As you can see, the technique of interpretation is a way of shifting the client's viewpoint about a problem. When the client understands the new viewpoint, he or she follows the appropriate treatment of that theoretical orientation.

Modeling as New Learning

Another way that clients change through new learning is by copying the behavior of the helper or other models. Bandura (1971) is responsible for sensitizing helpers to the role of modeling in psychotherapy. Modeling has been used extensively with children, developmentally delayed adults, and alcoholics; for training of helpers and parents; and for dealing with fear-related situations (Perry & Furukawa, 1986). Identification with the group therapist or with other group members is considered a major curative factor in group therapy (Yalom, 1995). A client can learn to be more self-disclosing, assertive, and spontaneous by seeing examples of these behaviors and trying them in the safe environment of the group.

Modeling can take place in counseling either as an intentional process or as an unexpected by-product. Some clients take on the listening mannerisms or even copy the clothing of the helper. Intentional modeling might include role-playing a specific behavior while the client watches or exposing clients to symbolic, biographical, or fictional models in books, tapes, and films (Milan, 1985). Through modeling, clients are able to see a successful performance of a skill. The client then attempts to reproduce the skill, getting feedback from the helper (Mitchell & Milan, 1983).

Stop and Reflect

Think about three of your favorite teachers. Write their names in the following chart and describe them as best you can according to the format shown:

	Teacher 1	Teacher 2	Teacher 3
Name	_____	_____	_____
What personal trait did you admire the most?	_____	_____	_____
	_____	_____	_____
	_____	_____	_____
What was this teacher's subject?	_____	_____	_____
	_____	_____	_____
Did knowledge of the subject change your ideas?	_____	_____	_____
What was the most important thing you learned?	_____	_____	_____
	_____	_____	_____
	_____	_____	_____
In what ways did this teacher influence you?	_____	_____	_____
	_____	_____	_____
	_____	_____	_____

- As you look over your answers, how do you feel the teacher influenced or changed you? Was it primarily through modeling, or was it through the subject matter that he or she taught?
- What role did the personal characteristics of the teacher play in how much you were influenced?
- Which characteristics of your favorite teachers do you think would transfer well to the therapeutic relationship? Are any of these characteristics particular strengths for you?

Using Metaphors and Stories

The use of metaphors, stories, parables, and tales are common means for stimulating new learning in clients (Barker, 1985; Gordon, 1978). For example, a helper once came up with this little aphorism for a client who was stewing about a situation over which he had no control: "You know, worry is like a rocking chair. It doesn't get you anywhere but it's something to do." A thought like this can gently suggest that the client think about his or her behavior.

Metaphors and stories engage the listener with imagery, suspense, and humor and are therefore effective in getting a client to accept a reframe. This was true in the case of Judie, a 35-year-old woman living in New York City who had grown up on a farm. Judie had considered marriage to several different men while in her 20s. Each time, she had ended the relationship when marriage seemed to be the next step. Judie was an only child and was quite close to her parents, whose marital relationship was quite poor. They had fought bitterly for years and she believed that they had stayed together for her sake. She admitted that she saw love as "chains."

Judie came for help because she had finally met a man that she wanted to marry. She was filled with confusion and had changed the date of the wedding twice. In the first few counseling sessions, reflective listening uncovered her fears, thoughts, and feelings about marriage and relationships. She felt better about her decision to get married after these sessions, but one night (a week before the wedding), she telephoned the helper in a crisis of doubt about whether to go through with the ceremony. On the telephone, her helper told her the following story: "When I was a boy, we lived on a farm, and we had a very healthy and strong mare. She was high-spirited, but gentle. She also had one peculiarity. She hated it when we closed the gate of the corral. In fact, she would run around in circles, rearing up, sometimes even hurting herself on the wooden fence. One day we discovered by accident that if we left the gate open she calmed down. And she never ran away. She didn't mind being in the corral. She just wanted to make sure that she could leave at any time."

The helper credited this story as the turning point in Judie's treatment and in restoring her sense of control. Although no interpretation was made, she apparently grasped that she did not have to feel imprisoned by marriage, that she could retain a sense of freedom. The helper used the farm story because of his knowledge about Judie's background. He used the metaphor of the corral because he knew that she saw marriage as a form of bondage. Through the image of the open gate, he was telling her that she could retain the option of leaving. Knowing that she had this option would help her enjoy her marriage.

Exposure to Avoided Stimuli

Fear reduction is one of the purposes for which the curative factor of new learning is most often employed (Morris, 1986). *Exposure* is the practice of facing feared stimuli (Emmelkamp, 1982; Foa & Goldstein, 1978). Exposure is an important treatment for all sorts of fears and phobias. Helpers set up hierarchies of feared situations and gradually encourage clients to face more and more difficult situations.

Clients learn important lessons from facing rather than avoiding fearful situations. They learn that many of their fears are groundless and that their perception of other people and the world may be erroneous. For example, many people fear that being more assertive will create worse relationships in their families. As they become more assertive, they learn from other people's reactions that most of the feared consequences of assertiveness never occur and that their relationships actually improve.

Humor

We know that learning is facilitated in a light atmosphere (Gardner, 1971). Humor also offers a subtle way to shift a client's viewpoint (Ansbacher & Ansbacher, 1956; Mosak, 1987). Like a metaphor, a joke tells a story and sometimes contains a philosophical shift, interpretation, or message.

One of the most common ways that helpers use humor to get clients to think about a situation in a different way is to use exaggeration. Exaggerating a client's situation sometimes helps to put it in perspective. Once, when a client was stewing about the fact that her divorce would become public, it was clear that she was making a mountain out of a molehill. The helper made the following comments, "Yes, undoubtedly this will make the front page with a big headline: 'Woman gets divorce—friends shocked.' Perhaps it will make the television news." The client laughed and later she was able to recognize her tendency to catastrophize.

Linguistic Changes

Linguistic changes are helper directives that suggest that the client use different language. Since language mirrors thought, what we say is a reflection of our world view. Often helpers suggest that clients use new jargon or use specific words that promote the ideas that the client is responsible for his or her own life, thoughts, and feelings. For example, when a client says, "I can't seem to get to work on time," the helper challenges the client's lack of responsibility by suggesting that the client rephrase as follows: "I won't go to work on time." Helpers also challenge clients when they engage in black-and-white thinking by using such terms as *always* and *never.*

Direct Instruction

Direct instruction is one of the most often used methods in helping. Direct instruction involves lecturing, discussion groups, modeling, and the use of films and demonstrations to provide new information to clients. These psychoeducational procedures are the stock-in-trade of alcohol treatment facilities, parent education, stress-reduction groups, anxiety management training, cognitive therapy techniques for depression, marriage enrichment seminars, and a myriad of other programs. Besides the educational material that is presented, clients benefit from the support and they learn vicariously from the experiences of fellow learners.

Direct instruction also takes place in the helper's office. Marriage counseling may involve training in good communication skills, and helpers often assign books and other reading material to educate clients about specific problems such as stress, substance abuse, dealing with anxiety or depression, proper parenting procedures, and particular social skills that a client needs to acquire.

The Technique of Reframing

Many of us are familiar with an advertisement for the Peace Corps that ran on television during the 1960s. It challenged viewers to determine whether they saw a glass as half empty or half full. This commercial was constructed to show that there are two ways of looking at a situation: in terms of its assets or its deficits. Reframing is the therapeutic technique of persuading the client to view the positive or healthy viewpoint: to see the glass as half full.

An even better example of reframing comes from Mark Twain's story of Tom Sawyer, who convinces his friends that painting a fence is fun and a privilege, not work. A more contemporary illustration comes from the movie *Moonstruck*. The hero of the story is rejected by his fiancée when his hand is severed by a bread slicer. The hero had always blamed his brother for distracting him at the crucial moment when the accident occurred. The reframing takes place when his new girlfriend convinces him that the real reason for the accident was his unconscious wish to stay single. She elegantly uses the metaphor of a lone wolf and accuses the hero of "gnawing off his own leg" to avoid the trap of marriage.

Helpers use reframes like this to help the client see the problem in a more constructive and responsible way. They move clients from blaming to taking responsibility, and from the victim's role to the survivor's role, by gently urging them to look at the world through a different lens.

Stop and Reflect

Figure 14-2 is a famous drawing you may have seen before. It can be seen as two separate portraits, one of a young woman wearing a feathered hat and a black neckband and another of an old woman with a long nose and a head scarf. Typically, it is easy to see one figure or the other. If you have trouble finding one of these faces, ask a classmate or teacher to help you. Notice that you can not see both portraits at once; you have to focus on each individually.

Looking at a drawing such as this is like looking at a problem situation (McMullin, 1986). Every issue has its positive and negative sides, depending on which you have

Figure 14-2
Old woman/young woman

been trained to focus on. By shifting your gaze, you can pay attention to one side or the other. Drawings illustrate to clients that reframing is not just pretending that the negative issues are not there; rather, it is simply more useful to learn that every cloud also has a silver lining and it is more productive to change one's outlook and to see the sides of the problem that are solvable and changeable.

An interesting technique used to develop the skill of seeing alternative viewpoints is called *relabeling*. Helpers use this technique in career counseling to help clients get in touch with their personal strengths. Have you ever noticed that it is easier to get people to identify their weaknesses than their positive qualities? In this exercise, clients make a list of their own undesirable traits and then of some undesirable traits of someone else they know. Then they try to think of another descriptor that puts a positive spin on the very same trait. Take a look at these examples and then make two lists of your own. First, make a list of personal qualities or traits about yourself that you do not like and then make a similar list about someone you know. Then, relabel them in a positive way.

Example:

Negative Viewpoint	Positive Viewpoint
Compulsive	Organized
Sloppy	Casual
Loud	Enthusiastic

Now consider the following questions:

- Is reframing like this just putting a coat of paint on a negative trait, or does it really uncover something positive about the tendency?
- As you look over your own list, would you really want to lose this quality? What would you be giving up?
- Does your relabeling another person's traits help you to see that person differently?
- Discuss some of these issues and your own reactions with your classmates.

How to Reframe

According to Watzlawick, Weakland, and Fisch (1974), reframing means coming up with a new, more constructive definition of the problem that fits the facts just as accurately as the old definition. To reframe a client's problem, the helper must appreciate the client's world view and then replace it with an acceptable alternative. To this end, it is useful to take the following steps.

Step 1   *Use the nonjudgmental listening cycle to fully understand the problem.* The nonjudgmental listening cycle gives the helper a firm grasp of the details of the problem, including the individuals involved, their relationships, and the environment where the problem exists. Before reframing, it is especially helpful to reflect meaning to discover the client's world view and values. In the following summary, the helper brings together a number of the feelings and meanings that the client, Arlene, has expressed during the session.

Arlene: "So that's the story: I have to move whether I like it or not. It's like being fired and I have no control over it. Either I move or I am out of work. I've never lost a job before. Sometimes I think it's their way of telling me they want me to quit."

Helper: "From what I have heard so far, what bothers you the most is the lack of control over the decision. That makes you mad. But sometimes you see this situation as your failure and at the same time a personal rejection."

Step 2   *Build a bridge from the client's viewpoint to a new way of looking at the problem.* Develop a reframe that bridges the client's old view of the problem with a new viewpoint that stresses the positive aspects of the problem or presents it as solvable. The important point is to acknowledge some aspect of the client's viewpoint while at the same time suggesting another way of looking at it.

Helper: "I wonder if you could start thinking about this move in a different way. You have always wanted to travel. A few months ago you were even considering a new job or moving to another state. Although you feel uneasy about this because you don't like it when the decision is made for you, I wonder if this may not be a blessing in disguise. How might this job actually give you a little more freedom?"

Step 3   *Reinforce the bridge.* A shift in perspective often develops slowly. One way of sustaining the perspective shift is to assign homework that forces the client to see the problem in a new light. Arlene, for example, might be given a homework assignment to do more research on the positive aspects of the move.

Problems and Precautions of Reframing

Reframing is most likely to be successful if the client is able to relate the significant aspects of the new frame of reference to corresponding features in the old frame of reference. For example, an algebra teacher used to try to reframe her examinations as "sharing experiences." The analogy was not successful and everyone groaned because "sharing" is not a graded activity (an important feature of a test).

It may be impossible to identify all aspects of a problem that might be important to the client; however, every effort should be made to imagine those that could be crucial. In a metaphor or story told by the helper, the basic elements of the tale must conform to the client's situation or risk being rejected.

Remember also that very simplistic reframing can be worse than none at all. One example that comes to mind concerns the reframes sometimes extended to people who are grieving over the death of a family member. Well-meaning friends are apt to say such things as, "It is God's will." Because strong emotions of sadness and loss are present, most people cannot accept a reframing that does not take into account the most salient feature of their experience—the grief itself. Reframing must be a well-considered move based on firm knowledge of the client, not just pat answers.

To summarize, reframing is a major technique in the art of helping in which the client learns to find alternative ways of looking at a problem. Reframing is more than just gaining a positive attitude. It involves thinking about the problem in a completely new way and focusing on what is changeable. Reframing is especially helpful in situations where direct action is not possible or advisable and a change of attitude is needed.

Variations on Reframing: Cognitive Restructuring

Cognitive restructuring (McKay, Davis, & Fanning, 1981; McMullin, 1986; Meichenbaum, 1977) involves modifying what clients say to themselves about their own abilities and capacities and about problem situations as well. (One aspect of cognitive restructuring was discussed when the technique of countering was explained earlier in this book.) Changing one's imagery or appraisal of a problem is also part of cognitive restructuring. For example, if a person has an image of butterflies in the stomach before a speech, he or she might be asked to develop a more powerful image, such as horses or bulls. The resulting feeling is one of confidence rather than fluttering weakness. Once the situation is restructured in one's thinking, it must be practiced to firmly establish it.

The term *cognitive restructuring* could also be applied to rational-emotive therapy. Catastrophizing is a type of irrational thinking identified by Albert Ellis (1962). It means accentuating the negative aspects of a situation and imagining the worst things that might happen. Ellis's approach is to frankly dispute catastrophizing by asking the client to see the real effect of the situation rather than the exaggerated view. For example, a client who imagines that he would be embarrassed to death if a woman refused him for a date would be challenged to see that he was catastrophizing. In reality, neither death nor serious injury would occur. A refusal would instead be inconvenient, disappointing, or a pain in the neck, not the end of the world. In subsequent sessions, a client's tendency to catastrophize would be confronted and disputed, perhaps with humor, until he or she became a partner in identifying the predilection to appraise events as catastrophes.

Stop and Reflect

One of the tenets of stress management is that solving a problem or acting is not always desirable or possible. Sometimes change is impossible; sometimes it is not the right time to act. In these situations, the best course is to deal with negative feelings by relaxation or by paying attention to the positive aspects of the situation. Consider the following example: Bob and Diane and their 5-year-old daughter live next to her parents. For Bob, this is stressful at times because he thinks his in-laws are around the house too much and that they take away from his own time with his family. On the other hand, for Bob, the benefits of living next to his in-laws outweigh these annoyances. The in-laws help with child care and provide help and support in many other ways. He likes his house, and his wife and daughter are happy to be near his in-laws. He does not want to move. In this situation, a helper might suggest that Bob change his outlook rather than his address. He or she might suggest that Bob pay more attention to the features of the situation that are positive and changeable, rather than the parts that are negative and not open to change. In other words, how can Bob find ways to be alone with his family without moving and to enjoy the benefits of living close to family?

- If you were helping Bob, how might you go about getting him to see the positive aspects of his situation? What aspects can you identify that put the situation in a different light?
- Is there a danger in being a Pollyanna? How might you avoid this?
- Do you think that showing Bob the old woman/young woman drawing might help him understand this concept? From what little you know about Bob, what other metaphors might you use to explain the concept of looking at a problem from different angles?
- Discuss your reactions to this exercise with your classmates.

Some Thoughts on Termination

In our discussion of new learning experiences, we have dealt with the final curative factor in the six-part REPLAN system. When the techniques derived from these curative factors have been applied, the helper's job is to evaluate their effects (see Figure 14-3). Did the technique work as it was designed to work? Were the helper and client able to reach the agreed-upon goals? If not, treatment must be replanned and helper and client must return to the goal-setting and treatment planning phase. Even if goals were reached, important new issues may have arisen; client and helper may wish to negotiate a new contract, and the process depicted in the cycle begins again.

If helper and client can agree that considerable progress has been made toward the goals, the helper may suggest *termination,* the discontinuation of the therapeutic relationship. Termination is not merely a process of leave-taking, but also a time to look back on the original goals and celebrate client success (Kramer, 1986). As the client and helper prepare to end the relationship, the helper encourages the client to focus on successes and also to become aware of other issues that have not yet been resolved and that may need work later on.

How to Tell Whether Termination Is Needed

Clients should be terminated when they have attained their goals, when they have been receiving counseling or psychotherapy for some time and have not made progress, or when there are signs that the client can handle his or her issues independently but has become dependent on the helper. Most professional organizations, including the American Counseling Association, the American Psychological Association, the American Association for Marriage and Family Therapy, and the National Association of Social Workers, state in their codes of ethics that a client should be terminated if he or she is not making progress. In such cases, the client should be told about alternate sources of help. The decision as to whether a client is making progress is not necessarily clear-cut; some of the signs that suggest that a

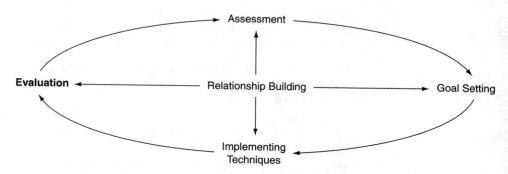

Figure 14-3
Stages of the helping relationship: Evaluation

client is ready for termination, such as missing sessions, coming late for sessions, or failing to do homework, can be signals of resistance or motivation problems as well.

How exactly do we know when helping has been successful? Should we consider success from the standpoint of the client or from the standpoint of the helper? Should we define success in terms of societal standards (dangerousness, employment) or from some ideal of mental health advanced by theorists? Mathews (1989) suggests reviewing one's caseload and asking oneself, "If I had a waiting list right now, would I be seeing this client?" (p. 37). Based on the work of Maholich and Turner (1979), Sciscoe (1990) identified five questions a helper might ask himself or herself to assess a client's readiness for termination:

1. Is the presenting problem under control?
2. Has the client reduced the initial level of distress by developing better coping skills?
3. Has the client achieved greater self-awareness and better relationships?
4. Are life and work more enjoyable for the client?
5. Does the client now feel capable of living without the therapeutic relationship?

The first four of Sciscoe's questions (1990) highlight improvements that have been made and goals that have been achieved. The last question is especially important, since it asks the helper whether the client is able to maintain the gains of helping without the therapeutic relationship. The answers to these questions can assist the helper in working through the knotty question of termination. Termination can be defined as that point in time when helper and client agree that mutually designated helping goals have been reached. The decision must be made based on the professional expertise of the helper and the personal experience of the client.

How to Prepare the Client for Termination

Most experts agree that sudden termination is not advisable (Brammer, Shostrom, & Abrego, 1989), but how soon should the topic of termination be brought up? Dixon and Glover (1984) recommend that at least three sessions in advance of termination be devoted to issues of termination, while Lamb (1985) recommends at least seven sessions. As much time as was spent in relationship building in the beginning of the therapy should be devoted to termination, say Cormier and Cormier (1985); and one-sixth of the time spent in therapy should be devoted to termination, according to Shulman (1979). In other words, there should be a period of preparation. How long this should take is a matter of judgment and should be determined by the length and quality of the therapeutic relationship.

During the preparation period, the helper leads the client in a discussion that reviews the counseling process and progress made. In general, it is important to emphasize the client's strengths and to end on a positive note; however, areas left untreated or unresolved must also be discussed (Anderson & Stewart, 1983). One way to review is simply to compare before-and-after client functioning from the viewpoint of both helper and client. Also, an early session in counseling might be discussed, or case notes read, to show progress. Finally, any unfinished business between client and helper should be addressed, and the client should be encouraged to think about how he or she will look back on the counseling experience in the future.

How to Explore and Ease Feelings of Loss

Gladding (1988) points out that loss is a two-way street. Helpers may drag their feet on termination because of their own attachments and feelings of sadness. Goodyear (1981) lists several possible reasons for this kind of reaction: the relationship may be quite significant to the counselor; the counselor may feel uncertain that the client will be able to function independently; the counselor may believe that he or she was not effective; the counselor may feel that his or her professional identity is challenged by the client's premature termination; the termination may represent a loss of continued learning for the counselor, who was looking forward to gaining experience from the client's peculiar problem; the counselor may miss the vicarious excitement of the client's exploits; or the termination may uncover historical events associated with loss in the counselor's life. A helper's feelings of loss at termination may also be due to a reliance on helping relationships to meet needs for intimacy (friendship) as well as a conscious or unconscious sexual attraction.

Kanfer and Schefft (1988) state that the helper needs to learn to accept the fact that termination inevitably occurs at a point far short of perfection. This discussion of helpers' feelings at termination suggests that they sometimes maintain therapeutic relationships to satisfy personal needs. They may even feel guilty and embarrassed by the importance they place on the relationship because it seems unprofessional (Mathews, 1989).

Krantz and Lund (1979) feel that trainees may have special difficulty with termination. Beginning helpers may keep clients too long because they like the client or because of a hope that the client will accomplish even greater goals. They may also be unprepared for their own feelings or for the powerful loss experienced by the client, no matter how much they are intellectually informed. A supportive supervisory relationship (Sciscoe, 1990) can help trainees through difficult terminations.

The general strategy to help clients deal with their feelings of loss at termination is to take time to prepare them and to ask them to identify both positive and negative feelings associated with the end of the relationship. Clients may be upset by termination because it is associated with other historical losses (Ward, 1984). Some suggestions to help prevent, explore, and resolve these feelings include the following (Cavanagh, 1982; Dixon & Glover, 1984; Hackney & Cormier, 1979; Munro & Bach, 1975):

1. Bring termination up early.
2. Reframe termination as an opportunity for the client to put new learning into practice.
3. Limit the number of counseling sessions at the very beginning.
4. Use a *fading procedure*: space appointments over increasing lengths of time.
5. Avoid making the relationship the central feature of helping. Although relationship building is crucial, it may be unwise to employ only this curative factor.
6. Play down the importance of termination; play up the sense of accomplishment and the value of independence.

7. Use reflective listening to allow the client to express feelings of loss.

How to Maintain Therapeutic Gains and Prevent Relapse Following Termination

The term *follow-up* refers to a brief contact the helper makes to determine how the client is progressing and to remind the client that the door is open if counseling is needed in the future (Wolberg, 1954). On the other hand, a number of helpers employ activities that go beyond a brief reminder. They are designed to help maintain therapeutic gains and are actually means for extending help after termination. Following are some suggestions (Cavanagh, 1982; Perry & Paquin, 1987).

Fading

Fading means scheduling follow-up sessions with longer and longer intervals spaced over a 1-year period. For example, a 6-week, 6-month, and 1-year follow-up can be planned during termination. When clients are learning specific skills, such as assertiveness training, stress management, and communication, these follow-ups can be called *booster sessions* or *refreshers* with the stated aim of reviewing learning. One benefit of planning for follow-up at termination is that the client need not later feel a sense of failure if a return to counseling is needed. If the client decides to cancel the later visits, this can be reframed as a sign of success.

Home Visits or Observation

A possible follow-up to marriage or family counseling is to review helping progress later with the family at home. Observing the family in this setting can convey a great deal about progress, though it is not an ideal therapeutic setting because of the many distractions.

Contacts with Paraprofessionals

Many agencies provide follow-up services for clients on a free or inexpensive basis. Many mental health clinics, for example, provide home visiting to monitor and maintain progress of clients suffering from severe mental disorders.

Self-Help Groups

Self-help groups, if improperly conducted, can be a case of the blind leading the blind. The quality of such groups is quite variable, so the helper must be familiar with groups in the client's vicinity before making a recommendation. However, as an adjunct to individual, group, and family therapy, they can provide an important means of maintaining gains by providing regular peer support.

Self-Monitoring Activities

Clients can also be encouraged to engage in continued self-monitoring activities, which they report at follow-up sessions. A less formal way to encourage self-monitoring and self-reflection is to teach the client to use a personal journal to explore thoughts and feelings (Kalven, Rosen, & Taylor, 1981).

Self-Management Skills

Clients can learn to use behavioral principles to reward their own positive behaviors and to punish negative ones (Kanfer, 1975; Kazdin, 1980; Rudestam, 1980). For example, students can learn to make watching a one-hour television show contingent on completing several hours of study.

Audiovisual Material

Both printed and recorded materials may be returned to the helper as evidence of practice on helping goals following termination. Clients can send in monthly self-monitoring forms or tapes of communication practice. Likewise, helpers can send clients reminders of their goal statements. Young & Rosen (1985) describe a group activity in which clients write a letter to themselves during the last session before termination. The letter reminds the client of the helping goals. It also contains a list that the client drafts that predicts some of the excuses the client may use to try to avoid achieving the goals. The therapist mails the letters to clients about a month after the completion of group therapy.

Summary

The final topic in this chapter and in this book is the termination of the client/helper relationship. While the door may be left open for future help, termination can evoke feelings of loss for clients and helpers. Developing a positive ending for the helping relationship helps clients celebrate their successes and can shape their attitudes about receiving help in the future. One important issue at termination is building in a follow-up system to help clients maintain change and prevent relapse.

Group Exercise

A recent innovation in family therapy involves reframing with a reflecting team. A family therapist meets with a family and gets their perspective on the problem facing them. Midway through the session, the therapist stops and consults with a group of observers who have been watching through a one-way mirror or on video. The observers suggest alternate ways of looking at the family's problem. The therapist then returns to the family and presents a reframe of their problem based on the suggestions he or she has heard.

In the following exercise, a small group of learners form a reflecting team as a way to practice reframing. Form groups of six or eight students. One person is designated as the helper, one as the client, and the remaining members form the team of observers.

Step 1   The client discusses a real or role-play situation with the helper, who uses the non-judgmental listening cycle to understand the problem as completely as possible in the 5–10 minutes allotted for this activity.

Step 2 Once the helper feels that he or she has a good grasp of the client's viewpoint and has summarized his or her situation, the client is asked to move out of earshot or leave the room for approximately 5 minutes. During this time, the team conducts a group discussion about alternative ways that the client's problem might be viewed. The team is encouraged to identify viewpoints that are consistent with the client's world view and values, but that are more positive and change-oriented than the client's current way of looking at the problem.

Step 3 The helper brings the client back into the presence of the reflecting team and delivers a reframe to the client. The helper chooses the best reframe for the client based on the client's own thinking and the thoughts of the reflecting team. The client is encouraged to respond to the reframe. When this has been completed, the role play is over.

Step 4 The client gives written feedback regarding the reframe that was presented by the helper and team using a 5-point scale, as shown in the Feedback Checklist.

Feedback Checklist: Reframing

Client Name_____   Helper Name_____
1 = Disagree
2 = Slightly disagree
3 = Neutral
4 = Agree
5 = Strongly Agree
_____1. The helper understood my problem completely.
_____2. The reframe was a more positive viewpoint than the original statement of the problem.
_____3. The reframe was a more constructive way of looking at the problem.
_____4. The reframe fit with my own personal outlook and values.

The exercise continues in order to allow several team members to have the opportunity to play the role of helper as time allows.

Additional Exercises

Exercise 1

Think of a problem situation in your own life. Suppose that you decided that drastic action on your part was unreasonable and you only wanted to change your outlook or attitude about it. When you have settled on a particular problem, answer the following questions:

a. What are the things about the situation that make you feel uncomfortable?

b. What other things about the situation are positive (not just bearable)?

c. What keeps you focused on the negative aspects of the problem?

d. Can you see this situation as an opportunity rather than as a problem?

e. What points would you need to focus on to keep your view of the situation positive?

f. When would it not be a good idea to encourage a client to change his or her perspective on a problem?

g. If you wish, discuss your answers with a small group.

Exercise 2

In a small group, two members role-play a client and helper discussing termination, which is to take place in a week's time. Observers give the helper feedback on the following:

a. Did the helper review the history of the helping process and the therapeutic relationship
   with the client?

b. Did the helper help the client celebrate success in attaining the goals?

c. Did the helper leave the door open while
   expressing confidence in the client's
   readiness to terminate?

Homework

Step 1 Before you record and transcribe a final
session with a client, take some time to review
the feedback you have received during group
exercises and your individual practice. Think
about each of the following building blocks and
for each skill, rate your current level of mastery.

> 1 = I understand the concept
>
> 2 = I can identify the skill and give exam-
> ples
>
> 3 = I can do it occasionally
>
> 4 = I do it regularly
>
> _____ Eye contact
>
> _____ Body position
>
> _____ Attentive silence
>
> _____ Voice tone
>
> _____ Gestures and facial expressions
>
> _____ Physical distance
>
> _____ Door openers and minimal encour-
> agers
>
> _____ Open and closed questions
>
> _____ Paraphrasing
>
> _____ Reflecting feelings
>
> _____ Reflecting meaning
>
> _____ Summarizing

Compare the scores with your answers in
Chapter 5. Where have you improved? Where do
you still need improvement?

Step 2 In Chapter 5, you recorded and tran-
scribed a session with a client. Now it is time to
make a final tape in the same way. Make a final
tape of 20 to 30 minutes with a classmate who is
discussing a real problem or who is role-playing.
During the taping, your goal as a helper is to:

a. Demonstrate the nonjudgmental listening cycle.

b. Demonstrate challenging skills.

c. Demonstrate goal setting skills.

d. Discuss with the client a possible treatment plan and what techniques you
   might use in subsequent sessions.

Step 3 Choose the best 15 minutes of the tape
and transcribe every word of both client and
helper, using the format of Table 5-2. It is important that the client's statements appear directly
below your helping responses so that the connection between the two can be examined. Be sure
you have permission from the client to record.
You can do this aloud on the tape and in writing.

Step 4 Listen to the tape or read the typescript
and make comments, naming each of the skills
that your response exemplifies. Sometimes, students describe their responses rather than categorizing them. It is important to identify the
skills you are using to determine their frequency
and appropriateness. Use only the names of the
building blocks and techniques you have
learned. The "Comments" column is a place for
you to reflect on your responses. Do not just
note weaknesses; identify strengths as well. In
the "Comments" column, you may also wish to
identify any other issues that come to mind as
you review the typescript.

Most important, reflect for a few minutes on your progress from the start of your training until now. Make some comments about your progress over the course of your training. What impact has it had on you personally, on your professional goals, or on your relationships with others? Learning the art of helping is a journey. What steps have you taken so far? What must you do now to go farther?

References

Anderson, C. M., & Stewart, S. (1983). *Mastering resistance: A practical guide to family therapy.* New York: Guilford.

Ansbacher, H. L., & Ansbacher, R. R. (Eds.). (1956). *The individual psychology of Alfred Adler.* New York: Basic Books.

Bandura, A. (1971). Psychotherapy based on modeling principles. In A. E. Bergin & S. L. Garfield (Eds.), *Handbook of psychotherapy and behavior change: An empirical analysis* (pp. 653–708). New York: Wiley.

Barker, P. (1985). *Using metaphors in psychotherapy.* New York: Brunner/Mazel.

Bernard, T., & Young, J. M. (1996). *The ecology of hope.* Easthaven, CT: New Society Press.

Brammer, L. M., Shostrom, E. L., & Abrego, P. J. (1989). *Therapeutic psychology: Fundamentals of counseling and psychotherapy.* (5th ed.). Upper Saddle River, NJ: Prentice-Hall.

Cavanagh, M. E. (1982). *The counseling experience.* Monterey, CA: Brooks/Cole.

Clark, A. J. (1995). An examination of the technique of interpretation in counseling. *Journal of Counseling and Development, 73,* 483–490.

Cormier, W. H., & Cormier, S. L. (1985). *Interviewing strategies for helpers: Fundamental skills and cognitive behavioral interventions* (2nd ed.). Pacific Grove, CA: Brooks/Cole.

Dixon, D. N., & Glover, J. A. (1984). *Counseling: A problem-solving approach.* New York: Wiley.

Elliott, R. (1985). Helpful and nonhelpful events in brief counseling interviews: An empirical taxonomy. *Journal of Counseling Psychology, 32,* 307–322.

Ellis, A. (1962). *Reason and emotion in psychotherapy.* New York: Lyle Stuart.

Emmelkamp, P. M. G. (1982). Exposure, *in vivo* treatments. In A. Goldstein & D. Chambless (Eds.), *Agoraphobia: Multiple perspectives on theory and treatment.* New York: Wiley.

Foa, E. B., & Goldstein, A. (1978). Continuous exposure and complete response prevention in the treatment of obsessive-compulsive neurosis. *Behavior Therapy, 9,* 821–829.

Gardner, R. A. (1971). *Therapeutic communication with children: Mutual story-telling technique.* New York: Science House.

Gladding, S. T. (1988). *Counseling: A comprehensive profession.* Columbus, OH: Merrill.

Goodyear, R. (1981). Termination as a loss experience for the counselor. *Personnel and Guidance Journal, 59,* 349–350.

Gordon, D. (1978). *Therapeutic metaphors.* Cupertino, CA: Meta Publications.

Hackney, H., & Cormier, L. S. (1979). *Counseling strategies and objectives.* Upper Saddle River, NJ: Prentice-Hall.

Kalven, J., Rosen, L., & Taylor, B. (1981). *Value development: A practical guide.* Ramsey, NJ: Paulist Press.

Kanfer, F. H. (1975). Self-management methods. In F. H. Kanfer & A. P. Goldstein (Eds.), *Helping people change* (pp. 309–355). New York: Pergamon.

Kanfer, F. H., & Schefft, B. K. (1988). *Guiding therapeutic change.* Champaign, IL: Research Press.

Kazdin, A. E. (1980). *Behavior modification in applied settings.* Homewood, IL: Dorsey Press.

Kramer, S. A. (1986). The termination process in open-ended psychotherapy: Guidelines for clinical practice. *Psychotherapy, 23,* 526–531.

Kramer, S. A. (1990). *Positive endings in psychotherapy.* San Francisco: Jossey-Bass.

Krantz, P. L., & Lund, N. L. (1979). A dilemma of play therapy: Termination anxiety in the therapist. *Teaching of Psychology, 6,* 108–110.

Lamb, D. H. (1985). A time-frame model of termination in psychotherapy. *Psychotherapy, 22,* 604–609.

Maholich, L. T., & Turner, D. W. (1979). Termination: That difficult farewell. *American Journal of Psychotherapy, 33,* 583–591.

Martin, J., & Stelmaczonek, K. (1988). Participants' identification and recall of important events in counseling. *Journal of Counseling Psychology, 35,* 385–390.

Mathews, B. (1989). Terminating therapy: Implications for the private practitioner. *Psychotherapy in Private Practice, 7,* 29–39.

McKay, M., Davis, M., & Fanning, P. (1981). *Thoughts and feelings: The art of cognitive stress intervention.* Richmond, CA: New Harbinger.

McMullin, R. (1986). *Handbook of cognitive therapy techniques.* New York: W. W. Norton.

Meichenbaum, D. (1977). *Cognitive-behavior modification: An integrative approach.* New York: Plenum.

Milan, M. (1985). Symbolic modeling. In M. Hersen & A. S. Bellack (Eds.), *Dictionary of behavior therapy techniques* (pp. 212–215). New York: Pergamon.

Mitchell, Z. P., & Milan, M. (1983). Imitation of high-interest comic strip models' appropriate classroom behavior: Acquisition and generalization. *Child and Family Behavior Therapy, 5,* 25–30.

Morris, R. J. (1986). Fear reduction methods. In F. H. Kanfer & A. P. Goldstein (Eds.), *Helping people change* (pp. 145–190). New York: Pergamon.

Mosak, H. H. (1987). *Ha ha and aha.* Muncie, IN: Accelerated Development.

Munro, J. N., & Bach, T. R. (1975). Effect of time-limited counseling on client change. *Journal of Counseling Psychology, 22,* 395–398.

Perry, G. P., & Paquin, J. J. (1987). Practical strategies for maintaining and generalizing improvements from psychotherapy. In P. A. Keller & S. R. Heyman (Eds.), *Innovations in clinical practice: A source book* (Vol. 6, pp. 151–164). Sarasota, FL: Professional Resource Exchange.

Perry, M. A., & Furukawa, M. J. (1986). Modeling methods. In F. H. Kanfer & A. P. Goldstein (Eds.), *Helping people change* (pp. 66–110). New York: Pergamon.

Rudestam, K. E. (1980). *Methods of self-change: An ABC primer.* Monterey, CA: Brooks/Cole.

Sciscoe, M. (1990). *The termination of therapy.* Unpublished manuscript.

Shulman, L. (1979). *The skills of helping individuals and groups.* Itasca, IL: Peacock Press.

Ward, D. E. (1984). Termination of individual counseling: Concepts and strategies. *Journal of Counseling and Development, 63,* 21–25.

Watzlawick, P., Weakland, J., & Fisch, R. (1974). *Change: Principles of problem formation and problem resolution.* New York: W. W. Norton.

Wolberg, L. R. (1954). *The technique of psychotherapy.* New York: Grune & Stratton.

Yalom, I. R. (1995). *Theory and practice of group psychotherapy* (4th ed.). New York: Basic Books.

Young, M. E., & Rosen, L. S. (1985). The retreat: An educational growth group. *Journal for Specialists in Group Work, 21,* 157–171.

Index